# JAGUARS OF THE DAWN

*Spirit Mediumship in the Brazilian Vale do Amanhecer*

Emily Pierini

**berghahn**
NEW YORK • OXFORD
www.berghahnbooks.com

First published in 2020 by
Berghahn Books
www.berghahnbooks.com

© 2020, 2023 Emily Pierini
First paperback edition published in 2023

**Library of Congress Cataloging-in-Publication Data**

Names: Pierini, Emily, author.

Title: Jaguars of the dawn : spirit mediumship in the Brazilian Vale do
Amanhecer / Emily Pierini.

Description: New York : Berghahn Books, 2020. | Includes bibliographical
references and index.

Identifiers: LCCN 2019042438 (print) | LCCN 2019042439 (ebook) | ISBN
9781789205657 (hardback) | ISBN 9781789205664 (ebook)

Subjects: LCSH: Ordem Espiritualista Cristã (Brazil) |
Mediums--Practice--Brazil--Vale do Amanhecer. |
Mediums--Practice--Europe. | Channeling (Spiritualism)--Brazil--Vale do
Amanhecer. | Channeling (Spiritualism)--Europe. | Spiritual healing and
spiritualism. | Mind and body--Religious aspects. | Vale do Amanhecer
(Brazil)--Religious life and customs.

Classification: LCC BF1242.B6 P53 2020  (print) | LCC BF1242.B6  (ebook) |
DDC 133.9/10981--dc23

LC record available at https://lccn.loc.gov/2019042438

LC ebook record available at https://lccn.loc.gov/2019042439

**British Library Cataloguing in Publication Data**

A catalogue record for this book is available from the British Library

ISBN 978-1-78920-565-7 hardback
ISBN 978-1-80539-117-3 paperback
ISBN 978-1-80539-366-5 epub
ISBN 978-1-78920-566-4 web pdf

https://doi.org/10.3167/9781789205657

Jaguars of the Dawn

# CONTENTS

# FIGURES

# ACKNOWLEDGEMENTS

This book is based on 36 months of ethnographic research conducted among the mediums of the Brazilian Obras Sociais da Ordem Espiritualista Cristã Vale do Amanhecer (Social Works of the Spiritualist Christian Order Valley of the Dawn). Most of my ethnographic research took place in the Templo Mãe (Mother Temple) of the Vale do Amanhecer near Brasília, firstly in 2004, then between 2009 and 2011, and in subsequent annual fieldworks. It also included Temples of the Amanhecer in Northeast and Southern Brazil, England, Portugal and Italy.

I am grateful to the Spalding Trust, the Read-Tuckwell Scholarship, the University of Bristol's Postgraduate Research Grant and the Royal Anthropological Institute's Sutasoma Award for funding the different stages of research upon which this book is based. I am immeasurably grateful to Fiona Bowie for her wonderful guidance at the University of Bristol and the fruitful conversations that gave rise to projects and networks in the subsequent years; she has certainly inspired intellectual insights and lines of research extending beyond the pages of this work. I also owe thanks to those who helped shape several parts of this work at different stages, providing insightful advice and constructive criticism on the earlier versions of these chapters: David Shankland, Bettina Schmidt, Margherita Margiotti, Judith Okely, Alberto Groisman, Diana Espírito Santo and the anonymous reviewers from Berghahn. The Faculty of Medicine of the Universidade de São Paulo (FM-USP, Medical Anthropology) offered institutional support during my fieldwork in Brazil in 2009–2011; I am particularly thankful to Maria de Lourdes Beldi de Alcântara and Carlos Corbett.

Chapter Three, Five, Seven, Eight and Nine have given me the opportunity to expand upon articles and chapters that were originally published in journals and edited books. Some sections of these chapters appeared in: 'Becoming a Spirit Medium: Initiatory Learning and the Self in the Vale do Amanhecer', *Ethnos* 81(2): 290–314 (2016); 'Embodied Encounters: Ethnographic Knowledge, Emotion and Senses in the Vale do Amanhecer's

Spirit Mediumship', *Journal for the Study of Religious Experience* 2: 25–49 (2016); 'Healing and Therapeutic Trajectories among the Spirit Mediums of the Brazilian Vale do Amanhecer', *International Journal of Latin American Religions* 2(2): 272–89 (2018); 'Becoming a Jaguar: Spiritual Routes in the Vale do Amanhecer', a chapter of the *Handbook of Contemporary Religions in Brazil* (Brill, 2016, pp. 225–32), edited by Bettina Schmidt and Steven Engler; 'Fieldwork and Embodied Knowledge: Researching the Experiences of Spirit Mediums in the Brazilian Vale do Amanhecer', a chapter of the book *The Study of Religious Experience: Approaches and Methodologies* (Equinox, 2016, pp. 50–70), edited by Bettina Schmidt.

Among the mediums of the Vale do Amanhecer, my deepest gratitude goes to Ana Paula, who introduced me to the Vale – without her this research would not have been possible – and to her family, Antonita and Saulo, who became my Brazilian family from the very first day of fieldwork. In the Vale do Amanhecer, I am thankful to the family of the founder, Neiva Chaves Zelaya (Tia Neiva), for embracing my research and welcoming me with warmth to the Vale. Particularly, to the Trino Ypoará Raul Zelaya, President of the O.S.O.E.C., for his kind support with all the permissions. To Vera Lúcia and Carmem Lúcia Zelaya for welcoming me into their homes, and Jairo Leite Zelaya Júnior for his precious friendship and endless conversations over the years. Living in the Templo Mãe provided me with the opportunity to meet some of the elder masters, who shared their stories of the founding of the Vale, the doctrinal knowledge learned with Tia Neiva and the technical explanations of mediumship and life beyond matter. First and foremost, I am deeply grateful to the Adjunto Ypuena Mestre Lacerda, a great friend and *adjunto*, whose contribution to this work in terms of knowledge, teachings and support has been invaluable. He passed away while this book was being finalized. The Adjunto Ypuena has permitted me to include in my research the philanthropic work of social assistance of the Casa Transitória Povo Ypuena (also known as Mansão Ypuena) and to approach resident and former patients, which allowed me to explore the therapeutic uses of mediumistic development. To Leonardo, Joaquim and all the staff and patients of the Mansão also goes my gratitude. To the Adjunto Yumatá Mestre Caldeira, who patiently clarified the technical aspects of the phenomenology of mediumship during the many afternoons spent sitting on the porch of his shop. I am grateful to the Trino Tumará Mestre José Carlos, Mestre Bálsamo, the Adjunto Amayá Mestre Guilherme, Mestre Vlademir, the Adjunto Adejá Mestre Fróes, the Adjunto Uruamê Mestre Fogaça, the Adjunto Gerulo Mestre Márcio and the instructors of the mediumistic development, for their patient explanations and teachings. I thank Mestre Itamir, who since my first fieldwork in 2004 has provided careful assistance with the technical issues of fieldwork and has always welcomed me with a smile, along with his wife Laura and the nymphs of the Falange Franciscana. I am grateful to Alisson, Edna, Jarbas, Alexandre, Marcelo Reis, Aldemir Júnior, Jerson, Jader, Valeria, Marco, Maria A., Socorro, Camila, Cláudio, Terezinha, Gilfran, Jacó, Guto, Íria, João, Venceslau, Xixico and Ana Maria, who over the years have shared their experiences, stories, knowledge and doctrinal materials with me. Some of them have been great friends and intellectual companions through the many nights and days of conversations fuelled by Brazilian coffee. I thank the mediums whose stories are part of this book but whose names have been changed for privacy purposes. I thank Thomas and Neuza for their caring friendship. I am grateful to Diego for his teachings and support, and his family, Brenda, Beto, Célia, David and Nayanna. I thank Vilela, the artist who paints the spiritual beings of the Vale, for authorizing the use of his images in this work. I am grateful to Laylson Coimbra for designing the image on the book cover, which is the outcome of a moment of creative insight that we shared after a ritual. I thank Márlio Kleber for authorizing the use of his illustrations of the ritual of *Tronos*. I owe thanks to the presidents and mediums of the Temples of the Amanhecer I visited in Brazil and Europe and to all those who guided me and taught me a lot in the field; those who welcomed me into their lives and homes, sharing experiences that contributed directly and indirectly to the pages of this book.

My family and friends have been extremely supportive in these years. I am especially grateful to my parents, Piero and Susan Ellen, and my brother Simone for their endless love and encouragement.

To all of them this work is dedicated.

# NOTE ON TRANSLATION

The names of the Vale do Amanhecer's rituals, sacred spaces, hierarchical classifications and spiritual beings have been kept in the original language, and, where possible, translation is provided in the text. Since some of the names are the proper terminology of the Vale do Amanhecer, they may not have a Portuguese translation either. In all the other cases, translations from Portuguese to English are the author's, unless otherwise stated.

# INTRODUCTION

## Towards the Vale do Amanhecer

*Rome, Italy, August 2003*

The crowd was gathering on the shore of the lake to wait for the fireworks. But something else was going on; along a small area of beach, a group of people were staring in another direction. Across the lake, there was a majestic pyramid-like mountain overseeing the waters, whilst a medieval castle reflected its lights on the surface. The growing moon above us was shedding a silver light on the dark sand. Ana Paula's white dress was leading the scene, floating as she entered the water, her eyes facing the horizon but her gaze somewhere else. What caught my attention was the silence of the people around her; the enchanted children seemed to perceive that something magic was going on, and an atmosphere of sacred expectation mixed with curiosity pervaded the scene. '*Salve Yemanjá!*', she exclaimed, greeting the Afro-Brazilian *orixá*[1] of the waters, this on the night of the celebrations for the Virgin Mary's Assumption on the Italian bank holiday of August 15th.

Ana Paula, a Brazilian woman, was someone I thought could provide me with some contacts while doing research on Brazilian religions. The first time I met her at that lake in Italy, she walked towards me squinting her eyes to focus me. She was in her mid forties and had golden skin. Her smooth facial features were surrounded by dark curly hair. 'Is it Candomblé that you are interested in?' she asked me, after introducing herself, 'I can probably help you, but we are not going to talk about Candomblé today, I am going to tell you about a different kind of Brazilian religion: it's called "Vale do Amanhecer" and I have the feeling that you are going to go there'.

She told me that seldom would she tell people about the religious aspects of her past in Brazil, particularly in a country like Italy, where people were not used to talking about, nor with, spirits. She was a medium of the Vale do Amanhecer (Valley of the Dawn) and during the 1980s had lived in the main temple near Brasília, while the founder was still alive. She helped with the opening of some of the first external temples in Bahia, São Paulo and Porto Alegre. It was sufficient enough to look at the images of the Vale that she showed me – with the impressive visual impact of the colourful ritual vestments and sacred spaces, which included a pyramid – to decide that Ana Paula's feeling would turn out to be correct.

I frequently visited Ana Paula for almost a year before leaving for Brazil. During our meetings, she patiently introduced me to the Ordem Espiritualista Cristã Vale do Amanhecer (Spiritualist Christian Order Valley of the Dawn), founded by the clairvoyant Neiva Chaves Zelaya (1925–1985). Towards the end of the 1950s, in the desert plateau of central Brazil, the new capital was built from scratch in only four years through a visionary project of President Juscelino Kubitschek. He envisioned it not only as the country's political centre but as a modernist city that would bring together Brazilian society in a sort of all-inclusive plan, which was then fed by millenarian narratives and prophecies that depicted Brasília as the capital of the third millennium. Thus, the new capital began to attract a variety of spiritual groups and host the centres of several religions, and it became known as the 'Capital of Esotericism and Mysticism' (Siqueira 2002), or 'Mystic Brasília' (Reis 2008). Among the workers in search of new opportunities, coming from all across Brazil to build this massive enterprise, there was a truck driver, Neiva, a woman in her thirties, widow and mother of four, who all of a sudden began to experience mediumistic phenomena that led her in 1959 to plant the seeds for what would later become a spiritual town of mediums on the outskirts of Brasília, the Vale do Amanhecer, which would flourish along with the capital and rapidly spread with temples throughout Brazil and worldwide. She held that her phenomena included astral travels through the spirit worlds and several historical times, as well as visions and instructions from spirit guides, which led her to the transposition on earth of the ritual vestments, spaces, symbols, words and movements that define the Vale do Amanhecer for the spiritual healing of patients and to assist humanity in the troubled transition towards a new era (N.C. Zelaya 1985). Among her main spirit guides were the Amerindian spirit called Pai Seta Branca (Father White Arrow), who presented himself as the same spirit who had an incarnation as Saint Francis of Assisi, and Mãe Yara (Mother Yara), who had incarnated as Saint Clare, both working with different groups of spirits of light such as the *pretos velhos* (African slaves), *caboclos* (Amerindians), German and Brazilian doctors, princesses, gypsies, knights and spiritual ministries among others, working under the aegis of Jesus Christ. She soon became widely known in Brazil as the clairvoyant Tia Neiva (Aunt Neiva), who, while channelling a Spiritualist doctrine and developing new, highly ritualistic forms of mediumship, was also grounding her spiritual work in charitable social assistance. The Temple of the Amanhecer is, indeed, understood as a *pronto soccorro espiritual* (spiritual first aid), where people find spiritual assistance free of charge for spiritual, emotional, material and health issues. In sixty years, the first community of Vale do Amanhecer grew into a town of 10,000 inhabitants, mostly mediums of the Vale. And around 700 external temples were opened in Brazil and abroad, spreading across North and South America and Europe.

Mediums, who call themselves 'Jaguars', understand their practice as charitable work for which they do not accept payment or offerings. Their voluntary work as mediums is also considered to be a way to redeem their karma from their joint past lives as a spirit group in specific historical times, such as in Ancient Egypt, Greece and Rome, as Mayans and Incas, and during the French Revolution and in Colonial Brazil. In rituals, mediums in a semi-conscious mediumistic trance incorporate spirit guides to assist patients with messages of hope and a spiritual cleansing called 'disobsessive healing' (*cura desobsessiva*). This involves the release of disincarnate spirits understood as affecting (obsessing) the patient. Differently from the spirit guides, these obsessing spirits are considered to be spirits of the deceased who remained trapped between the planes after death, and mediums regard as part of their spiritual work that of helping also those 'disincarnate patients' to be released into higher spirit worlds. Unlike some Spiritist groups, however, rituals in Vale do Amanhecer do not offer direct communication with departed relatives or friends, but only with spirit guides deemed to belong to high hierarchies, namely the 'spirits of light'.

One day Ana Paula opened a box and showed me some old photos of Tia Neiva, her original letters and the images of her spirit guides. She then showed me an essential part of her ritual uniform, the *colete*, the white waistcoat of the initiate, which in her case was turning yellow after years of mediumistic practice. The *colete*, she explained, was also used to indicate through its symbols the type of mediumship of the initiate. In a quite straightforward way, she said:

> We are all mediums. All human beings. It is not the belief in spirits that makes you a medium. It is within our body; we have different ways of perceiving other planes. In the Vale, we develop two kinds of mediumship: the *apará*, such as in my case, is the medium who incorporates spirits, and the *doutrinador*, is the medium who does not incorporate spirits but uses intuition and is able to elevate them to the spirit world.

Wearing ritual vestments and incorporating spirits, however, is not some-thing that happens so straightforwardly in some people's lives, and the notions that people have about being a medium are also quite vague. And this is true both for those who arrive in the Vale without any belief and those who arrive already manifesting spontaneous mediumistic phenomena. So how do they establish a relationship with spiritual beings? How do spirits become so relevant in people's lives? And how do these embodied encoun-ters with spirits influence people's notions of body and self?

Once one looks beyond the first impressions of the colourful ritual uniforms and the kaleidoscopic geometries of the sacred spaces, one may realize that behind this there are lawyers, doctors, scholars, artisans, traders, farmers and students, as well as retired and unemployed people, who do voluntary work as mediums in the temple during their spare time. Why would a professional after work in the city rush home to wear those uniforms and go to work spiritually in the temple? Why would they spend the weekend or their holidays working with patients and spirits? How is mediumistic practice meaningful for these people? Answering these questions will give us insight into a particular kind of religiosity, an extended notion of the self, an understanding of illness and healing, of life and death. The religious biographies of the mediums I met in my research recounted past routes across different religions in search of an active, participative, immediate and embodied relationship with the divine, which they describe as being fulfilled by their mediumistic practice. Others also revealed their therapeutic trajecto-ries unfolding between spirituality and biomedicine in the search for healing. Every scholar, and indeed anyone else visiting Brazil, cannot fail to note the incredible religious diversity and the fluidity of different religious trajectories and forms of religiosity that define the accents and rhythms of daily life. If Brazil offers a unique setting for researching mediumistic religions, the Vale do Amanhecer, one of the most visually spectacular among Brazilian religious forms, offers a remarkable opportunity for the study of a particular view of the wider processes of Brazilian religiosity, and especially of mediumistic phenomena that embrace core aspects of human experience.

## Approaching Spirit Mediumship

*Vale do Amanhecer, Brasília, October 2004*

On a full moon night, I stood by the pyramid photographing a ritual taking place in the open-air sacred space around the Lake of Yemanjá in the Templo Mãe (Mother Temple), the main temple of the Amanhecer near Brasília. I was with a medium receptionist, who was in charge of accompanying visitors, reporters and researchers. He suddenly pointed out his view on ethnography, explaining that as a receptionist he was used to people coming there for short visits and leaving with basic information about rituals, in many cases publishing articles in which they attributed to them labels and ideas that did not belong to the Vale. He lamented the fact that by being caught by the visual impact of rituals and mediums' uniforms seldom would they ask for their meanings. He had a different expectation regarding my ethnographic work: 'everyone here has a story to tell ... you are putting together this puzzle that composes the Vale do Amanhecer'. A similar concern that many researches face during fieldwork and in ethnographic writing, especially when writing about mediumistic phenomena, is with how we should deal with local categories when they clash against our own ones.

The earlier studies on spirit mediumship and possession were largely characterized by explanatory paradigms, which often led to pathologizing reductions, since they were informed by Western notions of a bounded self and driven by the mind/body dichotomy. Several anthropologists have repeatedly warned that the direct translation of a set of categories from one culture into another is often misleading (Evans-Pritchard 1976 [1937]; Lienhardt 1961; Goldman 2006; Holbraad 2008, 2009). The expression 'cognitive empathetic engagement' was coined by Fiona Bowie to describe an approach in which the ethnographer, rather than dismissing native categories, learns to think through these local concepts as they are lived through, although maintaining a situated and critical empathy (Bowie 2013). Phenomenological approaches to religious experience seek non-reductive ways to address religious phenomena that do not always fit into Western secular explanatory paradigms, with peculiar attention to how people come to experience them as real, particularly through the approach of embodiment – that is, conceiving the body not as an object but as a living entity through which we perceive and experience the world (Merleau-Ponty 1962; Csordas 1990; Desjarlais 1992; Stoller 1997; Desjarlais and Throop 2011; Knibbe and Van Houtert 2018). The phenomenological approach that I adopt in this work is interested in exploring the relations between the phenomenal and discursive (Ingold 2000; Throop 2003). I especially refer to Ingold's understanding of 'narratives' as being the ways in which lived, bodily and perceptual experiences are creatively interwoven and 'the ways in which the resulting discursive constructions in turn affect people's perceptions of the world around them' (2000: 285).

Talking about mediumistic practices often raises in the listener a mixture of fascination and scepticism, curiosity and fear, covering the phenomena with an aura of mystery. However, for many people in a great variety of societies around the world, including Western ones, these phenomena are part of an everyday life in which the boundaries between the world of the living and of the dead, spirits or deities are conceived as permeable. In different cultures, spiritual beings are variably considered enunciators of knowledge about the afterlife; or guides that bring healing and assist the living with their lives on earth or accompany the specialists of the sacred through the spirit worlds. Some spirits are otherwise understood as opposing forces or pathogenic agents that need to be exorcized or removed from a particular person or place. Whether welcome or not, these spiritual agents are understood as being able to communicate through, be embodied by or influence to different extents human beings. I refer to 'mediumistic practices', addressing the many ways and techniques through which this type of communication, embodiment or influence may happen in different cultures, in more or less controlled ways, assuming local features and conceptualizations. Being a spirit medium is understood as mediating the knowledge from the spirit world, and the body is the primary site of this mediation and process of learning spirit mediumship. While mediumistic experience is not exclusively a bodily experience, in the Vale do Amanhecer, the mediums' narratives of their mediumistic experiences prioritize the bodily dimension over belief – that is, their sense of transformation and belief passes through emotions and bodily feeling. But to be more precise, seldom would they refer to 'belief'; they would rather prefer to use the term *conhecimento* (knowledge), a kind of knowledge that is not only propositional but is 'felt'. What my interlocutors intended to stress was indeed that notions of mediumship should not be addressed independently from experiences, bodies, emotions, feelings and stories, which ultimately ground these ideas.

This book seeks to explore how conceptual categories intertwine with lived, bodily and affective experiences, especially in the process of learning spirit mediumship. In my approach, I draw upon two main scholarly threads: on the one hand on studies that approach the bodily dimension of spirit mediumship and possession (Stoller 1989, 1994; Desjarlais 1992; Strathern 1996; Halloy 2015); and on the other hand, on those that approach the process of learning religion, seeking to restore the prominence of the body (Goldman 2007; Berliner and Sarró 2009; Halloy and Naumescu 2012). The question of how notions of possession and the self are produced and transmitted is increasingly intriguing anthropologist working in the field of spirit mediumship and possession. Cognitive anthropology has extensively addressed religious transmission (Whitehouse 2000, 2004; Boyer 2001; Whitehouse and Laidlaw 2004), and as far as it concerns studies on possession, it has been mainly interested in the exploration of the underlying cognitive structures that may account for the cross-cultural recurrence of concepts of possession from a mind-centred perspective (Cohen 2007, 2008). As Andrew Strathern notes, the focus on 'embodiment represents a return to the sensuous quality of lived experience' (1996: 198). He considers 'the reentry of the body into the scene of social theorising' precisely 'as a result of a reaction against the mentalistic patterns of enquiry and explanation that have previously dominated' (ibid.). In this work, I understand 'learning' in Ingold's terms as a process of 'enskillment', as learning to sense the environment in culturally specific ways (2000). Halloy and Naumescu particularly suggested that when considering religious transmission, along with the cognitive architecture one should also take into account 'patterns of feeling and perceiving' and 'recurrent sets of affects and percepts' (2012: 168). They have identified a gap in the literature concerning a consideration of 'the way contextual factors shape cognitive, perceptual and emotional processes leading to possession expertise' (2012: 166).

The Vale do Amanhecer provides us with the opportunity to investigate ethnographically in depth these intertwinements given the conscious and semi-conscious modalities of mediumship developed in the temple, which allow mediums to describe different feelings and processes at work in their experiences of mediumistic trance. Provided that mediumistic development draws extensively upon bodily experience, throughout my discussion I look at embodied knowledge. More specifically, I am interested in how mediumistic development informs notions of the body and the self. Indeed, becoming a spirit medium in the Vale do Amanhecer involves the development of mediumistic skills through an education of perception, which draws upon discernment and may lead to the transformation of one's sense of self. My main argument is that the primacy given to bodily experience in the first stages of learning to become a medium articulates notions of a permeable body and an extended and multidimensional self, which also informs conceptualizations of mediumistic trance. Then, I will explore how such embodied knowledge informs spiritual and therapeutic experiences in a broader perspective. Specifically, I will present some cases of people who arrived in the Vale for therapeutic purposes and chose to develop their mediumship. I will propose that the notions of the self and bodily skills informed by their mediumistic development triggered their process of healing. Understanding the self as extended towards other lives and in other dimensions and thus interacting also with non-human spirits requires one to develop the skill of discernment. 'Developing a sense of self as separate from others is considered the cornerstone of human cognition and well-being. ... we define our selves through our past, present, future, and imagined involvement with people and things; our selves extend into these worlds, and they into us' (Ochs and Capps 1996: 29–30).

Concepts of the self articulated by a specific society inform an individual's self-image and the interpretation of their experiences, and the way the self emerges as a 'perceptible object' for an individual is all culturally oriented in a behavioural environment (Hallowell 1955: 75–76).

Moreover, according to Hallowell, the 'social' relations of the self may include more than its ordinary behavioural environment to encompass 'other selves', such as spiritual beings; thus, self-awareness emerges in relation to human and other-than-human beings (ibid.: 91). Scholars have assumed a direct correspondence between cultural models of the self and subjective experiences, as if cultural models were to encompass all aspects of the experiential self and be entirely integrated into everyday experience, and this discrepancy may be problematic (Hollan 1992: 285). For instance, Hollan shows how the cultural model of an impermeable bounded self in North American society was poorly accounting for the experiential self of his respondents, who in face of a loss of a relative experienced a 'death' of part of one's self: 'the self is at least partly constituted by the "others" with whom it interacts and ... the boundaries between self and other may remain somewhat fluid and indistinct' (ibid.: 289). Cultural representation alone may not account for the experiential self; both intersubjective experience and perceptual experience are indeed crucial factors involved in the way the self is constituted. The entanglement between these factors needs to be explored ethnographically. One remarkable exploration of the relation between the production of the self, cosmogony and mediumship was conducted by Diana Espírito Santo in her study on Cuban Espiritismo. Espiritismo is addressed as a 'technology of self-making', whereby the self is presented as discursively emergent and relational to the point that spirits of '*muertos* materialize their mediums as much as the other way around' (Espírito Santo 2015: 289).

The centrality given to the self in this book concerns the ongoing articulation of the self through the process of learning and practising mediumship and the encounter with spirit guides. One should note that this process of transformation may not be the initial appeal of the Vale do Amanhecer to participants. What leads people to develop as a medium may not be an ideal notion that one has to embrace or aim for, rather it may involve a variety of circumstances, ranging from health issues to relational ones, and the trajectories that emerge from my interlocutors' narratives of these experiences. In this sense, narratives are key in mediating self-understanding, in mediating between discourse and practice (Ochs and Capps 1996). Notions of the self, however, become relevant during the mediumistic development, as this process engenders forms of selfhood through the embodied encounter with spirits. Rather than transmitting notions of the self, the development 'grounds' – as one participant pointed out – and develops the self in the body through experience. Self is hereby understood as developed from the interaction between discursive and bodily dimensions. Moreover, since the self is also temporally oriented (Hallowell 1955), I will also consider the extended self in transhistorical terms through the narratives of mediums' past lives, often co-existing with the spirits with whom they work in rituals to bring along the forces left in the past for spiritual healing.

## Embodied Knowledge in the Field

*Vale do Amanhecer, Brasília, November 2009*

When I discussed my ideas about researching mediumship with Mestre Itamir, a medium who had followed my research since my first fieldwork in the Vale, he expressed his concern about the scholarly ways of approaching mediumship. His concern was specifically about the predominance of 'listening, seeing and writing' over 'sensing and feeling' in the research practice. 'This is what makes the difference – he said – listening and seeing are different from feeling. So be careful in paying attention to your own bodily feelings and sensations, as this is the only way to get in touch with this phenomenon and to understand its meaning for us, even if you don't incorporate spirits'.

In another case, my friend Pedro led me to observe the sense of impatience and frustration I was having when in the middle of a conversation he would often shut down in communication or drastically change topic. According to him, the problem was due to the fact that I did not understand how to use intuition. Although I always perceived myself as being open-minded, he defined me interchangeably as pragmatic, rational and 'with an apparent sensibility but not fully applied in life'. For him as a medium, these kinds of conversations on spiritual issues, rather than being based on question-answer strategies, implied other processes that regulated what could be said and what could not: these processes involved intuition and somatosensory perception, such as gut feelings. It was only with time that I came to understand the idea that energy was always in movement in each conversation; how a topic could change energy as much as energy could change a topic; and how an interruption in conversation may be interpreted as energetically influenced because the topic should not be discussed or because the interlocutor is not ready to understand it. Hence, Pedro pointed out that I had to question my own ways of knowing in order to enter into a process of communication and be able to conduct a conversation on spiritual matters. The ethnographic encounter implies far more than learning the local language to communicate; we should also become skilled in local ways of knowing and communicating, which may imply considering the embodied dimension of the encounter.

In subsequent fieldworks along the years, I shifted my focus from discourses to experiences once body and emotions emerged as relevant to understanding my interlocutors' narratives. I became interested in understanding how this transformation of perception occurred and how it was possible to learn this way of knowing. How do people learn mediumship? How do they learn to distinguish between different spirits? How does mediumistic experience inform notions of the body and the self? In the Vale do Amanhecer, these complex processes begin to occur in mediumistic development. Some patients are indeed invited by spirits to develop their mediumship for a variety of reasons, ranging from karma to health matters. Those who choose to do so in the Vale learn to become aware of their mediumship and control it through a practical and bodily training.

Whilst I began to pay attention to my own sensations in rituals, passing through as a patient, I realized that this position had little to tell me about mediumistic experience. Given the centrality of the body in mediumistic development, in an advanced stage of fieldwork and having extensively explored this possibility with the mediums' instructors and leaders of the Order, I began the mediumistic development and thus to re-educate my own perception and ways of knowing. I realized that by engaging my own body and discussing my experiences with mediums in a comparative way I could reach insights otherwise difficult to consider as outcomes of disembodied techniques of elicitation. The kind of participation I experienced in the field – fully involving my body in the process of learning mediumship – may not always be possible. Since the ethnographic practice requires the methodological choices to be drawn from both the research focus and the specific field circumstances, a method that may seem appropriate in a specific field may not be suitable in other fields. Therefore, I am not advocating that participation is the only means through which a researcher has access to the understanding of mediumship. It was in my case, at a certain stage of my research, the most indicated way to reach valuable insights into the somatic elements involved in the process of learning mediumship. It allowed me to discuss with mediums the relationship between somatic aspects of mediumistic practice and notions of the self. If embodiment was a way of knowing among mediums, the dimension of the ethnographer's bodiliness in the process of knowing the field had also to be tackled.

Scholars have noted how the questions of participant observation, bodily knowledge and reflexivity are hardly debated when researching on spiritual experiences; current debates seem to have rehabilitated such discussions by exploring the value of the researchers' awareness of their bodily, experiential and affective dimensions while participating in other ways of living (Goulet and Granville Miller 2007; Bowie 2013; Pierini and Groisman 2016).

Among the experiential turn in ethnography, Barbara Tedlock in her discussion of participatory approaches, which predominantly focuses on the aspect of ethnographic representation, critically notes that:

> What seems to lie behind the belief that 'going native' poses a serious danger to the fieldworker is the logical construction of the relationship between objectivity and subjectivity, between scientist and native, between Self and Other, as an unbridgeable opposition. The implication is that a subject's way of knowing is incompatible with the scientist's way of knowing and that the domain of objectivity is the sole property of the outsider. (Tedlock 1991: 71)

I propose that we need to question the assumption of 'going native' and understand participation as learning ways of knowing so as to ground intersubjectivity. In fact, bodily participation does not entail 'going native'. Firstly, the category of 'native' is neither bounded nor homogeneous, especially as participants in this spiritual practice have different sociocultural backgrounds and personal trajectories, thus not only my experience was informed by my background but all mediums' experiences are. Hence, if I am not assuming that the researcher's experience is identical to that of others, it is also the case that the instructors of the mediumistic development constantly alert newcomers that 'each medium is a different case'. Even when bodily experience in trance is similar, the anthropological insight emerges from the tension between world views, as Desjarlais (1992) maintains from his own apprenticeship with Nepali healers.

Secondly, participation can never be complete, as observation does not cease. Okely points out that 'The fear of total participation is the fear that observation will cease. Yet there is always the need to take notes … If note taking and the relevant anthropological analysis cease, then so does the research' (2012: 78).[2] Equally, participation does not automatically entail the researcher closing the 'ethnographic eye'. Indeed, I found myself engaged in an ongoing process of observation and interpretation even if my eyes were closed in rituals, which led me to develop an enhanced awareness of other ways of knowing. Furthermore, I have proposed that

> This kind of participation does not imply that the ethnographer accepts beliefs at face value, because not even mediums do so when they approach the practice. It rather implies reflecting critically upon one's bodily experience and the insights gained from it and discussing them with research participants establishing a particular kind of rapport (Favret-Saada 1990; Goldman 2003, 2005), and thus using this reflexivity as a common ground of interaction with research participants. (Pierini 2016b)

This common ground of interaction moved us to a new level of reflection in which both my questions and mediums' narratives gained in depth and nuances. Certainly, what our interlocutors are willing to share is informed by what they perceive the ethnographer is prepared to understand. But primarily, in reflecting upon and comparing experiences, we were making the effort to find ways to describe in words the felt immediacies of those experiences. Bodily knowledge allows moving beyond the limitations of verbal and visual modes of knowing, shifting from disembodied knowledge to the sensuous dimension of lived experience (Strathern 1996; Stoller 1997; Pink 2009; Okely 2007, 2012). Rather than reducing experience to a visual mode of understanding – particularly in cultural contexts where other senses may be more dominant than vision – 'sensory ethnography' affirms the multisensorial and emplaced character of learning in the field (Pink 2009: 64).

This level of ethnographic knowledge gained through participation and bodily involvement, rather than losing objectivity, may be valued for its reliability, as advocated by Goulet and Granville Miller: 'In this experiential perspective, reliable ethnographic knowledge is generated through radical participation and vulnerability, not distance and detachment. How else are we to grasp a "people's point of view", *their* relation to life, to realize *their* vision of *their* world (Malinowski 1953, 25)' (2007: 11). Detachment in search of objectivity during fieldwork 'is *more* likely to transform the context', as the ethnographer may be perceived as a threat or a critic; yet, involvement through participation may allow a greater 'invisibility' in terms of transforming contexts and, particularly, be understood as a sign of respect (Okely 2012: 77). The classic dichotomies of participation vs observation and subjective vs objective are indeed part of a false and misleading continuum, as one does not exclude the other (ibid.). Similarly, Csordas maintains that 'the attempt to define a somatic mode of attention decentres analysis such that no category is privileged, and all categories are in flux between subjectivity and objectivity' (1993: 146). Furthermore, I should point out that the kind of process of knowing in the field I am proposing should not reproduce dichotomies between intellectual and bodily ways of knowing, but eventually it should integrate the two.

'Ethnographic objectivity', as Fabian argues, should be pursued through knowing, where 'knowing' stands for 'acting in company' rather than contemplating, entailing an intersubjective and processual knowledge (2001: 29). Fabian understands the primacy of vision along with the displacement of ethnographic objectivity from the anthropological debate as a result of a shift of interest from knowledge production to representation: 'It is no longer possible to limit oneself to the concepts and images derived from vision when discussing questions of objectivity'; the body should be rehabilitated as involved in knowledge production, in intersubjectivity, and thus in grounding ethnographic objectivity (ibid. 30). Furthermore, objectivity should not be intended as a product of emotional detachment and distance from actions and interlocutors during fieldwork, it is rather a matter of analytical rigor applied to field notes, including the ethnographer's own experience as part of the data (Halloy 2016). Halloy, through an engaging discussion of the epistemological aspects concerning his full participation and his experiences of being possessed and initiated in Afro-Brazilian Xangô, maintains that analytical 'Rigor is not synonymous with cold indifference' and that 'emphatic resonance' and 'introspective expertise' are skills that should be cultivated in the ethnographic practice, ensuring the validity of data (2016: 20).

A closer look at bodily experience may further illuminate how foreign categories may not fit local experience and understandings. This often results in reductionist or pathologizing approaches, especially when the level of discourse is approached separately from the perceptual level, remaining on the level of 'belief', which is a territory of contested categories. Namely, 'concepts such as "knowledge" and "belief", "body", "self" and "person-hood", "health" and "illness" arise from the felt immediacy of the field' (Pierini and Groisman 2016). I therefore propose to move from belief to experience, reframing cognition within the bodily dimension of spiritual practice. Through this shift, the researcher's engagement with the field is cognitive and empathetic, and also bodily. Therefore, not only should we avoid bracketing out local experiences as not fitting into the Westerner framework, the researcher's bodily experience should also be tackled in order to convey in writing at which levels the intersubjective and embodied nature of the ethnographic encounter and knowledge was constructed.

My methodological approach of engaging my body in learning medium-istic ways of knowing – which could be seen in line with phenomenological approaches in anthropology that fall under the umbrella of 'apprentice-ship' – allowed me to unpack the multiple layers involved in the process of developing mediumship: embodied, intuitive, performative, concep-tual and intersubjective learning. It provided valuable insights into how participants developing mediumship in the Vale do Amanhecer are not transmitted a belief but learn to cultivate a particular mode of knowing through their bodies: spirits become real for people as they learn to experi-ence them through their bodies and in their everyday lives. Rather than being something transcendent, mediumship in the Vale do Amanhecer is understood as being grounded in the body, and thus one may develop ways of knowing through the body and cultivate a 'mediumistic body' intersub-jectively. The process of transformation that the medium undergoes during the development is indeed deeply felt at the bodily level.

This research contributes to studies on spirit mediumship and possession in that it shows how a focus on the process of learning illuminates the artic-ulation of bodies and selves as much as it informs therapeutic experiences. A multilayered process of learning mediumship also provides mediums with a multilayered articulation of the self: extended beyond the semi-permeable body, multidimensional and transhistorical. The study of the process of learning mediumship contributes an in depth view on several aspects of human experience, and particularly on how notions can be articulated and even transformed through bodily experience, and this has its implications for therapeutic experiences, especially if we consider that illness, addictions and emotional suffering bring about a rupture in people's sense of body and self. The embodied knowledge articulated through mediumistic development, the cultivation of bodily control and of an extended sense of self in relation to spirits, as mediums' narratives will show, may be highly transformative in people's trajectories of therapy. These therapeutic narratives significantly unsettle the early approaches that reduced spirit mediumship and possession to pathologies. Therefore, this study calls for a reconsideration of spirit mediumship as a fertile ground for exploring the entanglements between experience and discourse that are not exclusive of mediumistic phenomena occurring in small-scale distant societies but rather extend into urban industrialized societies and particularly into different domains of human experience.

## About the Book

This book is based upon extensive and intensive ethnographic fieldwork conducted at different stages since 2004 for an overall total of thirty-six months spent living in the temples of the Vale do Amanhecer. The longest period in the field involved living in the Templo Mãe in Brasília for fifteen months between 2009 and 2011, followed by shorter annual fieldworks in that community. Between 2011 and 2013, I spent seven months at different stages in several temples in Northeast and Southern Brazil. In Europe, I undertook short and long-term periods of ethnographic research in temples in England, Portugal and Italy between 2012 and 2018, which provided a significant view of consistencies and differences between experiences in different temples, enriching the ethnographic description. The relationships developed throughout those years with friends and research participants have constantly nourished my knowledge and insights on the lived dimension of the Vale do Amanhecer and contributed a valuable conversation about those research insights. Fieldwork in external temples of the Amanhecer allowed me to meet countless mediums, who spontaneously and informally shared with me their stories and experiences, and it gave me the opportunity to participate in a great variety of rituals and in unique processes such as: the transition of one temple from an initial stage to an advanced one, involving the physical construction of sacred spaces; the first initiations of European mediums in Portugal; and the opening of temples in Italy. Not all of these processes and experiences can be included in detail in this book, but they certainly contributed in many ways to this ethnography. Besides participant observation, which has been my leading method, and the ongoing conversation with the founders and elders of the Order, I gathered formal interviews and biographical narratives, and I conducted extensive research through the mediums' private and public archives of Tia Neiva's letters and audio recordings and the bibliographic production of those who have closely collaborated with her and interpreted her revelations.

Whilst descriptions of the phenomena of incorporation of spirits by mediums in development are quite vivid and detailed, these are focused upon mediums' accounts of their experiences, thus the specific ritual sequences, scripts, verbal initiatic keys and techniques that instructors used to develop mediumship, as well as the ritual of initiation, have intentionally been left out from this book. In order to protect the identity of some mediums who shared their experiences for the purpose of this research I use pseudonyms and they will appear with first names only. For mediums who hold high hierarchical ranks or are elders or founders, or mediums who are somewhat known as a 'public figure' in the Order, I use their hierarchical titles in front of their real names (e.g. Trino, Adjunto, or Mestre).

In terms of the organization of the book, I opted to include some rich ethnographic descriptions of the ritualistic setting and cosmology, both considering the current lack of literature in English upon the Vale do Amanhecer and to provide context to understand the mediums' narratives of their experiences addressed more in depth in the second part of the book. Chapter One guides the reader through the variety of practices involving encounters with spirits through mediumship in contemporary Brazil. I illustrate the contemporary features of Brazilian religiosity – in which the worlds of humans and spirits merge through an embodied, emotional and direct relationship that is sought more as an experience than as a concept – and trace the historical background of these practices. Indeed, Brazilians experience different ways of encountering the divine, defining their complex trajectories across different religions through their relations with spirits. Human and spirit trajectories thus entwine to form what I address as the Brazilian religious meshwork. I then narrow down the focus to Brasília and the foundational, millenarian narratives that attracted many spiritual communities to settle around the new capital of Brazil in the 1960s. It was indeed while Tia Neiva was working on the construction of Brasília that she began experiencing the mediumistic phenomena that led to the foundation of the Vale do Amanhecer. Tia Neiva's biography will be introduced in Chapter Two, along with the social and spatial organization of the temples of the Amanhecer, which will be presented as a materialization of her spiritual experience through her peculiar way of knowing.

Chapter Three presents Tia Neiva's revelations on the different reincarnations of the mediums of the Vale do Amanhecer as a spirit group called the 'Jaguars'. The past incarnations of the Jaguars play a key role in the mediums' articulation of a transhistorical self through their mediumistic practice. Tia Neiva's narrative of the past lives of the Jaguars evokes cosmologies of ancient civilizations, Christianity, Eastern religions, Spiritism, Amerindian and Afro-Brazilian religions, Gypsy cultures, theosophy and millenarianism. These different lines are brought together into healing rituals in which mediums call upon the forces from their joint past lives; thus the principle of reincarnation determines the global character of the Vale do Amanhecer. Tackling the mediums' mission of helping humans and spirits in the transition towards a new era, I propose that the Vale's millenarian discourse does not derive from the New Age Movement but is rather deeply embedded in the millenarian discourses of Brazilian indigenous and popular cultures. Chapter Four illustrates the multidimensionality of the self extending through different lives and dimensions, the processes of incarnation and disincarnation of spirits and the mapping of the spirit worlds. The interactions and exchanges between these worlds, which I present as an ecology of fluids and substances, provide a context to understand how the self and the temple are forged through these fields of relations and to grasp how mediums understand the notion of 'spiritual knowledge'.

Chapter Five explains the spirit-related aetiology of illness and the spiritual treatment through the ritual itinerary that patients undertake in the temple to address the physical, emotional or material matters in their lives. It discusses how spiritual and biomedical epistemologies are conceived as complementary and how mediums understand 'disobsessive healing' as a 'mediumistic science'. Chapter Six addresses the notion of 'mediumship' in the Vale in comparison with categories used in other mediumistic religions or Spiritualist groups, showing how it is closely related to notions of the body: mediumship in the Vale is considered to be universally originating from the body and thus can potentially be developed by anyone through a specific training. Mediumship is also related to karma, and thus has implications for the transhistorical configuration of human-spirit relations. Chapter Seven focuses on the body in the first stages of mediumistic development, exploring the role of emotions, feelings and senses in cultivating the relationship with spirit guides. I argue that newcomers are not taught about the existence of spirits; they are not passed a belief. They rather come to learn how to feel the presence of spirits and how to discern which spirit is manifesting, which is a specific mode of knowing that urges us to shift our analytical stance from 'belief' to 'experience'. Learning mediumship is hereby approached as a process of 'enskillment' (Ingold 2000), which implies situating the practice through the ongoing education of perception.

It is a process that articulates a particular kind of embodied knowledge, reshaping notions of the body and the self.

Chapter Eight expands the perspective to tackle the place the Vale do Amanhecer's mediumistic practice occupies within contemporary religiosity in Brazil. By presenting the experiences that led people to practise mediumship in the Vale, this chapter argues that the development of an embodied relation with the sacred and of a specific conceptualization of the body in the Vale do Amanhecer re-establishes spiritual commitment to an initiatic Order within a context of intense religious mobility. Chapter Nine traces the therapeutic trajectories that led people to the Vale; they were seeking a spiritual approach to their illness, alcohol and drug addictions, or mental disorders. It particularly refers to those patients who chose to develop mediumship for therapeutic purposes, proposing that their healing process was triggered by the embodied knowledge and bodily skills engendered by the processes of learning mediumship and then accompanied by the shift of the initiates' role from that of patients to mediators of healing.

Phenomena of spirit mediumship and possession have often been reduced to symbols of social order, mentalistic patterns or even pathologized through Western psychiatric categories. Mediumship, however, is not understandable exclusively in psychological, sociological or biological terms. Drawing upon the current debate in psychiatry concerned with the need to discern between spiritual and pathological experiences, I propose that an ethnographic approach that takes into account lived experience and modes of knowing may assist in making this discernment possible, showing how in some cases therapeutic trajectories may rather inform an initiatic path. Mediumship is a multidimensional phenomenon, and this multidimensionality may be illuminated through an approach that considers the process of learning mediumship as learning a way of knowing.

## Notes

1. A deity known all across Brazil in African-derived religions as the sea goddess.
2. According to Okely 'going native' is a cliché 'legacy of the colonial discourse ... passed on to anthropologists seemingly to avoid alignment with indigenous people' (2012: 78–79).

# Chapter 1

# WAYS TO EMBODY THE DIVINE IN BRAZIL

## Brazilian Religiosity: Between Categories and Experiences

Whilst in Brazil, I was struck by my acquaintances' accounts about the variety of combinations of faiths and the religious dynamics within their households. In most cases, religion did not seem to be bound by kinship. During my visit in São Paulo in 2004, for instance, I met a friend for lunch in the Avenida Paulista. She was a psychologist in her early thirties, and when it came to talk about religion she said:

> My mother is a Kardecist Spiritist; my father is Catholic. I could tell you that I am an atheist because of the clash between their religious beliefs. But I cannot deny the fact that I am searching for 'something'. I am interested in Buddhism, I also visited the Vale do Amanhecer, but I haven't found the one that suits me yet. I know everything about my parents' religions, and I do respect them, as much as I know that they respect my own choices. Many parents here are willing to leave their children free to experience their own religious paths. Whereas, if I am not wrong, in Italy religion is still acquired by birth, right?

Despite the idea of 'nominal' versus 'practised' religion, what caught my attention was the word 'still', as she seemed to imply an awareness that Brazilian religiosity featured a sort of anticipatory trend.

Greenfield (2001) and Motta (2001) identified the advent of a 'religious marketplace'[1] in Brazil with the end of the monopoly of Catholicism that articulated the passage from 'imposed faith' to 'chosen faith'. This dynamic, according to Greenfield, was marked by the proliferation of new religions as adaptive strategies to the demographic and industrial growth of the twentieth century (2008: 100). His conceptualization of 'marketplace' follows the logic of a patron-client exchange, arguing that the belief in the intermediation of a saint between human beings and a supreme god and the subsequent dynamics of exchange are cultural forms belonging to popular Catholicism. Consequently, he assumes that those religions that have 'syncretized' their beliefs and practices with Catholicism compete for believers by presenting their own model of interaction and exchange between devotee and supernatural being (Greenfield 2001: 57). According to Motta, the market economy presupposes 'entrepreneurs', who are 'understood as a person, or a group of persons, who bring new "products" to the (religious) market by introducing new (religious) goods and services, or by recombining previously existing ones to satisfy the changes in demand prevailing among consumers' (Motta 2001: 72). Similarly to Greenfield, Motta also insists on the contract of exchange, referring particularly to Candomblé, an Afro-Brazilian religion in which the initiate engages in offerings and sacrifices to his own *orixá*. During my fieldwork in Afro-Brazilian religions, a *pai-do-santo* (father-of-the-saint), a priest in Candomblé, stressed his distinction between Candomblé and Spiritism, which was epitomized by the nature of exchanges between spiritual beings and humans: 'Candomblé works with "energy of exchange" between *orixás* and human beings, differently from "charity" which is a feature of Kardecist rituals' (Pierini 2010: 72).

Although the metaphor of the marketplace with entrepreneurs engaged in satisfying the demand of consumers may appear sociologically intriguing, in this chapter I propose an approach to the Brazilian religious-scape that, alternatively to the idea of a 'market' of beliefs, is rather concerned with narratives of spiritual and religious experiences, moving beyond the idea of 'exchange' to encompass a non-mediated and embodied experience of the sacred. A focus on experience will also lead me to discuss the limits of quantitative data that aim to classify in fixed categories the religiosity of Brazilians, which rather features an intense mobility across religions. I will then explore the historical background of Brazilian mediumistic religions and how their current practices involve different ways of encountering and embodying the divine in Brazil. Subsequently, I will narrow the focus upon Brasília, looking at the foundational narratives of the new capital, known as the 'capital of mysticism', which is key to contextualizing both the rise of the Vale do Amanhecer in the 1960s and the current religious mobility across the Federal District. My point is that a perspective on the experiences of human-spirit relations may provide us with a less fixed classification of mediumistic practices, illuminating the entanglements of human and spirit trajectories and thus the transformative potential of mediumistic practices.

The narratives of the leaders of Afro-Brazilian religious centres in the Federal District presented me with a perspective that was slightly different from the 'marketplace' model: the 'offer' of religious leaders, instead of recombining different beliefs to satisfy the demands of 'consumers', as the marketplace paradigm would imply, was rather the product of their own past experiences and experimentation with different religions. What was considered experientially fulfilling for them regarding their relationships with spiritual beings and deities in those religions was then ritually shared with other practitioners. For instance, one *pai-do-santo* who was formerly a Catholic priest, besides his rituals and obligations in Candomblé Ketu, used to attend a Sunday Mass in a local church with some members of his *terreiro*. In another instance, the leader of a centre of Catimbó-Jurema was previously initiated in Umbanda, Kardecism, Jurema and Candomblé Angola. He then accommodated within the Jurema ritual practice a varied pantheon of spiritual beings, who have accompanied him along his past experience in those religions. Similarly, another *pai-do-santo* said he was brought up in a Kardecist family and then encountered a variety of Afro-Amerindian and Afro-Brazilian religions such as Catimbó in Northeast Brazil, Candomblé Omolokô, Ketu Opô Afonjá and Umbanda in Salvador da Bahia. He maintained that these experiences promoted a path to self-awareness through the relationship with his spirits and *orixás*. When he moved to Brasília as a father-of-the-saint, he founded his *terreiro* of Candomblé Ketu, although he included in rituals spirits of *pretos velhos* ('old blacks', spirits of African slaves), *caboclos* (spirits of Amerindians) and *ciganos* (gypsies). Hence, the religious experiences of these leaders defined the vast array of spiritual beings either worshipped or ritually incorporated through mediumistic trance as much as the identity, features and practices of their centres (Pierini 2010). Interestingly, these leaders' religious biographies trace the paths of spiritual beings as moving through different religious contexts with their mediums. Hence, some *terreiros* of Candomblé that would usually work with *orixás* would then hold ceremonies allowing the manifestation of other spirits, such as the *marinheiros* (sailors), *pretos velhos*, *ciganos* etc. Whilst these practices may be questioned by some other leaders, they are far from being an exception in Afro-Brazilian religions, considering that these religions rely more on the genealogy of priesthood rather than a centralized organization defining the practices.

Reflecting upon the diversification of religions in Brazil in terms of meanings, values, imageries, affects, rituals and therapies, Brandão correctly points out that such differentiation is offered even within a single religion along with different modalities of affiliation (2004: 279). The patterns of religious affiliation in Brazil are indeed changeable and subjective. A general overview of the census data on religious affiliation, which took place during my longest fieldwork in Brazil in 2010, shows that in the decade from 2000 to 2010 the number of Catholics decreased from 73.6% to 64.6%, whilst all the other groups increased or showed no changes: Evangelicals (including both Protestant Churches and Pentecostals) from 15.4% to 22.2%; Spiritists from 1.3% to 2.0%; Afro-Brazilians maintained a 0.3%; other religions from 1.8% to 2.7%; and atheists[2] from 7.4% to 8% (IBGE 2010b: 91). Drawing together the number of Catholics and Evangelicals overall, some 86% of all Brazilians identify themselves as members of Christian churches. The 2010 census contained one open-ended question on religion, 'What is your religion?' In that year, there were 2,068 different self-declarations, classified in 138 subcodes and distributed in 58 codes (Santos 2014). Nine hundred of these declarations belonged to Pentecostal denominations, implying great diversification in the way some Brazilians would declare themselves as being Evangelicals (ibid.).

The attempt to map the religious affiliation of Brazilians through an exclusively quantitative approach, however, has raised some criticism. On the one hand, scholarly criticism is especially concerned with the methodology for the elaboration of the 'table of classification', containing generic descriptive categories used to code the respondents' declarations (Camurça 2014). On the other hand, single Evangelical denominations criticized the inclusion of some other denominations within their own category (ibid.). Most importantly, although the census provided the category of 'multiple affiliation', it is difficult to grasp and to quantify the interconnectivity and fluidity of Brazilian religiosity in quantitative figures. The quantitative figures divided in the above-mentioned religious groups are not sufficient to map the Brazilian religious-scape, and they are even less able to reflect the phenomena and experiences that define it.

Although Catholicism is still the majority religion in Brazil, there is a great flexibility with respect to the Church. One may declare oneself a Catholic and attend a ceremony or a consult in an Afro-Brazilian *terreiro*, or a healing ritual in another religion. Among the thousands of people attending healing rituals in the Vale do Amanhecer, some people visit the temple weekly and consult *pretos velhos* as a patient for years without necessarily declaring themselves Spiritualists, and they even continue with another religious affiliation. Multiple definitions may emerge within the same spiritual group: a member of the Vale do Amanhecer may feel he or she may declare him or herself to be 'Spiritist', 'Spiritualist', or 'Christian'. So members of Umbanda may declare themselves to belong to an Umbanda centre called 'Centro Espírita' (Spiritist Centre) and their answer may be codified within the category of Spiritism or Afro-Brazilian. However, even though people are offered the opportunity to provide their religious affiliation, religious identity may be so complex that the coding of the responses within 'macro' religious groups is problematic. Similarly, one may argue that the place that mediumistic religions occupy in the Brazilian cultural and religious-scape is far more extended than the figures provided by the census. Eventually, if one were to address religious pluralism in Brazil, this should be considered as being so embodied in interpersonal dynamics, in the everyday experiences and personal narratives, so as to become an evanescent category.

## Mediumistic Religions in Brazil

In Bahia, I met Antonio, a fifty-year-old medium of the Vale do Amanhecer working as an accountant in Salvador. Raised Catholic, Antonio learned about his mediumship in São Paulo, where he experienced several mediumistic religions before encountering the Vale. Walking along the rail tracks of the small town of Cachoeira-São Felix, where he was born, he was telling me about his mixed European origins while describing this town – inhabited mostly by African descendants and where the Candomblé religion is widely practised – when he suddenly told me: 'you know, even in the veins of the white Brazilian flows the African blood, and in the depths of his being dwells the *caboclo*'.[3] His words resonated with the idea of the creative potential of human diversity as grounded in the formation of a Brazilian identity, proposed by Gilberto Freyre (1945, 1968, 1986 [1933]) and Darcy Ribeiro (1995). Indeed, ideas about cultural identity and religions in Brazil are better understood through a discussion of the process of colonization of such an extensive land and the associated need for labour. Stressing the peculiar character of Portuguese colonization, Freyre in particular approached the interpenetration between elements of local Amerindian culture, 'imposed' European culture and an 'imported' African one through the lens of a harmonious cohabitation and cultural reciprocity, which led to the formation of what he calls 'Brazils' in order to reflect the plurality of Brazilian regions (Freyre 1968: 127, 1986 [1933]: 83). Thus, according to Freyre, social distance in Brazil would be more 'the result of class consciousness, rather than race or colour prejudice' (1945: 97).

Despite Freyre's almost romanticized view, the idea that Brazilian society has been harmoniously constructed is questionable, since it fails to acknowledge the enormous genocide of indigenous peoples and the ethnic preconceptions that are historically tangible in both social relations and land rights disputes involving indigenous and African descent groups (Ribeiro 1995).[4] It would also be limiting to consider Brazilian society and religiosity to be derived exclusively from the colonial interpenetration between European, African and Amerindian cultures, as the process of migration that began in the mid eighteenth century and continues up until this day constantly feeds the diversity of Brazilian cultural and religious fields. Yet, a strong sense of pride seems to permeate ideas related to the interweaving of ethnic, cultural and religious patterns as a remarkable and defining value of Brazilian identity. Drawing upon these ideas, the Brazilian artistic avant-garde of the 1920s proclaimed 'anthropophagy'[5] against the mimesis of the culture of the 'civilizers', in particular Oswald de Andrade's *Manifesto Antropófago* (1928):[6] 'anthropophagy. The absorption of the sacred enemy. To turn it into a totem' (1928: 6).[7] Playing with the European imagery in which colonial Brazil was seen as an infernal mouth devouring European civilization and its representatives in the New World, the *Manifesto* encouraged the idea of swallowing everything that came from European culture, arts, languages and lifestyles to generate something designed to affirm a cultural identity distinct from the culture of the colonizer. Whether swallowed or flowing as blood through the veins, in many narratives these ideas about cultural identity are expressed as being embodied.

While being aware of the great variety of religious practices in Brazil, I am going to provide a brief overview of the historical development of some specific instances of mediumistic religions in Brazil, particularly focusing on the body and the variety of conceptualizations of the encounters and communication between humans and spirits. Such a focus also questions the category of 'possession religions', which is often used more by scholars – to address Afro-Brazilian, Afro-Amerindian and Spiritist practices in Brazil – than by participants, who present different articulations and definitions of their relations with spirits.

Brazil represents a distinctive context to reflect upon the emergence and rapid expansion of religions and spiritual practices based on spirit mediumship, particularly for what concerns their contemporary phenomena associated to religiosity, embodiment and healing practices; three aspects that emerge in this book as entangled. Furthermore, the ritual practice of embodiment of and communication with spiritual beings is key to Afro-Brazilian, Amerindian and Ayahuasca religions, Kardecist spiritism[8] and other Brazilian mediumistic religions – religions that originated in Brazil and that are currently spreading globally, undergoing new influences (Rocha and Vásquez 2013; Engler and Schmidt 2016).

The emergence of Brazilian religions was informed by the peculiar nature of Portuguese colonization. The imperialism of the colonizers and the process of religious conversion led by the Jesuit missionaries were closely related: converting the souls of the natives and the African slaves was a way to incorporate them within the dominant discourse of the colonizers. The religion of the colonizers was coercively imposed upon slaves, yet Catholicism in Brazil has exercised relatively weak control over African slaves and indigenous peoples, and so they were still able to practise their worship in the *senzalas* (slave quarters) in the shade of the *casas grandes* (slave owner's home). Christianity was presented as the only guarantee of salvation, and it was used at the time to measure the degree of civilization in human beings. Amerindian religions, inasmuch as the African ones, were reduced to the rank of 'primitive magic' or 'superstition'. These evolutionist concepts emerged from the uneasiness of colonial officers, missionaries and explorers, when European dualistic thought clashed with the ideas of the pervasiveness of the sacred, the interpenetration between matter and spirit, body and soul, human beings and gods, good and evil. African Yoruba religions present a life force called *axé*, which connects humans, non-humans and nature and is kept in movement between the worlds through ritual trances and offerings (Da Silva and Brumana 2016). This force is also hierarchically distributed. The highest degree of this hierarchy is occupied by the Supreme Being – the Creator often identified as Oxalá, Olodumarê, Lissa or Zambi – who is followed by a pantheon of intermediate forces represented by deities acting in specific domains of nature and human actions, who are sometimes held to have had an incarnation in the human world, or *Ayê* (earth), before inhabiting the world of the gods, or *Orum* (sky).

Scholars noted how the similarity of the domains of action of African deities and Catholic saints allowed slaves to merge them in their worship and to bring their religions over the Atlantic to Brazil (Bastide 1978). In the nineteenth century, in the north-eastern region of Bahia, the religion of Candomblé emerged based on the worship and embodiment of African deities called *orixás*, who were merged with Catholic saints. Hence, Afro-Brazilian religions have been widely approached through the category of 'syncretism' (Stewart and Shaw 1994; Leopold and Jensen 2004), a system of correspondences between African deities and Catholic saints: Yemanjá was worshiped as the Virgin Mary, Oxôssi as Saint George, Iansã as Saint Barbara and so forth. Scholars have also remarked how this system presented a great variation from region to region, characterizing this 'syncretism' as fluid and dynamic rather than fixed and crystallized (Bastide 2004). In researching among practitioners of Afro-Brazilian religions in the Federal District,[9] I found that this category was very differently conceptualized by my interlocutors as 'juxtaposition', 'correspondence', 'parallelism', 'interpenetration', 'hybrid' or 'blending' between African deities and Catholic saints (Pierini 2010). The term 'syncretism' has itself been under scholarly scrutiny: it is precisely the idea that in the African diaspora 'syncretism' was merely a way to mask African religions with Catholic elements that is questioned. Referring to Afro-Caribbean religions, Schmidt argues that 'the correspondence between African elements and Christian elements within the Afro-Caribbean religions symbolises a deep intimacy between the two categories but not a power relationship' (Schmidt 2006: 242). She addresses this process as 'polyphonic *bricolage*':

> Afro-Caribbean religions are neither created out of the mixture of two entities, nor frozen in a static moment. They are based on a constant re-arrangement of elements whose meaning can change according to the need of the believers – who in the end often speak with different voices and make contradictory, ambivalent statements about their own religions. (Ibid.)

Leaders of Afro-Brazilian places of worship in the Federal District would point out to me that African-derived religions are themselves a product of a process of merging of different local African worship practices. Indeed, the slave ships crossing the Atlantic transported a multiplicity of peoples, cultures, languages and religions that arrived on the Brazilian land at different moments of its colonization. Whereas in Africa each region featured the worship of a single deity called *orixá* (although deities often crossed the regional boundaries), in Brazil the forced cohabitation of slaves from different regions enabled the simultaneous worship of a pantheon of *orixás*, who danced together in rituals on a new soil. One *pai-do-santo* from the nation Omolokô suggested that this cohabitation of deities is reflected in the disposition of the sacred spaces of the *terreiro*: the disposition of the *quartos dos santos* (individual rooms of the saints) dedicated to their worship may be thought of as representing a reproduction of the different African regions with their own worship of the *orixás* (Pierini 2010: 82). Similarly, the sacred spaces of the temple have been interpreted as a reproduction of Yoruba extended families' living quarters (Da Silva and Brumana 2016). Many leaders would question the use of the term 'syncretism', as this category is regarded as being embedded in attributes of value somehow reproducing evolutionist ideas, measuring in this case the degree of authenticity to define a 'religion' and as such disqualifying many religious practices. Even the idea of 'bricolage' may be applicable in many cases but not always, as it implies an intentionality and pragmatism that may not be involved in the leaders' experiences that ground some of these practices.

Shifting the perspective to experience may illuminate key dynamics involving notions of the body and the self, conceptualizations of the encounter and communication between humans and non-humans, and especially the spiritual phenomena that rather than being one aspect of these mediumistic religions are often what grounds their rise and development, as the next chapter will elucidate. It is often the case that leaders of mediumistic religions in Brazil maintain to have received their 'mission' to open centres or initiate doctrines through spirit guides or deities, and then they seek their advice or follow their instructions throughout the process of development and management of these centres.[10] This may happen by different means, such as revelatory dreams, visions, communication with a spirit through a medium or embodiment of the spirit or deity. These phenomena are expressed and then cultivated in different ways according to the different contexts.

In Afro-Brazilian ceremonies, the *orixás* manifest with their specific dances through the practitioners, namely the *filho, ou filha, do santo* (son or daughter of the saint). The bond with their deity is strengthened through a long ritual initiation process called *fazer a cabeça* (making the head), in which the *orixá* is placed within the body, which has been purified from energies and diseases through cleansing rituals (*ebós*) and offerings (*bori*). The initiate is thus 'made' into a new being composed of material and immaterial elements, including parts of the deity; hence, according to this phenomenology, the initiate cannot be seen as 'possessed' by an external being but as 'becoming' an *orixá*, which is also 'made' within (Goldman 2007). Notably, in rituals, the initiate enters into an unconscious or semi-conscious spiritual trance when the *orixá* rises from within the body, completing its manifestation in outshining the human elements (Schmidt 2016). Each deity has its own natural domain, gestures and rhythm of the *atabaques* (drums) for its invocation, narrative of its life on earth and features of personality, which are seen as reflected in its son or daughter's personality.

Among the multiplicity of cultures of the African slaves, it is possible to distinguish two major linguistic groups – the Yorubá and the Bantu – that gave rise to the different nations of Candomblé: Yorubá or Nagô tradition (from Nigeria and Benin, such as the Ketu), Jeje (Ewe-Fon tradition from Benin, formerly Dahomey) and Angola (Bantu tradition, from Congo and Angola). Their deities are called respectively *orixás*, *voduns* and *inquices*. The religions of the Bantu ethnic group, originally from Congo and Angola, were concerned with the worship of ancestors. Undermined by the fragmentation of families and communities in the colony, similar worship was re-established through the encounter with the Catholic and Amerindian worship of the dead (Bastide 1978). The encounter with Amerindian religions found a fertile ground in the *quilombos* (independent communities founded by former slaves, regulated by their own social organization and productive system), whereby indigenous people, also escaping from slavery, joined with Africans in the seventeenth century. Both African and Amerindian practices sought the help of ancestors with healing. As Africans, Amerindians had practices of connecting with ancestors and spirits through the mediation of a *pajé* – meaning a shaman or healer in Amerindian cultures' Tupi language – a role acquired mostly by means of a 'initiatory illness', interpreted as a call by the spirits to learn to communicate with them, usually in shamanic trance by means of hallucinogens, or music and dances. In some groups, the shamanic calling may also occur in dreams or even at birth.

With the rise of Candomblé Congo and Angola, the worship of African ancestors shifted to Brazilian ones, namely the spirits of African slaves called *pretos velhos* ('old black') and of Amerindians called the *caboclos* (such as in the Candomblé de Caboclo). A number of Afro-Indigenous religions emerged in Northeast Brazil, such as the Pajelança in the states of Amazonas, Pará, Piauí and Maranhão, a religion that holds shamanic healing at the core of its practices. The Pajelança may be further differentiated in Pajelança de Caboclo and Pajelança Negra, working with the *orixás* (Engler and Brito 2016). Besides *caboclos* and *orixás*, in healing sessions the *pajé* also incorporates the *encantados* (enchanted spirits), spirits living in nature having animal or human-like forms – although they have not always been humans – carrying either dangerous or healing powers (ibid.). Another indigenous mediumistic religion in which spirits are incorporated for healing purposes is Jurema, also known as Catimbó. Jurema rituals involve the use of tobacco and the ingestion of a drink derived from the Jurema plant to induce spiritual trance and the incorporation of spirits of masters and *caboclos*, who provide the living with healing.

Afro-Brazilian and Afro-Indigenous religions spread across both rural and urban Northeast Brazil in the forms of Batuque, Tambor de Mina (in Maranhão) and Xangô (in Pernambuco), among others (Leacock and Leacock 1972; M. Ferretti 2001; S. Ferretti 2001; Cohen 2008; Halloy 2015). A wide variety of spirits populate the cosmologies of Batuque and Mina, including the *orixás* and *voduns* (Nagô and Jeje traditions), the *caboclos* and the highly evolved *encantados*, the enchanted spirits ranging from indigenous, Brazilians, Turkish, to the white European noble colonizers organized in families. Ritual ceremonies may often have a festive accent, such as in Batuque (Leacock and Leacock 1972), where they are occasions to maintain close relationships between humans and *encantados*. During a celebration featuring dancing and drumming, practitioners entering mediumistic trance may initially either lose balance or fall backwards, then, once back on their feet, the type of song and dance performed will suggest which type of spirit is manifesting (S. Leacock 1964). Each medium may incorporate two types of personal spirits: a *senhor*, as the main spirit guide manifesting in the medium with a serious personality; and a *caboclo*, who descends to enjoy the celebration through dancing, smoking, drinking, joking and occasionally being qualified as a trickster. This attitude seems to set Batuque apart from Pajelança-like traditions in which the appropriate indigenous spirit manifestation is associated to seriousness (ibid.). Besides dancing and singing, spirits would greet participants and offer consultations to those in need of healing. One may note that *caboclos* are not exclusively manifesting in *terreiros* of the Bantu tradition; although seldom publicly, they are also worshipped in *terreiros* and centres from different religions all across Brazil, sometimes raising issues of authenticity and differentiation between leaders of different *terreiros* (M. Ferretti 2001; Engler and Brito 2016).

Along with *pretos velhos*, *orixás* and saints, the *caboclos* have joined spirits of gypsies and cowboys (*boiadeiros*), white European gentlemen, prostitutes (*pomba giras*), sailors (*marinheiros*) and Bahians (*bahianos*) in Umbanda practices, which have been spreading since the 1920s among the middle classes in urban areas. Lacking a centralized structure, Umbanda centres present a great variety of spirits in their cosmologies and operate with great autonomy. The influence of Kardecist Spiritism – the Brazilian Spiritism that draws upon French Spiritism as systematized by the French educator Allan Kardec (pseudonym of Hippolyte Léon Denizard Rivail) – emphasized the idea of a process of reincarnation that would prepare the spirit to evolve morally along different lives and planes of existence, and that through mediumship spirits may communicate with humans to assist them with their lives on the material plane. Communication thus becomes a key aspect in Umbanda's ritual trance differently from Candomblé, where despite the manifestation of *orixás* through spiritual trance in ceremonies, communication with them is achieved mainly through private consultations involving divination practices such as the *Jogo de Búzios* (shells) and the Oracle of *Ifá*. In Umbanda, ceremonial elements like alcohol, cigars and tobacco are also a part of rituals as offerings to the spirits in exchange for their help. Regarding spirits' cosmology in Umbanda, as Diana Espírito Santo notes, spirits are understood as beings of light who clothe themselves with cultural imagery to constitute themselves; as such, spirits present an 'ontological plasticity' – that is, the ability to change themselves in relation to human culture (2016: 94). In such a relationship between spirit cosmologies and human culture, trance allows the opening up of the cosmos, providing proximity between person and spirit, especially when the cosmos is closed by a conceptualization of entities as transcendent, creating an 'ontological distance' (2016: 89). Therefore, she proposes to understand spirits' cosmologies in their own terms without reducing them to psychological projections or symbols of social order or Brazilian national identities (ibid.).

Spiritism has had an influential role in the definition of spirits' cosmologies and the development of mediumistic practices in Brazil. Introduced among white Brazilian urban elites of Salvador de Bahia and Rio de Janeiro towards the end of the nineteenth century,[11] Spiritism in Brazil developed peculiar religious and therapeutic features. In Brazilian Spiritism, rather than 'being possessed by spirits', mediums communicate in what they describe as a fully conscious state either with evolved spirits from other planes or with the recently deceased or suffering spirits, passing on messages to the incarnate ones (Engler and Isaia 2016). Different kinds of mediumship are developed in Spiritist centres, ranging from psychography (automatic writing) to conscious trance, channelling and spirit incorporation. Training mediumship in Kardecism involves many years of doctrinal study because of the scientific connotation of the Spiritist doctrine emphasized by its founder, which was aimed at explaining the influence of invisible forces behind matter (Kardec 2010 [1857]). There is a wide body of Spiritist literature illustrating life after death and the moral principles that lead to spiritual evolution, with a strong accent upon charitable work. Within this production, Spiritists would cite as remarkable the work of the medium Chico Xavier (Francisco Candido de Xavier, 1910–2002), who published over 400 Spiritist novels and books as authored by spirits and psychographed by the medium and was able to merge Brazilian Spiritism with popular Catholic culture (Lewgoy 2004).

The therapeutic features of Spiritist mediumship are expressed through various healing practices, such as ritual disobsession – that is, helping or subjugating suffering spirits to develop spiritually and forgive their human victims – and *passes*, involving the transfer of magnetic fluid from the medium to the patient. Its approach to well-being, which embraces spiritual and medical aspects, also led to the foundation of several Spiritist hospitals and clinics, providing patients with Spiritist therapies as complementary to medical treatment (Aureliano 2013). Another mediumistic practice born out of Spiritism involves spiritual surgeries performed by renowned medium healers, who incorporate spirits of physicians while in spiritual trance and often use scalpels without anaesthetics (Greenfield 2008), with followers claiming miraculous cures that are increasingly attracting patients internationally, such as the case of the medium João de Deus (John of God) in Abadiânia (Rocha 2017).

Social differentiation has historically defined the demographics of mediumistic religions such as Candomblé, Umbanda and Spiritism. Towards the end of the nineteen century, these mediumistic practices underwent a sort of hierarchization through moral criteria established in the juridical, social and medical fields. 'Low Spiritism' was a category used to define those practices that 'syncretically' merged African and Spiritist elements with healing practices through mediumship (such as candomblé of the Bantu groups, candomblé de caboclo) and that were accused of being illicit medical practices, against practices that were 'genuinely' African (such as candomblé of Yoruba groups, Ketu) and thus more evolved (Giumbelli 2003: 252). Moreover, Spiritism itself was drawing distinctions between 'true' and 'false' Spiritism' based upon the differentiations of charity vs charging for therapies and doctrinal study vs ignorance, in order to distinguish itself from other practices and respond to the repressive actions against mediumistic practices that were carried out at the beginning of the twentieth century (ibid.). Differently from Afro-Brazilian practices, Spiritism was associated with the white, educated middle class. However, once seen as a matter of resistance of marginalized segments of society, mediumistic religions in Brazil currently appeal to Brazilians with different socio-economic backgrounds, and they are even spreading globally in other cultures (Rocha and Vasquez 2013). The paradigm of marginality – especially Lewis's model (1971), which implied that lower-class members of society would seek empowerment through spirit mediumship and possession – was tested against Brazilian mediumistic religions through a quantitative analysis (Donovan 2000). Donovan compared the Brazilian national census data (1947–1980) on religious participation with demographic, economic, social and health indices. Results show that the correlation between these indices and religious participation in Spiritist practice is opposed to what is posited in Lewis's model (Donovan 2000). Furthermore, according to the Brazilian census of 2010, among all Brazilian religions, members of mediumistic religions – Spiritism in the first place (98.6% of its members) followed by Candomblé and Umbanda (96.2%) – are currently holding the highest literacy rate and level of instruction (IBGE 2010b: 102, tab. 16). Afro-Brazilian religions are currently not limited to African descendants or oppressed lower-class members of society but are increasingly opening up to members from different ethnic backgrounds.[12] In urban areas, such as the metropolis of São Paulo, groups of practitioners present a 'more diversified social and gender stratification' (Schmidt 2016: 437). The *terreiros* around Brasília in the Federal District often reflect a phenomenon known as *branqueamento* (whitening) and intellectualization, presenting an increase in white initiates and leaders holding higher education degrees or working as professionals (Pierini 2010).

Spiritism has informed mediumistic practices in Brazil to different extents: from the aesthetic dimension to the cosmologies, up to the conceptualizations of the phenomenology of spirit incorporation. Moreover, the migration flows from Europe and Asia in the twentieth century determined the expansion of other practices among urban middle classes and their influence across the Brazilian religious field. These practices included: Sufism, Buddhism, Hinduism, Seicho-no-Iê, Hare Krishna, Church of World Messianity, Perfect Liberty, Soka Gakkai, Bahá'í, Neo-paganism, Western Esotericism, and New Age among others.[13] The ways in which Brazilian religions interacted with spirits were informed to different extents by these influences. For instance, Santo Daime, Barquinha and União do Vegetal (Vegetal Union) are Brazilian religions based on the ritual consumption of Ayahuasca, a psychotropic substance originally from the Amazon used as a mean to communicate with the spirit world. Andrew Dawson

(2010) notes that the mediumistic repertoire in Santo Daime, once consisting of just consultations with spirits and healing, underwent changes according to the influence of Western Esotericism, and of Spiritism and Umbanda. Western Esotericism shifted the focus from the interaction with spirits to practices oriented towards the development of a 'higher self'. Spiritism determined what Dawson defines as 'private possession', where lower spirits of the deceased are incorporated, firmly controlled and encouraged to move further into the spirit world. Whereas Umbanda has informed a kind of 'expressive possession' involving the incorporation of highly evolved spirit guides, *caboclos* and *pretos velhos*, which besides its 'demonstrative and theatrical character', according to Dawson, has a less defined ritualistic function (2010: 143–44). Likewise, Alberto Groisman (2016) recognizes the influence of Kardecism and Umbanda on the mediumistic practice of Barquinha. However, he understands the ritualistic incorporation[14] of *pretos velhos* by mediums and their intervention in the life events of participants as a fundamental way to constitute the legitimacy and fluency of social and cosmic relationships, which he considers relevant when addressing spiritual healing and therapy in Daime religions (ibid.). Groisman proposes that to

> 'incorporate' an entity of the spiritual plane is not just a ritualistic event, but a full attitude toward the spiritual world, in which one assumes that the messages and guidance received from the consultation relationship with the entity may reverberate in one's life. In other words, there is a whole continuity between ritual life and social/personal life. (Groisman 2016: 65–66)

The repertoires of embodying spiritual beings and the forms of intertwining material and non-material worlds in ritual practices constantly proliferate in Brazil. An interesting feature of religiously inclined Brazilians, as elaborated by Greenfield, is that they 'see this world as part of a continuum that extends into and is a part of the other where power and authority is located' (Greenfield 1992: 43). In addressing mediumistic religions in Brazil, I have shown how a great variety of spiritual beings may be conceived as moving along this entanglement of worlds, sometimes working together in the same ritual and sometimes separately in different religions. Moreover, this entanglement of dimensions is experienced through the bodies of those engaged in mediumistic practices, engendering new ways of relating oneself to and manifesting the spirit world. The idea that emerges from this variety of mediumistic religions is that the thresholds that mediate the visible and invisible worlds are permeable and that mediumistic trance states – and mediumistic practices in general – are the means by which one may experience the interpenetration of these worlds. I will further address religious experience in Chapter Eight and Nine, where I relate religious experiences to therapeutic trajectories and argue that people undertake routes to encounter the divine look, on the one hand, for immediate and embodied ways to experience such an encounter, and, on the other hand, they tend to experience those religions that propose an idea of the multiplicity of the self.

## Brasília: 'The Capital of Mysticism'

About a year before travelling to Brazil, I was intrigued by the screening of Matthias Müller's film *Vacancy* (1998) at the Tate Modern in London. The fifteen-minute film was a montage of original faded images of the capital Brasília on its inauguration day on 21 April 1960. What appeared at first glance to be a small-scale cold architectural model of an entire city was all seemingly bought to life at once through crowds of people clapping hands along large avenues, cutting ribbons and entering the new monumental and residential buildings. The visionary and utopic project of President Juscelino Kubitschek was contained within those frames, that is, bringing Brazilian society together in large squares surrounded by modernist monumental buildings that emerged in only four years from the middle of the desert landscape of the Central Plateau. The frames in the film portrayed empty buildings and streets that produced overall a sense of artificial alienation, which, according to the criticism, was the paradoxical outcome of the urban planning. Such a sensation was not far off what I experienced the first time I crossed the Plano Piloto (Pilot Plan)[15] along the axis from south to north to reach the BR-020 that leads to the Vale do Amanhecer. The architecture conveyed an impression of the buildings as floating in-between the low white clouds in the blue sky and the intense red and green ground of the *cerrado*.[16] Even though Oscar Niemeyer's monumental buildings stood out as fascinating shapes in concrete, which were supposed to be inspired by the curves of nature, the residential blocks seemed to convey a monotonous sense of order.

A closer look at the ideas that drove the planning of the city will illuminate the two main narratives surrounding its foundation and informing the imagery of Brasília as 'capital of the third millennium'. These narratives are key in order to illuminate the context of the foundation of the Vale do Amanhecer, as much as how Brasília and the Vale share millenarian discourses and the idea of all-inclusiveness, considering that Tia Neiva was working as truck driver in the construction of the new capital when she began to experience the mediumistic phenomena that led her to develop the Vale do Amanhecer, as I am going to describe in the next chapter.

The idea of moving the capital away from the coast had been under scrutiny since colonial times, both for reasons of military defence and for the purpose of populating the interior of the country. The fundamental stone was set in 1922 near Planaltina-DF, only 2km away from where the Vale do Amanhecer is currently located. In 1955 Juscelino Kubitschek ran for the Presidential elections, with the main part of his programme being the construction in only four years of a new capital leading the progress of the country. In 1956, he became President, and the plans for the capital were commissioned to Lúcio Costa as urban planner, with Oscar Niemeyer being the public buildings architect and Roberto Burle Marx the landscape designer. The plan was composed of a simple cross: a vertical axis comprising residential 'sectors' perpendicularly intersecting with a shorter horizontal axis, the monumental one hosting the commercial, financial and political sectors. The eastern end of the horizontal axis, pointing towards the artificial Lake Paranoá, is Praça dos Três Poderes (Square of the Three Powers), where the government, Parliament and the Palace of Justice are arranged as an equilateral triangle representing the equivalence attributed to their powers. Since the shape of the cross resembles an airplane, this square has often been labelled the control cabin, and the vertical axis is currently addressed as Asa Norte and Asa Sul ('North Wing' and 'South Wing').

Brasília was presented as the 'symbol of a new age of Brazil' that was going to be produced by an urban plan and architecture aimed at transforming Brazilian society (Holston 1989: 3). Indeed, the planning was permeated by the idea of social equality: bringing together Brazilians of all statuses and incomes. The new capital was intended to be the symbol of a Brazil that was both plural and one at the same time; a point of confluence and integration for the different *Brasis* (Brazils) of different social classes and regional cultures (Freyre 1968: 190). However, the areas around Brasília where construction workers were sleeping grew rapidly into satellite cities that were not planned. The population of the city now far exceeds the original planned expectations, reaching 2,570,160 people in 2010 (IBGE Census 2010b). In order to preserve the original shape of the Plano Piloto as a UNESCO World Heritage Site, the majority of the population remains in the satellite cities, and living in the Plano Piloto has become expensive. According to Holston, the paradox of Brasília consists in the fact that since its conception it has created a duality in social structure and social disparities between the Plano Piloto and satellite cities: 'the successes of Brasília's order depend to on a considerable degree upon keeping the forces of disorder out of the capital and in the periphery' (1989: 29).

Many Brazilians associated the spectacular enterprise of building a capital in four years to what is known as the prophecy of Don Bosco. The Roman Catholic Saint John Bosco, founder of the Salesian Order and priest and educator of disadvantaged young in nineteenth-century Italy, was known for his prophetic dreams. In one dream on 30 August 1883, a young man guided him across South America, reaching a region near a forming lake between parallels 15 and 20. He told him that a promised land was going to rise there in about three generations, a land of inconceivable wealth, where milk and honey would flow.[17] Brasília was immediately interpreted as occupying such a location, with the forming lake being the artificial Lake Paranoá, and Don Bosco thus became its patron saint.

Whilst most foundation narratives draw on the role of Brasília for a new era, other narratives have linked the new capital to an ancient past. Egyptologist Yara Kern (1995) suggested that there were a series of correspondences between Brasília and the Ancient Egyptian city of Akhetaten. Kern was inspired primarily by the pyramidal shapes of the main public buildings of the modernist city, such as the National Theatre, the Temple of the Good Will Legion (Legião da Boa Vontade), the Messianic Church and the Rosicrucian Order; also by the fact that both Pharaoh Akhenaten and President Juscelino Kubitschek commissioned a new capital and then died sixteen years after its inauguration (Kern 1995; Kern and Pimentel 2001).

Narratives that link the creation of the capital both to millenarianism and an ancient past resulted in Brasília having the highest concentration of esotericism in Brazil (IBGE 2010b). It became widely known as the 'Capital of Esotericism and Mysticism' (Siqueira 2002: 179) or addressed as 'Brasília Mística' (Reis 2008). Aside from all the religions that have their centres in Brasília, new religious groups have cropped up in its surroundings and have grown into towns: the Vale do Amanhecer (Valley of the Dawn), the Cidade Eclética (Eclectic City), and the Cidade da Paz (City of Peace). Around the Federal District, sociologist Deis Siqueira has identified a number of what she calls 'non-conventional religions' or new 'Mystic-Esoteric groups' with an ecumenical and millenarian inspiration that identify themselves as 'centres', 'associations', 'institutes', 'brotherhoods', 'movements', 'societies', 'orders', 'temples' and so on (2002: 180).[18] Many other groups are located some 200km away near the Chapada dos Veadeiros National Park, which is the home of ecologically inspired communities and holistic therapy centres, who attribute healing powers to the area given the high presence of crystals in the land. Internationally, it is considered to be a focal point for new spiritual groups.

Afro-Brazilian religions need mentioning here to highlight their distinctive development in the capital. In Brasília, Umbanda settled before Candomblé because of the migration of the public administration employees from Rio de Janeiro, among whom Umbanda was widely practised. When Candomblé arrived from Bahia in the 1970s, practitioners of Umbanda migrated into various strands of Candomblé, frequently bringing with them elements of their former practice; in particular, their spirit guides, who would share the sacred ceremonial space with the *orixás*. A double trend characterizes Afro-Brazilian religions in the Federal District as the search for eclecticism and the longing for faithfulness to tradition (Silva da Silveira 1994). However, these trends are not mutually exclusive. Some leaders of *terreiros* of Candomblé Ketu were claiming for a return to the 'African way' of practising whilst including in their rituals, for instance, the worship of *caboclos*. Not always is the quest for 'tradition' synonymous with the quest for 'authenticity', but it may imply the aggregation of knowledge and practices from different religions by the leader of the *terreiro* (Pierini 2010).

The intense movement of people between *terreiros*, spiritual and holistic centres, eco retreats, new religious groups, churches and temples provides Brasília with a distinctive spiritual vitality, with people constructing their subjective spiritual routes creatively, which sometimes leads them to the entrance gate of the Vale do Amanhecer. Understanding the foundation narratives of Brasília and its spiritual vitality is indeed crucial to grasp the simultaneous development of the Vale do Amanhecer through the efforts of its founder, Tia Neiva.

In this chapter, I have shown how Brazilian religiosity is far more complex than the census figures may suggest, and people's religious biographies and experiences are too fluid to be contained in fixed categories and classifications. For the purposes of this work, I have focused my discussion on mediumistic religions in particular, considering the variety of ways in which people understand, relate to and embody spiritual beings and how these relations may give rise to the development of new mediumistic practices and the repertoire of spirit manifestations. Practices grounded in mediumistic trance involve ideas of permeability and the interpenetration of human and spirit worlds that are very much shared among these religions and involve non-mediated and embodied experiences of the relation with the divine that are sought by people engaged in this intense religious mobility.

Scholars have tried to classify the variety of mediumistic practices in Brazil through closed lines of development. One such example is Cândido Procópio Camargo (1961, 1973), who has articulated the variations in Brazilian Spiritist mediumistic practices in the theory of the 'mediumistic continuum' (*continuum mediúnico*) or 'Spiritist-Umbandist gradient' (*gradiente Espírita-Umbandista*). Kardecism and Umbanda are set at the poles of a continuum, which implies a common mediumistic practice and the cosmological principle of reincarnation. Between the poles, Camargo sets along the gradient the different Spiritist groups, which feature a great variety in the formal aspects of their practices. While weighting the influence of this theory upon the studies of Brazilian Spiritism, Camurça has proposed to expand the continuum in multiple directions and ramifications, not just between Kardecism and Umbanda but towards esotericism, theosophy, parapsychology and Ayahuasca religions and so forth to grasp the complex mobility of people between them and include the new forms such as Umbanda esotérica, Umbandaime and conscienciologia of the medium Waldo Vieira, among others (Camurça 2017). This expanded view of the continuum, in Carmurça's proposal, is aimed at overcoming the idea of a Brazilian religious field as divided in fixed compartments engaged in mutual borrowing (2017: 24); in this sense, rather than the idea of a network of connections, this view is closer to Ingold's idea of a 'meshwork of entangled lines of life, growth and movement' (2010, 2011: 65) in order to understand the flux of people and practices as constituent aspects of religions.

Developing this proposal, in the light of people's experiences of their relationships with spirits, I argue that we may expand even more the view to include in this entanglement not only the mobility of people but also of their spirits, sometimes following their mediums or triggering them to move on to new possibilities of becoming through experimentation with other religious practices, or to develop themselves new practices. What we may then understand as a Brazilian religious meshwork entwines 'ever-extending trajectories' (Ingold 2010: 11) born out of the relations between human and spirits. Spirits, moving along with their mediums, contribute to this ever-developing tapestry of ritual practices by manifesting in the sacred space of a *terreiro* or in a temple along with other spirits according to specific modalities; and this co-presence of trajectories of both humans and spirits nourishes the affective dimension and the transformative possibilities of mediumistic practices.

## Notes

1. For the concept of 'religious marketplace', see Berger (1967).
2. On atheism in Brazil see Montero and Dullo (2014).
3. The term 'caboclo' designates a person with mixed indigenous Amerindian and European origins, although it is also used to designate Brazilian Amerindians in general, particularly in Afro-Brazilian religions and in the Vale, where *caboclo* spirits are incorporated by mediums in rituals.
4. Darcy Ribeiro (1995) tackles racial disputes, historical genocide and slavery more directly than Freyre. He even reminds us that Brazilians are descendants of tortured African and Amerindians as much as of their torturers (1995: 120).
5. Cannibalism.
6. The 'Cannibal Manifesto' published in 1928 by Brazilian poet Oswald de Andrade, provokingly dated 'Year 374 from the Swallowing of Bishop Sardinha'.
7. Translated from the original in Portuguese.
8. I refer to Kardecism, the Spiritist doctrine systematized by the nineteenth-century French educationalist Léon Dénizard Hypolyte Rivail, also known as 'Allan Kardec', which is largely diffused in Brazil.

9. This fieldwork in Afro-Brazilian religions in the Federal District included fifty places of worship and was conducted between 2009 and 2010 as part of the Inventário Nacional de Referências Culturais (INRC) of the Afro-Brazilian places of worship in the Federal District, Instituto do Patrimônio Histórico e Artistic Nacional (IPHAN), Ministry of Culture, Brazil. The leaders of these places of worship were asked to define their religious practices, which resulted in eleven different denominations, with some *terreiros* practising more than one: Umbanda, Umbanda Iniciática, Umbanda Esotérica Oriental, Umbanda Ecumenico-esotérica, Quimbanda, Candomblé Ketu, Candomblé Jeje-Fon, Candomblé Angôla, Catimbó, Terecô and Omolokô (Pierini 2010).

10. See also Camurça (2003).

11. More specifically, the Federação Espírita Brasileira (FEB) was founded in 1884.

12. According to Roberto Motta (2001), African ethnicity, which once was at the core of group identity, is currently becoming the defining feature of the 'authenticity' of a religious product indistinctively offered to 'consumers' from different ethnic backgrounds. Paradoxically, 'the search for ethnic authenticity leads to its concomitant de-ethnicization' (2001: 79).

13. Since the focus here is on mediumistic religions, see Dawson (2007) for a study of new religious movements in Brazil.

14. Groisman notes that 'the *incorporation* of spiritual entities in Barquinha cannot be characterized by the notion of "spirit possession"' (2016: 60).

15. The part of the city that constitutes the original shape of the capital is commonly called Plano Piloto (Pilot Plan).

16. A savannah-like vegetation typical of this area of Brazil's Central Plateau.

17. Giovanni Battista Lemoyne, 1907, Vol. 16, Chapter 13.

18. For a nominal list, see Siqueira (2002: 180).

*Chapter 2*

# THE VALE DO AMANHECER

'One cannot speak about the Vale without beginning with Tia Neiva', a friend of mine and instructor of mediums used to say, constantly reminding the listener, including myself on several occasions, that her biography cannot be disentangled from any element of the Vale do Amanhecer, which originated from her daily relations with the spirit worlds through her mediumistic phenomena. Therefore, I will begin this chapter drawing together the mediums' narratives on Tia Neiva and thus addressing the foundation and development of the Vale do Amanhecer, followed by an ethnographic description of the current architectural and social organization of the Temples of the Amanhecer. While this chapter sets a more descriptive tone, it is intended to provide the reader with the context to understand the development of the doctrinal knowledge, mediumistic practices and experiences in the following chapters. In the previous chapter, I proposed an approach that is an alternative to the metaphor of a religious marketplace with entrepreneurs engaged in recombining existing beliefs to satisfy the changes in consumer demand. The perspective that I have proposed focuses on the narratives of religious experience and the transformative potential of human-spirit relations in mediumistic practices. In this chapter, I will contend that Tia Neiva's trajectory, defined by her encounters with spirits, was not only transformative for her biography, but I will show how human-spirit relations are considered to be able to give rise to the development of new forms of mediumistic phenomena and later on to inform its growth and transnational expansion. I will then address the development of Vale do Amanhecer as the materialization of Tia Neiva's spiritual experience.

## Tia Neiva

Hardly anyone can remain indifferent to an image of Tia Neiva (Figure 2.1), perhaps because of her deep, piercing eyes that seem to see right through you while they are lost somewhere else where time and space become vague memories of a distant reality. I saw people immediately captivated by her image and feeling a sense of familiarity, whereas others were felt uneasy in front of her images, either commenting on the intensity of her look or her exuberant style. As she passed away in 1985, I never met her personally, but I cohabited with the many aspects of Tia Neiva in daily life in the field. These aspects are tangible and embedded everywhere in the Vale. They are part of the collective construction of the sense of place and of the intersubjective sharing of spiritual knowledge. Mediums' narratives contribute to an ongoing portrayal of Tia Neiva, with their own styles, colours and nuances. These may be the memories and anecdotes reported by those who had lived with her: her family members and elder mediums. Or they may be the evocative narratives of the younger generation, who never met her, although they are still so emotionally charged. This portrayal is consolidated by the sources concerning her biography, mostly written by Tia Neiva herself then edited by her partner Mário Sassi (1974b, 1985, 1999, 2003) and the medium formerly responsible for the doctrinal archive, Mestre Bálsamo Álvares (1992).

She was born as Neiva Seixas Chaves on 30 October 1925. Her birth certificate was registered in Propriá, Sergipe, although her family claims that she was born in Ilhéus, Bahia. Brought up in a Roman Catholic family, she studied until the third year of primary school. She got married in 1943 to Raul Zelaya Alonso in the State of Goiás but she soon became a widow at the age of twenty-four. Solely responsible for the maintenance for her four children, she firstly opened a photo shop then worked as farmer and then eventually began working in freight transport, being the first woman to be issued a truck driver licence in Brazil. In 1957, she was invited to work on the construction of the new capital, Brasília, by Bernardo Sayão, friend of her former husband and director of the NOVACAP (Urbanization Company of the New Capital). Although being a woman driving a truck across Brazil in those times was a challenging enterprise in terms of both safety and gender issues, she was proud of her independence, passionate about her job and nomadic life and soon became widely respected among her colleagues. In the same year, she suddenly began to experience involuntary mediumistic phenomena, including visions, premonitions, spirit incorporations and out-of-body experiences (Sassi 1999: 11). Being apprehensive about the spontaneous and recurrent nature of these occurrences, she sought explanations in the Church, in psychiatry, Candomblé and Spiritist centres. Although initially refusing these phenomena, since they were intense, she began to listen to what those who claimed to be 'higher spiritual beings' were telling her. They began to instruct her in her mission to create a new doctrine that would gather a group of incarnated spirits called the 'Jaguars' and prepare them for the transition towards a new era. As part of this mission, she had to create the *doutrinador*, a new type of conscious medium able to clarify incarnate and disincarnate beings according to a 'spiritual science' (Sassi 1985).

It was through the encounter with a Kardecist woman, Maria de Oliveira, soon to be called Mãe Neném, that Neiva found help in situating her mediumistic phenomena through the Spiritist discourse. Mãe Neném assisted her in developing the technique of 'conscious transport' (*transporte conciente*), also known as 'astral travel', described as 'the ability to consciously leave one's body, leaving it in a state of suspension similar to natural sleep, and to dislocate oneself in other vibrational planes' (Sassi 1999: 11). Through this technique, from 1959 to 1964, her spirit was said to travel regularly to Tibet for her initiatory apprenticeship with a Tibetan monk, Master Umahã, whom she claimed to be alive in Lhasa until 1981 (N,C. Zelaya 1960; Álvares 1992: 133; Sassi 1999: 12). She maintained that not only was her clairvoyance the source of all the spiritual knowledge she received, but it also allowed her to live on different planes simultaneously. This included visiting different dimensions beyond matter and receiving instructions by spirits belonging to the highest spiritual hierarchies. Her main spirit guide was Pai Seta Branca (Father White Arrow), who manifested as a spirit of an Amerindian chief leading the mission of the Vale do Amanhecer. She claimed that he had an incarnation on earth as Saint Francis of Assisi. Along with Pai Seta Branca, she had a feminine spirit mentor Mãe Yara (Mother Yara), his twin soul who was incarnated with him in Assisi as Saint Clare. Among her main spirit mentors there was also Pai João de Enoque (Father John of Enoch), Tiaozinho and Amanto, who assisted her in establishing the material, ritualistic and doctrinal foundations of the Amanhecer, including the shapes and disposition of the sacred spaces and ritual vestments. Once Tia Neiva concluded her apprenticeship with spirit mentors, she was initiated into the highest spiritual planes with the title of Agla Koatay 108,[1] whereby '108' represented the number of forces (mantras) she had received (ibid.).

In November 1959, Tia Neiva, along with Mãe Neném and a small group of followers, founded the União Espiritualista Seta Branca (Spiritualist Union White Arrow) in the Núcleo Bandeirante of Brasília.[2] In the same year, the group moved to a rural area in the Serra de Ouro, near the city of Alexânia,

Goiás, where they built a wooden house to receive people in need and assist them through spiritual practices. Tia Neiva's charitable purpose also led to the foundation of the Orfanato Francisco de Assis (Orphanage Francis of Assisi), hosting some forty children. In 1964, the paths of Neiva and Mãe Neném parted ways, with Neiva wanting to develop mediumship away from the Kardecist practice that Mãe Neném preferred to follow. Neiva moved with the community to Taguatinga, changing the name to Obras Sociais da Ordem Espiritualista Cristã – OSOEC (Social Works of the Spiritual Christian Order). In 1965, the first wooden temple was constructed to host the rituals, and the orphanage was formally recognized as a legal entity by the National Council for Social Service – CNSS soon after in 1966. In the same year, Mário Sassi (1921–1994) joined the community, beginning his journey as both partner of Tia Neiva and co-leader of the community. At that time, Mário Sassi was invited by anthropologist Darcy Ribeiro to be the public relations advisor of the new University of Brasília. Former leader of the progressivist movement of the left-wing Catholic Youth Workers/ JPO with a background in philosophy and the social sciences, according to César Vicente (1977), a Catholic priest and anthropologist who carried out concealed fieldwork in the Vale in the 1970s, Sassi approached Tia Neiva in a troubled moment as he was at risk of being persecuted by the military regime after the military coup d'état of 1964. Sassi is often described by members of the Order as 'the intellectual' of the doctrine, both because of his academic background and because he interpreted and articulated Tia Neiva's revelations, producing the Vale's main doctrinal bibliography.

Four years after their settlement in Taguatinga, the community lost the right of ownership of the land, so in November 1969 they moved and definitively settled in an old farm south of Planaltina-DF, where the members of the Order began to build their houses and the temple and adopted the current name 'Vale do Amanhecer' (Valley of the Dawn). According to Tia Neiva's daughter, Carmem Lúcia, the location was indicated by the spirit mentors, who also called it Templo do Amanhecer (Temple of the Dawn). It was Tia Neiva that asked their permission to call it 'Vale' (Valley), given the geological shape of the site, which was surrounded by hills (C.L. Zelaya 2009: 143). People from all social backgrounds arrived in the Vale from all across Brazil seeking consultation with Tia Neiva's and spiritual treatment in the temple. Some patients remained and became mediums themselves. In order to accommodate the growing number of mediums and visitors, the temple was demolished and rebuilt several times, with the current elliptical one being the seventh temple since the beginning of the mission. All the work was carried out by mediums, who contributed in terms of labour and materials for the constructions. The community organization, doctrine and ritual practices were all developed during the 1970s and 1980s.

The Adjunto Yumatá Mestre Caldeira accompanied Tia Neiva in the development of the Vale do Amanhecer in the 1970s and described those years as follows:

> We had no instructors. Our instructors were Pai Seta Branca, Pai João, Mãe Tildes, Mãe Yara. They used to incorporate and pass on to us the instructions of what we had to do. There was no road from here to Planaltina, just ground – there was nothing else. That bridge was made with two logs; when it rained, the water would wash everything away so no one was able to cross over. Around 1972 and 1973 there were immense queues of people wanting to develop their mediumship; they used to come and go by foot because at the time there was no bus, no van, no horses here … nothing! I can't tell you how many times I came and went back by foot in the middle of the bushes at night.

The difficult conditions in the early years of the community are part of the memories of the elder masters. Municipal water arrived in the Vale in 1970 and electricity in 1973. The first temple made from stone was built in 1974, followed by the open-air sacred spaces: the *Estrela Candente* (name of a sacred space and ritual, literally meaning 'candescent star') in 1976 and the Lake of Yemanjá with the *Quadrantes* and pyramid between 1978 and 1979. Regarding the construction of the sacred spaces, Caldeira stressed to me that:

> The spirit called Tiãozinho is responsible for the constructions in the Amanhecer. All the *Estrela Candente* and the temple were marked by him. He used to stand in front of Tia, as she was the only one who was able to see him, tracing on the ground with a stick and saying 'here it will need to be these many metres, you will have to get this amount of bricks, it will be so high and so wide …' We used to do it and it was just right!

The community developed around the charismatic leadership of Tia Neiva, considered by mediums to be both the prophet and mother of the Jaguars. Sassi described her complex role as follows:

> Through the manipulation of forces from other dimensions, she cures and stabilizes abnormal situations and releases those beings who seek her out of distress; through the contact with other worlds, she gives us the most urgent news of our immediate future and through her apprenticeship with superior spirits, she transmits us the Christic teachings and prophecies. (Sassi 2003: 20)

In a research focused upon Tia Neiva, Cavalcante (2000) has defined her as a shaman for her ability to travel to other dimensions.[3] Certainly, Tia Neiva's phenomena should be distinguished from those of the rest of the mediums in the Vale do Amanhecer, since they do not have much in common with the types of mediumship she had developed for them – *apará* (incorporation mediumship) and *doutrinador* (indoctrination mediumship). Elder mediums often point out that her type of 'clairvoyance', which includes all known types of mediumship (apart from olfactory mediumship, as some mediums point out), appears only once every three hundred years. What they understand as 'clairvoyance' involves being simultaneously in different planes, and they distinguish it from 'voyance', intended as 'seeing' only. Mestre Caldeira described her as being completely unconscious during incorporations but also able to be in different physical locations simultaneously:

> One day Néstor[4] went to Pirapora [a town in Minas Gerais where they opened an external temple]. Tia was here incorporating a spirit, but she herself incorporated in Ivone [Néstor's wife] in Pirapora and gave a lecture to the people in that temple. Tia was a real, pure phenomenon! She had this conscious ability. She saw everything and she knew everything that happened over there. When she disincorporated here, she told us: 'I was in Pirapora and I incorporated in Ivone there and I said this and that ...' When Néstor came back to the Vale he confirmed what happened and what she had said.

The elder mediums' narratives of their lives with Tia Neiva often emphasize these kinds of episodes, especially when referring to the spiritual grounding and thus revelatory character of the doctrinal knowledge of the Amanhecer. The mediums I spoke to in the Vale presented me with different aspects of the personality of Tia Neiva. They described her as a gentle woman and called both *'tia'* (aunt) and *'mãe'* (mother) for her care of the children in the orphanage and hosting people in her *Casa Grande* (Big House). She expanded kinship ties in her everyday life by accepting those in need within her extended family, and hence she called everyone 'son' or 'daughter'. To this day she is referred to as *'nossa mãe'* (our mother) even by those who never met her. She is also remembered as a strong and independent woman with a passion for gypsy culture and dances, which she attributed to what she claimed to be her past life as a gypsy woman called Natacha. To revive her 'gipsy transcendental roots', she used to organize gypsy feasts in the streets around bonfires – something that is practised in the Vale to this day. Then, the gentle woman entered the sacred sphere as a prophet and priestess, reflecting what she presented as her past lives as a Pythia in Delphi's Oracle and the prophetess Veleda[5] in Vespasian Rome, infused with the charisma of Cleopatra.

The Adjunto Amayã Guilherme Stuckert, who was also the official photographer of the Vale until he passed away in 2005, told me that Tia Neiva used to call him at a moment's notice to do a photo shoot: 'she loved to be photographed', he said, 'but her eyes were always looking far away into other dimensions'. He would either capture her with the noble and proud gaze of a spiritual leader or lost in the deepest reflections, but primarily he would catch the expression of a loving and caring woman.

These qualities are echoed by the words of Mestre Guto, a medium who cohabited with her in the *Casa Grande* and assisted her especially through her later illness:

Tia was first of all a woman; she lived the life of a woman, and additionally she established all this. She was a woman in the 1960s. Imagine how a woman truck driver could be seen at that time. In silence and simplicity, she revolutionized what until then where the pillars of religion. She took Jesus off the cross and put him back walking among us. She took the idea of sin saying that it did not exist because each one is responsible for his trajectory and actions and that God does not come to punish and blame us. She was revolutionary in this sense. She didn't want mystic robots; she wanted the medium who felt moved by emotions, who cried and laughed ... and eat beans. She didn't want us to believe in her words, but she asked us to analyse and see if they suited us. I thought this was fantastic! The freedom that people have in this doctrine, where people come and go whenever they choose to do so.

**Figure 2.1** Tia Neiva. Photo: Guilherme Stuckert.

Tia Neiva was a contemporary of another Brazilian Spiritist medium, the automatic writer Chico Xavier. Tia Neiva and Chico Xavier gained the reputation of being the most popular mediums that Brazil has known because they are considered to have transmitted a considerable amount of knowledge from the spirit world while being the exemplary living principles of humility and charity. Indeed, Sassi described Tia Neiva's life as a testimony of 'an integral Christic existence' (2003: 11). In this sense, they contributed to characterizing spirit mediumship in Brazil more as a 'mission' rather than as a performance.

Tia Neiva and Mário Sassi led the Vale do Amanhecer until Neiva died in 1985 from tuberculosis, having spent the last years of her life dependent on an oxygen mask. Their joint work gave impulse to the development of the doctrine of the Amanhecer: Neiva had been transmitting the teachings from the spirit world and Mário interpreting and systematizing them into texts. Before addressing this doctrinal knowledge in the next chapters, I will tackle the description of the current spatial and social organization of the Vale do Amanhecer for what concerns both the Templo Mãe – that is the main temple near Brasília established by Tia Neiva in 1969 – and the external temples of the Amanhecer.

## The Templo Mãe in Brasília

Driving across the Brazilian *cerrado* with its savanna-like vegetation – along the BR-020 to Planaltina and turning right on the DF-230, and then right again on DF-130 – on the right side of the road one can catch a glimpse of a hill on the top of which is a symbol of an ellipse and the inscription in large letters *'Salve Deus!'* (Hail God!),[6] anticipating from a distance one's arrival to the Templo Mãe of the Vale do Amanhecer (the 'Mother Temple' being the main centre of the Valley of the Dawn). The entrance gate comprises tree columns, the symbol of the moon, the sun and the words 'Vale do Amanhecer' with a Jaguar symbol in the middle. Passing through the gate and proceeding forward, one will arrive at the sacred area of the temple.

It was there that on a spring evening in October 2004 that I took my first steps into the sacred grounds of the Vale, overwhelmed by its colours and symbols. The glowing orange sun was setting behind the 7m-tall image of Jesus to the right of the temple's stone facade. Rituals were being performed in external sacred spaces such as the *Estrela Sublimação* (Sublimation Star), a fenced area with geometrical forms featuring the most intense chromatic tones, among which was the symbol of a giant ellipse. Some mediums were sat around a table in the shape of a six-pointed star incorporating spirits, whilst the solemn voice of a medium leading another ritual reverberated through the speakers, merging with the gentle chants and mantras of some nymphs (female mediums) moving in a procession towards the temple. They wore glittering veils and their fluorescent-coloured vestments raised red dust from the ground as they passed by slowly, carrying lances.

The sacred area includes three external ritual spaces and a 2,400 square meter stone temple with an east-facing entrance (Figure 2.2). This is surmounted by the symbols of the moon and the sun connected by the arrow of Pai Seta Branca, and there is a jaguar symbol above the door. An enormous Star of David crossed by the arrow of Pai Seta Branca stands before the entrance and features an inscription in Portuguese that reads: 'Children! The man who tries to escape his karmic goal or transcendental oaths will be devoured or will be lost as a bird trying to fly in the darkness of the night. White Arrow'.[7] Among the three external ritual spaces, the one called *Turigano*[8] is contiguous to the left side of the temple entrance and hosts different rituals. The *Estrela Sublimação* (Sublimation Star) before the temple is a space dedicated to a ritual of healing, which draws on forces of past civilizations. The *Aruanda de Pai João* (*Aruanda*[9] of Father John, a *preto velho*) is an empty round space covered by a roof, functioning monthly as a sacred space during the week of the full moon to host the ritual of *Alabá*, which involves consultation with the spirits of the *pretos velhos* incorporated by mediums benefiting from the forces of the moon. Another focal point of the sacred area is Tia Neiva's former house, the *Casa Grande*, a blue and white house made from wood that after her death was turned into a museum of the history of the Vale do Amanhecer and covered with an aura of sacredness by mediums, who meditate in the room where she used to communicate with the spirit worlds.

The area in front of the temple is usually crowded with patients and mediums moving around rituals, and there are also cafes, restaurants and shops. The shops sell mainly accessories and uniforms, tailor-made. What catches the attention of visitors and mediums from other temples is the shop of Vilela, the artist that paints images of the spirit guides working with mediums in the Vale. The building opposite these shops hosts the offices of the President of the Order and the administration, which is conducted by mediums called *Filhos dos Devas* (Sons of the Devas). A cloakroom and changing rooms are also provided for mediums to leave their everyday clothes and put on their ritual uniforms.

When I first entered the temple, I felt a strong sensory impact. The extraordinary uniforms seemed to merge with the thick clouds of incense; there were multicoloured surfaces defining the ritual spaces and an intriguing mixture of sounds. Among these sounds, I could discern songs, the snapping of fingers, a variety of ritual invocations and the vocal expressions that later I attributed to the different spirits incorporated by mediums. This was all produced by the simultaneous performance of a dozen rituals, with several hundred people moving around the aisles. What initially seemed like noise and confusion sometime later unexpectedly produced a sense of calm in me. As I walked through the crowed aisles on an evening that featured the attendance of almost a thousand people, I was continuously brushed by the veils and cloaks of mediums rapidly passing from one ritual to another. The temple comprises of adjoining ritual spaces called *setores de trabalho* (working sectors) or *castelos* (castles) if they are rooms. The *castelos* are located along the perimeter, whereas the central axis hosts other *setores de trabalho*. The disposition of the spaces depends upon and also favours the flow of energy: one flow moves back and forth as a pendulum along the axis and the other moves clockwise along the elliptical perimeter. Mediums move across the temple according to these flows and stop and open the solar plexus as a reverence in the focal point whenever they cross the axis, such as in front of the statues of Jesus and Pai Seta Branca (Figure 2.3). Patients follow a therapeutic route through rituals, moving clockwise from the entrance to the exit (see Chapter Five for a description of these rituals).

Mediums describe the plan of the temple as an ellipse, which is one of the main symbols of the Vale, representing a portal between the worlds and also the flow of forces between the spirit and the physical world. Some mediums also compare it to a ship navigating between the worlds, with its command being the *Radar*, located in the middle of the left aisle. This is the place where three mediums (commanders) sit and direct the rituals of the day. Some *castelos* along the aisle are used by mediums to prepare themselves for rituals.[10] The main opening and closing of ritual sessions is done in the central area in front of the *Pira* (Pyre), which represents the Divine Presence in the temple. This area, which is visible to visitors but with access restricted to mediums only, includes the *Mesa Evangélica* (Evangelical Table), a triangular table (Figure 2.4) used for the incorporation and indoctrination of the *sofredores* (suffering spirits), which is derived from the Kardecist *Mesa Branca* (White Table) but differs from it in its form and ritual. The only hidden area of the temple comprises the Initiation Castles (*Castelos de Iniciação*), which are rooms located at the back of the temple protected by gates that are opened only to initiates for the ritual.

Apart from the sacred area of the temple, the other focal point in the town is an open-air sacred complex called *Solar dos Médiuns* (Solar of the Mediums) located at the bottom of the hill around an artificial lake called *Lago de Yemanjá* (Lake of Yemanjá), and it comprises three ritual spaces: the *Estrela Candente* (Candescent Star), the *Quadrantes* (Quadrants) and the Pyramid (Figure 2.5 and 2.6). The rituals of the complex are what mostly trigger the curiosity of visitors; the complex increasingly attracts tourists and the media with its giant symbols and spectacular choreographies performed by hundreds or sometimes even thousands of mediums.

The *Estrela Candente* is the setting of the ritual of *Estrela Candente* performed three times a day to transform the forces that are affecting humanity. The kind of disincarnate spirits passing through this ritual were described by Tia Neiva as leaders of lower spirit worlds causing major conflicts and epidemics on a large scale and who cannot be incorporated because their heavy energies could affect mediums. The ritual is guided by a commander invoking forces and directing ritual actions with a microphone from the *Reino Central* (Central Kingdom), a yellow cabin with the symbol of the sun. The preparation, called *Coroamento* (Crowning), entails a complex choreography in which mediums proceed in pairs of *doutrinadores* and *aparás*, male and female. Stairs and paths are coloured in order to distinguish the different routes they have to follow, passing around a waterfall on top of which is a triangle (symbol of the medium *apará*) and a giant image of Mãe Yara (Mother Yara, twin soul of Pai Seta Branca). Once preparation is complete, the pairs of *doutrinadores* and *aparás* are positioned along the 108 blue and yellow concrete slabs called *esquifes* (symbolically meaning 'coffins') that surround a small star-shaped lake. The *doutrinadores* lie down on the slabs to charge them with their ectoplasm, a magnetic force released from their initiatic plexus (Figure 2.7). Once they stand up, through their ritual actions, disincarnate spirits are attracted onto the *esquifes* to receive that force and to be indoctrinated and then passed over to the spirit world through a portal represented by an ellipse, which stands at the centre of the star. Finally, the *aparás* incorporate the spirits guides called the people of the water to cleanse the water of the lake. Since the energies are deemed to be strong, mediums participating in this ritual wear cloaks to protect their bodies, and in the evening they must participate in another ritual called *Entrega das Energias* (Delivery of Energies) in the *Turigano* to deliver the energies to the spirit world.

The second ritual space, called *Quadrantes* (Quadrant), is situated along the northern shore of the large lake and is divided into seven spaces, each comprising a line of *esquifes* and an image of a *princesa* (princess, spirit guides of the *doutrinadores*). Each space corresponds to the day of the week the ritual is performed, following a patter similar to the one of *Estrela Candente*. In the middle of the *Quadrantes* stands the giant image of Yemanjá, the deity of the water, whilst at the end of the line stands the third sacred space of the Pyramid. The Pyramid is said to act as the power plant of all the temples of the Amanhecer, thus it is opened daily, managed by two medium guardians assisting visitors, who go there to meditate or to drink the water, which is said to be infused with healing forces by a crystal hanging from the centre of the Pyramid. During the rituals of *Estrela* and *Quadrantes*, the Pyramid closes to the public, and the two guardians perform the same rituals outside the front doors facing the lake.

Walking along the streets of the town, one may easily come across some groups of mediums performing rituals at the crossroads. These rituals, called *Abatás*, involve five pairs of male and female mediums, *aparás* and *doutrinadores*, who position themselves in the shape of the ellipse and invoke forces to cleanse the energies in the streets. Rituals are indeed well integrated in the town outside the sacred area, as the town itself was originally developed by mediums constructing their houses around the temple. With its growth in the 1990s, people who did not belong to the Order also began to settle in the area, gradually contributing to its current uncontrolled expansion towards the south behind the hill. The southern half of the town, called Vila Pacheco, now features a Roman Catholic church and several Evangelical and Pentecostal churches, with members of the latter often distributing leaflets claiming to be carrying out the mission to 'convert mediums to Jesus Christ'.

According to the Brazilian census in 2010, the town of the Vale do Amanhecer counted 10,238 inhabitants (IBGE 2010a). Since my first time in the field in 2004, most roads have been paved, accommodation and commercial services have increased and internet connection has become available. Considering the Vale do Amanhecer as a whole (including the neighbourhood of Vila Pacheco), there are two schools, a small health centre, small supermarkets and commercial activities, a fitness centre and a football field. The area near the temple, comprising the first five streets parallel to the entrance, is mostly inhabited by members of the Order. It has a high concentration of commercial services, including two supermarkets, a bakery, several grocers, a pharmacy, hairdressers, internet points, restaurants and cafes. To accommodate visitors and mediums coming from other temples, there are around seven *pousadas* (guesthouses) and many private room rentals. In the same area, there is a remarkable concentration of shops for tailoring ritual uniforms and buying accessories, including sacred jewellery and images.

Some of my medium friends lamented the fact that the town lacks proper spaces for socialization. People often use the cafés in the temple area for this purpose, but being a sacred area, most mediums prefer to gather for a coffee in their homes. Indeed, many homes, besides the living room, have a backyard or a porch where people can entertain guests and organize barbecues. Young people can meet at the small park by the main entrance or at the gym. Although a number of social programmes offering classes of *capoeira* and various dances had been introduced, streets remained the main option for youth gatherings, but this was also risky. Safety indeed became a major concern when the police station near the temple was shut down. Consequently, in 2010 the criminality involving youth gangs and drug dealers had increased to a critical point, making it hard for mediums to walk the streets feeling safe, as armed robberies were happening weekly. The community put in several claims to the regional administration for a police station in the town, but the only result was a slight increase in police patrol in the streets. Some of my medium friends deemed it paradoxical that Brasília promotes its tourism and holds the Vale as one of its attractions yet the regional authorities do not provide basic safety protection for inhabitants and visitors. Houses are increasingly highly protected with gates, grates, electric circuits and other security measures.

Architecturally, apart from the sacred areas, the town of the Vale do Amanhecer does not differ from other small towns of the region, featuring simple houses differing from one another in colours and styles without following any prescriptive urban planning scheme, as one can buy a piece of land and build any kind of house within its borders. The majority of houses I visited were developed on one level and had a paved backyard. Mediums reserve a space in their houses, either a small room or a corner, for their private altar called *aledá*, to be used for daily prayers. The *aledá* represents a point where forces from the spirit world are projected in the house. It comprises a shelf or table with a white cloth, images of one's spirit guides, of Jesus, Pai Seta Branca and other spirits mentors, along with a white candle, incense, two small pots containing salt and perfume for cleansing and sometimes water from the temple, which is considered to be infused with healing energies. The disposition of objects and images varies, and some mediums may add other items such as crystals, a rose or even some accessories from their uniforms.

Household composition is also consistent with the Brazilian ones; there are no particular marriage patterns defined by the doctrine, although mediums may consider it ideal for partners to be *apará* and *doutrinador* because of their complementary functions of incorporating and indoctrinating spirits mean they can work together in all rituals. This is not the norm, however, as there are couples of two *doutrinadores* or two *aparás*. Couples may get married through a civil marriage and only then undertake a religious wedding in the temple (a ritual including the blessing from a spirit incorporated by a medium). Civil divorce is also recognized and remarriage is accepted as well in the temple. The couple's children may be baptized in the temple, and if they wish, they may participate in the Sunday meetings of the *Pequeno Pajé* (Little Shaman), a sort of catechesis where children are introduced to the principles of the Gospel. Children are not supposed to develop their mediumship before they are eighteen years of age, in order to favour the development of the body without the interference of some particular energies. There are, however, special cases in which teenagers spontaneously manifest mediumistic phenomena, and they may participate in the youth mediumistic development (which differs from the adult one in length) in order to learn how to control them. Children and teenagers also wear a uniform to participate in the singing around the temple. In any case, they are not required to follow their parents' religion if they do not wish.

Most activities in the town are based around the spiritual activities of the temple. The social composition of the Order in the Templo Mãe includes working-class members as well as a significant number of middle-class and professional participants either living in the Vale or coming from Brasília or its satellite cities. Because of the proximity to the capital, the most common employment sectors are the government offices, the public sector and the National Army. Among the professionals, there are lawyers, health practitioners and scholars from local universities. Young people have access to higher education and professional courses offered in the capital or in nearby towns. The high demand for ritual vestments means there are many artisans and dressmakers, some working in ritual uniform shops and others at home: some specialize in making veils, others in embroidering symbols, dresses and cloaks. There are also farmers, construction workers, cleaners, grocers, hairdressers and beauticians, schoolteachers and retailers, as well as a number of unemployed people. Many mediums of the Templo Mãe live in the Plano Piloto or in closer satellite cities and have houses in the Vale so

**Figure 2.2** The entrance of the Templo Mãe in Brasília. Photo: Emily Pierini.

**Figure 2.3** Mediums' reverences in front of the statue of Pai Seta Branca. Photo: Emily Pierini.

**Figure 2.4** The ritual of *Mesa Evangélica*: *doutrinadores* indoctrinating suffering spirits incorporated by the *aparás* around the table. Photo: Emily Pierini.

**Figure 2.5** Vale do Amanhecer. *Solar dos Médiuns* (*Estrela Candente*, *Quadrantes*, Pyramid and Lake of Yemanjá) and the town in 2010. Photo: Emily Pierini.

**Figure 2.6** Ritual of the *Estrela Candente*, *Quadrantes* and *Pyramid*. Photo: Emily Pierini.

**Figure 2.7** Ritual of the *Estrela Candente*: *doutrinadores* lie on the slabs to charge them with their ectoplasm. Photo: Emily Pierini.

they can spend the weekend participating in rituals in the temple. Besides the permanent inhabitants, there are many temporary residents from all over the country and, more recently, foreigners, who rent houses or rooms in the Vale for periods ranging from a weekend up to a year while they participate in rituals or undertake mediumistic development. The social composition of the members of the temple reflects the one of the locality in which the temple is located. Indeed, because of the proximity to the political capital of Brazil the social composition of the Templo Mãe differs from the temples I have visited in the rural areas across Brazil and from the temples in Europe that are located mainly in industrial areas.

## The Temples of the Amanhecer

### Foundation and Organization

Since its foundation, over 700 temples have been opened in Brazil and some opened abroad, including Bolivia, Guyana, Trinidad and Tobago, Japan, Portugal, Germany, Switzerland, Italy, the United Kingdom and the United States.[11] According to the administration of the Order, the register of the Filho de Devas counted 90,900 members initiated between 1996 and 2010, and during my long-term fieldwork in 2010, around 500 mediums were initiated at Templo Mãe. In 2019 the register counted 138,768 members.[12] Yet, they stressed that it is currently not possible to determine the number of initiated mediums across the temples of the Amanhecer, since not all temples send their registers to the Templo Mãe. Especially in the first decades following the foundation, not all mediums were formally registered. They further pointed out that it is not possible to determine the number of active members or members who have left or returned to the Order, as mediums participate on a voluntary basis and there is no record of how frequently they attended.

Although there are temples in every Brazilian state assisting patients locally, the Templo Mãe is attended by patients from across Brazil and beyond. More recently, indeed, the temple is often chosen by international groups of visitors – mainly from Europe, the US, Australia and New Zealand – as a destination of spiritual healing tours around the region of the Planalto Central, usually unfolding between John of God's healing centre (Casa Dom Inácio de Loyola in Abadiânia, Goiás)[13] and the many healing groups located in the National Park of the Chapada dos Veadeiros. As a result, foreign spiritual tourists often participate in rituals as patients and some decide to stay longer in order to be trained as mediums.

Temples abroad are founded either by groups of Brazilian mediums who have emigrated abroad or by foreigners who have developed their mediumship in Brazil and returned to their countries. In Europe, temples are rapidly growing and so is the number of new mediums, and they attract hundreds of patients in the weekly ritual sessions. In Portugal, ten temples were opened with over 2,000 Portuguese mediums being initiated between 2012 and 2015, an expansion that was facilitated by the Portuguese language. In fact, over several field visits, I noticed that linguistic accessibility was a major concern in the opening of temples in European countries. In England, for instance, the process of translation is still in progress. The two temples in Cambridgeshire and London are attracting primarily Brazilian and Portuguese members residing in the United Kingdom, as the main language in use is Portuguese, although consultations with spirits in English are also available to the English-speaking patients. Since 2015, I have followed the development of temples in Italy, where the spiritual work is entirely translated to non-Portuguese speakers, patients are assisted and new mediums are trained in Italian,[14] leading to the formal foundation of a first temple in 2016 with the subsequent initiation of Italian members, followed by another two temples in 2018.

The foundation of a temple is said to be received as a mission from spirit guides. Personal initiative not driven by a spiritual request is usually discouraged, even though it is not prohibited. Those who receive such a mission usually seek the guidance of both spirit mentors and their seniors in the hierarchy throughout the development of the new temple. The spiritual practices of the temple are not publicly advertised, since proselytizing is strictly forbidden and mediums understand it as clashing with the principle of free will and risking interference in people's karma. Therefore, patients usually hear about the Vale by word of mouth, and often they visit the temple accompanied by a friend or a relative. Some patients may then choose to remain and develop their mediumship, if invited by a spirit guide to do so. During the mediumistic development, some may also choose to be initiated, becoming members of the temple. As the community gradually grows, the temple may also develop both in space and in the number of mediums needed to perform specific rituals. In this sense, temples are categorized in 'stages' (*estágios*) designating their level of development. The first stage is a 'temple in projection' (*templo em projeção*) and the second stage is known as 'special work' (*trabalho especial*), with the temple working with the so called 'master stream' (*corrente mestra*), a special force acting in rituals. These stages vary in terms of opening and closing times of the temple's ritual sessions, the number and hierarchical classification of mediums, the types of rituals and sacred spaces required to be available, the disposition of ritual rooms and the presence or not of the initiation castles. While the Templo Mãe is open daily from 10AM to late at night, other temples may open on official work days (*trabalho oficial* – that is, on Wednesday, Saturday and Sunday).

In terms of financial organization, the temples of the Amanhecer are self-financed and thus monetary compensation from patients is not accepted, neither in form of payment nor offerings, as it is held to be against the principle of spiritual work as charity, a principle that is rooted in and quite widespread in Kardecism. Nor are mediums supposed to pay a percentage of their income to the Order. Rather, mediums contribute to the expenses of the temple to which they belong through voluntary donations, sometimes even anonymously. They may also contribute by participating in the several events organized by the temple's members to gather funds for paying the rent (where applicable), bills and maintenance and renovations of the sacred areas. In the Templo Mãe, a group of mediums organize a charity lunch in the *Casa Grande* on the first Sunday of each month, where mediums can donate food and cook. The lunch is sold at a fixed price (reflecting the average prices of the restaurants in town), and mediums can eat together entertained by some live music. Apart from donations, the other sources of funding rely on events such as raffles, second-hand markets and community parties with dances, games and food stalls. Another source of income is from the shop by the Templo Mãe belonging to the Order, where mediums buy the uniforms, vestments, accessories, badges, symbols and waistcoats of the initiation. There are other uniform shops belonging to the Order, although recently alternatives have appeared selling the same products. It is worth mentioning that given the growing number of external temples, they cannot be financially supported by the Templo Mãe, thus each temple since its foundation is entirely self-funded by its president and mediums.

### Hierarchical Organization and Gender

Each temple of the Amanhecer is managed by its president, a male *doutrinador* managing the administrative and ritualistic matters, and a coordinator,[15] a female nymph, preferably the partner of the president, whose function is to deal with the coordination of the phalanges (groups of mediums each with their ritual functions, uniforms and symbolism representing forces for the past), control the correct preparation of the ritual vestments and manage the social matters arising within the temple's community.

From a spiritual point of view, all the temples of the Amanhecer are considered to be fed by the forces of the Templo Mãe. Mediums would use the metaphor of a tree, whereby the Templo Mãe represents the root from which the force flows as water and nutrients to reach the branches, the external temples, and they would also refer to the pyramid in the Templo Mãe as being the engine of all the other temples. This idea of distribution of forces is also used to explain the hierarchical structure of the masterhood (*mestrado*), comprising the initiated members of the Order. The spiritual force distributed through the hierarchical pyramid is known as *força decrescente* (decreasing force).[16] Tia Neiva developed a hierarchical structure intended as a continuum of the spiritual hierarchy on the physical plane and conceived a leadership shared between four *Trinos Triadas Presidentes* (presidents) with different domains of action: Trino Tumuchy Mestre Mário Sassi (the administrative power), Trino Arakém Mestre Néstor Sabatovicz (the executive power), Trino Sumaná Mestre Michel Hanna (the healing power), Trino Ajará Mestre Gilberto Zelaya (the coordinator of external temples). They are called *Trinos* (Trines) for they are said to receive three rays of the Oracle of Simiromba (namely, a point of transmission of forces in the spirit world). These are followed by the Trino Regente Tumará Mestre José Carlos (Regent Trine) and the *Trinos Herdeiros* (Heirs), who are mostly members of the Zelaya family.

Below the *Trinos* there are the *Adjuntos Koatay 108 Arjuna-Rama Arcanos de Povo* (Adjunct Koatay 108 Arcana of People, unifying the Indian lines of Arjuna and Rama). Consecrated by Tia Neiva in 1978, they represent the roots of different peoples; indeed, they are also known as *Adjuntos Raiz* (Root Adjuncts). Each *Adjunto* was called by Tia Neiva to form his *Continente* 108 (Continent) distributing the forces of his spiritual Minister (the spirit guide they represent) to his people through his rays. The Continent had to be composed of: the *Adjunto*, representing his Minister; seven masters classified as '7th Ray', each with his nymph, godmother and godfather; for each 7th Ray, six masters classified as '6th Ray' with their respective nymphs; and three Regents (C. Zelaya 2009: 173). The *Adjunto Koatay 108* was then elevated to *Arcanos*, 7th Rays to *Rama 2000*, and the 6th Rays to 7th Rays, who along with three Regents, nymphs and masters altogether represent a decreasing force transmitted to their people (2009: 174).

Every medium after the third initiation must choose an *Adjunto de Povo* to which he or she will affiliate. In this sense, a medium who chooses to affiliate, for instance, to the Adjunto Ypuena Mestre Lacerda (whose spirit guide is the Ministro Ypuena), will belong to the *Povo Ypuena* (Ypuena People), receiving the forces of the Ministro Ypuena and having Mestre Lacerda as a reference point in his or her mediumistic life. If one 'component of the people' opens an external temple, he then becomes an *Adjunto* for the members of his temple. According to this example, the president would then belong to the root Ypuena but projects the forces of his own *Ministro* to his people. Members of that temple will then automatically affiliate to their Adjunct President of their temple upon their third initiation. For this reason, the *Adjuntos de Povo* consecrated by Tia Neiva in the Templo Mãe are the roots of different peoples; and in this way, according to Tia Neiva, the decreasing force would proceed and be distributed to all the temples through the hierarchy.

Mediums present themselves as having a spiritual genealogy and develop a strong sense of belonging to a people. In rituals, each medium calls upon the decreasing force by affirming their position within the hierarchy and spiritual belonging through the *emissão* (emission), an individual invocation of forces. Mediums alternate in invoking their forces so that their emissions form a meshwork of forces interweaving in rituals through their spiritual genealogies. These kinds of spiritual kinship ties or genealogies do not inform sociobiological kinship. Rather, if a female medium, a *ninfa*, belongs to a people different from her partner's, she must change people in order to follow her partner's *Adjunto de Povo*. The hierarchy is indeed composed of male medium *doutrinadores*.[17] Medium instructors and elders explained that Tia Neiva attributed the leadership of the Order to the *doutrinadores* because they are fully conscious in rituals rather than incorporating spirits, and they are especially men for physical reasons, as their bodies receive and transmit forces in a different way to women, which determines different ritual functions, positions and how they work in pairs. Male medium *doutrinadores* emit a *força geradora* (generative force); female mediums emit a *força giratória* (spinning force). Male mediums of incorporation emit both forces. Hence, pairs are usually composed of a male *doutrinador* and a female *apará*, or vice versa.[18] Tia Neiva stressed that the fact that hierarchical ranks are exclusive of male *doutrinadores* does not imply an inferior role for women but a complementary one: the function of the nymph is not that of commander, but it is 'in the line of "love gentleness", that we translate as invocation to the complement of forces' (*Lei do Adjunto*, N.C. Zelaya 1979a: 170), and she is responsible for bringing the Christic force into rituals; through male mediums only, rituals would be just technical and doctrinal. In external temples, the complementarity is more clearly expressed by the president in his leadership and executive role and the coordinator in her role of organizing the *falanges* (phalanges, see Appendix). It is in external temples that the person of the coordinator is more clearly perceived as being infused with attributes of 'motherhood' and caring for the community, reflecting not only the perception of the social domains of women in Brazilian society but especially perpetuating the attributes of Tia Neiva, the caring mother of the Jaguars. In the Templo Mãe, women belong to and are leaders of the phalanges (there being nineteen phalanges for women and only two for men), with every phalanx having a specific role indispensable for the performance of rituals, such as the invocation of transcendental forces from the past.

The question of gender in spirit mediumship and possession was extensively investigated through the perspective of social structures. These practices were approached by scholars as strategies employed by marginalized groups of society (lower-class or women) seeking empowerment and emancipation, the oppressed seeking resistance (Lewis 1971), or the disadvantaged responding to stressful events by enacting repressed and unconscious desires (Pressel 1974; Bourguignon 1989). Through this functionalist perspective, people in possession states would have freedom of behaviour justified by spirit affliction or would act through a socially recognized authority like an embodied spirit (Lewis 1971).[19] Other scholars regarded possession as a form of embodied critique of dominant discourses such as colonialism, nationalism, modernity and capitalism by a gendered and subaltern resistance (Comaroff 1985; Boddy 1988, 1994). Rather than attributing possession to women' s empowerment, several studies invite exploration of the reasons why in certain groups there is a predominance of female mediums and which cultural, religious and social aspects or gendered perceptions prevent men from participating (Lambek 1981; Schmidt 2010). In Mayotte society, for instance, Lambek (1981) explains the increasing involvement of women in healing rituals with the low participation of men, which is due to men's involvement with Islam, which inhibits trance behaviour. In Brazil, some religious centres presented a predominance of women and low social status members, and their mediumistic practices were interpreted as instruments of subaltern expression (Brumana and Martinez 1989; Cohen 2007).

However, in the previous chapter I have shown how the Brazilian Census data undermine the paradigm of marginality (Donovan 2000).

In the Vale do Amanhecer, both gender distribution and members' social-economic and educational background vary according to the context in which the temples are located. The gender role and hierarchical distinction established by Tia Neiva has never appeared to be an issue for any of the female medium participants in my research: firstly because it was understood as legitimized by the clairvoyance of Tia Neiva and secondly because it was conceived as complementarity. Marques (2008) also noted that women participants in his research in the Vale never felt that their position in the doctrine implied a gender imbalance. My female interlocutors – especially in the Templo Mãe, in temples near urban areas and in Europe – were mostly professionals in different fields, many of them holding a higher education degree. In fact, I found no relevant distinction in terms of education or socio-economic status between men and women – *aparás* (semi-conscious trance mediums) and *doutrinadores* (conscious mediums) – for both groups were internally heterogeneous. Therefore, the scholarly claims that marginal, uneducated women seek empowerment from their lower social status through possession did not apply to my interlocutors in the field, although one cannot exclude that this may be the case for some other mediums in other temples.

Some mediums explained the high prevalence of female *aparás* by saying that their sensitivity would enhance the preciseness of the interpretation of spiritual messages, marking a distinction between male and female respective attributes of rationality versus emotion. Others noted that some people (both men and women) could be *aparás*, but they may intentionally or unintentionally block their semi-conscious mediumistic trance for fear of losing control, thus they are trained as *doutrinadores* and may eventually become *aparás* in the future. Hence, the type of mediumship is not strictly informed by gender, nor it is unchangeable. Whilst in the Templo Mãe there is a prevalence of female *apará*, in other temples I visited there were more men incorporating spirits and women *doutrinadoras*. In this sense, Bettina Schmidt's argument is compelling when she asserts that gender distribution of possession mediums can change according to the social conditions (Schmidt 2010: 112–13). Further research drawing comparisons between the temples of the Amanhecer could possibly elucidate this issue.

In addition to defining hierarchical positions and specific ritual functions, gender also informs the type of spirits that *aparás* may incorporate: whilst female mediums may incorporate both male and female spirits, male mediums only incorporate male spirits. This distinction was determined by Tia Neiva in the 1970s (Marques 2009), although there were some instances in which I participated in rituals as a patient and a male medium incorporated a female spirit who was not necessarily his personal guide but who did manifest to leave a message.

Male medium *doutrinadores* receive new hierarchical classifications through consecrations, experience and practice, which, along with the mediumistic training (called 'mediumistic development'), are intended to prepare the body to support different forces. If on the one hand hierarchy is intended to distribute the decreasing force, on the other hand it is said to ensure control over and protection from troubling forces, an under-standing – as I will argue in Chapter Eight – that is embedded in a specific conceptualization of the bodily aspects of mediumship. Whether positive or negative, forces would reach those in higher ranks who are more prepared to handle them, and their intensity would gradually decrease protecting those in the lower ranks, such as new mediums, whose bodies would be less prepared to handle stronger impacts. High hierarchical ranks in the Vale are associated with increased responsibility and demand more commitment to others. Yet, some mediums noted that contrary to the principle of humility those positions are sometimes targeted as they provide the medium with a social status in the community. They pointed out, however, that this sort of appeal begins after years of involvement with the community, dismissing the idea that people would become a medium in the Vale to seek some kind of prestige that is not available to them in their society, as a medium in the first year of development would seldom understand the complexity of the hierarchical system.

After the founder died in 1985, major issues in the Order were raised in the highest ranks of the hierarchy. Following disagreements between the leaders in 1990, the Trino Tumuchy Mestre Mário Sassi left the Vale to found another Order, the Universal Order of the Great Initiates, although he returned shortly before he passed away in 1994. In 2009, a dispute arose between the two sons of Tia Neiva, the Trino Ypoará Mestre Raul Zelaya and Trino Ajará Mestre Gilberto Zelaya, over the approval of the Statutory Act of the Order. This dispute has determined the split of the Order into two administrative entities: the *Obras Sociais da Ordem Espiritualista Cristã* – OSOEC (Social Works of the Spiritualist Christian Order) currently admin-istered by the former in the Templo Mãe of Brasília, and the *Coordenação Geral dos Templos do Amanhecer* – CGTA (General Coordination of the Temples of the Amanhecer) administered by the latter and which includes a number of external temples. The CGTA already existed within the OSOEC as the coordinating body of external temples, but it was registered by the Trino Ajará in 2009 as an independent entity. The temples of the Amanhecer then affiliated to either one or the other administrative entity, sometimes shifting temporarily between the two. At the time of my fieldwork – which took place primarily in the Templo Mãe but also included visits to temples affiliated to CGTA – the differences between the two branches concerned the hierarchical ranks and thus were only noticeable to experienced mediums and not all temples were involved or clearly positioned on either side. Despite this administrative division, the Templo Mãe remains for mediums the 'energetic source' and 'root' of the doctrine of the Amanhecer. Mediums point out the uniqueness of the place, where details of the physical and practical aspects of the doctrine were channelled from the spirit worlds through the visions of 'the clairvoyant' and then physically constructed by the first members. It was the home of the Root Adjuncts but especially of 'the mother of the Jaguars', Tia Neiva, whose biography is inevitably entwined in the historical development of the Vale do Amanhecer.

## Materializing Spiritual Experience: The Making of the Vale do Amanhecer

It would be misleading to consider Tia Neiva as one of the 'entrepreneurs' assembling beliefs in a product prepared to be offered on the 'market-place'. This view, informed by a focus upon beliefs, would prevent us from understanding the role of the process of learning, and thus knowing, in the development of the Vale do Amanhecer and relegate mediumship to a secondary level of practice. Mediumship is rather at the core of this development. Hence, I have proposed an approach to experience that is better suited to address my interlocutors' narratives on the foundation of the Vale do Amanhecer.

In this chapter, Tia Neiva was presented as a woman with partial primary education who, rather than engaging in doctrinal study, had to re-educate her attention through her spiritual phenomena. She had to learn to master them initially with the help of a Spiritist woman, becoming aware of what the experiences of her self extending out of her body were allowing her to embrace. The initial years spent learning to control her phenomena with Mãe Neném have informed some features that derive from Kardecism, such as the principles of free will, karma, charity and the prohibition of charging for spiritual work and of proselytizing. However, she used to claim that most of her apprenticeship took place in mediumistic states of conscious-ness, through visions and out-of-body experiences in other planes and times, with spirits taking on the role of her mentors. Apprenticeship through spirit guides is widespread in Brazilian mediumistic religions, highlight-ing the 'pedagogical' character of some spirits instructing their mediums in different fields of knowledge (Camurça 2003). Camurça discusses the eth-nographic cases of the Comunidade Espiritualista Alvorada and the Templo Kundalini in which spirits acted as pedagogues of the leaders: speaking different languages fluently, teaching them spiritual works, recommending readings and introducing them to metaphysics and esotericism in order for them to found their centres (ibid.). Taves (2016) examines revelatory events (events claimed as revelatory, and thus with knowledge attributed to a superhuman source) that gave rise to spiritual paths and movements such as Mormonism, Alcoholics Anonymous (AA) and the network of A Course in Miracles (ACIM). Taves argues that 'These three spiritual innovations were produced by small groups that believed they were guided by superhuman presences and were able to generalize their experience so as to attract and incorporate others' (ibid.: 7). For Taves, this represents a creative act that implies shifts in self-identity, which expands to include non-human selves for a collective goal. In doing so, Taves embraces the material turn 'in which scholars have sought to undercut the presumed oppositions between spiritual/material and belief/practice, moving beyond studying beliefs about non-ordinary powers, entities, and worlds to examine processes – cognitive, experiential, and interactive – whereby people materialize what they view as non-ordinary in the ordinary world' (ibid.: 8).

The mediums who accompanied the early years of Tia Neiva's mediumistic phenomena assert that the Vale do Amanhecer was not a ready-made thing in the spirit world that she had to build on the earth plane, but it was gradually discovered day after day, year after year, through her mediumistic practice and phenomena; and thus it was developed and readapted through several attempts that included seven versions of the temple and many versions of the uniforms according to the available materials. In other words, the Vale do Amanhecer was not a fully formed representation in her mind, but it arose from the flow of her way of knowing through her peculiar attention. My use of 'knowing' is informed by Ingold's understanding of 'knowledge':

> Knowledge, from a relational point of view, is not merely applied but generated in the course of lived experience, through a series of encounters in which the contribution of other persons is to orient one's attention – whether by means of revelation, demonstration or ostention – along the same lines as their own, so that one can begin to apprehend the world for oneself in the ways, and from the positions, that they do. In every such encounter, each party enters into the experience of the other and makes that experience his or her own as well. One shares in the process of knowing, rather than taking on board a pre-established body of knowledge. Indeed, in this education of attention, nothing, strictly speaking, is 'handed down' at all. The growth and development of the person, in short, is to be understood relationally as a *movement along a way of life*, conceived not as the enactment of a corpus of rules and principles (or a 'culture') received from predecessors, but as the negotiation of a path through the world. (Ingold 2000: 145–46)

We are hereby moving beyond the idea of propositional knowledge to embrace the dimensions of feeling and affection involved in lived experience, as I will contend in my discussion on learning mediumship further on: as with Tia Neiva, mediums are not transmitted a corpus of propositional knowledge but rather learn a way of knowing through an education of attention.

Tia Neiva was constantly engaged in the attempt to materialize her spiritual experience, to make tangible spiritual substances and visions, to make perceptible the relationships with spirits through bodies, and to make people conscious of their own being as extended beyond the physical body in space and time. Along with her first followers, she was alchemically experimenting with substances, textures and different raw materials to give them the shape they had in the spirit world, to reproduce dresses and sacred spaces seen in the form of lights and different spiritual substances. In this sense, she was constantly engaged in a process of knowing and making. Again, Ingold's concept of 'making' is suitable to grasp this process. Ingold draws upon Deleuze and Guattari (2004) in considering matter in movement with artisans following the flow through active intuition: 'the process of making is not so much an *assembly* as a *procession*, not a building *up* from discrete parts into a hierarchically organized totality but a carrying *on* – a passage along a path in which every step grows from the one before and into the one following, on an itinerary that always overshoots its destinations' (Ingold 2013: 25). What was understood as a co-creation between Tia Neiva and her spirit mentors was then co-crafted through the available resources and materials in the environment of an emerging new capital, with the help of a community of people who mostly arrived in Brasília in search of new opportunities in the city and found themselves building what would develop into a spiritual town, with temples spread across the world. Tia Neiva's spiritual experience is therefore tangible in each new temple of the Amanhecer.

## Notes

1. In the Kabbalah 'Agla' is a divine name acronym of 'Athah, Gabor, Leolam and Adonai', meaning 'You are almighty and eternal, Lord'. It is attributed to those who went through the pains of descend on earth to face the tests of karma to achieve the wisdom to ascend to the highest spiritual planes (Silva 2010). 'Koatay 108' means 'Lady of the 108 mantras' (Siqueira et al. 2010: 267).
2. On the foundation of the Vale do Amanhecer, see also N.C. Zelaya (1985); Cavalcante (2000); Reis (2008); Galinkin (2008); Marques (2009); Siqueira et al. (2010); Pierini (2013); C.L. Zelaya (2009, 2014).
3. Both the doctoral researches of Cavalcante (2000) and Reis (2008) focus on Tia Neiva. Whilst Cavalcante approaches Tia Neiva's 'shamanism' as the founding principle of the

Vale do Amanhecer, Reis reviews bibliographic and media sources, as well as reports from elder mediums, to trace the life of the founder from a historical perspective.

4. Néstor Sabatovicz, one of the four *Trinos Triadas Presidentes* left by Tia Neiva to lead the Vale do Amanhecer.

5. On the life of Veleda, see Tia Neiva's letter (N.C. Zelaya 1980b).

6. 'Salve Deus!' is an expression used both in ritual enunciations and as a form of greeting people and spirits in the Vale.

7. According to mediums, this warning concerns the importance of following a life plan, or mission, decided before birth, which one may come to know by following one's own intuition or through spiritual revelation.

8. As with many words in the Vale, *'Turigano'* has no translation in Portuguese. Mediums claim that these words channelled by Tia Neiva belong to a spiritual language, and she could not provide any approximate translation.

9. Mediums refer to *'Aruanda'* as being a specific sacred space or a city (or colony) in the spirit world inhabited by the *pretos velhos*.

10. *The Castelo das Missionarias* (of the Missionaries), the *Castelo dos Aparás ou do Silêncio* (of the Silence) and the *Castelo dos Doutrinadores*.

11. For the temple in the United States, Atlanta, GE, see Vásquez and Alves (2013). At the time of my research, the temples in Germany and Japan were temporarily closed.

12. Source: *Sistema de cadastro dos Devas.*

13. For the international dimension of the John of God Movement, see Rocha (2017).

14. Only the main initiatic ritual keys (formulas), emissions (invocation of forces), chants and hymns remained in Portuguese.

15. In 1998, a new phalanx called Aponaras was created to gather the nymph coordinators of external temples; it is still active in the external temples affiliated to the Coordenação Geral dos Templos do Amanhecer (General Coordination of the Temples of the Amanhecer).

16. See also Chapter Eight for a discussion of how mediums understand hierarchy.

17. The only exception was the Adjunto Yuricy Mestre Edelves: the only woman consecrated by Tia Neiva as *Mestre Arcano Adjunto de Povo*.

18. In the ritual of communication with spirits (*Tronos*), two males of opposite mediumship (*apará* and *doutrinador*) may be allowed to work together. Two female mediums were initially allowed to work together, then the practice was suspended and reintroduced in 2013 in temples of the OSOEC.

19. Lewis (1971) distinguishes two forms of possession: 'central possession' (or ritual possession), which has the function of perpetuating social structures and moral values, and 'peripheral possession', which is concerned with marginal members of a society, with a high number of oppressed women, and involves foreign spirits whose moral behaviour does not conform to the values of that society.

# Chapter 3

# JAGUARS OF THE DAWN
## The Transhistorical Self

## Tracing the Transcendental Origins

When a medium wears a ritual vestment he or she is not just representing a hierarchical position or specific ritual function but embodying the forces from their past lives. When invoking Apollo or Amon-Ra, the medium is summoning the forces of the deities they worshiped in the past, to bring the sacred heritage of all humanity into the healing space.

Tia Neiva maintained that through her clairvoyance she could see a thread weaving together the past lives of the mediums of the Vale do Amanhecer, who were reincarnating together as a 'spirit group' called the 'Jaguars' (*Jaguares*). This thread is best understood in terms of the process of reincarnation and the concept of karma, which besides its origins in Eastern Vedic religions is also at the core of Spiritism. The idea is that spiritual beings reincarnate on earth in order to morally evolve themselves through the redemption of their karma; namely, the cumulative heritage of their previous lives. Therefore, present sorrows are interpreted as consequences of one's negative actions from past incarnations. Mediums address their practice as 'one way among others' to achieve karmic redemption, through the practice of the Christian teachings of humility, tolerance, love and charity that constitute the fundamental principles of the doctrine. The vivid colours and sumptuous vestments of the Vale do Amanhecer are an invitation to delve into the intricacies of Tia Neiva's visions, which not only evoke elements of different religions and cosmologies but present the encounters of mediums and their spirit guides as entangled in a common spiritual belonging and mission. This chapter retraces these joint reincarnations to tackle firstly the Vale's cosmology in its global and inclusive character; secondly the collective identity of mediums as belonging to the spiritual ethnicity of 'Jaguars'; third, its millenarian features, which I will present as embedded in Brazilian history and popular culture, rather than associated to the New Age Movement; finally, I will argue that through its discourses and practices the Vale do Amanhecer articulates a transhistorical self.

## The First Spirit Groups Shaping the Earth

In her visions – later elaborated on by her partner Mário Sassi in *2000, A Conjunção de Dois Planos* ('2000, The Conjunction of Two Planes') (2003) – Tia Neiva retraced the spiritual history of humanity, identifying its origins as dating back 32,000 years ago, when a civilization of spirits from the 'Planet Capella'[1] began incarnating on earth. In the Spiritist literature, Capella is considered to be inhabited by beings at an advanced stage of spiritual evolution. A group of spirits that was deemed still in need of moral evolution was exiled on earth, intended as a school where spirits would learn lessons through life challenges until they reached a stage that would enable them to return to their home (Armond 1986 [1949]; Xavier 2000 [1939]).

According to Tia Neiva, the civilization of spirits called the Equitumans incarnated in seven different locations corresponding to the current Andean region, Alaska, Mongolia, Egypt, Iraq and some parts of Africa. Their mission was to prepare the earth for future civilizations, acting on the topography, flora and fauna. Tia Neiva described the Equitumans as incarnated in physical bodies that were three times bigger than a human body; they were immortals, except in cases of drowning or physical destruction. Their children, however, were born with the body of common mortals, and by adapting to the environment in which they were living they began to differentiate both ethnically and linguistically. According to Sassi, some current indigenous groups still speak the ancient language of the Equitumans (Sassi 2003: 76). Theirs was a sun-centred cosmology: 'If historians would trace the trajectory of the Equitumans on earth, they should survey the religions and the peoples that worshiped the Sun' (ibid. 77). It was their longing for power that provoked the reaction of the Masters from Capella, who decreed the destruction of the civilization through a natural catastrophe caused by the passage of a spaceship called *Estrela Candente* (Candescent Star), which was guided by the Great Master Tumuchy, also known as Pai Seta Branca (Father White Arrow). According to Tia Neiva, the remains of this civilization are hidden in the depths of the Lake Titicaca between Peru and Bolivia.

The Great Tumuchy then began to gather the purest missionary spirits for them to reincarnate in the bodies of the descendants of the Equitumans and then they divided them into seven 'tribes' to distribute at the locations mentioned previously. In Sassi's words,

> Each tribe comprised of 1,000 spirits. So the hierarchies of the *Orixás* were created and the great chiefs had the virtue of communicating with the Masters. This Brazilian word is suitable, as it means exactly 'Intermediate Deity between the believers and the Supreme Deities'. Each *Orixá* had in his service other seven *Orixás* of a lesser degree, as each of these had another seven. (Sassi 2003: 78)[2]

The hierarchy of spirits in the Vale is articulated around the 'sevenfold organization of the spiritual phalanges', according to which a spirit may form a phalanx comprised of seven spirits united by vibrational affinity and working with the same name and aim. Each of these may have another seven affiliated spirits and so on. This type of organization of the phalanges of spirits, which is similar to that of Umbanda, explains the presence of spirits with the same name – thus considered to be working in the same phalanx – simultaneously incorporated in different mediums within the same ritual.

This second civilization of spirits guided by the Great Tumuchy incarnated on earth 30,000 years ago. Tia Neiva described the Tumuchys[3] as a group of scientists incarnating with the mission of building megalithic monuments to attract extra-planetary energies in different geographical points. Among these monuments, Tia Neiva maintained that the pyramids were originally built to function as centres for the manipulation of electromagnetic forces (Sassi 1999: 14). Likewise, the pyramid on the edge of the lake in the Vale do Amanhecer is said to attract and concentrate energies that purify the water used in rituals for healing and to work as an engine for all the Temples of the Amanhecer. The Tumuchys then established the 'scientific headquarter of the Planet and Centre of Interplanetary Communication' on the Isle of Omeyocan,[4] known as the Easter Island. The statues functioned as thresholds leading to underground chambers, and the Centre became the venue where 'they held the great conferences of the *orixás*, the top leaders of the civilizing planes of the Earth' (Sassi 2003: 87). According to Tia Neiva, as a result of geological irregularities the island began to be submerged, and the Tumuchys subsequently moved to Egypt; therefore, Easter Island as it currently stands would only be an emerged part of the ancient Omeyocan (ibid. 88).

## *The Jaguars*

After the spirit groups of the Equitumans, who incarnated to shape the natural environment, and the Tumuchys, who channelled cosmic forces, another group of spirits began to incarnate as human beings in order to organize the social forces: the Jaguars (*Jaguares*). According to Tia Neiva, the incarnations of 'the spiritual tribe of the Jaguars' on earth began between 15,000 and 25,000 years ago and continued along the millennia forming peoples and nations, leaving their symbol of the jaguar on several ancient monuments (Sassi 1999: 21). They were incarnated among the Assyrians, Persians, Hittites, Phoenicians, Dorians, Egyptians, Greeks, Romans, Aztecs, Incas and Mayans and gypsies in Andalusia and Eastern Europe during the French Revolution and in colonial Brazil, holding positions of leadership in the sciences, religions, arts, politics and wars and accumulating karmic debts along their various incarnations. The main purpose of the incarnations of this group of approximately 30,000 spirits originally from Capela was for their moral evolution and karmic redemption. In Sassi's narration:

> In this gigantic movement in time and space, we can trace the closest origins of the Spirits – who are now part of the mission called Vale do Amanhecer – from the Hittites, then the Ionians and the Dorians. Later we will meet them in Sparta, Athens, in Egypt and Rome. Mainly in Sparta and Macedonia began the path that may be called the 'Modern Era' of the Jaguars. From this origin, the destinies of the Jaguars converged in the Era of Pisces, with the birth of Jesus. Those who belonged to the phalanx of the Jaguar ... made their oath and began their new phase, this time under the aegis of Jesus and of His Law of Forgiveness. Jesus inaugurated the phase of Karmic redemption of the Christic System called 'School of the Way'... Therefore ... the civilising cycles were oriented in the sense of redemption, of compensation and of the return of the Spirits on the way to God. From this idea, wars, disasters and disappointments began to have a different sense, a reason, serving as a school and a lesson for the Spirits' individual training. (Ibid.)[5]

Described as having lived mostly as leaders, emperors, conquerors and tyrants (that is, in positions that disrespected the lives of others), the Jaguars had the opportunity to redeem their karmic debts through the process of reincarnation. Tia Neiva described the incarnation of the Jaguars as masters and slaves in colonial Brazil from a spiritual perspective, in which slavery represented a 'movement of redemption' of past debts for the Jaguars: slaves, deprived of their freedom and physically oppressed, felt the heaviness of their karma in their very flesh and were therefore forced to deepen in their individuality, to cede to the demands of their spirit (Sassi 1999: 24). Consequently, they began to practise spirit mediumship in Brazil, giving rise to Afro-Brazilian religions.

It is within this context that Tia Neiva introduced the stories of the main spirit mentors of the Vale, tracing the paths of redemption and evolution since their incarnations as Equitumans, Tumuchys and Jaguars that led them to occupy high hierarchical positions in the spirit worlds. Among the spirit mentors of the Vale, the *pretos velhos* (old blacks) are considered to be spirits of African slaves, keepers of the African roots and wisdom of the doctrine of the Amanhecer. They are the main spirit mentors of the *apará* mediums, who incorporate them to provide patients with spiritual knowledge and healing. Each *preto velho* might be called *Pai* or *Mãe* (Father or Mother) or *Vovó* and *Vovô* (Grandmother or Grandfather) and belongs to a specific people – that is, a spirit group such as: *Enoque* (Enoch), *Aruanda*, *Angola*, *Cachoeiras* (Waterfalls), *Águas* (Waters), *Pedreiras* (Stones), *Oriente* (East), Tibet and Congo, among others. Some of their names, such as Pai João de Enoque, Pai Joaquim de Angola, Vovó Catarina das Cachoeiras and so on are known in other Afro-Brazilian practices, such as Umbanda.

The spirit mentors of the *doutrinador* mediums are the seven *princesas* (princesses), namely: Jurema, Janaina, Iracema, Juremá, Iramar, Jandaia and Janara. According to Tia Neiva the *princesas* had incarnated in Ancient Pompeii and died in the volcanic eruption that destroyed the city. They reincarnated in colonial Brazil in the eighteenth century, six of them as creole daughters of slaves, whilst Janaina was part of a family of Portuguese colonizers. The six creoles escaped slavery followed by the white Janaina and settled near a waterfall in the middle of a forest. The site, which Tia Neiva called the *Cachoeira do Jaguar* (Waterfall of the Jaguar), became a gathering point for runaway slaves, in the style of a *quilombo*.[6] In that community, two *pretos velhos* known as Pai João de Enoque and Pai Zé Pedro used their mediumistic knowledge to perform healing and spirit materializations and to make prophecies (Figure 3.1).

Whilst on the coast of Brazil a new religiosity was flourishing, in the Amazon the Amerindian peoples were dwelling in vast forests full of the energies left by the ancient civilization and using the old power engines – now covered by the vegetation – as their sacred spaces (Sassi 1999: 27). These forces are said to be channelled for healing purposes in the Vale's rituals through the *caboclos* (Figure 3.2), such as Caboclo Pena Branca (White Feather), Cabocla Jurema, Caboclo Peito de Aço (Steel Chest), Águia Dourada (Golden Eagle), Tupinambá das Matas Virgens (of the Virgin Forests), Ubirajara, Pena Verde (Green Feather) and so on. As with the *pretos velhos*, some names of the *caboclos* are known in Afro-Brazilian religions.

Further west, near the current border between Brazil and Bolivia, the colonizers advanced, conquering new territories and destroying indigenous peoples. One Inca group asked for the intervention of a powerful *cacique*[7] Tupinambá, an Amerindian chief, with his army of 800 warriors. Through his diplomacy, the *cacique* managed to stop the invaders without causing any casualties. From the top of a hill facing the two armies lined up for battle, he lifted up a white arrow with both hands as an offering to god. His invocation echoed throughout the valley, and suddenly a sense of peace spread across the battlefield and the colonizers retreated as if under an invisible command. Having avoided genocide and promoted peace without any stain of blood on his arrow, he earned the name of Cacique Seta Branca (Chief White Arrow).

Besides the origin of his name, this episode highlights the main feature of the spirit considered to be responsible for the Vale do Amanhecer, Pai Seta Branca (Father White Arrow, Figure 3.3). According to Tia Neiva, this highly evolved spirit always incarnated with the mission of bringing messages of peace: as Tumuchy, as a Jaguar, the Egyptian pharaoh Tutankhamen, Saint John the Evangelist, Saint Francis of Assisi and finally as the Amerindian Cacique Tupinambá.[8] Other references found in the Vale do Amanhecer's literature mention reincarnations such as Tupac Amaru (Holston 1999: 617) and Master Kuthumi, or Mahatma Koot Hoomi (N.C. Zelaya 1985: 2). The latter is known in theosophy and was presented by Madame Blavatsky as her teacher and the inspiration behind the foundation of the Theosophical Society (Blavatsky 2011 [1888]). In the Vale do Amanhecer, Pai Seta Branca is considered a great *orixá* whose mission is to gather the 'spiritual tribe of the Jaguars' and prepare them for the transition towards a new era (Sassi 1985, 1999, 2003). Through this emblematic figure emerges a pattern of how the Amerindian, Egyptian and Catholic elements are articulated together by the principle of reincarnation. Complementary to Pai Seta Branca is his twin soul, the feminine spirit Mãe Yara (Mother Yara, Figure 3.3), who is said to have shared an incarnation with him as Saint Clare in the life in Assisi, Italy. Clare of Assisi was canonized by the Catholic Church, a process that included the recognition of the Eucharistic miracle of 1240, during the war of Assisi, when she prayed to Jesus, lifting up the Blessed Sacrament, and subsequently the troops of Saracens withdrew from the siege of the city. The narrative of the Eucharistic miracle overlaps in actions, purpose and outcome with Pai Seta Branca, defining the mission of these spirits through their faith. In the Vale, she is considered to be the daughter of Yemanjá, *orixá* of the Waters and the Sea and often identified as the Virgin Mary in Afro-Brazilian religions. Mãe Yara was the first mentor who manifested to Tia Neiva. She firstly appeared as the spirit of an elegant woman in a wheelchair, called Adelina, to reassure Tia Neiva when she was struggling to accept her clairvoyance. She then manifested as Mãe Yara along with Pai Seta Branca, instructing Tia Neiva in the creation of the Vale do Amanhecer. While in the spirit world she instructs highly evolved spirits, she plays a key role in the Vale as the godmother of the *doutrinadores* (Silva 2010: M; Sassi 1985).

Following the incarnations of the Jaguars, Tia Neiva's revelatory narrative moves back to the coast; this time to imperial Brazil at the end of the nineteenth century, in a region in Southern Bahia, which, according to her, was called Angical. It is the same setting where the seven princesses and *pretos velhos* incarnated in colonial times. The episode narrated occurred during the riots of slaves following the abolition of slavery in 1888 and depicts the contentions between two families of landowners readjusting karmic debts. Among those involved, Tia Neiva revealed the names of both *pretos velhos* and mediums working in the Vale, incarnated in that century as slaves and landowners. This is considered to be one of the last joint incarnations for most spirits belonging to the Phalanx of the Jaguars of Pai Seta Branca, which in Mário Sassi's words:

> comprises around 30,000 spirits, identified along the millennia as having the same trends and, currently, absolutely integrated within the Christic System. Some of them are leading the mission, alongside Pai Seta Branca, who is the one responsible for it. Others are incarnated as they are still in the process of karmic redemption and fulfilling their mission in the Vale do Amanhecer. Others still have to come, awaiting their turn in the etheric plane. Some are Mentors and Guides, others are incarnated mediums, and they all strictly follow the spiritual planning. Pai Seta Branca is the general leader, whilst the clairvoyant Neiva led the mission on Earth. (Sassi 1999: 28)[9]

Tia Neiva's revelations form a foundational narrative, the first part of which grounds the global threads of the doctrine through the description of the reincarnations of different spiritual civilizations on earth; whereas the second part localizes the Vale's roots geographically in Brazil, addressing the rise of Brazilian mediumistic practices in colonial times. As a foundational narrative, it clearly defines the positions of both spirits and mediums working in the Vale, whose paths cross intermittently across the centuries as members of the same spirit group. The spirit mentors in particular stand out as the main characters, realizing spiritual phenomena and bringing messages to humanity, in a succession of incarnations in which morality defines their destinies and position in the spiritual hierarchy.

The spiritual hierarchy is led by the Trinity of God the Father, understood as Absolute Truth, Jesus Christ, the wayfarer bearer of the Truth that leads to God, and the Virgin Mary. Jesus Christ is considered a medium both in the sense expressed in the Gospel –'I am the Way, the Truth and the Life. No one comes to the Father except through me' (John 14:6), a verse appearing at the temple entrance – and in the sense of being the healer, performing mediumistic phenomena. This results in the absence of an iconography representing Jesus on the Cross. One medium told me that 'other doctrines emphasize His sacrifice, whereas in our doctrine the central aspect is His life that serves as an example to us. For this reason, we use the symbol of the cross with the shroud, to represent Christ the wayfarer, alive and eternal'.

Pai Seta Branca and Mãe Yara occupy a hierarchical position close to Christ, leading the complex system of phalanges of spirits of light belonging to the Corrente Indiana do Espaço and the Correntes Brancas do Oriente Maior ('Indian Current of the Space' and 'White Currents of the Greater Orient').[10] Moving along the hierarchy of phalanges come the *ministros* (ministries of God) responsible for spirit groups and represented on earth by male mediums, who receive the title of *Adjunto* (Adjunct) of their

**Figure 3.1** *Pretos velhos*, Pai Jão de Enoque and Pai Zé Pedro. Painting: Vilela. Published with permission.

*Ministro* (e.g. the Adjunto Ypuena Mestre Lacerda is the representative of the Ministro Ypuena on the physical plane). Then there is the *Legião do Divino Mestre Lázaro*[11] (Legion of the Divine Master Lazarus) comprising the *cavaleiros da luz* (knights of the light), who are depicted as Roman centurions and represent specific healing powers that intersect in rituals. *Guias missionárias* and *cavaleiros* (missionary guides and knights) act as personal guides and protectors of female and male mediums respectively and rescue the spirits with a low evolution. The *cavaleiros de Oxossi* (knights of Oxossi), led by Oxossi, the *orixá* of hunting, are *caboclos* who have received a specific consecration in order to hunt with their magnetic nets the disincarnate spirits without light – who remain wandering on the etheric plane – in order

CABOCLO PENA BRANCA
EM CRISTO JESUS

**Figure 3.2** Caboclo Pena Branca. Painting: Vilela. Published with permission.

to bring them into the rituals so that they can be helped in pursuing their path of evolution towards the light.

The evolved spirits from Capella, namely the *Capelinos*, are also included in the high spiritual hierarchy with the mission of helping humans. Tia Neiva maintained that she interacted regularly with them through her clairvoyance and in her astral travels, especially with Johnson Plata and Stuart (Sassi 2003). Stuart was a sidereal engineer, who in his last incarnation in Brazil at the end of the nineteenth century was called Tiáozinho and died by drowning along with his twin soul Justininha. Mediums explain that he

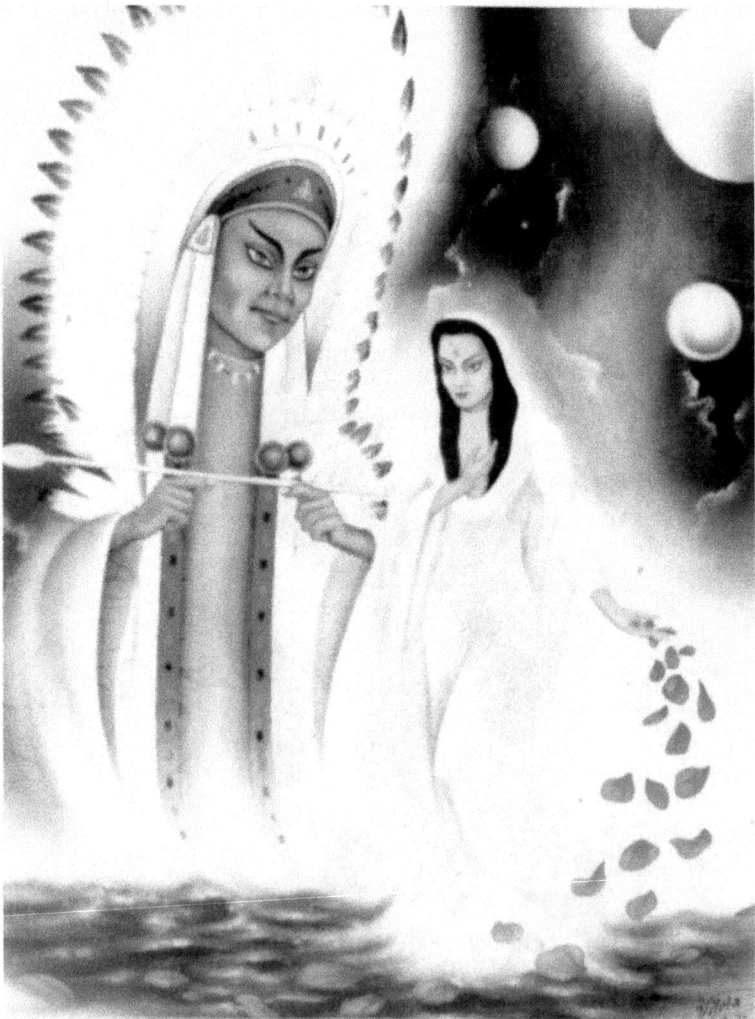

**Figure 3.3** Pai Seta Branca and Mãe Yara. Painting: Vilela. Published with permission.

used to incorporate in Tia Neiva to give instructions about the construction of the temple, manifesting as Stuart or Tiãozinho, and as Tiãozinho in particular he is concerned with issues of travel and relationships. They use this case to illustrate the ability of spirits to use simultaneously different manifestations according to the aim of their work (Figure 3.4).

Then there are the spirits that incorporate more frequently in mediums. Some are the spirit mentors that accompany *apará* mediums along their mission, incorporating as *pretos velhos, caboclos* and *médicos de cura*. The latter are considered to have had an incarnation as doctors in Germany, such as Dr Ralf and Dr Fritz (Figure 3.5), or in Brazil, such as Dr Bezerra de Menezes and Dr André Luiz. In Brazil they are known in Kardecism and other spiritualist lineages and are said to perform spiritual surgeries (Greenfield 2008; Rocha 2017). In the Vale, they incorporate in rituals such as the *Cura* and *Randy*, transmitting healing forces to patients. Other spirits of light might occasionally be incorporated by mediums in specific rituals. The work of the *ciganos* (gypsies) is aimed at healing and the resolution of material matters, and the *povo das águas* (people of the waters), comprising mermaids and other water spirits, are incorporated in rituals aimed at a collective cleansing. The medium of incorporation is called an '*apará*' after Nossa Senhora Apará, whose name, according to Tia Neiva, was a contraction of Nossa Senhora da

**Figure 3.4** Tiãozinho with Justininha in their manifestation in nineteenth century Brazil and as Capelinos (Stuart). Painting: Vilela. Published with permission.

Conceição Aparecida (Our Lady of Aparecida), patron saint of Brazil and worshiped in the Catholic Church. However, in the Vale she is referred to as the Our Lady Apará, described by Tia Neiva as having appeared on the slave ships to bring hope to the suffering of slaves crossing the Atlantic, and thus evoking the comfort and hope that spirit guides bring to patients.

*Pretos velhos, caboclos, médicos de cura, ciganos* and the *povo das* águas might be generally conceived as in transition across the Brazilian mediumistic religions and centres, working in different modalities according to the ritualistic setting within which they are incorporated by mediums, particularly in Umbanda, Candomblé de Caboclo, Terecô, Catimbó, Kardecism and Spiritualist clinics, among others. In the Vale, they share the sacred space with princesses, ministries, knights, spirits from Capella, and Tibetan and Hindu spirits, who work together in the lineage of the Great Amerindian

**Figure 3.5** *Médico de cura*, Dr Fritz. Painting: Vilela. Published with permission.

Chief Pai Seta Branca. Not only do these spirits with their trajectories enter the spiritual hierarchical structure of the Vale; for instance, when a former medium from Umbanda becomes initiated in the Vale with the same *preto velho* he or she used to incorporate in the other lineage, but they also turn out to be considered as part of a foundational narrative that recognizes them as playing an active role in the process of creation of the Vale do Amanhecer. The trajectories of spirits and their mediums are therefore entangled both in the foundational narrative and in their mobility through the Brazilian religious meshwork.

The Vale's foundational narrative articulates different religious traits through the principle of reincarnation, determining the global character of the Vale do Amanhecer, for it evokes elements and principles from Christianity, Spiritism, Amerindian and Afro-Brazilian religions, Eastern religions, theosophy, cosmologies from ancient civilizations and millenarianism (Pierini 2016a, 2016b, 2016d). In other words, reincarnation is the principle through which different religious elements, as much as individual experiences and a sense of self, appear to be articulated. Indeed, when this narrative becomes part of the collective imagery, it turns into memory, consolidating a sense of both the individual and collective identity of the Jaguars, providing them with a sense of self that is transhistorical and a strong sense of belonging to a spiritual ethnicity, 'the spiritual tribe of the Jaguars' (Pierini 2016b). Mediums in the Vale therefore understand the purpose of their current incarnation as being the redemption of their karmic debts from their past lives through the use of their mediumship to help others. Theirs is a spiritual mission of assisting incarnate and disincarnate beings in a time of crisis and change, providing them with the awareness of themselves as being on a path of evolution to return to God. Through their mission, they accompany the spiritual evolution of human beings through the 'dawn (*amanhecer*) of a new era', understood as a time of transition that began in 1984 and will unfold for an undefined length of time, depending upon the moral conduct of humans (Pierini 2016d).

## The Dawn

### The Army of Pai Seta Branca

On a Sunday afternoon in 2004, I assisted the complex ritual of *Turigano*, which takes place in the fenced sacred space adjoining the temple entrance. It featured the participation of almost one hundred mediums in phalanx vestments and holding lances. I was accompanied by the Adjunto Amayá Mestre Guilherme Stuckert, who was an Adjunto de Povo Raiz, consecrated by Tia Neiva as responsible for the Amayá people. He systematically recorded the history of the Vale using photography[12] until he passed away in 2007. Mestre Guilherme, commenting upon this complex ritual, told me:

> In the past, we have been leaders of armies, Spartan warriors, Roman centurions and gladiators. We have accomplished glorious enterprises, but we have provoked a great deal of suffering as well. Today, we are incarnated together in this place to work in the Law of Assistance of Jesus Christ, aiming to redeem ourselves from our past mistakes. Today we fight with different weapons: love, tolerance and humility.

He said that in the *Turigano* the Jaguars re-enact their past in Ancient Greece; particularly an episode that featured the encounter between the Pythia and King Leonidas, who, accordingly, are considered to be past incarnations of Tia Neiva and the Trino Arakém Nestor Sabatovicz. Besides the enactment of the dialogue between the main characters –which used to be performed by Tia Neiva and Nestor when alive – the ritual was accompanied by *mantras* (hymns), the individual emissions and chants[13] of the phalanges of missionary nymphs invoking the forces left in the past. The ritual featured the simultaneous incorporation of Yemanjá, Mãe Yara and of a Spiritual Minister to project their forces into the sacred space. Prayers were directed to Jesus Christ, and the forces of the Egyptian Akhenaton, Amon-Ra, and Ramses were also invoked by the Mestre who conducted the ritual. Mestre Guilherme explained that the Minister manipulates the forces of the present time, Yemanjá and Mãe Yara work with purifying forces, then, through the ritual enactment, mediums are able to recover the physical energies of the Greeks and Spartans and the spiritual force of the Pythia in Delphi. This energy left in the past life, called *charme*,[14] merges with the energy of the Amanhecer and is used for disobsessive healing.

In the ritual of *Turigano*, which is performed weekly on the Sunday by different mediums although always following the same script, the collective identity of the Jaguars is re-enacted and reaffirmed. The mediums participating in the ritual are not simply actors who interpret ancestral characters. Given their understanding of the past incarnations of the Jaguars, they *are* those characters, enacting aspects of their selves, of their past individual and collective identities of Jaguars. This ritual is therefore producing a 'performative reflexivity' – that is, 'a condition in which a socio-cultural group, or its most perceptive members acting representatively, turn, bend or reflect back upon themselves' (Turner 1987: 24). Reflecting upon their selves in the past, they reaffirm the present principles and meanings of the doctrine as well as their missions for the future assisting humanity in the transition towards a new era. Most importantly, I contend that they are multiplying the sense of space and time through a 'chronotopic switching' through which past and present become fused in rituals (Palmié and Stewart 2016: 219), which has crucial implications for the articulation of an extended self in a transhistorical sense. This transhistorical self is also mutable in that it is deemed to change its spiritual clothing every eighty days, adopting aspects of a specific past life, such as personality traits, vibrational pattern and karmic debts in the present life to determine different phases of the person's existence.

It is noteworthy to mention that at a spiritual level not all mediums, or people who arrive in the Vale, have a spiritual origin and past lives as a Jaguar. Some mediums told me that when they first participated as patients in rituals the spirit mentors revealed to them that they belonged to the 'spiritual tribe of the Jaguars', whilst others received this revelation after years of practice. Others again said that they were aware that even though they shared some past lives with the Jaguars they had a different spiritual origin and did not belong to the 'tribe' but nevertheless had a mission to pursue with the Jaguars, whether permanent or temporary. There were indeed cases of mediums that after years of practice were informed by Tia Neiva or the spirits that their mission in the Vale was temporary and that they had to receive the forces of the Amanhecer to prepare them to follow their mission elsewhere. Among these cases, I conversed with one woman who became Catholic, another one who opened her own Umbanda centre and a leader of a spiritualist centre that merges the Vale do Amanhecer with Afro-Brazilian religions. All three declared that they had no intention to leave the Vale at the time, but they now recognize their missions in the new religious context.

Those who remained, however, felt a sense of affinity with the Vale that seemed to be easily turned into a sense of belonging. This sense of belonging is reinforced especially when working in a missionary phalanx, since each phalanx represents the forces from different past incarnations and has its own narrative originating from the main foundational narrative (see Appendix for the phalanges' narratives and functions). By wearing the uniform and performing the function of her phalanx in the ritual, the medium is said to channel a specific force from the past, which is also the force of the Jaguars. A medium may choose to enter into a phalanx by affinity, or because they were revealed to have had an incarnation represented by a phalanx, as a medium told me: 'I always knew I had a strong gypsy transcendental heritage, so I felt I needed to manipulate this energy with the Ciganas Aganaras' (a phalanx working with gypsy forces). By 'strong transcendental heritage' she meant that a feeling of longing for that past was associated to the possibility of having had a particular incarnation considered to be more significant than her other lives. Another reason why a medium may choose to join a specific phalanx might be because they were called to it in a dream, as a nymph told me: 'I dreamt my missionary guide telling me that I had a mission with the phalanx of the Dharman-Oxintos' (a phalanx working with the forces of the initiations in ancient Egypt and now holding a role in the initiation of mediums). Elder medium instructors pointed out that the missionary phalanges were created gradually from 1975 to 1985 through the visions of Tia Neiva of their respective double in the spiritual planes. They represent the Jaguars' origins codified in their chants, uniforms and symbols as constituting elements of the ritualistic expressions of the Vale. In the ritual of the 1$^{st}$ of May, the twenty-one phalanges and thousands of mediums gather in the Solar dos Médiuns overnight to await the first rays of the sun of the *'amanhecer'* (the dawn) and take part in the major annual consecration of the Day of the Doutrinador (Figure 3.6). But it is especially in the ritual of Consecration of the Missionary Phalanges (*Consagração das Falanges Missionárias*), which is held every year in September, that the sense of belonging is consolidated; this is when all the phalanges – equating to thousands of mediums – gather inside the temple with their ritual vestments and their lances, forming the army of Pai Seta Branca, which re-evokes a distant past of being soldiers that is so vivid in mediums' narratives and which renovates their forces as missionaries engaged in a joint battle for spiritual evolution.

**Figure 3.6** The ritual of the 1st of May 2010, Day of the Doutrinador: thousands of mediums awaiting the dawn (*Amanhecer*). Photo: Emily Pierini.

### *The Mission in Times of Transition: Contextualizing Millenarianism*

The mediums of the Vale do Amanhecer refer to themselves interchangeably as 'Jaguars' or 'missionaries' because as they receive their initiations they gradually come to understand their spiritual practice as living through the mission of the Jaguars – that is, helping incarnated and disincarnated beings in the transition towards a new era.

Tia Neiva described the earth as a school of atonement where spirits reincarnate repeatedly in order to redeem their karma and learn the lessons they need to evolve morally. Once they have evolved enough so that incarnation becomes unnecessary, they can continue their journey of evolution in the spirit world and thus return to their origin, which for the Jaguars is Capella. Whilst spirits continuously reincarnate over the centuries, the course of history is considered to be divided into 'civilizational cycles' lasting approximately two thousand years each (Sassi 1999). The transition from one cycle to another features the overlapping of two different cycles over several centuries. This overlapping is deemed to cause situations of confusion, uncertainty and mistrust in institutions, which lead individuals to turn towards existential matters. The latest transition is considered to have begun in the eighteenth century and to have entered its final phase in 1984 (ibid.: 9). Tia Neiva maintained that this final phase of transition would culminate with the passage of Capella between the sun and the earth, leaving the latter in the darkness for three days, resulting in geological catastrophes. These catastrophes are intended as a process of cleansing for those spirits who have failed in their own process of evolution, preparing the earth plane for the launch of a new civilization. Nevertheless, according to Tia Neiva, the date of these occurrences depends upon the moral conduct of humanity, and rather than leading to the end of the world, this transition represents the 'Dawn of a New Era' characterized by a new way of thinking that will determine a new level of 'vibration', and thereby the earth plane will cease to be a place of atonement.

The mission of the Jaguars during this transition is that of preparing human beings to pass through this time of difficulties by comforting their sorrows and helping them to become aware of themselves and the processes of their spiritual evolution. In addition, it also entails releasing the disincarnate spirits remained trapped between the earth and the etheric planes after death. As Mestre Márcio, an instructor of mediums, explained to me, the vibration of the enormous amount of suffering spirits is causing a pressure upon the earth and humans, resulting in physical, spiritual and social imbalances. In rituals, these spirits are indoctrinated, their energy transformed in order to become light enough to be elevated to higher planes to pursue their evolution. The more spirits that are released, the lighter the earth plane will become, helping the transition. For this purpose, the Vale holds specific daily rituals, such as the *Mesa Evangélica*, for the continuous elevation of recently disincarnate spirits, and the *Estrela Candente*, aimed at releasing the spirits that cause major disorders, including wars, and so they are addressed as spiritual works in favour of humanity.

Mediums often presented the prophecy of the 'Dawn of a New Era' along with other prophecies associated to the creation of Brasília, such as Don Bosco's dream of a promised land for future generations, on account of the presence of what is known as the fundamental stone of the future Capital just behind the hill of the Vale; a stone that was laid in 1922 approximately 40km away from where Brasília was then built. Some mediums told me that this represented a meaningful connection between the two prophecies. Others discussed this connection between Brasília, the past incarnations of the Jaguars and their current mission in reference to the words of Pai Seta Branca in one of the messages that he used to pass through Tia Neiva every New Year's Eve in the Templo Mãe, dated 31 December 1973:

> Fair was Jesus, who through the evolution of your Spirits wanted you to be born in this country, where the Spartan Spirit governs, true and human, who allowed us to continue our journey. ... the initiatory [year] 1974 that is subtly preparing the human being for the Third Millennium, reminding the prophet and his prophecies, and affirming also your missions in this evangelical nation ... The year of prophecy and affirmations, of an old contemporary who saw lights, set his mark on this planet and also saw you on this land. His perfect vision is fulfilled. Do not be alarmed when the first signs appear in the Sky, for he who is confident will not be struck, because not a single son of this father can be missing! (Álvares 1991: 19)[15]

The 'old contemporary' prophet mentioned in this message is considered by mediums to be Don Bosco, and the incarnation of the Jaguars in this land is presented as a mission to assist the transition towards a new era. Tia Neiva's prophecy entailed that Brazil would become the 'barn of the World' after a transitional time featuring conflicts, unusual climate events involving snow and flooding, geological erosion, scientific discoveries of ancient civilizations and flying devices crossing the sky (N.C. Zelaya 1979b). Ideas of the creation of a new world 'usually involving the overthrow of the established order by natural or supernatural means' are features of millenarianism (Bowie 1997: 6). Hence, the passage from one order to another is often depicted as characterized by catastrophes. Alerts about catastrophic events have been scattered amongst the messages of spirit mentors in the Vale since the 1970s. Another two messages of Pai Seta Branca, dated 31 December 1972 and 31 December 1979, are often cited by mediums when referring to these events:

It is then that the Holy Comforter will expect your commitment for the final rescue. What will become of the Human Being without the Holy Comforter, seeing his greatness and his treasures being submerged by the ocean, when the fragile foundations of the mountains of ice will collapse, and turned into water they are going to release small beings, who will bring a struggle, and they will only be defeated by your scientific knowledge, my children! What will the enlightened man say when the great devices begin to appear in the Sky? The unceasing work will free you from pains ... This string encircling your chest, of Healing and Knowledge, symbolizes Christ on his path, a vivid frontier in the technique of salvation. (Álvares 1991: 18)[16]

My children, on this earth soon you will see birds with human faces, flying nearby, in physical sight, which will cross the beds of those who are asleep. Yes, when the time comes, you will see, on the other side of the path, tribes performing ceremonies and offering sacrifices on rich altars before images weighted by pageantry, by tradition and by fear. And proceeding further in the journey, you will see that without closing the door of your temple you will be dragged by the ocean! So, my children Jaguars, the human being will then see his great treasures, his traditions, his old papyruses, his laws and religious scriptures, everything, children, carried away by water or swallowed up by fire ... in a sort, son, of mourning and fear ... Is it a country? No, son, it is an enslaved power, in its phase of release. Yes, son, you made your way to the 5ft cycle without the contact of Capella; you resisted from the Equitumans to the Jaguar, you were and you are subject to the reaction of the laws because your hands and your feet are tight to your karmic destinies, until Eldorado will come, to the rigor of the three forces that will dominate with Science, the three Knights of the Apocalypse. Eldorado is the configuration of Master Sun, Master Moon and Nymphs. Equituman ... Sparta ... Jaguar. (Álvares 1991: 26)[17]

Both messages warn the Jaguars about catastrophes clarifying their mission, in which healing and knowledge are conceived as pivotal aspects of a Christic path that leads to karmic redemption, which in turn will open the doors to a new order. The first of these messages is in the temple beside the statue of Pai Seta Branca, a focal point of the sacred space.

The decades preceding the turn of the millennium featured the spread of several millenarian discourses, and then they were further associated with the end of a cycle of the Mayan calendar in 2012. Some forms of millenarianism are associated specifically to the New Age Movement, a network of eclectic, holistic, ecological, self-reflexive, spiritual ideas, practices and therapies aimed at transforming the inner world of individuals in order to help humanity to advance towards a new order (Heelas 1996). Elsewhere, I have proposed that the prophetic discourse of the Vale do Amanhecer, although consistent with the global discourses of the contemporary New Age Movement, is deeply embedded in indigenous millenarian narratives

(Pierini 2016a, 2016c). There are indeed striking parallels between the Vale do Amanhecer's prophecies and the Tupi-Guarani myth of the *Terra Sem Males* (Land Without Evil).[18] According to Egon Schaden (1974), the idea of a promised land is common to many Amerindian groups. Referring particularly to the Guarani, he notes how their religiosity is permeated by ideas of redemption and paradise associated with the belief in future cataclysm. Since 1820, these ideas have trigged group migrations toward the Atlantic coast in search of the 'land without evil', a land free from pain and death. Whilst he does not exclude that the belief in future catastrophes might have been informed by the Jesuit preaching about the Apocalypse, as set out in the Book of Revelation, Schaden affirms that 'in any case the belief in future disasters occurs also in the mythology of other tribes of the Tupi group, starting from the Tupinambá' and that this belief is diversely conceived: 'the Mbüa believe in an Imminent Flood, in a Universal Fire, or even in a prolonged darkness'; the Kayova 'in flying horses, in archer monkeys and other kinds of monsters' (Schaden 1974: 163). One may also note that the enunciator of the prophecy in the Vale is considered to be the spirit of an Amerindian chief Tupinambá, Pai Seta Branca.

From prophecies to tracing the spiritual heritage of the Jaguars, in drawing threads across time and civilizations, Tia Neiva made some remarkable references to the South American land, where the feline left its most vivid footprints and the mission of the Vale do Amanhecer flourished. Notably, she chose a stylization of a jaguar as a symbol to represent the medium Jaguars of the Dawn. According to her grandson, the Trino Herdeiro Elário Mestre Jairo Júnior Zelaya, in her travels in the spirit worlds, Tia Neiva used to see the iconography carved at the top of the Sun Gate in Bolivia, from which she drew the stylization of the symbol currently used in the Vale. The Sun Gate (Puerta del Sol) is located in Tiwanaku, the archaeological site of the pre-Inca Tiwanaku civilization featuring several similar gates as part of the Puma Temple (Pumapunku). The iconography arguably represents the Staff God, also known as Viracocha, pre-Inca and Inca creator deity who made the sun, the moon and the stars. His first creation of humans were giants, who he then destroyed with a flood. Tia Neiva's narrative about the Equitumans, destroyed by the Great Tumuchy then incarnated as a Jaguar and later as a chief Tupinambá crossing the Andes with his warriors to rescue Inca peoples from the colonizers, shows many parallels with Andean myths.

Looking at the symbolism of the Jaguar, the feline imagery is widespread in pre-Columbian Mesoamerican and South American societies (Saunders 1998): the Olmecs' were-jaguars; the Mayan, Inca and Aztec gods with jaguar attributes.[19] The *onça* (jaguar) crucially stands out in the myths of many Amazonian indigenous peoples, mainly in Tupí-Guaraní cultures in Brazil (Reichel-Dolmatoff 1975; Gow 2001; Fausto 2007). Albeit differently interpreted according to the local contexts, it is worth noting two main attributes of the jaguar in these myths that have become salient in the Vale do Amanhecer's understanding of their designation as Jaguars. On the one hand, the strength and prestige attributed to warriors and hunters characterize also the history of the 'spiritual tribe of the Jaguars': depicted as warriors, kings and emperors, considered to be civilizing heroes and creators of social institutions in the past. On the other hand, another set of attributes of the jaguar related to shamanic powers seems to character-ize a new phase of the history of the 'spiritual tribe': the present time in the Vale as mediums between the physical world and spirit worlds. As part of his exploration of the jaguar imagery across the Americas, archaeologist Nicholas Saunders (1998: 32) focuses upon the association between jaguars and shamans, whereby the former – a companion spirit and protector of the latter – is the 'embodiment of physical and spiritual power'. Hence, the shaman undergoes a transformation in order to become a jaguar and minister cures against illnesses caused by spirits: 'Transformation is a key element of shamanic power, where things are hardly fixed or permanent, but rather in constant flux, a "state of becoming" that is structured by myth and calibrated by ritual' (ibid.). Likewise, through the process of medium-istic development in the Vale, mediums undergo a process of inner trans-formation that entails an ongoing articulation of their sense of self in the encounter with the spirit world, while they learn to manage, as Jaguars, the transitions between the worlds.

My contention here is to show how millenarian discourses in the Vale do Amanhecer are not derived from the New Age Movement; they are rather deeply embedded in the millenarian discourses of Brazilian indigenous and popular culture. Even mediums in different temples of the Amanhecer in both Brazil and Europe pointed out that the idea of a new era in the Vale should not be confused with the New Age Movement. Rather than a New Age centre, they describe the Vale as an initiatic order of missionar-ies. Indeed, associating the Vale to a New Age Movement [20] – or even to 'Popular New Age'[21] – could be problematic. Although the Vale might share many discursive connotations with the contemporary New Age Movement, it cannot be understood solely through the category of New Age – or Christianity or Spiritism – or reduced to any of its single elements that evoke other religions, and thus it avoids misleading categorizations (Pierini 2016d). In fact, in this chapter I have shown how these different lines articu-lated through the principle of reincarnation are brought together in healing rituals, which determines the global character of the Vale do Amanhecer. This distinction becomes clear when shifting the analytical focus from doctrinal discourses to mediums' experiences as initiates, a point that will be developed more extensively in Chapter Eight.

Brazil features more than sporadic, isolated and exceptional instances of millenarian communities. Brazilian millenarian discourses and practices are depicted as constantly in flux across movements from the Portuguese legacy – 'as a foundational state narrative and technology of colonial rule' – throughout colonialism, rural resistance and folk Catholicism, and is thus embedded in Brazilian history, popular culture and religiosity (Pessar 2004: 8).[22] Furthermore, 'millenarian communities that were once decried as backward and fanatical are now marketed as centers of religious and historical tourism' (ibid.). Considering the character of resistance or rupture with mainstream society that some movements have incarnated, Holston depicted the messianic and millenarian religions in the backland of Brazil as violently destroyed by the dominant order after engaging in conflicts and disputes over land, for instance. Among these movements, he mentions 'The Enchanted Kingdom of King Sebastian in Pernambuco (1836–1838), the Muckers in Rio Grande do Sul (1872–1898), the New Jerusalem at Canudos of the prophet Antonio Conselheiro (1893–1897), the Holy War of Contestado in Santa Catarina (1912–1916), and the Miracle of Padre Cicero at Juazeiro (1872–1934)' (1999: 608). However, according to Holston, the Vale do Amanhecer represents an exceptional case, for it hardly calls for political mobilization or resistance, and differently from other millenarian groups, even though its members cannot actively participate in other religions, it does not involve forms of escapism, sectarianism or isolation from the rest of society (differently from the near community of the Cidade Eclética also set in the District Federal) and its rituals are public and inclusive and accommodate difference through spiritual healing (ibid.: 610). Holston, examining the Vale with its bureaucratic idiom in the hierarchy of offices as embedded in the institutions of the new capital Brasília, remarks that also Brasília's modernist plan is grounded in millenarian ideas: transforming the present by creating through architecture and urban planning 'new forms of perceptions and experience' (ibid.: 614). He argues against explanations that present the emergence of popular religions, and people's engagement in them, in terms of deprivation/compensation, as imitations of institutions of secular society, and proposes that Brasília and the Vale do Amanhecer 'are performances of the same paradigm of modernity', although the Vale presents an 'alternative modernity', but both 'manipulate the course of history' (1999: 606). While considering Holston's view of the Vale as 'alternative modernity', in this chapter I have discussed the Vale's knowledge about the past, which, although it contains elements from different religions, through mediumistic practice produces its own articulation of history, namely an alternative history. Palmié and Stewart (2016: 226) invite anthropologists to address ways of conceiving and making history alternative to the Western framework that may be sensed affectively and 'do not necessarily take shape through conscious, rational reflection, or receive expression in writing'. By taking on this invitation, I suggest that discursive, performative and affective reiteration of this alternative history in the Vale informs the mediums' sense of belonging, and it especially engenders new extended configurations of the self as transhistorical. In addition to this conceptualization of the self as transhistorical, extending diachronically through time, in the next chapter I will explore another attribute of the self – that is, multidimensionality and its extension or coexistence in different dimensions.

## Notes

1. *Capela*, to which the Vale do Amanhecer refers to, is the star Capella (Alpha Aurigae) from the constellation Auriga (or Charioteer) located forty-two light years from the earth. Previous references to Capella as being the original home of spirits incarnated on earth came from Spiritist literature, namely *A Caminho da Luz* (2000 [1939]) a book claimed to have been channelled by the notable Brazilian medium Francisco Cândido Xavier (Chico Xavier) from the spirit of Emmanuel, and *Os Exilados da Capela* by Edgar Armond (1986 [1949]) is claimed to have been telepathically received by the author from spiritual beings. Some mediums in the Vale claimed that the spirit of Emmanuel, Chico Xavier's guide, used to be one of Tia Neiva's mentors, although manifesting under the name 'Amanto' (Silva 2010: A). In astrophysics, Capella is known as a star, but in the Spiritist's discourse it is considered a planet inhabited by beings and presents a molecular composition that is radically different from earth.
2. Translated from the original in Portuguese.
3. As a name of a spiritual civilization, it is not translatable.
4. In Mayan and Aztec cosmology, Omeyocan is the highest layer of the thirteen heavens. Inhabited by Ometeotl, the God of duality and creator of all existence, Omeyocan itself is known as the 'place of duality'. This reference, however, is not mentioned in the Vale.
5. Translated from the original in Portuguese.
6. Autonomous villages founded by runaway slaves.
7. A term denoting the role of leader among several Amerindian peoples.
8. Mediums often referred to the incarnations of Pai Seta Branca as Tutankhamen and Saint John the Evangelist, despite there being no reference in the archive. Those that stand out in the doctrinal narrative are the incarnations as Saint Francis of Assisi and as the Amerindian chief Tupinambá. The visual representation of the mentor of the Vale, however, is rather closer to that of a North American Indian.
9. Translated from the original in Portuguese.
10. *'Corrente'* might be translated both as 'Current' and 'Chain', and it is understood in both senses by mediums. The *Corrente Indiana do Espaço* is described as a Christic force projected by the Great Indian Initiates, whereas the *Correntes Brancas do Oriente Maior* represent the joint action of the earthly forces from the Himalayas and the rays projected from the Oracle of Obatalá (R. Zelaya 2009). The spirits working in the Vale do Amanhecer are positioned along these two rays.
11. 'Mestre Lázaro is Arakém, the third of the seven rays of Xangô ... bearer of the Force of the Earth, in the African line as well as in the line of the Amanhecer' (Silva 2010: L).

12. His photographs are part of the Vale do Amanhecer's archive and are exhibited in the museum of the *Casa Grande*, in front of the Temple.
13. The emission (*emissão*) is an invocation of forces that is unique to the medium, whilst the chant (*canto*) is an invocation of forces common to mediums belonging to the same phalanx.
14. An English translation as 'charm' may lead to a misunderstanding, since *charme* is the divine energy that links the spirit to the foetus and remains on earth after bodily death, thus it is understood as karmic energy from past lives.
15. Translated from the original in Portuguese.
16. Translated from the original in Portuguese.
17. Translated from the original in Portuguese.
18. For studies concerning the myth of the *Terra Sem Males*, see also Métraux (1927); H. Clastres (1978); Nimuendajú (1987); P. Clastres (2003); and Pompa (2004).
19. An earlier version of this paragraph was published in *Ethnos* (Pierini 2016a).
20. For the New Age Movement, see Heelas (1996).
21. Oliveira (2007) approaches the Vale do Amanhecer through the analytical category of 'Popular New Age', understanding New Age in a context of local Brazilian religiosity of the Brazilian lower class. It should be noted, however, that the social composition of people attending temples of the Amanhecer may vary according to their geographical location and, more specifically, to their proximity to urban areas.
22. Pessar's study is particularly concerned with the cases of the Canudos, Contestado and Juazeiro Movements.

*Chapter 4*

# SPIRITS IN TRANSITION
## The Multidimensional Self

Walking along the streets of the Vale do Amanhecer and its sacred grounds, whether it be the majestic open-air space around the Lake of Yemanjá or the temple, one may often feel a sense of moving in-between the ground and the sky. The low white clouds floating fast across the Central Plateau feed this illusion of being on board of a giant ship navigating between the known and the unknown. Upon entering the temple, one's perception is increasingly challenged by a proliferation of sensory stimuli while one shares the sacred space with hundreds of bodies manifesting the descent of spirits to earth and their elevation to the spirit world through specific gestures and postures. Ideas of transition, multidimensionality and extensibility that permeate discourses in the Vale seem to reverberate through the landscape, the environment and people's bodies. This chapter explores these ideas, tackling the notion of the self, the process of incarnation and disincarnation and the mapping of the spirit worlds. The interactions and exchanges between these worlds and their inhabitants, which I will present as an ecology of fluids and substances, provide a context to understand the uses of ritual spaces, symbols and vestments in the mediums' everyday spiritual practices, as much as to grasp how they understand doctrinal knowledge. Therefore, I will explore the movements, entanglements and field of relations that forge both the self and the temple.

## The Multidimensional Self

The Vale do Amanhecer's conceptualization of human beings builds upon the idea of 'multiplicity'. 'Multiplicity' is not intended here to mean 'multiple personalities' but the extension of the self through different dimensions, hence 'multidimensionality'. Tia Neiva referred to the 'three worlds of human nature': body, soul and spirit. The body, or physical plexus, is based on the system of physical memory (genetic), and it is considered 'the main basis of reception and emission of energies from different planes, is the plexus responsible for the redistribution of these forces to the micro and macro plexus' (N.C. Zelaya 1984: 105).[1] The soul, or micro-plexus, is considered to be the 'psyche' connected to the nervous system. In Tia Neiva's words,

> The soul is the small body; it is located in our physical body in between the waist and the head. The soul ... reveals itself through our thoughts, is that who receives and emits the vibrations. It is the soul that is the place of feelings, this I, the core of decisions. It is within the soul that lives my transcendental individuality, emitting my transitional personality. (Ibid.)[2]

The spirit, or macro-plexus, is considered to be based on the system of spiritual transcendental memory and enveloped in a subtle body called 'perispirit', which has the record of the evolution of the spirit. Through thought, the perispirit is able to shape its body. The term 'perispirit' first appeared in Allan Kardec's *The Spirits' Book* (2010 [1857]), and it is also known in Kardecism as 'fluidic body' and in theosophy as 'astral body' (Blavatsky 2011 [1888]). By means of thoughts, the perispirit shapes the appearance of the spirit, thus when not incarnated the spirit might use a past life appearance (N.C. Zelaya 1984: 105). The Three Worlds are located in the solar plexus, forming the 'Inner Sun' (Sol Interior) that emanates seven rays of energy distributed through the organism, each one ending in a chakra. The Three Worlds are described as three spheres enveloped and separated by a membrane called *ectolítero*, which contains the *charme* – the energy that links the spirit to the body – and thus both remain on the physical plane after bodily death, whilst the disembodied being is composed of soul and spirit. The *ectolítero* is actively involved in the process of production of a fluidic energy called 'ectoplasm', which flows through the body and determines the person's mediumship, as Chapter Six will illustrate. Besides matter, Tia Neiva envisioned 'particles of a fluidic system' constituting the human being: 'as anti-matter, they sustain us and transmute themselves ... giving us all the varieties of sensory perceptions'

(N.C. Zelaya 1981). Concepts of invisible fluids and substances marked the discourses about mediums from the nineteenth century. In fact, the term 'ectoplasm' was coined in parapsychology by the French physiologist and Nobel Prize winner Charles Richet (1850–1935) to designate the 'exteriorized substance' coming out from mediums' orifices in physical mediumship séances. The German physician Franz Anton Mesmer (1734–1815) maintained that all objects and living beings had a magnetic fluid – 'animal magnetism' – running through their bodies and that an imbalance of this fluid was the origin of diseases; hence, he developed his healing method known as Mesmerism, aimed at re-balancing the body's magnetic fluid.

Mário Sassi illustrated the notion of selfhood in explaining how humans exist on different existential planes:

> On Earth's surface, on the physical plane, in the cellular organization called matter, we are a physical being; in the etheric world, we are an etheric being; in the astral world, which is still molecular, we are an astral being; in the subtle and atomic world of the spirit, we are a spiritual being. And so on, being something, until God! (Sassi 2003: 50)[3]

Body and soul determine the state of *estar* (being), concerning the actual positioning of the self in the current life or 'personality'; the spirit determines the state of *ser* (to be) or 'individuality', which transcends the current life. The self is conceived as a 'broad field of consciousness' not reducible to the physical being. The 'higher self' embodies different modalities of being, or 'minor selves', the different personalities adopted in past incarnations or simultaneously acting on other planes (ibid.). When minor selves are working in the same direction, the individual is balanced. Otherwise, when they undertake different paths, they provoke a state of imbalance or suffering that in turn may extend to the body. It is, however, through this state that the individual may become aware of the multiple dimensions of the self: self-observation entails perceiving one's own actions on the physical, psychological and spiritual levels. Sassi envisioned the aim of the Vale do Amanhecer as that of providing individuals with the spiritual knowledge necessary to become aware of their selves, of their missions and their paths in their present life in order to relive their suffering, to align their personality to their individuality (ibid.). Much of this awareness of a multidimensional self is learned in the process of mediumistic development, where the medium experiences how different dimensions are weaved together in the body. Spiritual knowledge in this process, as I will argue further on, entails learning a specific mode of knowing.

## The Processes of 'Incarnation' and 'Disincarnation'

The idea of multidimensional layers of existence implies that something that may have a shared meaning on the physical plane simultaneously acts beyond physical matter in the spirit worlds. The temple's siren works as a system of encoded messages in an on-off tone through which particular kinds of communication are directed both to the community of mediums and to specific spiritual planes. The siren sounds at the beginning and conclusion of the morning, afternoon and evening sessions of the *trabalhos* (rituals), articulating likewise the rhythms of daily life around the temple in town. It may call mediums for a *trabalho especial*, a 'special ritual', to attend a patient's emergency case during the night when the temple is closed. In case of death of a medium in the community, the siren might ring every thirty minutes along the day to alert the spiritual planes of the passing of a Jaguar.

At the beginning of July 2010, the siren rang repeatedly almost every day. Several members of the Order passed away, including a *Trino Herdeiro*. There is no formal funerary ritual in the Vale; rather, the family of the deceased organizes a wake. The wake and the subsequent burial are accompanied by prayers and hymns (called mantras) aimed at projecting forces to strengthen the spirit of the deceased to continue on his or her path in the spiritual planes. Mediums attending the wake wear their Jaguar uniform without the *armas*[4] – that is, they only wear the black shirt and the brown trousers or skirt without the symbols and waistcoat, as a sign of mourning.

Several assumptions regarding those passings spread quietly across the village. Some people even mentioned that every time a medium classified as *Arcano* or a *Trino* dies he or she is followed by up to seven other mediums. Others considered the timing more significant, for it occurred during the week of the anniversary of the storming of the Bastille. Every year that particular week is considered somewhat of a sensitive time in the Vale because according to Tia Neiva a group of Jaguars participated in the storming of the Bastille in a past incarnation and thus felt the effect of a 'fluidic connection' with that life and its karmic debts. Remembering might then open a bridge to the past through which disincarnate spirits in search of their debtors may pass and have the opportunity to be elevated to the spirit world through the rituals of the Vale. However, as the nephew of the *Trino* pointed out to me on the day of the wake, what those cases of passing had in common was that their time had come. He said that before incarnating in the body the spirit makes an incarnatory plan (*plano encarnatório*) that also includes the time and modality of leaving the physical body. The date of death, however, may not be foreseen exactly, as this life plan is dynamic, being subject to the person's free will, attitudes and choices.

Birth and death are understood as processes of *reencarne* and *desencarne*, namely 'reincarnation' and 'disincarnation' of the spirit, which in Portuguese literally means re-entering and leaving the 'flesh' (*carne*), and thus implying the different layers of composition of the being. The Adjunto Gerulo Mestre Márcio, a special instructor of mediums in the advanced course of *Centúria*, during a lesson explained to me that both the processes provoke a rupture in the spirit's usual affective and social relations: the spirit experiences as much sadness in leaving its spiritual family when incarnating on the physical plane as leaving the physical plane to enter the afterlife. These are liminal phases, moments of transition for the spirit in and out from the physical body, whereby death is also considered to be a new birth. Mestre Márcio went on explaining these dynamics in more detail. Before reincarnating, the spirit, fully aware of its karmic path from its past lives, plans its incarnation assisted by its spirit guides during a period that lasts about eleven months. All spirits incarnate on the physical plane with a plan they need to accomplish, which involves experiencing different modalities to redeem the debts accumulated in past lives through social relationships, life events, bodily or psychological issues, missionary attitudes and so forth. Family members or those closest to them are the people they choose to reincarnate with; they may be their creditors or debtors from a past life with whom they need to readjust. In these terms, mediums understand their most difficult social and affective relationships and consider forgiveness and love to be the main means for karmic readjustment and thus spiritual evolution. Nevertheless, some spirits may incarnate with a mission, alongside the plan they need to accomplish, which may involve helping others to evolve, including family members, human groups or even disincarnate spirits. As Mestre Márcio continued to explain, the spirit's life plan is then evaluated by the Ministers of the Reincarnatory Legion (*Legião Reincarnatoria*),[5] and once approved, two months before conception occurs on the physical plane, the spirit enters a five-month long phase called 'cultural sleep' (*sono cultural*) during which the transcendental memory of the spirit is erased. From conception until the third month of gestation, a team of spiritual doctors connects the spirit to the embryo through the chakras and the plexus, forming the foetus.

What the spiritual doctors take three months to connect during the process of incarnation has to be disconnected within twenty-four hours during the process of disincarnation. As the Trino Tumará explains, in cases of death by accidents – where the body may suffer major injuries, complicating the process of disconnection – the process is said to begin as early as twenty-four hours before the event (Silva 2010: D). Since spirits are disconnected from the body before fatal accidents, they rarely keep any memory of physical traumas. In all other cases, after the first metabolic changes, a special team of spiritual doctors begin to assist the spirit along the process of disconnection. The spirit is said to leave the physical body through the throat chakra and to rise one meter above the body, in an inverted position head on feet. From this position it takes twenty-four hours to absorb from the physical body the magnetic fluid necessary to pass over to the spirit world (ibid.).

Proceeding in his description of the passage of spirits to the spirit world, drawing upon Tia Neiva's visions, Mestre Márcio pointed out that all spirits, except those who disincarnate as children, spend seven days in a dimension called White Stone (*Pedra Branca*) gradually awaking from the unconscious state in which they remained during the disincarnation. Here the spirit has the opportunity to observe its incarnation passing through a screen projected in its consciousness, self-evaluating whether it accomplished its plan or not. In that environment of isolation, the spirit gradually gains awareness of its condition, assisted by the voice of its spirit guides, and might fall into a state of frustration and depression. On the seventh day, the guides accompany the spirit to visit those loved ones it has left on the physical plane. After the limited time of the visit, the spirit has the free will to decide to follow the guide to the spirit world. Supposing that the spirit chooses not to follow the mentor – either because it is not accepting physical death, or will not let go of life on earth or it rejects the belief in the afterlife – the guide leaves and, depending on the situation, the spirit may begin to wander around its house or family or to seek revenge. It might be aware of its condition of being disincarnate or, as in most cases, continue to live an illusory life unaware of having left its physical body. Because of the emotions that characterize this situation, this kind of spirit is referred to as a suffering spirit (*sofredor*). Wandering alone without the protection of its mentors, it becomes the prey of the space bandits (*bandidos do espaço*), those who capture wandering spirits and sell them as slaves to the chiefs of the lower dimensions, called the *exus*. The spirit is then expected to accomplish missions for its chiefs, unless it deserves to be rescued by those spirits of light called 'knights' (*cavaleiros*) and taken to higher dimensions.

If the spirit follows the mentor and leaves the physical plane, it is taken to the Red Channel (*Canal Vermelho*), a dimension for the spirits' adaptation between lives, where it can remain for a maximum of seven years. If the spirit has not accomplished the plan of its incarnation, still having karmic debts to redeem, it enters the queue of spirits awaiting the opportunity to reincarnate. Otherwise it joins a spiritual colony to be prepared to continue its evolution in the spirit worlds, in order to return to its spiritual origin.

Mediums in different Spiritist contexts are held to be able to channel spirits' descriptions of the process of disincarnation and life in the colonies – accounts that proliferate in the Spiritist literature and are often turned into movies and series distributed across the Brazilian media industry. One such example is the vivid account of life in a colony provided in the book *Nosso Lar* ('The Astral City: The Story of a Doctor's Odissey in the Spirit World'), about the spirit of a doctor called André Luiz and its adaptation to the colony of Nosso Lar and subsequent work as a spirit guide, channelled by Chico Xavier (2000 [1944]). The spirit of André Luiz also incorporates as a *médico de cura* in the healing rituals of the Vale. *Nosso Lar* became a bestseller of Spiritist literature, reaching over twenty-five editions in Brazil and abroad and later adapted into a movie (2010). Another Brazilian bestselling channelled book is Vera Lúcia Marinzeck de Carvalho's *Violetas na Janela* (Violets on the Window) (2002 [1993]), about a spirit learning to live as a disincarnate being in the colony of São Sebastião. Both accounts are consistent with descriptions provided by Tia Neiva and the spirits incorporated by mediums in the Vale. Mediums attribute the overlaps between Tia Neiva's visions and Chico Xavier's texts to a common spirit guide, manifesting under the name of Amanto to the former and Emmanuel to the latter.[6] Besides the two mediums having lived at the same time in Brazil, without meeting each other in person, the Spiritist concepts are very much present in the Vale's discourse also because of Tia Neiva's contact with Spiritism during her first mediumistic experiences under the guidance of Mãe Neném.

## Mapping the Spirit Worlds

Several spirit worlds are meticulously depicted by Tia Neiva in the accounts of her astral travels to different dimensions beyond matter. These are spread across the Vale's literature (Sassi 1974a, 1999, 2003; Álvares 1992), represented in the paintings of the Vale's artist Vilela[7] and articulated in advanced mediumistic teachings. Tia Neiva described the spirit worlds as hierarchically organized in a scale of evolution according to the type of vibrations of their inhabitants; and the visible world as separated from the invisible ones by a barrier called *neutrom*,[8] a cloud of variable thickness protecting humans from seeing disincarnate spirits. As Mestre Márcio explained, incarnate spirits produce the energy they need through their physical body in the form of ectoplasm. Disincarnate spirits from the Dark Worlds (*Mundos Negros*) feed themselves with this energy produced by incarnated beings. It is this basic need of ectoplasm that induces spirits from the lower worlds to set up and maintain a complex set of relationships with humans. These relationships might be of an 'obsessive' kind, in which humans are not aware of the actions of these suffering spirits upon their bodies and lives. Or, they may be based on the negotiation of mutual favours. According to Mestre Márcio, one such negotiation might involve sacrifice, which generates ectoplasm through blood, in exchange for material favours to the person: 'ectoplasm in these lower planes equals fuel for life in the physical plane', he said.

Since surviving alone in the lower planes could be difficult, these spirits usually seek affiliation with phalanges. 'Like in the physical world where there are gangs specialized in bank robbery and others in drug trafficking, in the dark worlds each phalanx has its aim'. Hence, the spirits of the lower planes are categorized by phalanges according to their actions upon incarnate beings: spirits of space bandits that hypnotize their victims; spirits wearing a black hooded cloak that wander around sucking the remaining energies in corpses; spirits similar to vampires, sucking vital fluids from human bodies and sometimes causing death; spirits described as puppets with large heads approaching groups of people in the streets and getting them to provoke each other so that they can feed themselves with the energy generated by discussions and fights; or spirits coming from the parties of the Roman Empire, feeding themselves with large amounts of sexual energy generated from environments that involve orgies and prostitution. A particular phalanx of spirits known as the *falcões* (falcons) is said to include spirits who have participated in political plots and intrigues within the centres of power of many societies and could now influence current governments and political decisions. The highest position in the hierarchies of the lower planes is occupied by the valley of the shadows (*vale das sombras*), which includes spirits who stood out on earth as politicians, scientists and religious figures but who morally deviated from their original missions and, once disincarnated, refused to reincarnate and began to build their cities or kingdoms. They are said to recruit only those spirits that will serve them; scientists and doctors who know the structure of matter and the human body, and politicians who are able to mobilize the masses. They act upon incarnated scientists in order to produce diseases in laboratories or weapons of mass destruction, and they influence leaders in politics and religion to provoke wars and genocides.

The *falcões* and the *vale das sombras* cannot be permitted to incorporate, as Mestre Márcio pointed out, because their vibrations would be dangerous for the medium's body, and thus the ritual of *Estrela Candente* was created to allow the passage, indoctrination and elevation of such spirits to a higher plane without the need for their incorporation. When their negative charges decrease they can then incorporate in an *apará* in the ritual of *Trono Milenar* (Millenial Throne) in which one *doutrinador* cleanses the negative impregnation of the spirit whilst another *doutrinador* talks to the spirit about God and uses discourses about redemption and forgiveness to try to persuade the spirit to move on. Only designated mediums can participate in this ritual, Mestre Márcio told me, as the spirits may be firm and challenge the *doutrinador*: 'some spirits are harder than others to indoctrinate as they often already have full knowledge of whatever sacred text or doctrine'. In many instances, when explaining about the function of the ritual of *Estrela Candente*, several elder mediums recalled an episode that occurred during the Falklands War in 1982, when Tia Neiva called mediums through radio and television announcements to perform a special ritual of *Estrela*, at the end of which she told mediums to go home and watch the news the day after. The next day the news announced that the Argentine commander had signed a surrender document, and Tia Neiva explained to the mediums that through her clairvoyance she had seen two *falcões* acting upon Margaret Thatcher and the Argentinian President Galtieri and that through the ritual these spirits had been passed to the spirit worlds.

Another lower plane is called Umbral. Literally, *Umbral* has two meanings that might be translated into 'threshold' and 'penumbra', designating a dark place of transition in the spirit worlds that is known in the Brazilian Spiritist literature, particularly in the works of Chico Xavier (2000 [1944]). Tia Neiva described Umbral as a dark and cold dimension located close to the earth's surface where a magnetic barrier blocks the sunlight. Spirits with low vibrations who died with feelings of hate and revenge might be imprisoned in that place of desolation, wandering around for an indefinite time or rolling in mud. Although it is a lower dimension, there are some points of assistance provided by evolved spirits ready to rescue those who seek the light. As part of this dimension, there is the valley of the suicides (*vale dos suicidas*), where spirits of suicides have to experience a condition of isolation for the rest of the time originally planned for their incarnation because incarnation is considered to be a rare opportunity for which spirits may queue for ages; therefore, suicide is firmly discouraged and sanctioned in the spirit worlds.

### *The Red Channel: Transdimensionality and Multidimensionality*

One particular dimension of the spirit world considered to be directly involved in the spiritual work conducted in the temple is known in the Vale do Amanhecer as Red Channel (*Canal Vermelho*).[9] Mestre Márcio explained to me that, according to Tia Neiva, before Jesus disincarnate spirits wandered on the etheric plane awaiting incarnation, causing a pressure on the physical world that often resulted in wars between civilizations. Jesus was sent to earth to establish a Christic system (*sistema Cristico*) grounded in the principles of love and forgiveness through which spirits could alleviate their karma. Moreover, as part of his mission, he also had to build a system in the etheric plane able to manage the reception of disincarnate spirits and the process of reincarnation, as well as the transition of more evolved spirits to other planes. Tia Neiva maintained that Jesus accomplished this mission during the years missing from the Gospels' narrative, when Joseph of Arimathea took him from age twelve to thirty to Tibet, to be initiated by the Great Initiates. The discourse of Jesus's stay in Tibet is consistent with the esoteric and theosophical literature from the late nineteenth and early twentieth centuries – some of which claims to be channelled by authors from the great masters from the spirit world – that depicts Jesus as having received guidance in a monastery by members of the Great White Brotherhood (Blavatsky 1999 [1877]; Notovitch 1916 [1890]; Dowling 1908). According to Tia Neiva, with the help of the Great Initiates, Jesus created the system of the transitory houses (*casas transitórias*) of the Red Channel. She described this dimension as the first level of light, similar to the physical plane in its appearance but differing from the earth because of its molecular composition. Functioning as a centre of interdimensional connection, the Red Channel features a Universal Station (Rodoviária Universal), managing the departures and arrivals from different planes and dimensions of the universe. Transport is carried out by *amacês* and *cassandras* – which would also transport the forces of the spirit world for the ritual of the *Estrela Candente* – depicted as what are popularly known as space ships,[10] but belonging to the etheric plane they would be invisible to incarnated beings.

Mestre Márcio described the Red Channel as comprising approximately twenty-one departments intended as separated worlds at different stages of evolution, to which recently disincarnate spirits are attracted according to the energetic frequency they achieved in their evolution. He said that according to Tia Neiva's accounts of her astral travels to the different departments, there are hospitals and asylums for the recovery of spirits, as well as universities. He explained that while mediums are asleep, their spirit extends out of their body and reaches the Red Channel in order to continue to assist spirits in the transitory houses, because as incarnated beings they have the capacity to bring their ectoplasm with them in order to treat the suffering spirits, completing the work they began in the rituals; hence, they say that 'the Jaguar works 24 hours a day'.

Continuing his description, Márcio mentioned the Square of Religions (Praça das Religiões), a department where recently disincarnated spirits coming from different religious backgrounds may find the appropriate vision of passing that they have learned from religious teachings on the earth plane, in order to help them readapt to their etheric existence. Thus, a Catholic would be received by the spirit of a priest, who would gradually introduce the recently disincarnate to the dynamics of the afterlife. The description of the Square of Religions holds similarities to what Bruce Moen, an author trained in out-of-body experiences at The Monroe Institute in the United States, describes as the 'Beliefs System Territories' to which one is attracted in the afterlife (Moen 1998: 89, 2005: 141–47). Mediums in the Vale also refer to this department to explain the different views of the afterlife in different religions and the cases of differing reports of Near Death Experiences (NDEs) in different cultures. They understand religions as human interpretations of the teachings of Jesus and other 'Great Initiates', each representing different means to reach God, and they consider the system of spirit evolution beyond matter to be common to all spirits.

Tia Neiva described endless queues of spirits extending across the Red Channel waiting for their turn to access the departments regulating the incarnations: the Reincarnatory Legion, a department for life planning; the 'cultural sleep' where they prepare for incarnating; and the Palace of Justice, where a Council of Ministers also evaluates the possibility to interrupt an incarnation when it is threatening the mission and evolution of a spirit.

The higher dimensions of the Red Channel and the astral plane are described as peaceful environments responding to the energy vibration of their inhabitants, featuring mansions, spiritual colonies and cities, with an architecture similar to the wealthy neighbourhoods on the earth plane. Some villages are inhabited by spirit guides such as *caboclos*, *pretos velhos* and *ciganos*. Spirits who have paid their karmic debts once disincarnate do not need to reincarnate and may go directly to their colonies, where they will be waiting for all their spiritual family members to reach the same stage of evolution in order to depart together towards their world of origin, which in the case of the Jaguars is Capella. Spiritual kinship is held to be based on mutual help toward evolution, meaning that the spiritual parents may be those who brought up the spirits. The spirits' life in the colony is marked by spiritual assistance to human beings or work in the hospitals of the Red Channel, earning bonuses that may be used for their evolution or to help some family members still incarnated on the earth plane. Mestre Márcio emphasized how this dynamic applied to the work of spirit mentors in the temples of the Amanhecer. These spirits were trained in a dimension of the higher astral plane called Mayanty, described as a university where spirits may study to become spiritual doctors working with mediums or learn how to work in rituals of the temple, because guides are required to adapt to the ritualistic systems of different religions in order to work on the earth plane.

Mestre Diego suggested that as opposed to the category of *espíritos sem luz* (spirits without light), who feed themselves with energy produced by human suffering or negative emotions, the *espíritos de luz* (spirits of light) feed themselves only with the light of the higher planes, turning to human energies only to produce healing phenomena. Moreover, whilst spirits from lower planes cannot enter higher dimensions because of the density of their low vibrations, spirits from higher planes can pass through all dimensions, reaching the lower ones in rescue missions or to assist humans on the physical plane.

To descend to lower planes, the spirit of light has to protect itself from the increasing density of the vibrations. A spirit called Pai Joaquim das Cachoeiras, a *preto velho* incorporated by an *apará* in a ritual, explained to me that 'as humans use atmospheric diving suits in order to protect themselves from pressure variations when deep diving in the sea, so we need to mould a kind of spiritual bodily appearance, which protects us as spirits while making us recognizable to humans'. Hence, this body should also be culturally recognizable within the religion in which the spirit manifests, drawing on those human representations that include attributes and functions similar to those of the spirit group. The *pretos velhos*, for instance, are spirits of African slaves, represented, in Brazil, by attributes of humility, unconditional love and deep wisdom. These attributes are involved in the dynamics of the *Tronos* (Thrones), the ritual of communication in which the *pretos velhos* incorporate in mediums to listen to patients, bring comfort and orientate them in their lives. Pai Joaquim also explained to me that,

> The spirit worlds are something like a reflection of the physical world, with societies, buildings, and so on … like physical life continuing in the spiritual plane, although I have a different body, which is astral, so in order to communicate to humans I need to use the physical body of this medium. God holds all the system of incarnated and disincarnate beings. Imagine a theatre where God is the director, the physical plane is a stage and humans are the actors expected to enact their role. Everyone incarnates on the Earth with a mission. You have yours, and once you accomplish it you will continue your journey in another plane, with other missions, since we are continuously working for our evolution, walking on the path which leads us to return to God through humility, love and tolerance.

The spirit mentioned the close connection of his words with Hindu teachings contained in the *Bhagavad Gita*, a reference that became clear afterwards when I asked him if he had had an incarnation as an African slave in colonial Brazil. He explained that African slaves deported to Brazil had to use all their knowledge of mediumship to incorporate spirits in rituals to assist the others suffering in the condition of slavery, bringing them hope and relief. They passed to the spirit world as highly evolved spirits acting together on the same vibratory condition, and their goal is now to assist incarnated and disincarnate beings. Although most *pretos velhos* had incarnations as African slaves in Brazil, some did not. Other spirits at the same stage of evolution may join the phalanx to work in assisting humans in the *Tronos*. He himself was a spirit whose last incarnation was in India, and he had no previous life as an African slave. 'I give you an example to understand how it works – imagine yourself as an anthropologist collaborating with a historian to give your contribution with your knowledge … belonging to two different origins but working with the same common goal'. The example itself was interesting, since I had initially introduced myself as an anthropologist, but I did not mention that in fact at that time I was collaborating with a historian on another research project. The scenery he presented me with was that of phalanges composed of local spirits who had at least one incarnation on that land and affiliated spirits that adopt culturally recognizable 'clothing' to work within that specific cultural setting and with a specific ritual function, in order to evolve themselves along the spiritual planes. I later understood that this perspective was not limited to the phalanx of *pretos velhos* but was also extensible to other phalanges. This discourse of spirits moulding their appearance is also common to other Brazilian mediumistic religions, such as among some practitioners of Umbanda Sagrada, where spirits are beings of light using cultural imagery as materials to 'clothe' their bodies, and thus are overcoming the dichotomy between ontology and cultural construction (Espírito Santo 2016: 88).

As the spirit evolves closer to God, it loses the definition of its shape, expanding its consciousness to merge with the divine principle. To illustrate this, Lucas, a *doutrinador* medium, showed me the image of a minister spirit guide painted with a few evanescent face traits merging his appearance with the highest spirit worlds. 'Look at this minister – he has worlds within him … he *is* the worlds. The mental dimension only maintained the face traits so that his medium could identify him, but his consciousness is already with the Father in different dimensions'. The idea of a multidimensional self was powerfully illustrated by that image – an extended self encompassing different layers of composition and merging with other worlds and beings.

### In-Betweenness: Managing the Exchanges between the Worlds

Descriptions of the spirit worlds reflect different shades of light, from the darkest dimensions of the *Vale Negro* (Dark Valley) rising towards the enlightened worlds, where matter becomes increasingly subtle and the spirit more transparent until – at even higher stages of evolution – it is transformed into lighter energy merging with God. The Vale do Amanhecer represents the 'dawn', the point where spirits that live in the darkness of the *Vale Negro* are transformed to reach the light in the spiritual planes.

The Adjunto Yumatá Mestre Caldeira, an elder master leader of the People Yumatá,[11] would usually sit outside his porch facing the street conversing with the mediums and visitors that occasionally visited him to listen to his stories about the fifteen years he spent witnessing the spirits manifesting through Tia Neiva or her accounts of her astral travels. Besides showing her letters and his several photo albums depicting the historical physical and ritualistic development of the Templo Mãe, he would eloquently clarify doubts and deepen her teachings about the spirit worlds. In one of our meetings, he explained to me that whilst the spirits of the dark worlds work in five dark planes, the Jaguars work in seven planes of light, namely: physical, etheric, astral, mental, Holy Spirit, Son and Father. They are hierarchically structured in ascending order, with the three highest ones being known as the Christic Planes or Divine Word. According to Caldeira, this relates to the recurrence of the number seven in the Vale. Each plane is divided into seven dimensions, each of which is held by different laws. Recalling Tia Neiva's descriptions, he said that there are dimensions in which the spirit has no need to move but attracts things through its own vibration (telekinesis), whereas in other dimensions the spirit may travel via mentalization (teleportation). He located the Red Channel in the first dimension of the etheric plane as being just above the physical plane; whereas entities such as the knights and missionary guides inhabit the mental plane, and the *pretos velhos* and *caboclos* may work in all planes. The seventh plane comprises the Central Kingdom (Reino Central), formed by the union of various oracles (*oráculos*), which are 'points of emission of forces' projected upon the earth plane as rays acting upon the mediums' bodies in rituals (R. Zelaya 2009: 59–65).

A slightly different understanding of the spirit worlds' structure was presented to me by the Trino Herderio Elário Mestre Jairo Junior Zelaya, grandson of Tia Neiva. He envisaged the earth as composed by seven spiritual dimensions. The three lower worlds, which are less evolved than the physical plane, are located beneath the earth's surface and include the Dark Valley, the Valley of Shadows, and Umbral. An intermediary plane, the non-material fourth dimension called the etheric plane, is located parallel to the physical plane. If a disincarnate spirit remained on earth, it would be in the etheric plane. Since mental energies generated by thoughts circulate in the etheric plane, this might also be referred to as the Mental Plane. Around and above the earth there are three other highly evolved planes: the third is the Astral Plane, comprising the Red Channel; the second is the Spiritual Plane; and the first dimension is called Divine Plane or Higher Astral. Whilst Pai Seta Branca and the Oracles reside in the Divine Plane, according to their individual evolution the *pretos velhos* are partly in the third and first plane but mostly in the second, and some are Great Initiates disguised. Likewise, the spirits incarnated on earth may belong to all seven planes and find themselves readjusting their debts with each other or on a mission to help humanity. Jairo pointed out that these planes only refer to the earth, since they are worlds inhabited by disincarnate spirits constantly interacting energetically with spirits on earth. Every planet has its own set of planes of evolution.

> Capela, which is in the constellation of the Charioteer, has its own scale of evolution, so for us the Divine Plane is the most evolved, but in Capela there are even more evolved planes. Most planets are inhabited, albeit on different dimensions, thus with a different composition of matter. Mars, for instance, is inhabited on the same vibrational frequency as our second plane, but from here on the fourth plane we cannot perceive it.

His conception of the structure of the spirit world, as he explained, is the result of his own understanding after joining together the information spread all over the doctrinal archive.

The Trino Tumuchy Mário Sassi noted that

> most initiatory groups make a division into seven planes: the physical, the etheric, the astral, the mental and the three Christic or Buddhic planes (Father, Son, Spirit, or God, Word and Universe), descriptions that vary according to each group. All, however, keep the number seven as a base. But for our understanding of mediumism, we just need the three planes. (1974a: 35)

Sassi was more concerned with those vibrational planes that were close to the mediums' experience, so he focused on the physical, psychological and spiritual plane, referring to body, soul and spirit.

These three different views of the structure of the spirit worlds may be attributed to the spread of doctrinal information across the archive and to the limited written systematization of doctrinal knowledge. What seems well systematized, however, is the structure of the Red Channel, for it is considered the plane directly connected with the work of the Vale and the first transition point for most rescued spirits. Such an interconnection is particularly emphasized in symbols and ritual spaces. Mestre Caldeira explained to me that Tia Neiva conceived the specific points of the physical construction of the temple as directly connected with sectors of the Red Channel. In the ritual of *Mesa Evangélica*,[12] mediums sit around a triangular table and continuously incorporate recently disincarnated spirits, indoctrinated by mediums and elevated to the spiritual plane, during each 15–20 minute session. Each side of the triangle is associated with a different region of the Red Channel, where the spirit is sent when elevated. In a bidirectional movement, energies are projected from specific sectors of the Red Channel into the core points of the ritual spaces, whilst spirits released in different rituals pass through 'portals of integration-disintegration' to different areas of the Red Channel.

The double process of receiving and releasing spirits that defines the practice of mediumship in the Vale do Amanhecer is represented in its main symbol: the ellipse. Even when the medium invokes his or her forces through the *emissão* (emission), this is said to open a channel through the different dimensions of the spirit worlds, so the elliptical shape illustrates the flow of energy transmitted from the spirit worlds to the Jaguar (appearing at the bottom of the symbol), used for healing on the earth plane and then ultimately returned to the spiritual planes (Figure 4.1). This shape recalls the 'mandorla' (in Christian iconography, this is an aura in the shape of an almond) or *vesica pisces*, while it could also be associated with a symbol of the feminine, transmitting a sense of the generative character of doctrine and the transition towards a new life. The ellipse is also considered a portal itself, a transformational *limen* between two worlds, which is related to the idea that a spiritual body passes through different systems of vibration by disintegrating and reintegrating according to the molecular composition of the dimension. One day, Mestre Itamir took me up the hill of the Vale to show me from above the system of four ellipses in the Vale. He described these portals as being interconnected by an energetic flow that descends from the ellipse on top of the hill, passing through the ellipse at the bottom in the middle of the *Estrela Candente*, and the one inside the temple in the middle of the *Mesa Evangélica*, before rising to the spiritual planes through the ellipse in front of the temple beside the ritual space of the *Estrela Sublimação*. The different symbols that appear within each ellipse represent the interaction of forces (indicated by arrows) – which differs according to the plane (represented by the stars) – and its effect on the medium's body (the chalice). The elliptical shape is used in the temple's plan as well as most structures of the sacred spaces; patients can undertake an elliptical therapeutic route through rituals, transforming their energies from negative to positive. Collectively, it appears in the ritual vestments of some phalanges, and it is individualized in its representation in the form of yellow and purple string that diagonally encircles the medium's body (the *fita*). As a mandatory part of each uniform, the *fita* is said to act on the medium's body as a portal of disintegration, protecting it from specific energies. By wearing it, the medium also carries on the body the meanings of mediumistic practice, wisdom and healing (or science and faith), respectively codified in the yellow and purple colours.[13]

Sacred spaces are considered to be visible extensions on the physical plane of wider structures of management of disincarnate spirits in the spirit worlds, namely the transitional houses (*casas transitórias*). Elder mediums claim that from structures to colours each detail resulted from either the clairvoyant's visions of these details in the spirit worlds or from

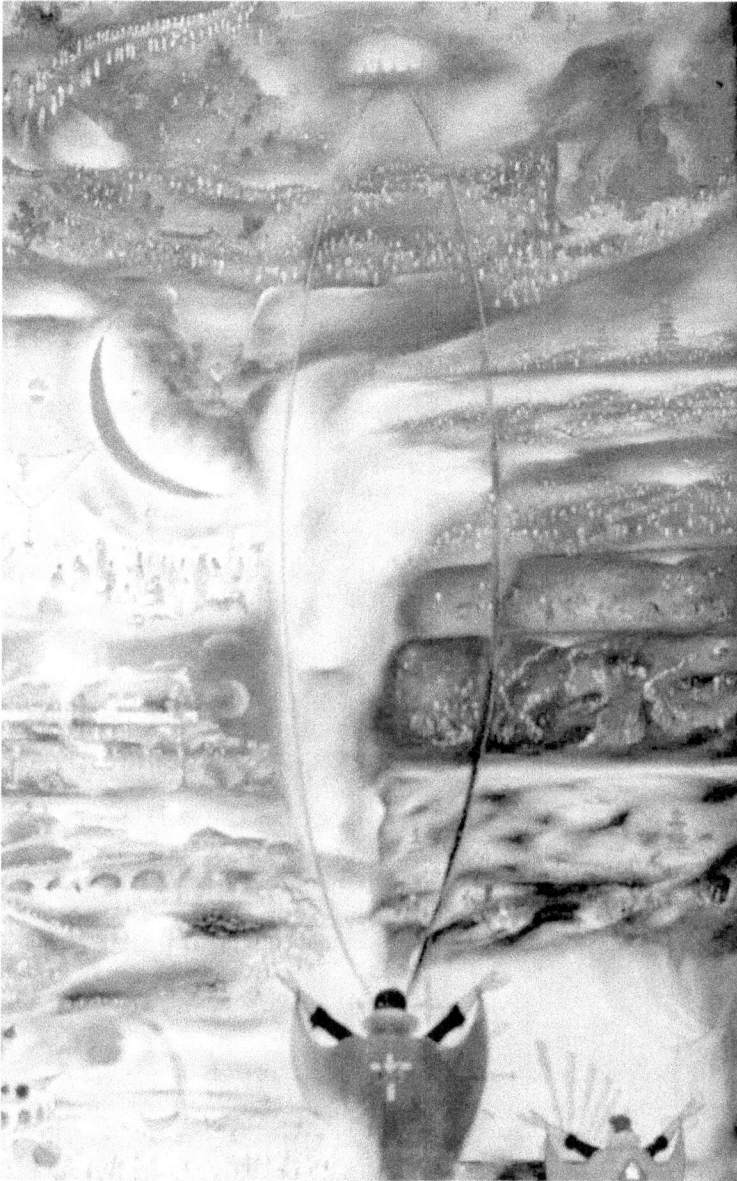

**Figure 4.1** The action of the mediums' *emissão* (invocation of forces) beyond matter, opening a channel through the different dimensions of the spirit worlds. A detail from the painting of the spirit worlds displayed in the *Casa Grande*. Painting: Vilela. Published with permission.

the instructions received by the spirit mentors she used to incorporate. The creation of the uniforms and vestments of the different phalanges may well illustrate the nature of her visions as reported by Mestre João Santana, an elder medium who was Tia Neiva's tailor from 1972 until she died and was commissioned by her to tailor most of the ritual uniforms. While sewing male uniforms in the sewing salon beside the temple, Mestre João told me that according to Tia Neiva the dresses came from the Kingdom of Zana (*Reino de Zana*), a region of the higher astral plane inhabited by the spiritual phalanges represented in the Vale. The *ninfas* are representatives on the earth plane of their spirits called missionary guides on the astral plane, just as the *mestres* are representatives of their knights: 'they dress like them to get closer to their guides', he said. He described the first creation of the uniforms as a process of approximation to Tia Neiva's visions, requiring long experimentation with materials. For instance, they had to look for the right material to reproduce the glittering lights she used to see on the dresses of the spirit guides, so they used different materials through the years until they got hold of sequins, which represented the visions most appropriately. He said:

> We made a lot of dresses that we then had to change or readapt according to her visions. We made three versions of the *pente*[14] to get the right one. She used to tell us that seeing a missionary guide straight away was not an easy task. It is a spontaneous phenomenon; there are times when you want to see and you just can't and times when you don't expect it and it simply happens! You don't always see them closely. Sometime they appear far away as if beyond a screen. Moreover, she used to see the guide sometime turned on her side, sometime on her back, so that she couldn't see whether she had any symbol on the front, until the entity manifested in a straightforward way. Imagine that in the very first ritual of *Elevação de Espadas*[15] the dresses of the *ninfas sol*[16] were not ready so they went through the initiation wearing the brown skirt and a cloak like the one of the *mestres*.

João's report of his experience of working with the clairvoyant highlights the partial, multi-perspective and episodic way in which knowledge from the spirit world is said to be acquired. Likewise, Ramon Sarró notes that 'the problem with revelation is the same as the problem with invention: while both are seemingly "sudden" acts, psychologists of creativity, as well as religious scholars of revelation, know that they are very slow processes, often accompanied by long periods of incubation and with meanders and hesitations' (2018: 62). Sarró refers to the long process of the creation of Mandombe, a graphic language system invented by David Wabeladio Payi in Congo, which was claimed to be inspired by a revelation received in 1979 while praying for nine months in front of a wall and then developed along Wabeladio's life. Wabeladio's inspiration came by looking at the bricks of the wall in front of which he was praying or even at chicken and ducks' footprints. His revelation was then validated by his prophetic dreams. During the long process of creation of this language, also intended as a Messianic form of art, he used the raw material of schemes composed by bricks to extract form (Sarró 2018). Tia Neiva's process of creation, as discussed in Chapter Two, implies attempts to materialize her spiritual experiences of visions, experimenting with raw materials to reproduce the shapes they had in the spirit worlds. Tia Neiva's accounts of visions and her descriptions of the spirit worlds that she reported to have visited in different times over the years are scattered throughout the audio recordings and letters she distributed to mediums, which has resulted, for the most part, in a fragmented archive, which leads us to a discussion on the status of doctrinal knowledge.

## Doctrinal Knowledge: Between Legitimation and Systematization

Several attempts to map the structure of the spirit worlds in particular, and to systematize what mediums call doctrinal knowledge in general, are indicative of a body of knowledge with a revelatory character and grounded in the mediumistic experiences of the founder. Unlike Kardecism, in which mediumistic development is grounded in the doctrinal study of written texts, knowledge transmission in the Vale, as Chapter Seven illustrates, is grounded primarily in practice and first-hand experience and shared intersubjectively following the logic of 'mestre ensinando mestre' (master teaching master). Only in an advanced stage of mediumistic development may instructors pass on to new mediums a more or less standardized description of the spirit worlds. Those interested in deepening the study may then undertake a personal search in the archives of elder masters or consult their *Adjuntos de Povo*.

Over the years, the Trino Tumará Mestre José Carlos has put together an archive structured as a dictionary of the Vale. It is known as *Observações Tumará* (Tumará's Observations; Silva 2010), which he freely circulates among mediums. In presenting his work he states:

I feel that our doctrine was brought to us gradually, depending on each one's understanding, and being more Science than Religion, many things were partially revealed, and we need to join the parts. It is like a huge jigsaw puzzle where the pieces were delivered, distributed to all the Jaguars. But some have the pieces that others do not. Therefore, my concern was that of joining together as many pieces in order to compose the picture. The general picture is incomplete, but we can see already, with greater coverage, many of its aspects. (Silva 2010)[17]

Mestre José Carlos considers his work as 'observations', emphasizing his experience of living side by side with the clairvoyant, listening and reading about the phenomena from which this doctrinal knowledge resulted, albeit treated according to his own interpretation. Likewise, the Trino Tumuchy Mestre Mário Sassi has emphasized the role of individual experience in understanding and conceptualizing the spirit worlds, particularly in the Vale, where descriptions of life beyond matter were received by means of revelations made by spirits or through Tia Neiva's clairvoyance, although he noted that every attempt to provide a conceptualization that goes beyond this information might run 'the risk of being entirely anthropomorphic' (1974a: 37). Primarily for this reason, Tia Neiva's clairvoyance – which differently from other mediums entailed the simultaneous awareness of different times and planes of existence – is considered by mediums to be the main source of legitimacy, not only with regards to discourses concerning life beyond matter but of all doctrinal knowledge.

Historian Marcelo Rodrigues dos Reis stresses this point effectively in his doctoral thesis on Tia Neiva:

> The inspiration and materialization involved in the knowledge and the spiritual work all dependent on her speech or her legitimating clairvoyance, which acted as a privileged communication channel with the transcendent dimension once she was recognized by those of the community as a vessel of superhuman powers. (Reis 2008: 264)[18]

In this respect, one may note that after Tia Neiva's death, the modification of the forms of expression of the doctrine left by the founder (whether visual, verbal or ritualistic) with the addition of new elements, especially from other religions, may be regarded by mediums as an attempt to challenge the legitimacy of her clairvoyance. Major changes have resulted in both a separation among the mediums and have given rise to internal controversies (such as the schisms of the Order of 1990 and 2009). Nevertheless, the doctrine maintains its dynamism and capacity to adapt to different contexts and conditions as exemplified by external temples, where the formal rituals may be adapted to the limited availability of physical spaces and mediums, although these decisions belong to the temples' presidents, who are invested with this responsibility by a centralized hierarchy that guarantees the maintenance of the formal aspects of the ritualistic system. At the time of transition from the generation of the founders to a second generation of mediums trained by them, statements such as 'at the time of Tia Neiva it used to be this way' or 'I was here at the time of Tia Neiva' are commonly used to legitimize assertions concerning the doctrine.

This stance does not assume that members of the Vale do not seek a dialogue with other religions, but neither does it mean that the doctrine is a hybrid product of an accommodation of elements increasingly contributed by new members arriving from other spiritual contexts. Indeed, since Tia Neiva's death up until today, such contributions have been firmly discouraged (see Chapter Eight), and changes are more likely to be driven by mediums holding the highest offices in the hierarchy. From the foundation of the Vale, the search for parallels in other religions was aimed at understanding Tia Neiva's mediumistic phenomena; however, even Mário Sassi's interpretations and systematizations were still subject to Tia Neiva and her main spirit guides' verification and approval.

The tension between conservatism and renewal of meanings is emphasized in moments of crisis or major transformation in the social order. It so happened that I was conducting fieldwork during two such moments of transformation for the Order. My first fieldwork began in October 2004, a few days after the death of the Trino Arakém Nestor Sabatovicz, who represented the executive power of the Order left by Tia Neiva. This determined the beginning of a process of succession that led in 2005 to the nomination of the Trino Sumaná Michel Hanna as head of the Order. My second fieldwork began in 2009 at the time of a dispute over the Statutory Act of the Order. This led to the current division of the Order into two administrative entities, respectively led by Tia Neiva's two sons, differing in the offices that some members occupy in the hierarchy. These transitions led to an interest in systematizing doctrinal knowledge, mostly expressed by second-generation mediums as a response to the uncertainties brought about by these changes.

During a focus group I organized in 2004 with young mediums who were born and raised in the Vale, they discussed possible projects aimed at joining together Tia Neiva's writings spread among elder members of the community to make them available to those interested in deepening their doctrinal knowledge through her writings. These projects materialized in 2005, when Tia Neiva's grandson, Mestre Jairo Júnior Zelaya, founded the Library of the Jaguar (*Biblioteca do Jaguar*), providing free access to texts on the Vale and copies of mediums' personal archives, as well as Spiritist literature and texts on other religions. This material was also used by a study group formed by mediums, whose discussions eventually lead to the publication of a free-press publication *Journal of the Jaguar* (*Jornal do Jaguar*) and was disseminated across temples. Jairo told me that the *Jornal*, in addition to mediums' articles grounded in Tia Neiva's writings, published scholarly perspectives of the Vale as much as articles on other cultures and religions, as both could provide insights to understand the complexity of the doctrine. Two years later, Jairo Júnior and some members of the study group of the library were actively involved in field research for the National Survey of Cultural References (INRC) of the Brazilian Institute of Historical and Artistic Heritage (IPHAN) as part of the process of recognition of the Vale do Amanhecer as Intangible Heritage of Brazil. Their work resulted in hours of footage and included interviews with elder mediums about Tia Neiva and the foundation of the Vale as well as a survey of ritualistic and symbolic expressions of the doctrine (Siqueira et al. 2010).

Whilst both the library and journal are not currently active as projects, the centralized attempt to systematize the doctrine by drawing upon archival sources – Tia Neiva's letters and audio recordings – is still in progress and may define the future way in which doctrinal knowledge is presented to mediums in advanced courses. This process could also be seen in parallel to, and presumably as a reaction to, the proliferation of social network pages and groups opened individually by mediums to disseminate doctrinal texts and audio recordings. The digital space does not escape the tension between new interpretations and claims for original narratives grounded in Tia Neiva's legitimizing clairvoyance as a source of doctrinal knowledge from the spirit world. It magnifies this tension to the extent that some instructors in mediumistic development warn new mediums to avoid seeking information about the Vale on the internet and instead refer to Tia Neiva's sources, which may be provided by instructors.

In practical terms, not many mediums engage with doctrinal knowledge beyond what is passed on in the advanced training courses. From the first classes, they learn that knowledge arises through mediumistic practice and the engaged encounter with the spirit guides, who often share teachings and technical instructions. In this lies the capacity of the Vale to speak to and be accessible to people from the most diverse walks of life. In Northeast Brazil, I spent several months in a temple situated hours away from the city on the slopes of a mountain. Most of the mediums walked 6km down and up the mountain almost every day to work at the temple until late in the evening. They would not be able to explain the meaning of their phalanges, their vestments or ritual actions. They held a little knowledge of the descriptions of the spirit worlds or the categories of spirits. What motivated these mediums was not the intellectual aspect of this complex doctrine; it was the affective dimension of the encounter between humans and spirits and what they described as the sense of fulfilment given by an accomplished mission of working with the spirit worlds to assist the long queues of patients seeking hope and healing for their various afflictions. Knowledge in the Vale is less a representation of a disembodied mind, but it is generated through experience as engagement with a field of relations between humans and spirits.

## Ecologies of Fluids, Substances and Invisible Forces

This chapter presented precisely this field of relations as extending beyond physical experience. Ideas of extensibility, trans- and multidimensionality define the notions of the self, the geographies of and movements between the earth and spiritual planes and the sacred spaces of the temple. These ideas resonate with the cosmologies of invisible forces of the late nineteenth and early twentieth century. Simone Natale (2011) analyses the invention of X-rays in 1895 and wireless communication in 1896 as inserted in the cosmology of invisible forces proposed by the theories of psychical research and Spiritualism of the late nineteenth century. What these technologies had in common with occultism, Mesmerism and Spiritualism was that they were associated with an idea of invisible forces acting on physical reality and able to collapse distance, and to an idea of invisible substance, the ether, which would act as a medium for forces, magnetic waves, electricity and light (Natale 2011). The idea of ethereal fluids was popular in nineteenth-century occultism. One of these substances was called 'od' by Karl Ludwig Freiherr von Reichenbach and later described as an 'odic force' in the writings of Johannes Gerber, a German former Catholic priest who became a Spiritualist. Gerber, who published his communications with spirits (1932), describes an 'odic force' as similar to a power current, conducted by the blood of physical beings and if in excess it may create disorders. They describe the material body as 'od' condensed into matter, distinguished from its dissolved forms such as the 'odic body', the 'astral body' or the 'fluid body'. 'Od' may also be used by spirits to shape their bodies. Odic vibrations in humans may be influenced by the thoughts of the spirit or by other beings, as much as they can be felt by others. 'Od' may also be transmitted to others, both human and non-human, or infused in substances, and healing is based on a reciprocal transmission (ibid.).

Gustavo Ruiz Chiesa (2016) examines magnetism, ectoplasm and para-surgery in terms of connections, relationships, processes, flux and movement. Mesmerism, which shares commonalities with humoral medicine, was based on the idea that the body is composed of fluids and substances that need to be in balance. The body can be affected by others by means of these invisible fluids. Similarly, Richet envisioned vibrations emanating through thoughts that extend into others and the environment, whereas Spiritism posited that spirits may use fluids to affect thoughts. Chiesa draws parallels between the cosmologies and perspectives on science proposed by Franz

Mesmer's animal magnetism, Charles Richet's views on metaphysics, Waldo Vieira's Conscienciologia and the ecological approaches proposed by Bateson and Ingold. These epistemologies, according to Chiesa, share common features such as 'The *complexity* of living systems (ever interconnected and contextualized), the *instability* of the organic world (in terms of a *process* or a permanent *becoming*), the *intersubjectivity* in the constitution of reality and in the possibility of its understanding (whereby "subject" and "object" only exist relationally)' (2016: 249).[19]

The Vale do Amanhecer's complex human-spirit ecology of fluids and substances interconnects the different dimensions through the relations and movements of their inhabitants. Highly evolved spirits feed themselves with the *prana* of the highest dimensions but use human ectoplasm as a vehicle for their energies to heal human beings. In Vedic traditions, *prana* is the universal energy or life force. Also known as 'ether', 'prana is not a particular form of energy, but is rather the ultimate essence of all energies. Heat, light, electricity, gravity, that is, all the forces that act on matter, in their multiple activities, are expressions of prana' (Tumará 2010: P). Spirits at a low stage of evolution need to feed themselves with human magnetism and thus they may enter into a relation of dependence, attaching themselves to a particular person and sucking their magnetic animal fluid, especially when infused with alcohol and toxic substances that create addiction. Humans are therefore entangled in these fluidic relations with spirits and also with other humans; through thoughts and emotions, they may affect or be affected by other people's energies. This human-spirit ecology is what defines 'disobsessive healing' in the Vale do Amanhecer, as the next chapter illustrates.

These discourses share many commonalities with Spiritism and occultism from the late nineteenth and early twentieth century; however, their physical and ritual expression is unique of the Vale do Amanhecer through Tia Neiva's process of knowing and making. Furthermore, these human-spirit ecologies are not just fluidic; in the Vale they are also embedded in a transhistorical configuration, as they may be based on affinity or the readjustment of debts established in previous lives that are then managed in rituals.

In the previous chapter, I discussed the transhistorical extension of the self. In this chapter, I have explored its multidimensionality – how it extends through its composition, its fluids and relations through different dimensions. Substances like ectoplasm or vibrations through thought are extensions of the self beyond the body in the environment, which in the Vale may also encompass other worlds and fields of relations. The notion of body takes a multidimensional articulation as well, considering that the physical body is just one layer among many, as the spirit forges its envelop through a substance (perispirit) according to its vibration and dimension. Therefore, the self is made of fluids, membranes and substances that connect what may initially seem to be separate parts –body, soul and spirit – but are rather a field of relations in flux, corresponding to Ingold's approach to the human being as 'organism-person', growing entangled in and affected by an environment of relations with others (2000: 4).

The Vale do Amanhecer itself may be conceived as an organism with forces from the spirit world connecting its parts, its peoples and temples through the hierarchy, moving through the spaces in specific directions, linking ritual sectors and attracted to and redirected by ritual uniforms and symbols and materializing through bodies. The physical body as the physical temple is the centre of manipulation and transformation of forces, energies and substances, constantly made and sustained by these movements and relations from which it cannot be thought of as separated. The next chapter addresses specifically how these movements of fluids, substances and relations inform the aetiology of illness and the therapeutic intervention through disobsessive healing through the different rituals in the temple. This will be followed by a discussion in Chapter Six on the bodily grounding of the Vale's notions of mediumship based upon this movement of substances and its implication for the transhistorical configuration of human-spirit relations.

## Notes

1. Translated from the original in Portuguese.
2. Translated from the original in Portuguese.
3. Translated from the original in Portuguese.
4. The symbols that appear on the uniforms are called *armas* ('weapons'), most of them used as protection from different forces.
5. According to Tia Neiva, the time between one incarnation and the other could be at least five years, and only in some special cases may ministers allow the spirit to reincarnate before, although once back on the physical plane they may have memories of the past life.
6. A reference to this correspondence in the Vale's literature may be found in Silva (2010: A).
7. Vilela's paintings of the spirit worlds are exhibited in the *Casa Grande*, the former house of Tia Neiva, which is the current museum of the Vale.
8. The word *'neutrom'* has no relation to the 'neutron' of physics.
9. The red colour in the Vale represents disobsession – that is, spirit release.
10. Journalists' sensationalistic reportages usually depict the mediums of the Vale as people who worship UFOs, misrepresenting their views.
11. The Povo Yumatã is one of the largest groups to which mediums affiliate after the third initiation to work under the aegis of Ministro Yumatã, the spiritual minister

represented by Mestre Caldeira, who was consecrated by Tia Neiva among the first Root Adjuncts in 1978.

12. The ritual is similar to the Kardecist *Mesa Mediúnica*, although the spirits incorporated in the *Mesa Evangélica* do not pass on any communication.

13. Another interpretation is that the yellow and purple represent science and faith, respectively.

14. The *pente* is the veil used by the *ninfas*; they also wear gloves with their uniforms. According to the Mestre José Carlos (Silva 2010: P), it represents the energy projected from the spiritual planes flowing through the coronary chakra. The base of the veil, which is fixed to the hair, is shaped like an elliptical cone and is aimed at concentrating energies on the crown chakra.

15. 'Elevation of Swords', the second initiation.

16. 'Nymph Sun', or *doutrinadora*, the female indoctrination mediums.

17. Translated from the original in Portuguese.

18. Translated from the original in Portuguese.

19. Translated from the original in Portuguese.

# Chapter 5

# Disobsessive Healing

⁓ꙮ⁓

## Spiritual Obsession

One day, my friend André and I went to visit the Adjunto Ypuena Mestre Lacerda, an elder master in his late 70s who was among the first Adjuntos de Povo Raiz to be consecrated by Tia Neiva in 1978. He managed the *Casa Transitória Povo Ypuena* (Transitory House Ypuena People), also known as *Mansão Ypuena* (Ypuena Mansion), a charitable institution to assist people recovering from alcohol and drug addiction, and he is the spiritual leader of the People Ypuena, one of the largest groups of mediums in the Vale. In his office in the courtyard of the *Mansão*, he organized the daily activities, including the charitable social lunch served to those in need, and provided both patients and members (*componentes*) of his people with spiritual support under the guidance of his spirit mentor, Minister Ypuena. When we arrived, we sat down on the sofa ready to engage in an intense doctrinal conversation. He handed us several pages each and insisted that we had to read them out loud. One was a commentary on one of Tia Neiva's letters and the other was a transcript of a course delivered by the Trino Arakém Nestor Sabatovicz. After a while, I found myself feeling quite impatient, thinking that perhaps I could read it later at home and employ our time together listening to his stories. But his insistence suggested a hidden agenda. André read the following:

Koatay 108 said that in this doctrine the medium of the Amanhecer has the condition, thanks to the indoctrination of his *cobradores*, to release in this incarnation what would need four or five incarnations in the case he would not be in the Vale do Amanhecer. The karmic law is smoothened through the work in the law of aid. The incarnation is precisely an opportunity for readjustment. Spiritual life is the best way to readjust with our victims from the past.

'Nothing happens by chance', Lacerda interrupted, 'we are here on the earth plane to pay our debts'. André commented, 'When you see that everything is going well and suddenly it all goes wrong then it is the *cobrador* arriving'. 'He wants to see you suffering as you made him suffer', Lacerda noted, '… and we feel his actions when everything is so difficult and annoying …You have to fight against yourself because your ego would not accept this at all'. 'And how would you do that? How would you control your ego?' I asked. 'The doctrine is here for this, to help you', Lacerda said,

> If you are suffering there is a reason. If you made someone suffer, this person that you wounded is going to hate you. Tia used to tell us that when you have a good job or business and the *cobrador* arrives, he will suggest that the employer tell you that you're not worth anything, that your job placement was given to someone else. This is what she used to tell us, that if we don't change we are going to suffer.

'The action of the *cobrador* may reach you', said André, but if you have a certain posture and conduct, if you were working on your inner self, leaving your egoism and vanity aside, leaving your personality to encounter your individuality, the *cobrador* cannot do anything; he cannot move you to attack anyone. But if he is not able to access me or Lacerda, he may act upon me because I got annoyed and have lowered my vibrations.

Lacerda looked at me and said, 'My daughter, if we would be in peace with ourselves we would be in peace with everyone. The secret is in simplicity'. 'In sum, do you mean that the essence of the doctrine is the opportunity for re-adjustment?' I asked. André explained, 'he is saying that the Jaguars may be those more indebted and these consecrations may help them readjust more easily to what they've left behind, as there is also the adjustment through love'. Lacerda added, 'If someone doesn't like you, go to the Temple and pray that he can receive the forces he needs. The *cobradores* are also God's children and he demands us to release them'.

He suddenly asked us to stand up and then recited the Prayer of Simiromba, in which he asked God to transform through disobsessive healing those who were there listening to us and to guide them and release them through the spirit mentors. I then understood that since the beginning Lacerda had intended the reading and the conversation we had to be spiritual work, a lesson attended by the disincarnate suffering spirits around us.

When mediums in the Vale refer to disincarnate spirits as suffering spirits, they point out that this is because they recognize that feelings of hate, rage or rancour originate from suffering, wounds or lack of understanding and love. The temple is intended as a spiritual hospital where these spirits are welcomed and it is explained to them where they are, which state they are in (as some of them may not be aware of their death), how to overcome their situation of suffering through forgiveness and that they will be guided by spirit mentors towards the hospitals situated in the spirit worlds. This conceptualization grounds the practice of disobsessive healing, whereby 'obsession' (*obsessão*, a term derived from the Kardecist terminology) refers to the action of a disincarnate spirit influencing different aspects of a person's experience. Thus, disobsession might be intended to heal the physical, affective, social or material aspects of the person's everyday life.

This chapter illustrates an aetiology of illness and the therapeutic treatment of patients in ritual healing, illuminating how mediums understand disobsessive healing as a 'mediumistic science'. In discussing the conceptualizations of illness as based upon human-spirit relations and the ecology of fluids and substances, I point out the relational dimension of healing. I examine the ritual itinerary of patients through the temple, highlighting the transitional mode of participation and the progressive work of cleansing the body, which involves removing layers of affecting energies and the projection of healing forces through ectoplasm. In addressing my own bodily experience and how mediums responded to it, I show how spiritual and biomedical epistemologies are lived through as complementary and how the 'evidence' and 'validity' of mediumistic practice are the result of meaningful patterns of discourses and occurrences emerging through the unfolding of life. I will argue that the ideas of 'complementarity' and 'mediumistic science' as developed in the Vale, in a specific historical condition and through a process of learning, focused more on practice than on theoretical study, determined an all-inclusive character that was able to attract different segments of the population.

## An Aetiology of Illness

Illness is understood in the Vale as having a twofold process, beginning in the spiritual dimension and then manifesting in the physical one, with bodily dysfunctions to be treated by means of conventional medicine.[1] Mediums claim that treating the spiritual cause may facilitate the healing of issues that do not find effective relief in biomedicine. The spiritual aetiology of illness may involve different factors: a) the payment of a karmic debt from a past life (*cobrança carmica*); b) a mediumistic disorder, namely an over-production of ectoplasm concentrated around the chakras, affecting the person's organic and psychological conditions, and thus requiring medium-istic development; c) an obsession (*obsessão*) through vibrational affinity, namely when the person's feelings of hate, rage or dissatisfaction attract disincarnate spirits in line with those feelings. These spirits are said to bind their victims, projecting their vibration upon their organs, mind or neu-rovegetative nervous system, leading to disease and imbalance. Obsession may also take the form of a chemical addiction, when the spirit attaches itself to the victim and feeds on the energy produced by alcohol and drugs.

Causal agents of obsession are the so called 'spirits without light' (*espíritos sem luz*), and they are distinguished into three main categories: *sofredores* (sufferers), disincarnate beings who have not yet realized or accepted they have died and wander on the physical or etheric plane causing emotional imbalance or physical pain to humans (also known as 'errant' or 'wandering spirits' in some Spiritist and Spiritualist groups); *obsessores* (obsessors), spirits that are in need of human ectoplasm and act with a more or less constant vibration upon the person, establishing a relationship based on an energy exchange; *cobradores* (debt collectors), spirits linked to the person's past incarnation who died with a desire for revenge and thus obsess over the person directly or cause difficulties in their life. A particular form of a *cobrador* is the *elítrio*, described by Tia Neiva as a spirit deformed by rage into the shape of a monkey head, incarnating together with the person in debt from a past life; they are attached to their aura and adhere to an organ or the nervous centre. Sassi illustrated its action as being subtle, beginning with imperceptible symptoms until it suddenly starts sucking the victim's energy, first from an organ and then expanding throughout the body, leading to critical medical conditions (1974a: 63). Its actions are associated with illnesses such as epilepsy, if the *elítrio is* positioned in the head, or cancer (or other diseases) that does not improve with biomedi-cal treatment. Obsession may not always be the cause of a mental disease, but it may be a secondary effect of an undeveloped mediumship. As the instructor explained, mental disorders may be part of a process of karmic redemption determined in a past life; or they may result from an accu-mulation of ectoplasm in the head, leading the person to become more perceptive to spirits, a case that could be treated through the development of mediumship.

In this sense, these categories are as fluid and interconnected as it is the relationship between karma, spirits, persons, illness and health that deter-mines disobsessive healing as healing relations between humans and spirits or between humans with the help of spirits. In the latter case, in order to reach the person who caused its suffering in a past life, a *cobrador* may act through someone close to this person – as Mestre Lacerda illustrated in the above mentioned conversation – or it may incarnate within their circle or as someone who the person may temporarily cross paths with at a certain moment in life, demanding payment within a relationship, which could be affective, financial, professional and so forth. This sort of action may not directly form the basis for a physical illness, but it may socially, emotionally or materially affect the person's well-being. In the rituals of the Vale, spirit guides may then assist the patient in addressing this relationship in such a way that the *cobrador* might reduce its actions through the principles of love and forgiveness. This relational dimension of healing was also illustrated by Groisman, addressing ritual interventions of spirit guides in Brazilian Barquinha. Engaging with participants in problem management and 'dislocating and relocating' the way they perceive the world constituted a sort of 'epistemological healing' and a 'framework for the fluency of social and cosmic relations' (2016: 54–57).[2] In the Vale do Amanhecer, the temple is organized ritualistically, architecturally and aesthetically around the broad scope of disobsessive healing, so that patients can undertake an itinerary of different rituals, each addressing particular needs.

## Spiritual Treatment of the Patients

Disobsessive healing is understood as a process acting upon the spirit and, according to the multidimensionality of the self and to the patient's specific case, its consequences may reach the physical and psychological dimension. This process may occur in a single ritual, in a series of different rituals or it may require a longer attendance involving several visits to the temple. Patients undertake an elliptical therapeutic ritual itinerary clockwise around the temple (see Figure 5.1) during which several rituals are performed by mediums to gradually transform the patient's energies from negative to positive. The expression 'to pass into a ritual' emphasizes the conceptualization of a transitional mode of patients' participation along an itinerary of rituals. The continuous movement of patients and mediums from one sector to another, the queues outside the ritual spaces and the simultaneous performances of different rituals are far from being associated with a religious temple. Indeed, the analogy with a hospital emergency unit is often used to describe spiritual work in the Vale, and mediums refer to the temple as a *pronto soccorro espiritual* (spiritual first aid), where patients firstly receive first aid and are then optionally referred to receive further treatment in specific rituals.

Given the high flow of patients, particularly in the Templo Mãe, seldom is information about the doctrine or the spiritual work passed on to them before they undergo the rituals. When one arrives at the temple, one is immediately instructed by receptionist mediums on where to seat to wait for one's turn and how to proceed from one ritual to another. Anamnesis, diagnosis and triage – terms borrowed from the medical discourse used by my interlocutors in several descriptions of the ritual – happen in the ritual of *Tronos* (Thrones, Figures 5.2 to 5.5), which takes place in a sacred space composed by one sector with red tables and benches, or another with yellow ones, whereby the patient seats and receives first assistance from the *preto velho* incorporated by an *apará*. The *preto velho* examines the patient's spiritual and karmic situation, cleanses the energy around the body, feels the vibrational imbalance of the body reflected in the aura (Figure 5.3–5.4) and attracts the *obsessores* and *sofredores* attached to the patient to be incorporated by the *apará* and then indoctrinated and elevated by the *doutrinador* (Figure 5.5). In case the *preto velho* perceives that the physical side has been affected, the spirit advises the patient to consult an 'earth doctor', who can complement the healing process with biomedicine. Spirits manifesting in the Vale are not allowed to prescribe any treatment or remedy (or to advise

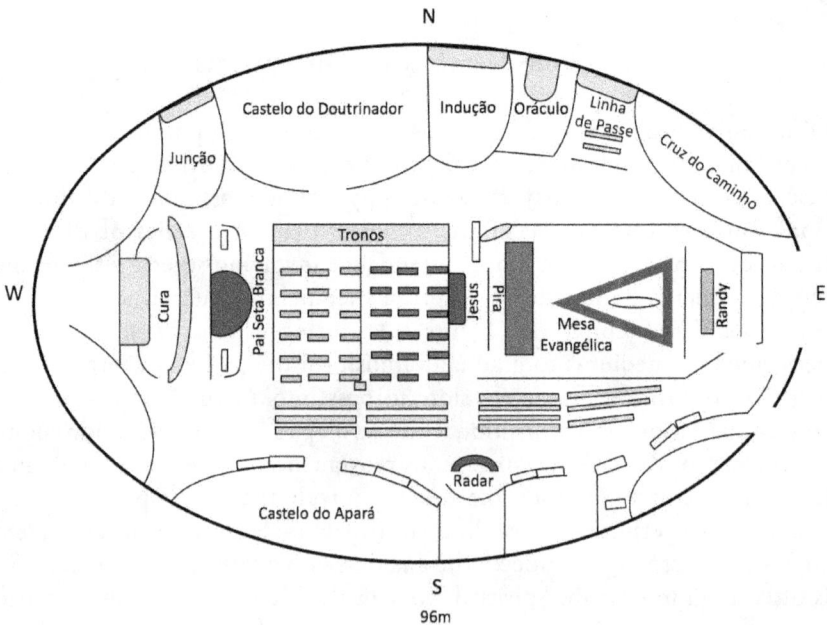

**Figure 5.1** The plan of the Templo Mãe with its main ritual spaces. Figure by: Emily Pierini.

a patient to stop any medical therapy), including natural ones such as herb teas or baths. Treatment through material means is limited to using salt and perfume in rituals, considered to have cleansing properties, and drinking the water from the temple, which is said to be 'fluidized' by spirits – that is, infused with healing forces. When the spirit identifies undeveloped mediumship, the patient is advised to undertake mediumistic development either in the Vale or in other spiritual groups of his or her choice.

The communication with *pretos velhos* may sometimes require the intervention of the *doutrinador* to add further explanation for the patient to understand the message of the spirit. Only after a few consecutive visits may the patient be able to draw together the information received and to get a sense of the doctrinal discourse. Towards the end of the consultation, the *preto velho* may suggest patients pass into those rituals that are best suited for their situation. From then onwards, there is no further verbal communication with spirits guides, and patients are asked to position themselves in a receptive mode – namely seated with hands palms up on knees – and think of their illnesses and suffering, their homes, material lives and people in need so that the action of the energies manipulated in rituals is not limited to patients but moves beyond the physical ritual space to reach other aspects of their lives. When the physical presence of the person in need is not possible, the *pretos velhos* may suggest a relative or a friend leave the person's name in rituals for distant healing.

**Figure 5.2** Ritual of *Tronos*. Photo: Emily Pierini.

After the *Tronos*, the patient may be directed to the sector on the west end of the temple, behind the Statue of Pai Seta Branca, to pass into the ritual of *Cura* (Healing), whereby the *aparás* incorporate the *médicos de cura* so as to cleanse the patient's chakras to re-establish the magnetic balance of the body and project forces for the release of the *obsessor* (Figure 5.6). The ritual of *Junção* is thought of as an extension of the *Cura* in using the forces of the spirits of *médicos* in conjunction with those of the *doutrinadores* projected into patients through the application of seven magnetic *passes*. Derived from Mesmerism, the *passe* is used in the Spiritist practice as the imposition of hands to transmit fluids, but it differs in the Vale for the specific gestural sequence required for its ritual application. Instructors explain that the *passe* is an infusion of the *doutrinador*'s magnetic fluid to rebalance the organism energetically. In the *Junçaõ*, it widens the intra-molecular spaces of the obsessing spirit, or *elítrio*, so that it can become lighter, losing adherence to the body, and be elevated. Mediums insist that only patients advised by the *pretos velhos* are allowed to pass into this ritual. This is because some people's

**Figure 5.3** Illustration of the Ritual of *Tronos* and its spiritual effects beyond physical matter: the patients carrying suffering spirits, the spirits elevated by the *doutrinadores* and the spirit guides standing beside the *aparás*. Digital painting: Márlio Kleber. Published with permission.

**Figure 5.4** Illustration of the ritual of *Tronos*: the patient, carrying an *obsessor* spirit, consults the medium *apará* incorporating a spirit guide while the *doutrinador* pays attention to the spirit manifestation in the *apará*. Digital painting: Márlio Kleber. Published with permission.

**Figure 5.5** Ritual of *Tronos*: one *apará* incorporating a *sofredor* spirit and the *doutrinador* behind her performing the elevation of the spirit to the spirit worlds. Photo: Emily Pierini.

incarnations may be aimed just at the redemption of a specific *elítrio* and so its premature release may determine the end of that incarnation.

The ritual of *Indução*, performed in a sector along the northern aisle, is aimed at removing the negative charges affecting the patient's material life. These charges are said to be attracted to the sacred space by the invocations of the *comandante* (commander – that is, the medium directing the ritual); they pass through a chain formed by mediums holding hands and are broken by their solar plexus, then they are manipulated by the *pretos velhos* incorporated by the *aparás*. Some patients may be advised by the *pretos velhos* to stop by the *Oraculo de Pai Seta Branca* (Oracle) to drink the blessed wine (non-alcoholic grape juice). The Oracle is in a room accessible through a gate opened by the nymphs of the phalanx Muruaicy (female mediums who are guardians of the sacred doors), where selected male mediums receive the spirit of Pai Seta Branca projecting his forces in the temple. Following the therapeutic ritual itinerary, patients may pass through the adjoining room called *Sudálio* to attend the ritual of *Defumação*, performed through the use of incense and the invocations of the *doutrinador*, so as to remove those negative charges produced by feelings of hatred and envy that the person may have received in daily life. The same ritual sector also hosts the ritual of *Linha de Passe*, where *aparás* incorporate the *caboclos* to perform their disobsessive healing. The *caboclos* beat the medium's chest with their right hand,

**Figure 5.6** Ritual of *Cura* (healing): the *aparás* incorporating their *médicos de cura* standing behind the patients and transmitting to them the healing forces. Photo: Emily Pierini.

chanting and greeting other spirit guides, then pass their hands around the patient's body and snap their fingers to disintegrate the last negative charges.

As part of their therapeutic indications for the day, patients may also be advised to participate in the *Cruz do Caminho* (Cross of the Path), a ritual in which the forces of the *médicos* and Yemanjá, the deity of the sea incorporated in *aparás*, are said to be crossed with those of the *cavaleiros da luz* (knights of the light) and Ramses, acting altogether as a powerful healing device. The last ritual of the therapeutic itinerary inside the temple is the *Randy*, where patients either lay on a cot or sit on the side while the mediums form an elliptical circle around them, firstly calling for the forces of the *cavaleiros da luz*, then incorporating two *médicos de cura* to perform an invisible spiritual surgery on the etheric bodies and finally incorporating the people of the water to cleanse the energies.

Besides the rituals inside the temple, the *pretos velhos* may suggest participation in the rituals of *Estrela Candente* and *Estrela Sublimação*. The latter is aimed at healing through the forces of the Oracles, the knights of light, Apollo, Ramses and Amon-Rá and those from the past lives of the Jaguars. The aesthetic dimension of the sacred spaces is also considered to participate in the therapeutic process by transmitting and attracting specific forces through the vibration of the different colours in a chromotherapy-like conception.

Rituals are formally defined by opening and closing verbal formulas enacted by the ritual commander and are distinguished from one another by different combinations of single elements, such as *emissões* (emissions) – namely the invocations of forces expressed by the enactment of the individual spiritual genealogy of each medium; the distribution of magnetic *passes* and elevation of obsessing spirits by the *doutrinadores*; and the incorporation of spiritual mentors by the *aparás*.

The therapeutic process involves the single or combined use of a) disobsessive healing – that is, the release of causal spiritual agents affecting the person; b) patient-spirit communication, which may bring along awareness of one's self and advice on life matters; and c) development of mediumship, involving bodily and psychological control over spirits. Furthermore, when the action of a suffering spirit has affected the physical body, patients are advised to seek parallel treatment through biomedicine. Factors that may interfere in the healing process are primarily understood as karmic, as being part of a path of an individual spiritual evolution involving a redemption of karmic debts through illness. The stage of illness is also a determinant, as Mestre Lacerda explained, when the organ of the patient is damaged by the continuous projection of the causal agent, it might be hard to find relief. However, if the patient arrives at an initial stage of illness, the causal agent may be released in time. Generally, mediums attribute to faith an important role in determining positive thoughts to enhance the vibrational pattern of the body, which thus allows access to healing forces. In this stands the mission of the Vale, which, ultimately, is to transform suffering via hope and faith and develop in the patient an awareness of their own forces.

## Special Rituals of Disobsession

It was around half past one in the morning when the temple siren rang repeatedly, calling for the intervention of mediums residing in the town for a *trabalho especial* (special work). This ritual occurs when special cases of obsession arrive in need of urgent assistance at times when the temple is closed (during the night until 10AM). I had recently gained permission to access the temple at night to observe this ritual, so I rushed down the street, meeting a couple of mediums on the way wearing casual clothes and carrying just the *fita* with them, as the uniform is not mandatory for this kind of work. I spotted a car parked in front of the entrance; I could hear someone screaming inside. I had previously seen patients arriving at the temple in a condition recognized by mediums as 'strong obsession', although not often. They usually threw themselves to the floor before the temple door or hit those who accompanied them. Some manifested a muscular strength above their ordinary abilities or twisted their arms and fingers in a way that forced the joints to perform unusual rotations. Mediums who are receptionists are trained to deal with such cases by calming them down and ensuring that no one gets hurt. Through specific techniques, the obsessing spirit was transferred to the body of an *apará*, who is trained to control it. Once the patient had calmed down, they were accompanied inside the temple to continue the special treatment.

All the cases I had previously witnessed arrived during the daytime amid a crowded temple with all the rituals fully working, so that within that context their screams were somehow mixed with and alleviated by other familiar sounds. At night, however, those screams echoed throughout the empty temple, in an atmosphere of uneasiness. The doors were ajar. The medium receptionist on duty told me that they were awaiting the arrival of some other *aparás* to open the ritual and advised me to sit right at the back to avoid getting involved with the energies of the *trabalho*. I entered and walked through the penumbra of the aisle, as only a few lights were turned on. I could see a group of six mediums standing in front of the ritual space of the *Tronos*. As I approached, I also saw two *aparás* sitting on the side, and the patient, a woman probably in her fifties, lying on the floor experiencing epileptic-like convulsions while two other mediums tried to protect her from self-injury. Suddenly, the *aparás* incorporated simultaneously two *obsessores* and the patient instantly calmed down; it was if she had woken up after fainting. The *doutrinadores* were indoctrinating the spirits until the other mediums arrived in pairs and completed the numbers needed for the *trabalho*. The mediums took their positions into the *Tronos*, the *pretos velhos* manifested in the *aparás* and then the patient was passed into each *Trono*. While she was receiving the cleansing (*limpeza*) from one *preto velho* in a *Trono*, the other *aparás* were alternating incorporations of *pretos velhos* with those of *sofredores*. Every so often, the *obsessor* took over control of the patient again. In some cases, another *doutrinador* might have to intervene to indoctrinate the spirit incorporated in the patient or the *obsessor* might be transferred from the patient to the *apará*. In this instance, the patient gradually regained control over her body until she was able to walk out from the temple with her family.

Strongly obsessed patients may present seizures as symptoms; however, mediums are able to distinguish between physical epilepsy and spiritual obsession. The former is physical (albeit believed to be caused originally by an *elítrio* spirit in the head) and the patient may report a history of the illness, while spiritual obsession manifests often in a single episode or for a limited time in the person's life and is immediately responsive to disobsessive treatment. Neurobiological investigations by Brazilian psychiatrists are undermining the supposed relationship between mediumistic phenomena and temporal lobe seizures. One investigation in particular tested nine Brazilian mediums in what they defined as a 'trance state' with electroencephalography (EEG), which was 'suggestive of neither epileptic discharge during mediumship activity nor a clinical history of seizure disorder' (Hageman et al. 2010: 104). This kind of discernment between spiritual and pathological experiences will be discussed further on in addressing specific cases of people undertaking mediumistic development in the Vale for therapeutic purposes.

There is another form of *Trabalho Especial* that often takes place during usual daytime ritual consultations in the *Tronos*, when the spirit of the *preto velho* feels that the patients need their energies to be further worked by two more *pretos velhos* in another *Trono*. This special work may be used in cases of both strong obsession, such as the one above, and patients not particularly manifesting any visible reaction to an *obsessor* spirit. Mediums consider it usual for humans to be carrying some kind of suffering spirit attached their aura, thus the ritual of *Tronos* is there ready to be employed in the release of these spirits, even when patients attend the ritual with no particular problem and are there just to listen to a word of hope or encouragement by spirit guides. The ritual is perceived by patients as being a moment in which to fully experience their current emotions in such a confidential and safe manner that they even bring their children to receive the blessing of spirit guides.

In passing as a patient through rituals, I was familiarized with the *pretos velhos* way of cleansing me, which was usually by interrupting the conversation to remove and release suffering spirits. One day, however, one *preta velha* unexpectedly advised me to undergo a *Trabalho Especial*. I had felt particularly weak and tired during the day, and Pedro, a friend of mine, suggested that I walk down with him to the temple that evening. The length of the queue to pass into the ritual of *Tronos* was quite discouraging, but we sat in the line. Once my turn arrived, I introduced myself to the *apará* medium, a woman in her thirties, who was incorporating the *preta velha* Vovó Catarina das Cachoeiras (Grandma Catherine of the Waterfalls), her eyes closed and a calm smile on her face. She began to do a cleansing, shaking her hands around my body and snapping fingers to discharge the heavy energies, and then suddenly gave passage to a suffering spirit. While the *doutrinador* was indoctrinating the *sofredor*, the *aparà* had her arms crossed on the table and her hands were tightly contracted to control the spirit, but she seemed as if she was having difficulties in holding firm that position. Facing my direction, she rested her head on her arms and coughed intermittently until the spirit was elevated by the *doutrinador*, then the *preta velha* came back to cleanse the *apará*'s body from the negative charges left by the spirit. She then turned to me and greeted me, but suddenly another *sofredor* gained access to the *apará*'s body to be indoctrinated and elevated, followed by another six spirits, thus it was not possible to build a proper communication with the *preta velha*. She told me I had carried them to the temple; that they were attached to my body and sucking my energy. She then asked the *doutrinador* permission to manifest a *caboclo* to further cleanse me with the native energies from the forests and proceeded to incorporate the Caboclo Pena Branca (White Feather), beating strongly on her chest with her hand and then passing both hands around my body while snapping her fingers. The spirit was emitting an Amerindian chant interspersed with greetings to the forces of nature: 'Hail the forces of nature! Hail the forces of the waterfalls! Hail the forces of the forests! And thank God! Eeeh-eeeh-eeeh! Praised be Jesus Christ! And thank God!' These greetings (*saudações*) to other spirits working in the Vale are the way in which spirits call on different forces in rituals. I was feeling heat waves entering my body whenever she placed her hand on my front or between my shoulders. Then the *caboclo* passed on a short message about the fact that I had recently returned to the Vale. When the spirit of the *preta velha* came back reincorporated by the *apará*, she gave me her blessing and recommended that I should pass into another two *Tronos*, since I needed more disobsessive treatment.

I waited until another *Trono* was free. When a patient left a *Trono* in the opposite row, I sat down where a male *apará* in his sixties was incorporated with a *preto velho*. As soon as I introduced myself he incorporated a *caboclo* instead and began to beat his chest with his hand. The *caboclo* introduced himself as Caboclo Pena Branca, the same one who passed into the first *Trono*. Apparently continuing the message that I received earlier in the other *Trono*, he told me about the obstacles I had found along my path of return to the 'House of Seta Branca', and said I had demonstrated my strength. He gave passage to a couple of *sofredores* to be indoctrinated, whilst I gradually began to feel a sort of relief from tiredness. Eventually, he said 'you have one *Trono* left to pass through, don't you? Go with my blessing, another spirit of light will attend you there'. After examining in rapid sequence the possible ways in which the information could be passed from one *Trono* to the other by conventional means, I realized that the only two involved in both rituals who had access to this information were the spirit of the *caboclo* and myself. Still, with this issue in mind, I passed into the third *Trono*, where a young woman *apará* was incorporating Vovó Maria Conga. She did some more cleansing, and since I felt better, she blessed me and said I could leave. Soon afterwards, I commented upon the work of the *caboclos* with my friend Pedro, and he told me that in his view it was the same *caboclo* conducting the ritual in the first *Trono*, and since the work became so disobsessive, the *caboclo* needed to change the energies at play using another *apará* and *doutrinador* to switch the work from disobsession into communication. Thus, the spirit manifested in another medium to pass on his message. This dynamic involving the manifestation of the same spirit in different mediums or on a different occasion was not as exceptional as I expected, as Pedro informed me, which impels us to consider the therapeutic work of spirits as not entirely bounded in the single ritual event.

## Complementary Epistemologies of Healing

When in a more advanced stage of fieldwork I began the mediumistic development, I could look at the different dimensions of the process of learning mediumship, but mostly I was able to grasp the primacy of bodily experience within this process, as I will further discuss in Chapter Seven. Concurrently, my own bodily experience was fully involved in the process of knowing in the field, and by sharing my accounts of unexpected events and sensations with my interlocutors and listening to their interpretations I could reach new insights. This enhanced attention to my bodily sensations was not confined to the mediumistic development but encompassed my participation in rituals as a patient as well as my daily activities outside the temple.

On one occasion while participating in a ritual, I suddenly felt a pain on the right side of my abdomen. I initially thought that this kind of pain was transitional, thus I had not given it much importance. However, since the pain persisted, that evening my friend, Mestre Diego, advised me to pass as a patient into the *Tronos*. After receiving a cleansing by the *preta velha*, she told me that the pain was caused by a *sofredor*; although it had been elevated to the spirit worlds, in the previous ritual it had left an 'impregnation', a residue in my physical body, so I had to drink the water from the temple. She told me not to worry, because the spiritual cause was solved, but that I should refer to an 'earth doctor' for the physical side. Three days later, I decided to see a doctor because the pain was reappearing intermittently. Diego took me to a hospital in Brasília, where I had all the relevant tests. A doctor walked in with the results and Diego noted how curious the name written on his badge was – 'Dr Ralf' – and winked at me with a hilarious smile to indicate that he had the same name as the spirit of Dr Ralf in the Vale, a *médico de cura*. The 'earth doctor' told us about the German origins of his family. He then showed me my test results; nothing relevant had come up so he said that the pain was probably a residue left in my body by a virus. He recommended that I drink plenty of water and said I could take some painkillers if needed. The resonance of his words with those of the *preta velha* was seen by Diego as confirming the spiritual diagnosis.

My bodily experience illuminated how spiritual and biomedical epistemologies were perceived as complementary rather than in conflict, not just ideally but in the everyday life of mediums. The ethnographer may learn through his or her body how to interpret the world through the categories of the people he or she studies with, as Paul Stoller suggested after he became ill during his fieldwork among the Songhai of Niger and learned to interpret his illness as embedded in a system of sorcery in which he was also implicated as an apprentice sorcerer (Stoller 1997). Through my experience, and the way my medium friends responded to it, I was training myself to see these emerging patterns of meaningful interlacements between spiritual messages and life occurrences and how these patterns grounded what mediums deemed as the validity of their practice.

'The science that denies faith in God is as useless as the faith that denies science', these being the remarkable words of Tia Neiva (N.C. Zelaya, 1977), written outside her former house, the *Casa Grande*, as indicative of the Vale's stance towards mainstream science. This position was embodied in the character of Mário Sassi, remembered by mediums as being 'the scientist' of the doctrine, both because of his background in the social sciences and his attempt to systematize Tia Neiva's revealed doctrine through personal research into mainstream science. Sassi envisioned a complementarity between science and Mediumism:

> Medicine is perfectly equipped for its mission of healing, and Mediumism's only aim is to act as spiritual nursing. Mediumistic work should refer to

doctors, the patients free from *elítrios* and ectoplasmatic pressures. But, for the two processes to work in harmony, it is necessary for the admission by the medical conceptualization of the existence of these invisible factors of illness. Medical science and spiritual science complement each other perfectly. (Sassi 1974a)[3]

Sassi considered Kardec's classifications and Charles Richet's analysis driven by a scientific method to be two valid interpretations of the same phenomenon that, taken individually, are partial 'philosophical conceptualizations' that gave rise respectively to the religious dimension, namely Kardecism, and to parapsychology (1974a: 20). He envisioned the potentiality of Mediumism to become the common denominator between science and religion. In this sense, when referring to the Vale some mediums use the term 'doctrine' to mean a body of revealed principles, a 'doctrine of the spirit world'. In his doctoral thesis on Tia Neiva, the historian Marcelo Reis (2008) observes that in the Vale 'The scientific treatment does not materialize in everyday life, because a large number of mediums keep apart from conceptual discussion. Conversely, these religions are dedicated to the practice, a sort of *empiricist Spiritualism*. On the other hand, validating and reaffirming their tradition, they imagine themselves as scientists, seeing themselves as deep *connoisseurs of the Spirit Worlds*' (Reis 2008: 176).[4]

As a matter of fact, in our conversations, mediums repeatedly affirmed that 'the doctrine is more practical than theoretical', and this becomes clear in the process of mediumistic development, whereby a practical-empirical learning prevails over what Whitehouse (2004) defined as a 'doctrinal mode' of religious transmission. What, then, is a 'spiritual scientist'? Some instructors referred to the 'spiritual scientist' as 'an initiated medium able to transform negative energy into positive, producing phenomena of integration and disintegration of molecules from one plane to another'. The 'spiritual scientist' is thus understood as the medium who has gained practical knowledge of the laws that are said to connect the material and non-material planes of existence and of the ways to intervene on phenomena understood as extending beyond physical matter. He or she administers a set of techniques, methods and explanations that altogether form a method of investigation that has been developed and empirically tested over the years through the experiences of the clairvoyant and founding members.

Differently from Anglo-Saxon mediumship, mediums in the Vale do Amanhecer are not concerned with providing patients and visitors with evidences of the validity of mediumistic science and phenomena. My interlocutors referred to the 'evidences' experienced within their practice more in terms of how these had been key facts grounding the validity of this practice for their own lives rather than trying to prove the existence of a spiritual life beyond matter. Thus, 'evidence' may refer to an event (single or recurrent) or a process (short or long term) involving a transformation as a result of a spiritual phenomenon, a new situation clearly different from the previous one. The term 'confirmation' was also frequently used. 'Evidence', or 'confirmation', may involve synchronicity, an event occurring after being announced by a spirit, or spirits reporting information not accessible to the medium in whom they incorporate. It may involve the same spirit incorporating in different mediums and rituals, or the same specific message transmitted by different spirits over time, as in the instances provided so far. These cases in particular – that may be approached as a form of triangulation – produce a cumulative effect, weaving narrative threads through a sequence of interrelated spiritual events that gradually strengthen the validity of mediumistic practice for mediums' lives.

The effectiveness of healing was also claimed as 'evidence'. Individual narratives included cases of a patient being cured after receiving spiritual treatment in the Vale for illnesses that had found no solution in biomedicine, and in many cases they became a trigger point for individual spiritual experience. These cures were intended by my interlocutors more as 'evidence' rather than as 'miraculous' or 'paranormal' experiences because they are addressed by Mediumism and thus they become part of the ordinary everyday practice and experience of thousands of mediums. As Fiona Bowie notes, 'The notion of miracle is embedded within a particular language and cosmology, and in dealing with the miraculous, the contravention of our rules of science or the breakthrough of unseen powers into the material world we need to recognise that there might indeed be nothing miraculous, nothing unexpected or anomalous, for the people in question' (Bowie 2011: 172).

One might argue that the notion of a mediumistic science within the Vale is a legacy of Spiritism. However, unlike Spiritism, which has a long tradition in developing the scientific aspect – using psychical research and aiming at the acceptance of its therapies from the medical profession – the Vale does not promote any study or seek any medical recognition of its treatments, 'the practice of Mediumism and spiritual science' being its focus. Analysing the history of the Spiritist movement, David Hess identified alternate moments of development of religious-evangelical and scientific discourses. Class divisions were also played out in the discursive division, with the educated middle class using the scientific discourse over the religious one (1987: 29). In the Vale, theorizing was less developed precisely because of the lack of those factors that informed the development of the scientific aspect in Spiritism, that according to Hess were the pressures by the Roman Catholic Church and by the medical profession; the state repression under Vargas's dictatorship; and the necessity to 'reinforce' its differentiation from Afro-Brazilian religions (Hess 1987: 29).

Primarily, the Vale emerged in a historical moment in which mediumistic religions were in a process of rapid growth, and, differently from Spiritism, its development occurred without experiencing any relevant external pressure or episodes of religious intolerance frequently experienced by Afro-Brazilian religions. Despite clearly differentiating its notions of Mediumism from those developed by other spiritual groups, in evoking elements from different religions while seeking a complementarity with mainstream science, the Vale do Amanhecer presents itself as a mediating discourse. As such, the plurality of discourses multiplies the segments of society they may address. As a matter of fact, bringing together the scientific and religious discourse with a focus on practice rather than on the theoretical study has attracted various segments of the population, from middle-class professionals to the semi-literate.

The need for complementarity between science and faith proposed by the Vale is also embedded in culture, where healing is sought in both conventional and non-conventional institutions. We should not assume these dimensions to be definite, since their boundaries are regularly crossed by both patients and healers. Particularly in the latter case, Brazil offers some examples also of medical professionals open to Spiritist discourse who operate both in public medical institutions and Spiritist medical centres. Beyond their professions, some may choose to participate in mediumistic activities or also develop their mediumship, whereas patients may sometimes become involved in the spiritual therapies they undergo or learn a spiritual practice as part of their therapeutic process.

## Notes

1. An earlier version of some sections of this paragraph was published in the article 'Healing and Therapeutic Trajectories among the Spirit Mediums of the Brazilian Vale do Amanhecer', *International Journal of Latin American Religions* 2(2): 272–89.
2. Groisman (2016) draws upon Bateson's notion of 'epistemological correction' (1972).
3. Translated from the original in Portuguese.
4. Translated from the original in Portuguese.

*Chapter 6*

# MEDIUMSHIP

## Positioning the Discourses around Mediumship in the Vale do Amanhecer

It was almost midnight when on my way back home from the temple I came across my friend Pedro, who was just returning from the city. He invited me to join him at his sister's house to meet a *mestre* who was visiting them and who I would call José, a medium in his late forties, initiated twenty-four years earlier and a renowned instructor of the course of *Centúria*. His invitation was a pre-warning of one of those overnight doctrinal conversations that occur in the intimacy of mediums' homes in the Vale. We walked up from the temple; the streets were populated only by stray dogs and the odd white horse rummaging in the garbage. When we got to the house, Pedro clapped his hands in front of the doorway and his sister let us in to the courtyard. A small group of close friends were gathered in the porch drinking coffee and sharing memories from over a decade earlier. I knew most of them already and so was immediately handed a cup of coffee and invited in to the conversation. I was always intrigued by how these kinds of conversations would suddenly turn from hilarious recollections of spiritual episodes to the serious handling of doctrinal knowledge. José, directing his attention towards me, pointed out:

> The Vale makes a distinction from what is understood as mediumship in Spiritism, Spiritualism and the paranormal. If you ask a North American

medium about mediumship, he would report on mind powers, telekinesis, psychokinesis and so forth. It is cultural. If you ask in Umbanda and Candomblé, they will mostly speak about those who incorporate spirits. Our definition is so direct that it may be disappointing: 'mediumship is a biological factor resulting from blood circulation in all human beings'. It indicates an active molecular production of blood in the body, which is transformed into energy – that is 'ectoplasm' or 'magnetic animal fluid'. It is ectoplasm that makes all human beings mediums, not spirit incorporation, which is just one among many mediumistic manifestations. What leads just some human beings to experience the sensorial is an overproduction of ectoplasm that has accumulated around the contact points of the body – the sixth, seventh, eighth, ninth senses that are the chakras – which makes the person more receptive to or perceptive of the vibrations emanating from the etheric plane.

When discussing mediumship, my interlocutors used to carefully position what is intended as 'mediumship' in the Vale in respect to categories used in other mediumistic religions or Spiritualist groups. Proceeding from José's words, it is important to clarify the Vale's categorization of different spiritual phenomena so as to avoid confusing the terminology with other sets of categories proposed in anthropological literature. In the Vale do Amanhecer, the term 'obsession' (*obsessão*), which derives from Kardecism, refers to the agency of action of a disincarnate being (at a low stage of evolution) on a person, which is more or less continuous and produces psycho-physical imbalances. 'Incorporation' (*incorporação*) instead may be either voluntary or involuntary. In the first case, a developed medium may incorporate and control both spirit guides bringing guidance and healing and those spirits bringing suffering. In the case of undeveloped mediumship, the person may not be able to control an obsessing spirit, in some cases experiencing an involuntary incorporation accompanied by negative feelings; the scholarly literature from different cultural contexts has variously described this as 'unsolicited', 'negative', 'unexpected' or 'involuntary' possession (namely, Lewis 1971; Bourguignon 1979; Claus 1979). The categorical differentiation relies on the volitional control over the phenomenon.

The variability of control is indeed widely used in the anthropological literature to define different typologies of spirit possession. Lewis (1971) provides a wide-ranging comparative investigation of mystical experiences involving shamanism and spirit possession in different religions. He draws a distinction between 'unsolicited possession', which is involuntary and uncontrolled, and 'solicited possession', which, conversely, is voluntary and controlled. These types of spirit possession may also be approached as two consequential phases. The 'primary phase' is understood in many contexts as being a sort of mystical call from spirits involuntarily manifesting in the person, in some cases involving an illness that requires therapeutic action.

In a 'secondary phase', the person gradually learns how to control the spirit's behaviour for purposes of communication, or to heal spirits afflicting others (Lewis 1971: 55).

In a cross-cultural survey, Bourguignon (1967) focuses on the presence or absence of 'trance behaviour', distinguishing between: 'possession trance', which implies an 'altered state of consciousness' featuring the loss of conscious awareness, with a spirit taking over a person's body and producing observable changes, and 'possession', when a spirit produces changes in the person's behaviour or health but the 'altered state of consciousness' is absent. The kind of social response to a behaviour attributed to a supernatural being would then determine a further distinction as 'positive possession' for being socially valued, or 'negative possession' for being socially abhorred.[1] Although still widely used in the literature on possession, this scholarly distinction focusing on trance is considered problematic. Most studies on mediumship and possession, particularly the psycho-physiological ones, are focused primarily on 'trance' as the tangible indicator of the relationship with the spirits. However, the relationship with deities and spirits is more complex and changeable than these studies seem to imply.

The 'desirability' or the 'legitimacy' of these phenomena determines the classification proposed by Peter Claus in his study on the Siri and Mayndala practices in Southern India (1979). He describes 'spirit mediumship' as the 'legitimate, expected possession of a specialist by a spirit or a deity, usually for the purpose of soliciting aid ... for human problems'; and 'spirit possession' as the 'unexpected, unwanted intrusion of the supernatural into the lives of humans ... [which] generally creates disturbance and is regarded negatively with concern and apprehension' (ibid.: 29). Psychological and sociological determinants may only be secondary aspects of these phenomena. According to Claus, it is the religious explanation, the ideology of the context, that may enhance understanding of the cause and cure of spirit possession (ibid.: 49).

The exploration of the underlying cognitive structures that may account for the cross-cultural recurrence of concepts of possession is currently a major concern of cognitive anthropologists addressing these phenomena. Emma Cohen has proposed two types of possession:

> *Pathogenic* possession concepts result from the operation of cognitive tools that deal with the representation of contamination (both positive and negative); the presence of the spirit entity is typically (but not always) manifested in the form of illness. *Executive* possession concepts mobilise cognitive tools that deal with the world of intentional agents; the spirit entity is typically represented as taking over the host's executive control, or replacing the host's 'mind' (or intentional agency), thus assuming control of bodily behaviours. (Cohen 2008: 103)

Cohen maintains that in 'pathogenic possession' the spirit is perceived as a contaminating substance, and beliefs about contamination are universal and accompanied by conceptions of purification. She also recognizes that 'executive possession' may be a prescribed treatment for 'pathogenic possession', a consideration that is in line with the above-mentioned consequential phases described by Lewis, and later by Bourguignon. Cohen makes a further distinction within 'executive possession' concepts. Exploring spirit possession in the Afro-Brazilian religion Tambor de Mina in Belém, she distinguishes between the modes of 'displacement', where the spirit's agency replaces the person's agency and takes control of the body (and the medium's identity is perceived as sleeping or journeying out of the body); and 'fusion', where the agencies of the medium and the spirit are merged in the person's body and the two entities form another being (Cohen 2007, 2008). In both cases, the medium is in a state of unconsciousness. Cohen's approach, however, raised criticism regarding the disentanglement of conceptual categories from the embodied and perceptual dimension as if they were the product of the acquisition of concepts by disembodied minds. Such criticism maintains that whilst Cohen claims for a context-sensitive analysis, she does not adequately address how the process through which concepts are transmitted may vary contextually and how social, cultural and religious interactions produce changes in the conceptualizations of possession (Espírito Santo et al. 2010).

One should point out that the term 'possession' is hardly used in the Vale do Amanhecer given the conceptualization that the spirit does not fully enter the body and physically possess it but projects its vibration into the body. Indeed, my interlocutors used to stress that the term 'possession' is not applicable to the Vale's spiritual practice. In other words, although it is possible to compare or contrast mediumistic practice in the Vale to 'possession' in other contexts, it would be misleading to categorize it as such. The implications of this require us to move beyond the Western classificatory systems of the body and the self, which might not reflect those assumed to be the Western conceptualizations, as the next chapter will show in its discussion of mediums' experiences. The focus of this chapter is thus to explore how the discourse on 'mediumship' is articulated and used by mediums in their everyday practice. My point here is to show how notions of mediumship in the Vale do Amanhecer are grounded in the body rather than in being products of a disembodied mind, as cognitive approaches would suggest. In this chapter, firstly, I illustrate how mediums talk about mediumship and how their descriptions and categorizations involve the body as they are based upon the movement of substances. Secondly, I examine their conceptualization of mediumship as related to the transhistorical self, and thus to human-spirit relations, through a description of specific rituals in which mediums faced spirits from their past lives. Then, I introduce the process of learning mediumship as articulated through various initiatic steps, so as to prepare the reader to grasp the experiential and bodily aspects of this process discussed in the next chapter.

Mediums use the term 'mediumistic trance' (*transe mediúnico*) (Sassi 2003) to refer to one aspect of their spiritual practice concerning a 'mediumistic state of consciousness', which is achieved through a practice of concentration, namely 'mediumization' (*mediunização*), in which mediums become more perceptive of spiritual phenomena, thus facilitating their connection with spiritual beings. Mediumistic practice in the Vale uses exclusively two states of consciousness that mediums define as 'conscious' and 'semi-conscious mediumistic trance' (Silva 2010: M). These are all aspects of 'mediumship' (*mediunidade*), which is considered in the Vale as the universal human ability to connect to the spiritual planes, to receive and transmit different forces – that is, all human beings are natural mediums, manipulating energies mostly in a subconscious way with their feelings and thoughts, whereby 'manipulation' means 'putting into motion' and transforming energy.

The Trino Tumuchy Mestre Mário Sassi described mediumship as 'the basic and instrumental force of religions and the main factor of religious attitude' (1974a: 22). Sassi explained that once physical development is completed the need to balance the production of ectoplasm could arise if it accumulates in the body, as this could give rise to psycho-physical imbalances, a sense of dissatisfaction and sometimes diseases. This energy produced in excess, however, may be distributed for the healing of others. By means of rituals, most religions provide people with a technical and doctrinal system called 'mediumism' (*mediunismo*), aimed at balancing mediumship (ibid.). For this reason, when *pretos velhos* advise patients to develop their mediumship, they specify 'in this doctrine or another', presenting the Vale as just one means among others.

In the Vale's mediumistic development, one may learn how to become aware of and gain control over one's mediumistic forces and to balance them through their distribution in healing rituals. The phenomenology of the production of ectoplasm is explained by Tia Neiva (N.C. Zelaya 1980: 29), the Trino Tumará Mestre José Carlos Silva Nascimento (Silva 2010) and mediums instructors. The process of emission of ectoplasm, called *ectopía*, begins in an energy membrane (*ectolítero*) that surrounds and separates the three dimensions of the solar plexus (body, soul and spirit). This membrane emits an energy called *ectolítrio*, which acts as a continuous flow throughout the body, determining the vibratory pattern of the individual. The *ectolítrio* then triggers the throat chakra, allowing the medium to issue his or her ectoplasm (Silva 2010: E). Instructors claim that what distinguishes a medium of the Vale from other types of mediums is the specific development and initiation of the solar plexus, which determines the kind of disobsessive healing that mediums perform in rituals, with the solar plexus considered to be responsible for the reception and emission of forces and their transformation from negative into positive ones.

A medium is far from being considered an exceptional human being gifted with unordinary abilities, as José explained to me. 'There are human beings who have an increased *ectopía* – that is, they produce more ectoplasm than others. They incarnated with a mission that will partly be developing mediumship in favour of the others'. He then pointed out that whilst mediumship is understood as 'universal' and 'biological', the form of the practice of mediumship is cultural. In this sense, the formal aspects of its practice are understood as being culturally shaped by means of a specific 'mediumistic development' according to the purpose for which it is used.

In British and North American Spiritualism, a distinction is often made between a 'psychic' and a 'medium'. Whilst psychics claim to be able to tune in to someone's aura and read the information contained in it, the mediums tune in to the higher vibration of the spirit world to receive and transmit the information usually aimed at providing evidence of survival after death. The difference lies in a) perception, whether it is horizontally or vertically oriented; b) the referent, whether human or spiritual; and c) the aim. Members of the Vale do Amanhecer may be understood through the category of 'mediums', but their communicative exchanges with the spirit world are not aimed at providing evidences of survival after death, since these evidences are intended as implicit in their practice of spirit manifestation. Neither does this practice involve divination as in some spirit possession practices around the world, because revealing details about future events is seen as possibly interfering in the person's free will. Since the specific purpose of mediumistic practice in the Vale is disobsessive healing (the release of disincarnate spirits trapped on earth) and obsessing spirits need to be controlled by mediums, two forms of mediumship are developed in the temple, which are addressed as the semi-conscious mediumship of the *apará* – the mediumship of *incorporação* (the incorporation of spirits) – and the conscious one of the *doutrinador* – the mediumship of *doutrina* (doctrine). One may develop either one or the other of these forms of mediumship, since they are complementary, with disobsessive healing based upon the joint work of *apará* and *doutrinador*. These two types of mediums are defined by the concentration of ectoplasm in the body and the specific state of consciousness that one is more likely to develop, verified by instructors able to identify the specific traits of each type of mediumship, resulting in the relevant type of training.

Since the Vale puts the emphasis on disobsession, mediumship in the Vale may be positioned more closely to the Spiritist practice (Kardecism) than to the Afro-Brazilian ones. One may also note a continuity with a Kardecist idea of 'mediumistic development'. Mediumship in the Vale, however, differs from Kardecism both in practice and in mediumistic development, for being primarily practical, experiential and highly ritualistic. Whilst in Shamanism one may enter a restricted group of specialists of the sacred through an initiatic call, mediumship is understood in the Vale as universally originating from people's bodies and thus considered to be something that can be developed by anyone through a specific training.

## Complementary Forms of Mediumship: The *Apará* and the *Doutrinador*

The degree of consciousness retained by the medium and the points of concentration of ectoplasm in the body define the categorization of mediumship in the Vale (Sassi 2003). The *apará*, also called *mestre* or *ninfa lua* (master or nymph moon), is the medium of incorporation, who works with eyes closed. According to the Trino Tumuchy Mestre Mário Sassi, the *apará*

> Is the medium whose ectoplasmatic charge is higher in the solar plexus, in the umbilical plexus … [This mediumship] belongs to the autonomic system, also called neurovegetative … The ectoplasm, activated by the solar plexus above the normal tonic, produces a series of phenomena, resulting in the so-called incorporation … The blood flowing with more pressure in this region impoverishes the brain irrigation, thus it attenuates the main senses. (Sassi 1974a: 47)[2]

Instructors explained to me that the spiritual being establishes contact through the central nervous system: while *aparás* prepare to alter their state of consciousness, the spirit starts to radiate its vibration into their nervous system, either from another plane or by approaching the medium's vibratory field. Once the blood flow decreases in the head, the medium partially loses consciousness. José described this phenomenology as beginning with the projection entering from the crown chakra on top of the head and descending through the spine until it reaches the solar plexus then expanding into seven rays of light, with one ray reaching the throat chakra, which is deemed responsible for the vocal enunciation of the transmitted message. Then, he explained to me, he will begin to receive not voices, not hallucinations … the centre of emotions is here, the plexus, not here, the heart, because when you feel something bad at first you feel butterflies in the stomach, which then move to the heart. He will receive here [in the plexus] what the projection is sending as a message, so he begins to feel like a will to say that, and this will become so clear because he sees that the reasoning behind that answer is not his … he realizes that he doesn't have that answer.

The *aparás* spirit is said to be partially displaced one and half a metre out of the body, leaving room for the spirit's projection, but maintains a connection. This thus leaves two considerations: the first is that the medium is thought to be, and frequently referred to as, an *aparelho*, namely an 'instrument' or 'device' prepared to tune themselves in to the frequency of different categories of spirits; thus, this process is usually described through the metaphor of a radio or a television. The second is that even though the spiritual being does not fully enter and possess the body, the phenomenon is still considered to be incorporation (or embodiment), since the entity is said to project into the body of the medium. The *apará* incorporates spirits of light in order to cleanse energies, pass on communications and remove suffering spirits from patients so that they can be indoctrinated and released by the *doutrinador*. During the incorporation, the medium is said to be in a 'semi-conscious state', during which he or she partially maintains awareness and agency over the body in order to control the spirit.

Whereas the *aparás* ectoplasm accumulation and blood flow are said to be concentrated around the solar plexus, facilitating the shift to semi-consciousness, different features are said to determine the complementary form of mediumship of the *doutrinador*, or *mestre* or *ninfa sol* (master or nymph sun). The *doutrinador* is the medium of indoctrination, described as having ectoplasm concentrated in the upper part of the body, particularly in the head, which allows the senses to operate above the ordinary levels and become more alert. The *doutrinadores* are also known as the 'mediums with opened eyes' as they do not incorporate spirits. However, they are also said to develop their crown chakra along with the solar plexus, increasing the blood flow in the area of the head, through which they establish connection with their spiritual mentors. According to Sassi, 'The communication made through the cerebral process, by means of the sensitivity of the endocrine system, centred in the pineal gland, and of the nervous system, shifts the focus of consciousness, although the senses remain alert' (Sassi 2003: 35).[3] The Vale defines this phenomenon as a 'fully conscious mediumistic trance' characterized by enhanced perception and intuition. When indoctrinating suffering spirits, the *doutrinador* is said to emit ectoplasm through the mouth, carried by their words, in order to heal these spirits, and they then remove negative charges with their hands, leaving the spirit lighter to be elevated to the spiritual planes. In contrast to the emotional attributes of the *apará*, the *doutrinador* is described by instructors as being a mix of reason and intuition, which allows the medium to indoctrinate disincarnate spirits, distinguish between different forces, recognize interferences in incorporations in order to invoke, balance or transform forces, protect the incorporated medium *apará* and administer the *passe* (pass), which acts as a transfusion of magnetic force into the patient's body. Male *doutrinadores*, in particular, are those in charge of the control and command of rituals, the development of new mediums and the administration of the Order, occupying roles of responsibility or leadership in the hierarchy.

It is worth mentioning that other mediumistic religions divide positions and ritualistic roles between mediums who incorporate spirits and those who do not. In Candomblé, for example, in contrast to the *Elégùn* or *filho de santo* ('son of the saint', an initiated medium manifesting the *orixá*), the *Ekédis* and the *Ogáns* do not manifest the *orixás*; they rather hold high position in the hierarchy of the *terreiro* (cult house) and they are responsible for summoning and taking care of the *orixás*.

Primarily, however, the function of the *doutrinador* is to indoctrinate suffering spirits through the Christic principles of love and forgiveness and elevate them to the spiritual planes through specific verbal codes called 'initiatic key'. When mediums assert that the *doutrinador* was a new kind of mediumship created by Tia Neiva as part of her mission on earth, it is because they conceptualize practices of exorcism other than Spiritist and Spiritualist ones as just removing the spirit from the patient's body and leaving it to wander on the physical plane. Thus, they consider the *doutrinador* to have a specific ability to break the barrier (*neutrom*) that divides the planes and to 'elevate' the spirit to a higher plane. Mediums also make a distinction from the type of *doutrinador* that operates in Spiritism by drawing on their ability to manage the transitions between different planes. Indeed, Mestre Jairo Júnior Zelaya explained to me that they share similar functions of indoctrination, aimed at passing on the spirits to another plane. Yet, he said that the specific development of the plexus and chakras of the *doutrinador* in the Vale determines a peculiar 'physiological' process that once linked to ritualistic formulas allows for the human ability to open the portals between the planes, a function that is usually said to be attributed to spiritual beings. Through these attributes, the figure of the *doutrinador* is brought to the core of the doctrine of the Amanhecer, shifting the main focus of mediumistic phenomena from the incorporation of spirits to a 'conscious mediumship' aimed at disobsession.

The scholarly literature has increasingly focused on the shifts in the discourses of participants in mediumistic religions concerning the different states of consciousness – especially in the emphasis attributed to conscious mediumship – and the interplay between group expectations and individual accounts of mediumistic experiences. Daniel Halperin (1995) conducted fieldwork in Tambor de Mina in Northern Brazil exploring mediums' discourses concerning memory and states of consciousness in spirit possession. Halperin notes that mediums associate 'unconscious possession' to the perception of authenticity of the deity's manifestation in the medium's body, and the phenomenon is expected to be followed by amnesia; 'incomplete possession' is often associated with 'fake', simulated possession. However, Halperin provides some ethnographic examples of 'conscious' possession. Interestingly, some mediums reported that in certain cases they are not completely unconscious but are only experiencing the spirit 'radiate' its energies during rituals, thus they are aware of what is happening around them while in trance. That is to say, they describe their experiences of incomplete possession as a radiation of the spirit, which leaves an intuition in the medium's mind about what to say and do. These experiences, which do not meet the common expectations of total unconsciousness, might lead mediums to doubt the authenticity of their possession, and seldom would they publicly admit it. Some mediums, however, suggested that conscious mediumship may be conceived as a more developed form of mediumship as it does not allow spirits to dominate and control the medium's body. Halperin attributes the transformation in the conceptualization of possession, and thus the growth of the phenomenon of 'conscious mediumship', to the influence of the spread of Kardecism in Brazil. Such a transformation was also noted in Umbanda by Diana Espírito Santo, who related the increased emphasis on conscious possession to a new generation of mediums, showing a new attention to the self (2017).

Frigerio, arguing against the mutual exclusivity of the categories of 'possession state' and 'normal state', explored the grey areas in-between them as they emerged from the perspectives of Umbandistas in Argentina (1989: 5). These mediums do not conceive trance as 'a uniform state'. They rather distinguish different levels of trance that may be interchangeable even within a single interaction with spirits: *irradiación* (irradiation), when the medium perceives the energy of the spirit through bodily sensations and intuition; *encostamiento* (to be beside), when the spirit approached and 'touches' the medium's body, causing a halfway possession featuring a loss of control and memory of the event; and *incorporación* (incorporation), when the spirit fully enters the body producing a complete possession. Levels of *irradiación* and *encostamiento* may occur outside of rituals, in mediums' daily lives, with the latter being the most commonly reported as experienced during Umbanda ceremonies (ibid.). Hence, when using the variable of altered states of consciousness to draw categorizations of these phenomena, scholars should take into account that trance states are far from being fixed and unchangeable but contextually present their internal variability (Frigerio 1989; Cardeña 2009; Pierini 2016a).

We should consider that the distinction between 'normal' and 'altered state of consciousness' or 'trance' is itself controversial in the scholarly literature as there is no agreement on what a 'normal' state is. Thus, while I use the Vale's definitions of 'mediumistic trance' and its distinction between modalities of 'conscious' and 'semi-conscious' that mediums use to describe their experiences, I also point out their variability. In fact, it should be noted that mediums' accounts of their experiences highlight that semi-conscious states may vary from medium to medium, and even from one incorporation to another; and also *doutrinadores* may report variations in feelings and perceptions, as the next chapter will illustrate. There are also cases in which one medium may change the type of mediumship they employ, even after years of practice, and have to develop the other type from the beginning. Moreover, in the Vale do Amanhecer, semi-conscious mediumship was a degree of consciousness gradually developed by Tia Neiva and the first group of *aparás* with the first initiations in order to gain increased control of disobsessive rituals, as the next chapter will discuss.

Other mediumistic forms may manifest spontaneously in some mediums, such as visual or auditory mediumship or mediumistic writing or painting. Some mediums I spoke to said they had experienced these phenomena since childhood although they did not often admit this to other *mestres*, since mediumistic development only addresses the two forms of *doutrinador* and *apará* that are employed in rituals. The complementarity of *doutrinador* and *apará* is visually represented by the symbols used to identify their type of mediumship in rituals, respectively the golden sun and the silver moon. The *doutrinador* is also identified by the symbol of the cross with the shroud. Some mediums interpreted this symbol as the forces that descend vertically from the spirit worlds and distributed on the physical plane horizontally, an idea of movement of forces that is embodied by the ritual postures adopted in invocations – that is, standing with opened arms forming a ninety degree angle. Other mediums suggested that the cross on the cloak represents the responsibility and karma carried on one's back (the higher the position the medium occupies in the hierarchy, the bigger is the symbol of the cross on the back of the cloak). The symbol of the *apará* is an opened book, the Gospel, inside a red triangle, representing spiritual evolution through Christ's teachings. The triangle is also representing the ritual *Mesa Evangélica* and the mission of the *apará* of helping suffering spirits to continue their evolution in the spirit world. These symbols appear on the mediums' waistcoats, cloaks and the *fita*.

*Doutrinador* and *apará* work in pairs as 'master sun' and 'master moon'. Sometimes mediums seek to work with specific others, such as partners, relatives, friends or other mediums with whom they have worked before, having also established a relationship with the spirits manifesting through those mediums. In these cases, a medium may combine participation in a specific ritual beforehand. In other cases, a medium may wish to participate in a specific ritual, or he or she may be asked by the commanders to help to complete the necessary number of mediums to perform a ritual. Then the medium may ask anyone with the complementary form of mediumship to partner with them for the performance of that ritual. During the spiritual work, spirit mentors are said to use the *apará's* ectoplasm as a vehicle to heal the patients, whilst the *doutrinador* emits his or her animal ectoplasm to indoctrinate and heal the suffering spirit. Hence, the joint action of the ectoplasm of the *apará* and that of the *doutrinador* interacting with the ectoplasm of the patient and the energy of their spiritual mentors determines the phenomenon of disobsessive healing.

## Mediumship and Karma

When one is invited by spirits to develop mediumship, a nymph of the phalanx Dharman-Oxinto explains the implications of mediumistic practice, particularly that in the Vale it means working with humility and love to help those disincarnate spirits that seek the payment of one's debt from past lives. Thus, mediumistic practice is presented as a means by which one may redeem karma, or at least relieve its consequences in the present life. Understanding the relationship between karma and mediumship has indeed been a crucial aspect of mediums' practice in the Vale, grounding both its ritualistic and experiential dimensions. This relationship is deemed to be established when the spirit plans its incarnation, having the option to choose to redeem part of its karma in helping others through the charitable practice of mediumship. In this sense, not only is mediumship considered to be 'a biological factor', but it also takes the form of 'a mission'. The ritual expression *'a minha missão é o meu sacerdócio'* (my mission is my priesthood) invests the mediumistic practice with added value. Instructors explain that when mediumship is part of an incarnation plan, at a certain point in life it will manifest requiring its development. Symptoms of undeveloped mediumship may range from an anxious spiritual quest to recurrent physical disturbances around the chakras, up to the spontaneous manifestation of mediumistic phenomena. Failing to develop a manifested mediumship that is linked to a mission is said to result in an accumulation of ectoplasm or actions of the disincarnate creditors from a past life (*cobradores*) that may affect the person physically, psychologically or their material life – a situation that is relatively similar to Shamanism, in which ignoring a shamanic call may result in an initiatory sickness (Eliade 1964; Lewis 1971).

Some mediums, referring to the karmic law of cause and effect, pointed out that 'the seeding is optional, whereas the harvest is mandatory', thus spiritual work may alleviate the situations that one has to face as a result of karma. Instructors explain to the mediums in development that as part of their charitable spiritual work they earn spiritual bonuses (*bonus horas*, namely hourly bonuses) in each ritual, which are administered by the mediums' spirit guides – the missionary guide for the *ninfa* and the knight for the *mestre* – to pay their debts to creditors from past lives, providing these spirits with the amount of energies expected for their release and evolution. However, the bonuses alone are not sufficient and should be accompanied by a visible change in the moral conduct of the person, which ultimately determines if the medium is forgiven by the *cobrador* spirit. The complex relationship between mediums and their *cobradores* is grounded in morality and it also informs the relationships between humans because they may interfere in the person's material life, social relations or psycho-physical health. Mediums may participate in specific rituals to release particular *cobradores*: the rituals of *Angical*[4] and *Prisão* (Prison) may be accessed by mediums only and require the use of specific uniforms. In these rituals, experienced mediums holding at least two initiations, through their specific preparation and ritual actions, may directly face their own *cobrador* and try to readjust their karmic relationships. These rituals are filled with a strong emotional charge for both mediums and spirits, whereby moral change occurs through sorrow, forgiveness, love and a sense of freedom, and the principles of the doctrine are felt and lived through quite intensively.

Whilst the ritual of *Angical* occurs on a monthly basis, it is up to the medium to choose when to do the ritual of *Prisão*; it is based on having the feeling that one's life is being persistently affected by the actions of a *cobrador*. However, instructors indicated that every three months the person tunes into the energy of a specific past life, potentially attracting *cobradores* from that life, so the ritual of *Prisão* is available to help release them. This work entails becoming 'prisoners of the high spirituality' for seven days[5]– that is, performing rituals in order to gather energies entirely directed towards one's own *cobradores* from past lives. The time dedicated to this work during that week varies according to the medium's personal life commitments outside the temple. Prisoner mediums gather in the external area of the temple in front of the *Turigano* wearing specific uniforms and collect signatures and names in their notebooks from other mediums. Mediums may write their names or the names of people in need of healing, each of which counts as a 'bonus of light' – that is, units of energy to be directed to both the *cobrador* and the names of the persons mentioned in the notebook, who may receive distant healing. By participating in *Prisão* rituals, mediums may collect between three hundred and one thousand bonuses according to the type of ritual. The total amount of bonuses are said to be used by the medium's spirit mentors to negotiate the payment of a debt with the *cobrador*, so that the spirit is energetically strengthened to pursue the journey of return to the spiritual planes. When a medium chooses to undertake the *Prisão*, the spirit mentors – namely the knights specifically designated for this function – are said to bring the *cobrador* closer to the medium, so that the spirit can observe how he or she has changed in the present life in working in aid of others to pay karmic debts.

When Júlia, an *apará* in her thirties, discussed with a *preto velho* her decision to undertake the work of *Prisão*, he advised her to be careful about every vibration she emitted through her thoughts and words, so that besides testing her concentration in sending the *cobrador* energies from the rituals, this prison work could also be a chance for her to learn intensively doctrinal conduct in her everyday life. She said that in fact during her week as a prisoner medium her conduct was continuously tested by people approaching her with quite unusual and unsettling issues. One day in particular, she went shopping in the town market and without any apparent reason began to feel a sort of irritation towards her partner. As she returned home, she also felt sadness and heaviness, which soon turned to anguish, and she broke down in tears. Suddenly she felt she could not breathe because of a pain around her neck, as if someone were strangling her. She described the symptoms as being similar to a panic attack. Her partner, a *doutrinador*, gave her magnetic *passes* until she felt well enough to wear her uniform and go to collect bonuses in front of the temple. In the evening, the sadness came back along with the tears. 'You know', she said, 'Tia Neiva used to say that "your vibratory pattern is your verdict". As you lower your vibrations, you attract and give access to those spirits in the same vibration'. She explained to me how the proximity of a *cobrador* could affect the mood and sometimes the body of the prisoner medium. In fact, other mediums reported that during the week of *Prisão* they had symptoms such as depression, fever and body pains. One medium said he was not able to walk properly given the pain in his legs; another had strong back pain. These symptoms were usually accompanied by emotional breakdowns manifesting at some point during the week.

Prisoners may gain freedom through two different rituals: the *Julgamento* (Judgement), directed at the *cobradores* with whom the medium had a direct confrontation in a past life; and the *Aramê*,[6] aimed at the release of groups of *cobradores* with whom mediums had no individual confrontation but rather a collective debt; for instance, as a result of wars involving the disincarnation of many soldiers and innocents or violent land occupations. These rituals are held on alternate Saturday nights in the ritual space of the *Turigano*, where around one hundred prisoners gather. They involve a spiritual trial, with two designated *mestres* representing the prosecutor and the defence for the group of prisoner mediums under judgment that week. Whilst the prosecutor's speech usually follows a discursive pattern focused on faults in the Jaguars' past lives, the defence emphasizes how they are trying to improve their attitudes in the present life through charitable work. These rituals aimed at spirit release collectively reaffirm what should be individually and intimately experienced by mediums during their week as prisoners, namely moral values grounding the doctrine and practice of mediumship leading to their spiritual evolution. After the lawyers' speeches, medium prisoners participating in the *Julgamento* communicate individually with a *preto velho* incorporated by *mestres aparás*. The *preto velho* evaluates the quality of the work for the release of the *cobrador* and may free them or, in some cases, suggest continuing for another week. Depending on the case, he may also give the *cobrador* the chance to incorporate and communicate directly with the prisoner medium.

When Júlia participated in the *Julgamento*, the *preto velho* told her that her bonuses helped release her *cobrador* along with an entire phalanx of spirits, so she herself was also released from the prisoner work. However, about one month later, on the day of the *Angical*, she experienced the same strangling sensation that she compared to a panic attack. On the same night, she participated in the ritual in which mediums have the chance to converse directly with their own *cobradores* from past lives incorporated by the *aparás*, helping the spirit to shift from feelings of rage to forgiveness, presented as the only possibility to move on and evolve. Júlia said she chose a medium she did not know and the spirit of her *cobrador* manifested. The first thing he asked her was how she was dealing with the episodes of feeling suffocated. He told her he was causing that feeling, being the same spirit who passed in her *Julgamento* with his phalanx, but since he could not speak then, he had the opportunity to come back and tell her how she treated those spirits in a past life. After the indoctrination, the spirit said he was satisfied with the bonuses he had already negotiated with the blonde lady on her side – identified as Júlia's missionary guide – so he would forgive her, then he was elevated. She said that the most rewarding aspect of the ritual was to see the spirit's transformation arriving with the heavy energy of the accuser infused with rancour then becoming lighter while the mediums explained to him his condition, providing words of hope. She said that *aparás* may feel the spirit's transformation in the body, regaining beauty through the emotion of seeing the light reappearing after centuries of darkness.

A medium called Beatriz described her latest work as prisoner as being quite unusually filled with positive emotions and blissful sensations pervading her body during rituals along with a sense of gratitude. When she had the opportunity to converse with her *cobrador* in the *Julgamento*, the spirit said it was her conduct and vibrations that mostly favoured his forgiveness. 'As things are more complex than they seem', Beatriz said, 'the tests began the day after the release'; she began losing concentration in rituals, feeling restless, often losing sensitivity in her legs and waking up with a sense of oppression during the night. She worked as much as she could and then decided to pass as a patient into the ritual of *Tronos* to seek the advice of a *preto velho*. While the *preto velho* was performing a cleansing on her, he gave passage to a *sofredor* spirit, who was promptly indoctrinated by the medium *doutrinador*, but instead of moving on with the elevation, he said 'My phalanx is coming down'. Suddenly, she saw the mediums in the four *tronos* next to theirs incorporating *sofredores* altogether, and even the patients sat on their side – whom she recognized were mediums participating as patients – were incorporating, with one of them falling from the chair. She said she gave a puzzled look to the *doutrinador*, who was continuing with the indoctrination, while other *doutrinadores* commanding the work rushed to indoctrinate the spirits incorporated in the patients. Then the *sofredor* incorporated in the *apará* on her side said 'My phalanx is going to be elevated, but we will meet again', and immediately all the *sofredores* disincorporated at once. When the *preto velho* came back, he told her that the spirit was the *cobrador* she met in the *Julgamento* who wanted the opportunity to pass a phalanx of spirits related to him, and it was the perception of these spirits that was causing her sleep disorders and a sense of anxiety.

On the night of the *Angical*, the *cobrador* returned to converse more extensively with her. She began to indoctrinate the spirit – in the *Angical* the *aparás* indoctrinate their own *cobradores* with the help of the *doutrinador*, who ultimately elevates the spirit – explaining the special opportunity given by the spirit mentors for them to meet again, readjust and be released from their karmic issues. She said she felt a powerful sense of love emanating from her words towards the spirit. The spirit calmly recounted his story and how he acted upon different aspects of her life. When he observed closely her spiritual work in those rituals, he decided to forgive her and also asked her forgiveness as he realized that she did not deserve all that revenge. She shared with him her gratitude for his forgiveness, and she asked the *doutrinador* to elevate the spirit. 'The objective of this doctrine', Beatriz said 'is the evolution of spirits, the release of karmic debts, because nothing is just good or evil but everything is in transformation'.

Intense emotional aspects stand out from these mediums' narratives about their experiences, along with three main threads that connect the different rituals. Firstly, the aetiology of the episodes they experienced – identified as similar to a panic attack, anxiety or nervous disorders – as attributed to the agency of a *cobrador* spirit and linked to their morality in a past life and vibrations in the present. Secondly, the practice of moral principles through mediumship as a condition for release. Thirdly, the recurrent narrative used by the same spirits manifesting in different and usually unrelated rituals. These threads intertwined to ground narratively, phenomenologically and affectively these mediums' understanding of how their mediumship is related to karma.

## Mediumistic Development

The mediumistic development (*desenvolvimento*) is a complex process through which one learns how to become aware and control one's mediumship and to use it to help others. Following almost the same standardized pattern in every temple of the Amanhecer,[7] the process of learning mediumship consists of a series of initiatic steps, each of which is considered to be a particular stage of preparation for receiving an increasing amount of forces and responsibility. One instructor explained to me that

> Initiation means taking up responsibilities. Once you own a certain kind of knowledge and you are able to discern forces, you become fully responsible for your thoughts, actions and their consequences. You are responsible for any time in which your thought is not aligned to the Christic principles of love, tolerance and humility. You cannot say that this or that force has taken over your control and acted through you, as an initiated medium knows that nothing happens without his permission. You are also responsible for your own victims of the past, your *cobradores*, whether incarnated or disincarnated, and aware that the way to pay a karmic debt and release them is through unconditional love and incessant mediumistic work devoted to helping others.

Those who enter the development have previously passed as patients through rituals and received an invitation by the *pretos velhos* incorporated by the *aparás* in the *Tronos*. Indeed, in some cases, the *pretos velhos* may advise patients that they need to develop their mediumship when they identify an excessive production of ectoplasm that may lead to physical or psychological imbalances, or when they see that the practice of mediumship is part of a person's life plan. Most mediums describe their first encounter with a *preto velho* or the moment they received the invitation as: 'highly emotional', 'a spiritual call', or as 'being involved by an energy of pure love'. The Adjunto Uruamê Mestre Fogaça, in recalling his first time as a patient in the *Tronos*, thirty-five years earlier, said that as soon as he sat beside the *preta velha* incorporated in an *apará* and she introduced herself as *Vovó Catarina de Aruanda* (Grandma Catarina of Aruanda), he began to cry and laugh, 'feeling in heaven and simultaneously at home'. He told me he understood these mixed emotions as his mediumship arose.

The *pretos velhos* make it clear to patients that their development may be undertaken either in the Vale or via other doctrines, since all religions are intended as having their own systems for the 'manipulation' and balancing of mediumship: namely, to become aware, manage, put into motion, transform and distribute one's forces. Seldom do they point out that a mission should be undertaken specifically in the Vale. When this happens, they say that those patients might be a 'son or daughter of Pai Seta Branca' and thus belong to the 'tribe of the Jaguars'; or they might not be Jaguars but nevertheless 'adopted' if they need the Vale's particular forces and techniques for their spiritual development. Sometimes patients might specifically be informed that their mission is not in the Vale, which happened to one of my colleagues, who, after researching and participating in Candomblé, visited the Vale and passed through rituals as a patient but after being welcomed in the House of Seta Branca was told by the *preto velho* that he was a son of an *orixá*, who was waiting for him to work in the African line.

Once the patient is authorized by the *pretos velhos* to begin the development, he or she is directed to the *Castelo Dharman-Oxinto*, a small room in the temple where a nymph from the phalanx *Dharman-Oxinto* explains the details of the *desenvolvimento* and issues the authorization paper for the 'test of mediumship' to be taken on the Sunday. Not all patients are invited to develop mediumship – explained Tatiana, a *Dharman-Oxinto*:

> All humans are mediums, but while some people incarnate with different missions linked to material, social or emotional life, and others to read-just their karma with particular people or within their families, those who incarnate with this energy in excess have also a spiritual mission. And this spiritual mission should involve distributing this energy to others through charity; I am not referring to material charity, but helping others to alleviate their sorrows.

Every Sunday morning, the temple rituals are suspended for both mediums and patients, and activities are dedicated exclusively to mediumistic development. As in all rituals, each development class is approached as spiritual work happening through the interchanges between the physical and spiritual planes. The session begins with a general thirty-minute lecture

(*Palestra*) briefly presenting the doctrine, which follows the same script each Sunday, although delivered by a different instructor.[8] Mediums at all stages of development attend this lecture in order to absorb the energies that are said to be conveyed by it. There were around two hundred mediums in development attending when I was following the *Palestras* in the Templo Mãe, with about ten or fifteen new arrivals each week. In the lectures, the instructors delivered general introductory information about things such as Tia Neiva, Pai Seta Branca and the spirit mentors working on the Vale and the centrality of the principles of unconditional love, tolerance and humility in the doctrine. They described mediumship and its relationship to karma and presented disobsessive healing as the aim of the practice of mediumship in the Vale. Instructors always reminded people about the responsibilities and duties of a medium. They stressed that proselytizing is strictly forbidden along with accepting payments or offerings in exchange for spiritual work, since these would clash against the principles of free will and charity respectively. Likewise, it was pointed out that in the Vale no one has the obligation to work in the temple and that it is possible to leave the doctrine at any time during or after the development without the need to inform anyone. They also warned that alcohol or drug consumption, as well as the active participation in rituals from other lines, would affect the body of the medium, which is prepared through the development to accommodate specific forces for disobsessive healing. Consequently, those practices would alter the forces, with consequences for the healing transmitted to patients and disincarnate spirits. These two warnings are informed by the specific notion of preparing the medium's body and thus deserve a more extensive explanation, which will be provided in Chapter Eight.

As soon as the lecture ended, each medium followed his or her group to another sector of the temple for another class, each one numbered one to seven. Each class had three instructors, *doutrinadores*, prepared to deliver a lesson that would follow a specific list of topics. Each Sunday, the group attending for the first time undertook the *Teste de Mediunidade* (Test of Mediumship) – also called *Triagem* (Triage). They were taken to the area of the *Mesa Evangélica*, where instructors appointed for the test through a specific ritual verified if the spirit mentors of the newcomers had manifested, and thus whether one was more likely to develop either a conscious or semi-conscious mediumship. These instructors were specifically trained to recognize even without the manifestation of the spirit if the person presented specific signs or symptoms of spirit incorporation. In the case of a spirit manifestation or projection, the newcomer was registered as *apará* or otherwise as *doutrinador*. The instructors explained that as something that is determined by the pre-incarnation life plan, the specific form of mediumship is not attributed during the test but has the chance to manifest in the test. There were also cases in which mediums changed their type of mediumship during the development or after years of practice and had to restart the development, as with an experienced *doutrinador* in my class who suddenly turned into an *apará*.

After the test, *aparás* and *doutrinadores* are divided into two groups, and they attend the respective lessons for seven consecutive Sundays,[9] during which they are called *aspirantes* (aspirant mediums). These classes entail the practical and technical preparation: the *apará* learns to incorporate the *pretos velhos*, the *caboclo* and the *médico de cura* and to control the *sofredores*, whilst the *doutrinador* learns how to indoctrinate and elevate spirits. They both learn how to perform the opening and closing rituals of their working sessions and to work in the rituals of *Tronos*, *Cura*, *Linha de Passe* and *Mesa Evangélica*. During this stage, male *aspirantes* wear a white shirt and black trousers, and females wear a white dress, and they both wear the yellow and purple string (*fita*) around their chest. The instructors explained that each item of clothing and each accessory and colour that mediums wear at each stage is aimed at their protection from specific energies. After seven lessons, the *aspirantes* conclude the first stage with the *Emplacamento*, in which they receive a badge (*placa*) with the name of their main mentor: a princess intuitively chosen among Janaina, Jurema and Iracema for the *doutrinador*; and the main *preto velho* or *preta velha* manifesting and identifying with a name for the *apará*, along with the *médico de cura* and the *caboclo*. There were also cases in which the first stage lasted for more than seven lessons; for instance, when the three main mentors of the *apará* were not giving their names. *Emplacado* mediums, also informally called 'de branquinho' (in white) because of their uniforms, are permitted to begin working with patients in the rituals of *Tronos*, *Cura* and *Linha de Passe*. Five hundred new mediums *emplacados* were registered in the Templo Mãe of Brasilia[10] in 2010.

## *The Initiatic Steps*

*Aparás* and *doutrinadores* who have received the *Emplacamento* join the same three preparation classes for the initiation, which merge learning the practice of other rituals with more theoretical explanation. The ritual of initiation in the Vale is called *Iniciação Dharman-Oxinto*. Tia Neiva used to explain to the mediums that '*Dharman-Oxinto*' in the spirit world means 'On the Path to God' and that the first to receive this initiation was Jesus Christ when he was thirteen years old. Through her visions and astral travels, she used to address the gap in the Gospels concerning Jesus's adolescence, situating him in Tibet, where he received this initiation by seven clairvoyant monks, including the Dalai Lama, who covered Jesus's face with a hood as a sign of respect for his spirit, perceiving the highest spiritual evolution for the son of God. During the ritual, he received seven mantras of force, and he was later instructed about his mission on earth. The initiation in the Vale is considered to be an oath of the medium's commitment to the responsibilities of the mission in front of God and the spirit worlds. Instructors explained that the medium receives seven 'mantras of force' from the spirits of the Great Initiates, namely initiatic forces that open all the chakras and that especially mark the solar plexus, transforming its nature so that the spirit would always be recognized as initiated in the spirit worlds or in future incarnations. The ritual of initiation takes place every two weeks in the Templo Mãe on the Tuesday night,[11] when the initiands are accompanied by their godfather or godmother (initiate mediums) into the *Castelos de Iniciação* (Castles of Initiation) of the *doutrinador* or the *apará* accordingly. Access to the initiatory rooms is permitted only to the initiands and the *Corte de Iniciação* (Court of Initiation, the masters who are prepared to initiate them). What happens in the rooms constitutes the only 'doctrinal secret' in the Vale, and mediums must not reveal or even discuss it between them. High emotion surrounds the mystery involved in this initiation; it marks the liminal phase in which the initiand is separated from the community and later reintegrated as a new subject, when he or she comes out from the ritual wearing the *colete* (waistcoat). The white *colete* represents the initiate and identifies, on the back, through the symbol of the cross the mediumship of the *doutrinador*, or through the red triangle with the Gospel the mediumship of the *apará*. The name of the main spirit mentor is written on a badge pinned on the right side of the waistcoat. Subsequently, at each classification mediums will receive and apply to the waistcoat other symbols that as a whole are called *armas* (weapons), since they are used for protection from different energies. Initiates are authorized to assist patients also in the ritual of *Indução* and *Junção* and may choose to follow another four Sunday classes in preparation for the second initiation. During these classes, they learn about the meanings and uses of the uniforms, doctrinal conduct and how energies are received and manipulated in each phase of the ritual of *Estrela Candente*. In order to practically learn this complex ritual, after class they participate in a special session called *Estrela Aspirantes* (Star for Aspirants), during which they have the possibility to perform its different phases by learning ritual actions.

Unlike the first initiation ritual, the second one is open to the public and takes place approximately every two months[12] in a space called *Aledá* (a sort of dais behind the *Pira*). The ritual takes its name, *Elevação de Espadas* (Elevation of Swords), from the *doutrinador*'s symbolic act of raising a sword in front of the image of Jesus located at the centre of the ellipse as a confirmation of his or her oath and initiation. The sword, used in major consecrations, is a symbol of faith, struggle and the Jaguars' achievements through the Christic principles in their present mission. After the oath, the *doutrinador* turns towards the *apará*, who is sat on his or her knees, and summons the *preto velho* to incorporate in the medium. He then exchanges a rose with the manifested *preto velho* and pronounces the key to spirit elevation. During the ritual, the mediums are said to receive another seven mantras of forces from the Great Initiates and the Divine Dalai Lama, whose presence is invoked at the opening of the ritual. The mediums' 'energetic structure' is further altered, and they are subsequently able to participate in a greater number of rituals, including the one of the *Estrela Candente*.[13]

Subsequently, mediums enter the masterhood: male mediums are called *mestres* (masters) and female mediums, who are also masters, are called *ninfas* (nymphs). They receive the name of the *falange de mestrado* (phalanx of masterhood) to which they are going to belong. These represent a specific force in rituals and they can wear the uniform of jaguar. The *mestres* wear brown trousers with a black or brown belt, a black shirt with yellow crosses on the arms, the waistcoat and the *fita*. Some rituals require mediums to wear the cloak, intended as a protection from energies. This may be brown with a yellow cross for the *doutrinador* or green with a red triangle for the male *apará* – who is called *ajanã* from the second initiation – with the colour of the internal lining corresponding to their classification. The *ninfas* wear a long brown skirt with a black or brown belt, a black lace blouse with yellow crosses on the arms, the waistcoat with the symbol of her mediumship and the *fita*. Instead of just wearing the cloak, as the *mestres*, in specific rituals women wear the *indumentária de ninfa* (nymph vestment), consisting of a dress with golden detail and a symbol of the sun for the *doutrinadora* or silver detail and a moon and stars for the *apará* as well as a cloak in organza and the *fita*. The *indumentária* is later added to with accessories such as the *pente*[14] with veils and gloves.

Once part of the *Mestrado* (Masterhood), mediums may choose to follow the preparation course for the third initiatic step, called *Centúria*. The course consists of another seven classes, which take place once every two weeks in the temple. These advanced classes are theoretical rather than practical and prepare mediums with the doctrinal knowledge about the composition of the spirit worlds, spirit evolution, the processes of incarnation and disincarnation, moral conduct, the action of forces and in depth explanations of what happens beyond physical matter in the performance of specific rituals. At each lesson, the mediums are said to receive one mantra of force in their solar plexus – differently from the previous stages, in which the seven mantras were received altogether in the initiation rituals – and they are advised by instructors to work on this force through mediumistic practice between one class and another, so as to facilitate its accommodation in the body and thus their balance. A developed medium is indeed expected to be able to maintain balance at any time, distributing one's mediumistic force when this is produced in excess, otherwise when this excess accumulates around the *chakras* it is said to affect the medium physically, whereas when distributed to others it is said to heal both them and the medium.

The *Consagração de Centúria* (Consecration of *Centúria*) is the third initiation ritual by which the medium becomes a *Centurião* (Centurion). The term '*Centúria*' derives from the Latin *centurio*, which refers to the unit of the Roman military legion, composed of one hundred soldiers. Roman terms are used in the Vale as a symbolic reference to the past incarnation of the Jaguars, creating similarities and oppositions between past incarnations of military conquests and massacres and a present incarnation of spiritual conquests and redemption. Thus, a medium centurion who has duly learnt the laws of rituals and with moral conduct is considered to be worth a hundred mediums. He or she is also expected to be aware that his or her life occurs simultaneously on the physical, etheric and spiritual planes.

The ritual takes place twice a year in the same area as that of *Elevação de Espadas*. Mediums pass individually under six swords crossed by six *mestres* stood in pairs, one pair in front of the other. They then receive a *morsa* (a white cotton scarf similar to the Tibetan *kata*) and open their solar plexus in front of the image of Jesus situated at the centre of the ellipse before drinking a glass of non-alcoholic wine, symbolizing Jesus Christ's blood. Each medium receives other *armas* (weapons) to attach to the waistcoat: *Povo* (people) the name of a spirit group working in the spirit world; the *lança*, the symbol of a lance; an *estrela* (star), which is said to project its forces into the medium; and the *radar de centúria*, symbol of the medium centurion. Soon after, in the ritual of Classification, the medium is asked to choose: an *Adjunto de Povo* (People's Adjunct), becoming part of a People (*Povo Ypuena, Yumatã, Yucatã* and so forth);[15] a missionary phalanx; and a *Turno de Trabalho* (Working Shift), which is related to whichever ritual the medium feels the most affinity (mediums would prioritise this work in case there is a need for participants to perform it). *Mestres* also choose between two spirits of knights (Reili or Dubali) and *ninfas* between two missionary guides (Sabarana and Doragana). They also acquire a personal minister and knight or in the case of a *ninfa*, a personal missionary guide. These spirit guides protect mediums and deal with their *cobradores*. The *mestre* adopts a title according to the name of his personal minister, becoming Adjunct of that minister on the physical plane. These *armas* are considered not only as protection but also as sources of forces that the medium is going to invoke and bring into rituals through the enactment of his or her *emissão* (emission), which becomes a constitutive element of the structure of rituals.

The *emissão* states the individual features and spiritual origins of the medium, such as the type of mediumship, phalanx of masters, people, missionary phalanx, people's adjunct, classification, knight or missionary guide, star and working shift. Its enactment is considered to be a presentation of the medium's individuality before the spirit world, which is able to open a channel that reaches the highest dimensions of the spiritual planes, permitting the passage of forces that will be projected from there into the rituals.

After the *Centúria*, mediums may attend the course of *Sétimo Raio* (Seventh Ray) to further deepen their knowledge of the topics addressed in the preparation for the *Centúria*. That of *Sétimo Raio* is the highest classification a *ninfa* may achieve, whereas the *mestre* may proceed along five further steps of hierarchical classifications. These re-classifications are appointed by *mestres* called *Filhos de Devas* (Sons of the Devas), who are said to receive the forces of the *Devas* from the Oriental line, guiding them through intuition to appoint classifications and thus making them responsible for all the initiations.

## Conceptualizing the Encounters between Humans and Spirits

The categories of 'possession', 'mediumship' and 'shamanism' appear to be used interchangeably in the anthropological literature on these phenomena of encounters between humans and spirits in different societies. A classical categorization proposed by Raymond Firth in his study on the Tikopia of Melanesia distinguished between three different phenomena: 'spirit possession', when the spirit is controlling the person's actions, provoking abnormal behaviour; 'spirit mediumship', which is the use of 'abnormal' behaviour to communicate with the spirit world; and 'shamanism', where the person is controlling the spirit (1967: 296). However, different forms of mediumship and possession are described as being accompanied by out-of-body experiences or astral travels, or as mastery of spirits, which are features of the classical categorizations of shamanism. Similarly, shamanic practices are not limited to 'ecstatic' kinds of conceptualizations, but they may include the incorporation of and communication with spirits. Through the category of 'possession', scholars have addressed a variety of practices involving crossing the physical boundaries of the human body, which variably features channelling spirits or mediumship; however, not all practices that involve a direct relation with the spirit world are locally understood as 'possession'. In Brazil, for instance, the category of 'possession' is not commonly used or understood everywhere in the same way (Goldman 2007; Pierini 2013, 2016b; Groisman 2016; Engler and Isaia 2016), given the widespread influence of Spiritism and its conceptualizations of human and spirit relations on different religious practices. Participants often refer to these ritualized relations as 'mediumship' (*mediunidade*) or 'mediumistic practices' (*práticas mediúnicas*). When the relation is interpreted negatively, it is referred to as 'obsession' (*obsessão*) by a spirit. Not only Spiritists but also members of the Vale and leaders of some centres of Umbanda and Candomblé I visited did not use the term 'possession'. Whereas, in Europe and North America the term 'mediumship' is often associated with a practice of communication with the dead, in Brazil mediumship involves a great variety of practices, including spiritual healing and practices in which the body mediates between different dimensions or beings.

The scholarly debates on spirit mediumship and possession increasingly reveal the difficulty in and the inadequacy of providing an exhaustive conceptual classification or systematizing these phenomena in one single theoretical framework. Current developments in these studies suggest a tendency to move from labels to descriptions of common features (Taves 1999), and especially to move beyond pre-constructed dichotomies – from Eliade's classical distinctions between 'trance' and 'possession', to the gender role distinctions in ecstatic practices, to the Western dualistic body-mind paradigm (Huskinson and Schmidt 2010: 12) –through an interdisciplinary approach that promotes a dialogue between different perspectives (ibid.). 'There are a few human phenomena that carry the complexity and ambiguity of possession: it challenges the notion of a unified, immutable self; of a facile distinction between "acting" and reality: of who or what is the source of one's actions; even of humans as single, isolated entities' (Cardeña 1989: 16). In this sense, these phenomena open up new avenues to explore core aspects of human experience, as this debate highlights the extensive character of a phenomenon able to embrace and embody heterogeneous experiences, meanings, values, needs, practices and discourses within the same process. This is a complex phenomenon that is related, but not reducible to, identity, morality, ethics, social organization, history, politics, notions of the body and the self, conceptualizations of the afterlife and different modalities of relation to the sacred of each particular society. In sum, the scholarly comparison should not only consider the context and environment in which these phenomena occur, but what I urge is that it should account for the different conceptualizations of body and self. Thus, we need more phenomenological description.

I have pointed out the bodily grounding of notions of mediumship in the Vale. After illustrating how mediums conceptualize the mediumistic practice and the articulation of the process of learning mediumship through the different initiatory steps, I propose a discussion of the experiential aspects of this process in relation to the technical features of mediumistic practice. Since spirits need to be controlled by mediums for the purpose of disobsessive healing, the process of mediumistic development draws largely upon bodily experience. The next chapter focuses on the body in the first stages of mediumistic development and the role of emotions, feelings and senses in cultivating the relationship with spirit mentors. My aim is to illuminate how in the Vale's mediumistic development ritual practice and bodily experience precede and ground conceptual knowledge. I thus approach the process of learning mediumship as learning a specific way of knowing, exploring the interrelation between the cognitive, sensory and emotional dimensions and then looking at what kind of knowledge this process engenders. Through the lens of this knowledge, which involves specific notions of the body and the self, I will then be able to analyse its implications for the dynamics of mediums' spiritual routes and therapeutic trajectories.

## Notes

1.  Bourguignon (1967) takes a pathological stance and treats 'negative possession' as linked to a dissociative identity disorder (DID). The discussion of current research and the therapeutic trajectories that I will propose in Chapter Nine seek to question these early approaches to the study of spirit mediumship and possession.
2.  Translated from the original in Portuguese.
3.  Translated from the original in Portuguese.
4.  The name *Angical* comes from an area in the state of Bahia, where, according to Tia Neiva, the Jaguars shared an incarnation as masters and slaves in imperial Brazil.
5.  In some external temples, the work of *Prisão* lasts two weeks, given the fact that unlike the Templo Mãe most external temples are not open seven days a week.
6.  Mediums could not provide any Portuguese translation for this name.
7.  The structure of classes and teachings is contained in a Manual for Instructors.
8.  In the Templo Mãe, the instructors interchange in delivering the *Palestra*, whereas in other temples the *Palestra* is delivered by the president or the vice-president.
9.  Since 2014 in the Templo Mãe, *aparás* should attend fourteen classes to be *emplacado*.
10. Data from the registry of the *Filhos de Devas* (mediums in charge of the registration of the members of the Order).
11. In external temples, initiations take place once or twice a year, according to the geographical location, when appointed *mestres* from the Templo Mãe travel to initiate other mediums.
12. In external temples, the ritual of *Elevação de Espadas* takes place the day after the first initiation. For logistic purposes, mediums travelling from different temples to the main temple of their region undertake all the classes in preparation for the initiations and then receive the consecrations altogether.

13. When mediums participate in their first *Estrela Candente*, they complete the consecration of their second initiation.

14. The missionary guides project energies into the *pente* with veils for the *ninfas*. The *pente* is always accompanied by gloves that leave the chakras of the hands uncovered for the projection of energies. The lining of the cloak varies according to the hierarchical classification, and the most internal layer represents the colour of the missionary guide of the *ninfa*. The number of stars on the dress of the *apará* may vary between seven and twenty-one, according to the number of layers of the cloak.

15. In external temples, mediums are automatically affiliated to the Spiritual Minister represented by their Adjunto, who is the president of their temple.

# Chapter 7

# LEARNING SPIRIT MEDIUMSHIP
Ways of Knowing

## The First Stages of Mediumistic Development: Reshaping the Body

Mediumistic experiences in the Vale do Amanhecer are initially framed by the mediumistic development; hence, examining the process of learning mediumship is crucial to understanding the dimensions in which learning operates. Since this process is primarily practical and draws largely upon bodily experience, in an advanced stage of fieldwork I fully engaged my own body in the process of knowing, participating in the mediumistic development classes, exploring in depth the somatosensory aspects that underpin this embodied encounter with the spirit world. Discussing my bodily experience with fellow participants, instructors and experienced mediums provided valuable insights into how learning mediumship was not limited to the transmission of a set of notions and techniques, but, as I argue in this chapter, it entailed learning a specific mode of knowing through enskillment – that is, attending to bodily sensations and feelings.

When I was about to begin my mediumistic development, I just needed to go to the Castle of Authorization, a small room in the temple where a female medium, a nymph belonging to the phalanx Dharman-Oxinto, would issue a paper authorizing access to the training. That was the first formal step that anyone invited by spirits to develop mediumship would have to go through. In addition, as a researcher, I had already extensively examined and agreed upon this option with the mediums responsible for the development, the leaders of the Order and with the *pretos velhos* – who are ultimately the spirits deemed responsible for suggesting and authorizing which patients should take part in mediumistic development. The authorization issued by the nymph Dharman-Oxinto is in some sense a formalization on earth of the spirits' authorization. But while I was sitting on a bench in the temple awaiting my turn to talk to the nymph, I was struck by a strong headache. All of a sudden, I saw Antonita walking along the aisle dressed in her Jaguar uniform and our eyes met. She had no idea I was there to get the authorization.

'Something says I need to sit down with you', she said. 'Something says I need to go home … this headache is unbearable', I replied, standing up and grabbing my bag. With a caring but firm attitude, she suggested I sit down instead and tell her what was going on; she perceived that something was affecting me energetically, so she patiently accompanied me through the process of getting the authorization. From that day and throughout the first month of my development, I was affected by strong headaches. The sensation was analogous to a drill piercing my temples, a kind of pain that was unfamiliar to me and seemed to be resistant to painkillers. I experienced some relief after the Sunday development classes and thus my instructors – elder masters who were going from class to class in pairs – attributed my headaches to the opening and cleansing of my head chakras. In sharing my concern with fellow participants in the development, it immediately became clear that bodily reactions to the mediumistic development were not confined to learning the practice, but to a different extent they could manifest outside the classes, as most of the participants had experienced headaches, fevers, back pain or disturbances of the digestive system, which they attributed to the development of the solar plexus. The instructors explained that mediums' bodies undergo changes during the development, and the effects of these changes are felt in a different way by each medium. These aches and pains are considered to be independent from the disturbances related to what the Vale refers to as 'mediumistic disorder' or an illness that may lead to mediumistic development. They also differ from the symptoms of obsession, which in turn may involve depression, uncontrolled crying and other emotional responses.

Even experienced mediums had vivid memories of these body pains related to the development or the initiations and described them as a cleansing process: the development prepares the medium to accommodate the forces of the initiations, and these forces alter the body of the initiate. Therefore, episodes of vomiting or dysentery were frequently reported by initiands on the day of initiation and interpreted as a body cleansing. Stomach cramps and headaches were interpreted as caused by the action of the forces upon the *chakras*. I had noted that the same symptoms were also experienced by initiands in the temples of Portugal and Italy.

Cláudio, a *doutrinador* in his thirties who developed his mediumship in the Templo Mãe, said,

> Everyone has his own reactions depending on the amount of energy that one receives. The week before my initiation, I felt abdominal pains and fever, which was unusual for me. When I reported it to my instructor, he said I was 'in the ritual' because it is a process. This happens to all mediums because they will never be the same again; we are in a constant development … the body, the mind and the spirit are all involved in this process.

Mediums described the forces of the initiations as pervading the whole village, and they said that they could also be felt by visitors. My friends in the Vale used to point out that, even as a researcher, since I was living in the Vale, my body was immersed in that energetic environment and it was being reshaped by those forces. The first time they mentioned this dynamic was during my fieldwork in 2004, when I was affected by high fevers every two weeks; Antonita pointed out to me that it was happening on the day of the initiation ritual but that the fever would disappear the morning after. I was again reminded of this association by another friend of mine when in 2009 and 2010 I suffered abdominal pains every two weeks while the ritual was taking place in the temple. Bodily reactions and pains seemed to reinforce among mediums in development the idea of the reshaping of the body and the inscription of the solar plexus by the initiation forces. The development was therefore 'felt' as acting simultaneously upon the different dimensions of the medium, producing a transformation, a sense of becoming.

The new notions of the medium's body articulated by the process of learning mediumship involved ideas of cleansing and pollution. Indeed, the instructors repeatedly warned that the use of alcohol or drugs 'in any dosage' may not be combined with this kind of mediumistic practice for physical reasons rather than moral ones, based upon the conceptualization of mediumship as being grounded in the body. Firstly, the alcohol's concentration in the blood would interfere in the production of mediums' ectoplasm, which is used by spirits in healing rituals and would consequently affect and pollute the patients. Secondly, alcohol and drugs would affect the nervous system, which a mediumistic trance state relies on, and therefore mediums learn to enter a conscious or semi-conscious without any inducing substance. Some instructors also proposed an additional spiritual reason: these substances are known to attract a particular kind of obsessing spirit that feeds itself with the magnetism of those substances, rapidly causing addictions in humans. Thus, they recommended that when one is not prepared to abstain from these substances before beginning the development, the person should continue passing through rituals as a patient until quitting their consumption.

*Cruzamento de corrente* (crossing forces) involves participating actively in the rituals of other religions or spiritual groups and is another thing that can affect mediumistic ability. According to instructors, each religion works on a different frequency of energy, and the body and plexus of the medium are developed to work on specific frequencies, thus mixing frequencies may result in a shock that may unbalance firstly the medium and subsequently the patient.

The centrality of the body in mediumistic development implies increased attention to emotions, feelings and sensory perceptions. But how do people – including those who are unfamiliar with mediumistic phenomena – learn to enter the mediumistic state of consciousness called *transe mediúnico* (mediumistic trance)? How do they learn to discern, manifest and control spirits? In this chapter, I will compare the experiences reported by both *aparás*, the mediums incorporating spirits, and *doutrinadores*, those who work in tandem with the *aparás* in order to release suffering spirits. These mediums I spoke to have a diverse cultural and experiential background – most are Brazilian but some are foreigners, including those who at the time of my fieldwork were in development in the Templo Mãe and Italians developing mediumship in a recently opened temple I visited in Italy. My own experience of bodily engagement in learning mediumship will also be analysed comparatively with other mediums in development. I will show how newcomers are not taught about the existence of spirits; they are not passed a *belief* but rather come to learn how to *feel* the presence of spirits and how to discern which spirit is manifesting, through an ongoing education of perception.

*Learning to Feel Spirit Guides:*
*Affect, Emotions and Feelings in Spirit Incorporation*

Even though during my fieldwork I had heard many descriptions of mediums' experiences of what they call 'semi-conscious mediumship', my first experience of it helped me realize that my ideas and expectations about what would happen during these states did not fully acknowledge my interlocutors' accounts. As soon as I entered the temple on the day of my test of mediumship, I felt an insistent pressure upon my forehead; my head felt like it was expanding and contracting, and my hands felt like they were swelling. We were sat in line with our eyes closed when the instructor opened the ritual and called for the spirit mentors to manifest. My heartbeat increased, and I felt shivers running along my body up to my hands. What best describes that sensation is the feeling of being on a rollercoaster. When the instructor asked the spirit to move away from my body and told me to open my eyes, I felt like someone who having got to the end of the roller-coaster ride and still pervaded by a sense of excitement asks the attendant 'can I have another go?'. I wanted to understand more about that feeling, as I realized that whilst some unfamiliar reactions were going on *through* my body, I did not switch off as I somehow expected; I was still there aware of the sensations, even though when I was asked to open my eyes I felt as if I was waking up from dream sleep. The fact that one retains a certain level of awareness during the phenomenon means that mediums may often recall the emotions, feelings and sensations involved in such mediumistic states. That was the first step into the re-education of my perception to these new sensations.

Rather sublime feelings marked Alexandre's understanding of his experience, as he said 'imagine what it feels like to be touched and then embraced by an angel. Your life is never going to be the same afterwards'. In the first stage of development, the *apará* incorporates one mentor at each session, beginning with the *preto velho*, the spirit of an African slave, then once familiarized with that energy they pass to the manifestation of the *caboclo*, the Amerindian spirit, and then of the *médico de cura*, the doctor. Each medium has his or her own spirit mentors although they may have similar names given their energetic affinity with a particular phalanx of spirits. For instance, there may be two mediums who have their personal spirit guide identifying itself as Vovó Catarina de Aruanda (Grandma Catherine of Aruanda).

In contrast to the sublime and calm manifestation of the *preto velho*, the *caboclo* is perceived as highly physically engaging, as Pedro described it:

> I found everything quite funny at the beginning of the development up until the day of the incorporation of the *caboclo*. I began to visualize the forests and the *caboclo* when my body began to transform. I felt tachycardia, but this wasn't necessarily a bad sensation. I felt a voice inside of me wanting to come out as a hoarse cry. I held it so much that I put a lot of strength into my hands placed on my knees. When the instructor called for the presence of the *caboclo*, I felt a strong slap on my chest, and since my hands were on my knees, I thought someone had hit me! I then realized that it was actually my own hand banging on my chest! Then … I saw him standing there, three times taller than me with naked chest, and he was not alone but accompanied by other *caboclos*.

Similarly, an *apará* in his thirties at the beginning of his development in Italy, after the incorporation of the *pretos velhos*, looked at me and said: 'Could you ask the instructor if I can repeat the test of mediumship? To be honest I don't feel anything, I think that maybe I am not a medium of incorporation but I'm a *doutrinador*'. As soon as I turned around to call him, the instructor was already invoking the *caboclos*, and I heard this *apará* screaming loud behind me, and as I turned back again there was the guy firmly banging his chest with a very serious expression on his face. When he disincorporated, he looked at me amazed and said 'Maybe, I don't need another test …'

The body and its invisible substances are stimulated as conductors of forces. A common feature in mediums' descriptions of the incorporation of the *caboclo*, along with shaking legs, is an expansion of the chest, provoked by a feeling of a force running along their back. This expansion is followed by a sensation of their hand slapping their chest, which instructors say is used by spirits to increase the heartbeat and blood flow in order to produce more ectoplasm to cleanse patients. The ectoplasm is also said to be distributed through the voice, through the cries of the *caboclos* and the *saudações* (the greetings to other entities used in the spirit's work of energy cleansing). The manifestation of the *caboclos* is sometimes perceived as being stronger in the development, becoming more subtle after the initiations, when the body has been prepared to handle more forces so the medium may be able to manifest the spirit for a longer time in rituals dedicated to patients' assistance.

In following the development of mediums in a temple of the Amanhecer in Italy, I noticed how also those who approached the phenomenon for the first time holding no previous spiritual beliefs and apparently not manifesting any particular bodily reaction to the external observer reported to the instructors, after disincorporating the spirit, the most various emotions and inner reactions, ranging from heatwaves expanding from the plexus to the throat, tingling along the limbs, pressure on the head, a sense of peace, or the will to laugh or cry. Others were instead surrendering to a sensation of bliss, opening their arms to embrace the encounter that they seemed to be longing for, often leading to a contagious emotional cry. Some of them pointed out that for the first time they realized they could be worthy of that experience, as even though they had previous spontaneous mediumistic experiences they said that in their predominantly Catholic culture a closer encounter with the sacred was perceived as being exclusively accessible to the clergy. The Brazilian instructors in Italy have indeed noticed that rather than 'uncontrolled mediumship', the Italians arriving at the temple were presenting mostly cases of 'inhibited mediumship', which was causing either anxiety with their material and physical lives, or anxiety for a spiritual quest. In their first development classes, some of these *aparás* said they had previously seen or even incorporated those spirit mentors of the Vale in past spontaneous mediumistic experiences, but until then they had no idea of how to contextualize and use those gestures and images within their culture.

This was the case of a man who after his first incorporation described his sensations to the instructor along with his vision of an old man with a white beard sat bending over with a stick behind a waterfall, adding that he had had the same vision years earlier. The instructor turned towards me and identified the spirit as a *preto velho do Povo das Cachoeiras* (a *preto velho* from the People of the Waterfalls) but chose not to tell him and to wait for the spontaneous identification of the spirit, relying on the fact that there were no images of mentors in the first setting of the Italian temple.

In some cases, *aparás* were crying at each incorporation, but the instructors felt it was not a suffering spirit incorporating, it was rather the spirit guide approaching and the *aparás* were feeling the emotions too strongly, a reaction that would then gradually be attenuated through practice. Indeed, in addition to the highly evolved spirits guides, aspirants are also trained to incorporate *sofredores* in the ritual of *Mesa Evangélica*. Each medium feels this to a different intensity. The incorporation of *sofredores* is described as an uncomfortable sensation, which could be more or less heavy. A medium *apará* may give passage to ten or more different *sofredores* during the one Mesa session, each of which carries a different energy and emotion, ranging from suffering to rage, to just being annoyed. When the medium *doutrinador* after a brief indoctrination elevates the *sofredor* to the spirit world the *apará* opens their closed fists to release the spirit. When the bell rings to alert participants of the end of the manifestation of *sofredores* and the *aparás* disincorporate, some look exhausted and others as if they had just woken up. Even though their bodies would feel tired they often claimed to feel lighter than before.

*Gestures and Expressions*

During the first classes of mediumistic development, the *aparás* are instructed on the different modalities of expressing the energy running through their bodies through the gestural and verbal codes of the Vale. Once spirits manifest through the *aparás*, the instructors teach spirit mentors how to express themselves according to the culturally recognizable manifestation they choose to assume. This is due to the understanding that there are spirit guides accompanying the person throughout her life and others joining later for specific purposes. Instructors say that some spirit guides may come prepared to work in the Vale, while others may need further training if they have been previously working in different lines. This would apply, for instance, if the person was previously practising another mediumistic religion and his or her spirit guides were manifesting according to the codes of that religion, thus both medium and spirits need to be trained according to the codes of the Vale. Thus, the spirit mentors are said to be prepared to then instruct their mediums. Instructors may then ask the *pretos velhos* to cleanse the *apará*'s body and snap their fingers to disintegrate negative charges, or the *caboclo* to slap the medium's chest to increase the production of energy, and the *médico* to stretch the arms in front of the body to transmit healing energy. The *preto velho* and the *caboclo* also learn to release their voice while they are cleansing energies by greeting other forces and spirits of light through the *saudações* (greetings). They may do so using expressions such as: 'Hail the forces of the forests!' 'Hail the People of the Waters!' 'Hail Pai Seta Branca!' 'Hail the force of the *pretos velhos*!' 'Hail the forces of the *caboclos*!' 'Hail the Healing Forces!' 'Praise Our Lord Jesus Christ!'.

There are, however, local nuances in the ways of manifesting spirits in different temples, as I was able to note through my visits to external temples. While the general manifestation of *pretos velhos* and *caboclos* largely follows the same pattern across temples, some accents and details of their expression may be specific among mediums belonging to a particular temple. In some temples of Northeast Brazil, I noticed that mediums manifesting *caboclos* in the ritual of *Linha de Passe* frequently used in the *saudações* a long cry, 'eeeeeeeeehhhh, Caboooclo!!!!', with a peculiar intonation that was absent in the expressions used in the same ritual in the Templo Mãe at that time.

Some *aparás* may initially manifest what is called an *incorporação cruzada* (crossed incorporation), when they are said to receive the simultaneous projection of different mentors without being able to discern them, thus mixing their gestures (for instance, manifesting a *preto velho* slapping their chest like a *caboclo*). Hence, they learn to concentrate on one mentor at a time, familiarizing themselves with that specific energy while the instructors provide the spirit with corresponding instructions. In later sessions, the *aparás* learn to switch from the incorporation of one spirit to another without disincorporating. Switching from one spirit manifestation to another is comparable to switching from one language to another in speech. However, this case involves not only the verbal dimension but also the bodily one, with different perceptions of energies, different emotions, feelings, gestures and postures, which together allow for the recognition and communication of the spirit's identity.

Among the group in the development classes I attended, some *caboclos* used to arrive with such intensity that some *aparás* stood up or others felt they wanted to sing. In these cases, the instructors intervened to reframe the spirit manifestation within the Vale's pattern, pointing out that differently to rituals in some Afro-Brazilian religions *caboclos* in the Vale incorporate in the medium whilst seated and they must be controlled. Spirit manifestations are culturally shaped, and these patterns mark the Vale's ritual identity. However, the initial conformity of the gestures among aspirants undergoes a kind of personalization along with the practice and establishment of a relationship between medium and mentor. Once the medium begins to visualize her spirit mentors and gain confidence in releasing their expression, the mentors may highlight specific traits of their expression or particular features of their way of working the energies. Elsa, who has been working for two years with the *preto velho* Pai Francisco de Oriente (Father Francis of the Orient), noted that he cleanses the energies of patients by making the shape of the pyramid with her hands and invoking its energy, which he told her 'catalyses the healing forces of the oracles'. Some gypsy spirits manifested holding a fan, so the hand of the medium opened waving the fan, whereas other gypsies clapped their hands to dissipate the energy.

Whilst the manifestation of the mentors and spirits of light features a wide range of personality expressions, suffering spirits such as the *sofredores*, *obsessores* and *cobradores* are generally contained in their verbal and gestural expression. *Aparás* are indeed instructed to close their fists to secure the spirit's energy controlling them while the *doutrinador* informs them that they are deceased and should leave this plane to follow their journey, and then elevates them to the spirit world. To perform the indoctrination of the spirit (*doutrina*), the *doutrinador* learns the techniques to cleanse the aura (*limpeza*) of the suffering spirit incorporated by the *apará* by passing his or her hands around the *apará's* head and shoulders and discharging the heavy energies removed from it by snapping their fingers towards the ground. While the *doutrinador* does so, he or she talks to the spirit, calling him 'brother' (*irmão*) and welcoming the spirit to the House of Seta Branca, making him aware of his death and of the cause of his suffering, rage or hatred, which is the lack of love and forgiveness. Eventually, the *doutrinador* informs the spirit that the spirit guides are giving him the opportunity to be released from this plane to be healed and continue his evolution in the spirit worlds, and through an initiatic key they elevate the spirit. Much of the first stage of development of the *doutrinadores* is devoted to learning the ritual gestures appropriate to their functions, such as how to administer a magnetic pass (*passe magnético*), how to connect his or her plexus to the *apará* in preparation for receiving a spirit mentor (a process called '*ionização*'), how to project a *sofredor* spirit into the *apará's* body for indoctrination (*puxada*), how to indoctrinate a spirit (*doutrina*), how to cleanse the aura of the spirit (*limpeza*), how to elevate the *sofredor* to the spirit world (*elevação*) and how to disincorporate the *apará*. Each of these skills require a set of formalized and ritualized gestures and postures accompanied by prefixed sacred enunciations called 'keys' (*chaves*) that the *doutrinador* must be able to perform correctly before being allowed to assist patients. The only part of their performance where personal variation is allowed is in the words used to indoctrinate the *sofredor*. They are provided with a sample pattern of the 'doctrine of the sofredor' (*doutrina*), which they are able to increase with other words, drawing upon the Christic principles of love and forgiveness through which the spirit can be released and follow his evolution in the spirit world.

Both *apará* and *doutrinador* learn to perform the specific gestures that compose the ritual and contribute to its efficacy. A precise set of movements and gestures constitute the opening and closing of a mediums' session of spiritual work and of each ritual they perform. The way the medium moves around the temple is different from the way a patient or visitor would move around. Mediums move clockwise following the direction of forces in order to protect themselves from different energies. Particularly until initiation they walk with their arms crossed behind their back to protect the development of the solar plexus. They open their plexus through a reverence – that is, by placing their hands on the solar plexus and then opening their arms, bending them in a ninety-degree angle – on entrance and exit from the temple and in front of the focal points. Thus, there are specific techniques that are used to open and close the body whether mediums need to receive forces or to protect themselves, which raises the question of the body's permeability.

### The Skills of Discerning and Controlling Spirits

For several months during fieldwork, I stayed in a guesthouse near the temple, where people, mostly mediums, were renting rooms for short or long stays while visiting the Vale, working in rituals or developing mediumship. The rooms were aligned along a small hallway, which was a place for socialization between guests. Given the friendly atmosphere among long-term residents, we used to leave room doors open and often eat together and share stories and accounts of works in the temple. On a few occasions, some guests in development experienced uncontrolled mediumistic phenomena, and in these cases they were either brought to the temple or *doutrinadores* would promptly intervene. In one case, I was just returning to my room when I noticed a young woman in her twenties, an *apará* in development, who was in the hallway with other guests. She was lamenting stomach pains, had difficulty standing up and looked as if she was going to faint. She began to cry and said that she was feeling the action of a *sofredor* spirit. A *doutrinador* told her to take some deep breaths; he then began to pray to Jesus Christ and asked for the forces of the spirit mentors to cleanse the energy she was feeling. Then he stood behind her to give her a magnetic *passe* to rebalance her, putting his hands on his plexus so as to transfer his magnetic force to her by laying his hands near her plexus, on her front and her back between the shoulders. When the woman looked as though she was feeling better, he asked her, with a concerned tone, how she could have allowed the spirit to act upon her so much by lowering her vibrations.

On another occasion, another *apará* in development said that all of a sudden he began to feel deeply sad and progressively cold. He asked for a blanket, even though the outside temperature was over twenty-five degrees. He was lying on the bed with the blanket rolled over his body when the fingers on his right hand twitched and stiffened; he asked for the help of a *doutrinador*, saying that he could not move and that the sensations did not belong to him. The *doutrinador* from a nearby room rushed in and performed a *puxada* – literally 'pulled' – a technique to project the *sofredor* spirit into the *apará*'s aura so that it would manifest and be indoctrinated. Then, through the appropriate initiatic key, he elevated the spirit to the spiritual planes, and the *apará* recovered immediately afterwards.

Mediums learn that incorporation of spirits outside the temple is not safe because of the lack of protection usually provided by the sacred space and ritual, and that *aparás* should retain enough consciousness to guarantee control over the forces thereby not allowing the spirit to incorporate without permission. Cases of involuntary incorporation could happen during the first stage of development if the *apará* still doesn't feel confident in his or her ability to control the phenomenon and remains vulnerable to different kind of energies. In contrast to the pains attributed to the body in development, involuntary incorporation may begin with a sort of body pain but is accompanied by unexpected negative emotions and feelings, tiredness, headache, nausea or losing sensitivity of the limbs. Studies on Shamanism have addressed these symptoms as part of the Shamanic apprenticeship and have highlighted the question of control (Lewis 1971, Hutton 2001). Lewis has emphasized the mastery of spirits as being at the core of the healing process. Spirits that would otherwise be dangerous, instead of being exorcized, are domesticated and become spirit helpers (Lewis 1971). The Vale's cosmology, however, does not suggest that an obsessing spirit might be domesticated to become a medium's spirit helper. Indeed, in the Vale there is a definite distinction between the category of spirit mentors and those suffering or obsessing spirits that belong to a different dimension of evolution. Obsessing spirits are controlled only for the purpose of being indoctrinated and released from the physical plane, whereas spirit mentors are said to already belong to the higher spirit worlds and to rarely incorporate without the medium's permission, and they are associated with positive emotions and feelings.

Instructors stressed that the *aparás* must develop the necessary level of control in order to avoid episodes of involuntary incorporation, for they will not always have the presence of a *doutrinador* by their side in daily life outside the temple. Allowing a force to take over a medium's body is regarded as a lack of preparation on the medium's part, a form of imbalance or vanity. Vanity was a frequent consideration of some mediums when an *apará* incorporated suffering spirits in the *Mesa Evangélica*, banging on the table, yelling or laughing at each manifestation. Indeed, given the number of spirits incorporated by mediums at each 15–20 minute long session of the *Mesa* (fifteen or more) and their variety, the medium may feel a wide range of emotions and react in a different way to each incorporation. While they recognized that some spirit manifestations may be more intense and difficult to control than others, some instructors pointed out that some mediums may seek visibility by manifesting all *sofredores* by acting fiercely and view this as proof of their ability to support similar forces in their bodies. Then they explained that a loud and uncontrolled incorporation does not define any social or spiritual hierarchy; it would rather reveal the lack of preparation of the medium. Others suggested that some mediums may be playing out some kind of 'demonic imagery', belonging to other religions. There were, however, cases of mediums developing as *aparás* who told me that they were previously 'unconscious mediums' in Afro-Brazilian religions, so they initially had difficulty in retaining enough consciousness to control spirits. A president of an external temple suggested that there are also cases of *aparás* who are mainly 'disobsessive' – that is, they might be 'predisposed by mission' to incorporate *obsessores* more frequently and might feel those forces more intensely than other mediums, and thus show less control.

The basic assumption was that nothing happens during incorporation against the *apará*'s will, especially after the initiation, when the *apará* has already learned what is considered to be appropriate or not in the spirits' manifestation and to contain inappropriate behaviour. This assumption implies a specific difference with the practice in many Afro-Brazilian religions, whereby the behaviour of the spirits or *orixás* remains partly unpredictable as it is considered to depend upon the spiritual agent rather than upon the medium.

Although members of the Vale consider mediumship to be a natural and universal phenomenon, control and discernment are skills to be learned. Discernment for an *apará* works at different levels: firstly, discernment between the medium's thoughts and those of the spirit; secondly, between his or her spirit mentors; and thirdly, between the mentors and the interference of a *sofredor*. From several discussions with *aparás* at different stages of development, it emerged that the process of discernment is informed by the joint action of three factors during incorporation: emotions and feelings, the content of messages and the access to information about patients. Exploring these three levels of discernment in more detail through the experiences of mediums, at the first level, the presence of a spirit of light, for instance of a *preto velho*, is perceived to be clearly discernible from the presence of a human being, given the feeling that it provokes, firstly and most strongly in the *apará*, then in the *doutrinador* and often in the patient. This feeling is often described as 'a love that embraces you that does not belong to this world', a non-ordinary feeling that is said to pervade the whole body. Then, *aparás* claimed that the content of the communication passed from the spirit implies a much more complex level of spiritual knowledge than mediums ordinarily have. For instance, it is not unusual for an *apará* in the very first stage of development to incorporate spirits passing on highly elaborate descriptions of life beyond matter and the spiritual teachings of a master. In this sense, *aparás* discern themselves from spirits, overcoming the doubts that some of them may experience as a result of their semi-conscious incorporation. Gloria told me that, being a professional psychologist, when she incorporated her spirit mentors, although she did not exclude their projection upon her body, she sometime wondered whether or not it was her 'unconscious' speaking rather than a spirit. What was helping her discernment during the incorporation, however, was the fact that as soon as the patient sat at her side during a ritual she suddenly felt she already held the knowledge of the past, the present, and the future of that patient, what he was in need of, and the appropriate language to use. She pointed out that in her professional life as a psychologist, she needed to listen to patients, encourage them to bring forth information and then analyse it and make connections, which was a process requiring several sessions of therapy, whereas in the ritual, she noted, it frequently happened instantaneously and often without any patient intervention. Some *aparás* describe this kind of access to the knowledge of the patient's life (or past lives, in some cases) as a movie scene manifesting in front of them whilst they are incorporated with a spirit. In other cases, they say that the spirit may conceal the wider picture of the patient's life to *aparás*, but they then realize that the messages passed on are accurate descriptions of the patient's situation.

At a second level of discernment between their own mentors and other spirits of light, *aparás* need to become familiar with the particular energy and feelings provoked by the spirit mentor. Additionally, in order to identify their mentors, some mediums rely on specific verbal or gestural features through which their spirit mentor works. Others make this discernment through an expression or a smell, such as in some cases in which mediums said that they could smell a scent of roses while incorporating their *pretos velhos*.

The third level involves both *apará* and *doutrinador* in discerning spirits of light from suffering spirits. If the *apará* perceives a drastic change in the feeling of a *preto velho*, resulting in an interruption in the flow of words or a sensation in the body similar to a sudden power outage in electricity, this is interpreted as interference caused by a *sofredor* or *obsessor*, to which the *apará* responds by closing his or her fists and preventing as much as possible the verbal and gestural expression of the spirit. For instance, Marilza said that if while incorporating her mentor she felt her tongue jam and a contraction of the abdomen around the solar plexus, she automatically closed her fists and felt rage or the will to cry. Indeed, *aparás* learn that as soon as they feel a change in energy and a presence of a *sofredor* during a communication in the ritual of *Tronos*, they should allow its incorporation to be indoctrinated and elevated, so as to avoid its possible interference in the message passed to the patient.

Since the *apará* is not completely aware during incorporation, the responsibility of determining the authenticity of or interference in a spirit manifestation relies on the *doutrinador's* ability of discernment. This ability is held to increase when the *doutrinador* is focused upon the ritual in what one instructor defined as a 'state of conscious mediumistic trance', as consciousness that extends to embrace his spirit guides and those of the *apará*. The conformity of the styles of manifestation helps this process of discernment. In other words, the concurrence of a culturally recognizable configuration of elements, such as gestures, emotions, tone of voice and postures in the performance of spirit manifestation, along with the content of messages, suggests to the *doutrinador* the kind of manifesting spirit. Instructors explained that some spirits, such as the *obsessores*, may be able to mimic the gestures of the spirits of light in order to play tricks upon the patient or interfere in messages. These interferences may be identified, since *doutrinadores* and *aparás* share knowledge of the ethics of communication with patients, which strictly forbid: diagnoses of physical illness (the spirit may tell the patient to seek advice from a medical consultation with a doctor instead); prescription of chemical or natural remedies, or diets (they may only suggest participation in rituals or drinking the temple's water); interference with a doctor's prescription or treatment and any type of intervention in the patient's free will. In any of these cases, the *doutrinador* must block the communication and indoctrinate the *obsessor* spirit that is interfering. A key aspect that defines the *doutrinador's* mediumship and enhances spirits' discernment is intuition. Lucas, a *doutrinador* in his mid thirties with almost twenty years of experience, described how intuition intervenes in rituals in these terms:

> In my case, the energy of a spirit of light is a shiver and at the same time that fire that refreshes – it is pleasant. And when the energy is not sublime and satisfying … it's an energy that squeezes the heart, rather a less pleasant sensation. Even unenlightened, that spirit is an individuality with a history. Once, a spirit of my *cobrador* in an *Angical* had no hatred of me and even called me brother, but I couldn't speak really, and I just wanted to do the doctrine and elevation; I didn't want a dialogue, and he went. And then the *apará* began to greet the entities and apparently there was a *preto velho*, but I still felt that presence, and I saw that he had not gone and made the *puxada*, and he came and said

'it's difficult to trick you right?' Sometimes the *doutrinador* doesn't feel, but he has an incredible intuition. Intuition has no interference; it is a certainty, and whenever you go against it you always regret it.

When I asked Mike, an American *doutrinador* who developed his mediumship in Brazil, how he recognized what kind of spirit is manifesting in the *apará*, told me,

> I definitely feel the differences. First, it's like a gentle kind energy or a stern, heavy one. If it's stern, I feel this energy in my lungs, in my ability to breathe. From there, it's masculine or feminine. And from there, it's how I am reacting to it; sometimes I might get defensive over it, sometimes I feel peaceful – there are different variations, like being mad, being sad, being happy, joyful, feeling like a kid, feeling powerful. A gentle, calm, controlled kind of feeling is more feminine, and being the one more kind of confident is masculine, I would say. Every time it's a different experience for me.

The emotional response that a spirit provokes within those in its presence contributes to determine the authenticity of the spirit manifestation. It is also an intersubjective response acting upon the emotions of the *doutrinador*, the *apará* and the patient involved in the ritual. Halloy and Naumescu address possession as a 'cultural expertise', for it 'requires an expertise both from the observers, who perceive it in relation to shared social values and aesthetic and normative criteria offered by that particular culture, and from the possessed person who has to make sense of her own experience' (2012: 166). Even Pentecostalism features a cultivation of the senses, with the church regulating bodies through self-vigilance and discipline in the highly emotional experience of the action of the Holy Spirit, teaching balance between spontaneity and control over this force and the involuntary movements it produces in the body – as losing control is interpreted as demonic interference (Rabelo 2007).

The modalities of discernment in the Vale, which are based upon emotions and feelings, bodily manifestation and content of messages, are partially passed on by instructors in the development, but mostly they are skills acquired by the *aparás* and the *doutrinadores* during their experience in the practice and familiarization with the spirit mentors. The process of discernment is culturally informed and locally defined; involving both legitimized gestural and verbal patterns of spirit manifestation and the interpretation of emotions, feelings and intuition. There are parallels with Tanya Luhrmann's suggestion in her study on the ways in which Evangelical Christians learned to discern the presence of God in their everyday lives that 'discernment is clearly a social process, in that there are socially taught rules through which God is identified' (Luhrmann 2009: 90).

Group identity is then constructed through shared feeling – which resonates with the expression 'mediumistic body' (*corpo mediúnico*), used to address the community of initiates in the Order – in which emotions and senses are cultivated so as to provide a particular kind of access to and encounter with the spirit world.

## Ways of Knowing the Spirits: Conscious and Semi-conscious Mediumship

*How Semi-conscious Mediumship Was Developed in the Vale do Amanhecer*

What is defined as a semi-conscious state of incorporation was developed in the Vale do Amanhecer with the specific purpose of allowing control. Elder mediums narrated that this grade of control was developed over many years. Mestre Guto, an *ajanã* who lived close to Tia Neiva and assisted her in the *Casa Grande* from 1974 until she passed away, explained to me that because of the disobsessive work of the Vale, the incorporation medium could not be developed as in Umbanda or Candomblé. In his view, mediumship along these lines was a door to the African forces that were rather less controlled. He explained to me that,

> Tia Neiva received from the spirit world the authorization to call the medium of incorporation '*apará*'. It seems something simple, but it is not, because she was able to place the medium of incorporation in the line of Nossa Senhora Apará (Our Lady Aparecida) so the energy changed, the line changed; the new line did not conform to the previous model. After this process of adaptation, which lasted one decade from 1973 to 1983, our mediumship began to change. It was necessary to create filters. With the arrival of the initiation in 1973, the *apará* was placed directly in the Christic system. Before then, we had a heavy incorporation – it was difficult to manipulate energies; some experienced pains in the body because of the dense energies and we could not remember things afterwards. We were almost unconscious so we had problems because the suffering spirits did not accept what the *doutrinador* was telling them and there were cases in which the *apará* would stand up and jump against the *doutrinador* because it was his *cobrador*.

Similarly, the Adjunto Yumatá, Mestre Caldeira, used to tell me of episodes from the early times in the Vale, when mediums incorporated with *sofredores* and climbed on the ellipse of the *Mesa Evangélica*, or ran out of the temple and into the woods with *doutrinadores* running after them, yelling out the intiatic keys to release the spirits. He used to say that the technique was so perfected over the decades that nowadays these cases are not acceptable anymore.

According to Guto, semi-consciousness began to appear in the initiated *aparás* but with the consequence that mediums began to doubt their incorporation as they were remembering what happened during the process. He said that 'it was the beginning of a no-return process, either you adapted to it or there was nothing that could be done. From what was said to the patient I could remember some incomplete sentences from the first paragraph then it jumped to the last one, but I could not form the whole story afterwards'. He continued explaining to me that with the coming of the second initiation of the *Elevação de Espadas* in 1975, they became *Raio Lunar* (Moon Ray), a direct ray of the oracle of Olorúm, and what was understood as a 'traditional medium of incorporation' was then left behind, followed by the *Mestre Lua* (Master Moon). 'A master is a profound connoisseur of his craft', he said, pointing out that this consecration applied to both male and female *aparás*, giving them 'the autonomy along with their spirit guides to decide what could be said or not to the patient as they have control over this, and also physical control as mediumship is physical'. He continued,

> Then it came, the *ajanã*, master and nymph *ajanã*. It was the spirits that gave this name; it wasn't a name created by Tia. They told her that from that day the incorporation medium of the Amanhecer would be known in the spiritual planes as *ajanã*. When she asked them about the meaning of the term, they answered that it's the scientific name for the mediumship of incorporation in the spirit world. That is, Tia Neiva was able to place the mediumship of incorporation in the spiritual scientific line. So in the early 1980s, the classification of 5ft Yurê arrived for male *ajanãs*, which means the fifth ray of the oracle of Olorúm, a medium apt to solve any situation and with absolute control over his incorporation and the energies around him. This was visible as we radically changed in the sense that we began to make decisions and sustain the forces.

> You see a great musician from an orchestra – he picks up his instrument, he tunes it up, he tries to keep that instrument as perfect as possible to perform the music he wants, so we, *aparás*, are instruments. If he plays a higher or lower note, he will disharmonize the whole orchestra. But that musician sits with confidence, knowing that he has prepared the instrument – which can always give a problem, but he did his part – so he sits there and will harmonize with the other instruments, within the system of the temple that is a power plant with forces coming in and going out, and all this passes through the *apará* when he is in the temple, incorporated or not.

Interestingly, Guto illuminated the collective development of the mediumistic body of the *aparás* across a decade, passing from what he defined as the African line to the Christic-scientific line in terms of modes of consciousness and control. With the notion of 'mediumistic body' again I am referring here both to the individual body and collective one in terms of shared skills and modes of knowing.

## Mediumization and Mediumistic Trance

Altered states of consciousness (ASC) have been the locus of interest particularly of earlier anthropological studies on spirit mediumship and possession. As a matter of fact, a variety of classifications of possession phenomena were driven by criteria such as the presence or absence of trance states, along with the level of control retained by mediums (Bourguignon 1967, 1979; Firth 1967; Lewis 1971). However, the debate highlighted that trance is merely one aspect of spirit possession, as argued by Michael Lambek (1981) in his study of possession in Mayotte society (Comore Islands). Lambek describes possession as a relationship between humans and spiritual beings that encompasses the everyday life of the person (what he defines as 'latent possession') and that becomes 'manifest' in rituals of spirit possession – that is, when the deity manifests itself actively possessing the host's body (ibid.). Likewise, Janice Boddy calls for a reconsideration of spirit possession as not confined to the 'extraordinary' and dramatic manifestation of spirits in rituals, for it is rather embedded in the experience of 'ordinary', everyday lives of the subjects (Boddy 1988). In the Vale do Amanhecer, the relationship between mediums and their spirit guides is cultivated in their everyday lives. However, it is initially through mediumistic states of consciousness – what mediums call 'conscious and semi-conscious mediumship' – that new mediums learn their spirits, and it is only through experience that this relationship is gradually extended into the everyday life beyond such states of consciousness. For this reason, my discussion focuses upon mediumistic trance in order to explore phenomenologically the various layers involved in the process of learning mediumship and how this process informs a transformation in the articulation of the body and the self.

In addressing the experiences at the core of mediumistic practice, it is firstly necessary to illustrate the preparation that mediums undergo for either their conscious or semi-conscious mediumistic trance states. In mediumistic development, instructors used to stress that the medium *apará* is considered to be analogous to a radio device (*aparelho*) that needs to be tuned to gain access to different channels, and this tuning is achieved through a preparation that is technically known as *mediunização* (mediumization): a process of *concentração* (concentration) through which one becomes an intermediary between planes, enabling the contact with spirits. Since in the Vale mediumistic states of consciousness are not induced by any substance, mediums need to become skilled in this technique. In some rituals, the *mediunização* is guided by the medium directing the ritual with brief narrations focused on visualizations of scenes. These visualizations include landscapes, natural elements, forests and waterfalls, and they tune in to the energy of spirits such as the *caboclos*, the people of the waters and mermaids, who are then called to manifest in the *aparás* through specific keys (sacred formulas). Places of suffering and people in need can also be visualized so that the forces in the rituals can reach them for distant healing. These visualizations are aimed at establishing connections through thought, but they are also crucial for the medium to enter a mediumistic state of consciousness.

In most rituals, however, mediums are individually responsible for their own *mediunização*. Before participating in a ritual, mediums prepare themselves by sitting with eyes closed on the benches in the Silence Castle (*Castelo do Silencio*), the area of the temple in front of the *Tronos* dedicated to the practice of mediumization. Both *aparás* and *doutrinadores* learn to focus on their spirit mentors, but they are also encouraged to find their own way of establishing a connection with the spirit world, and thus there are various ways in which mediumization is experienced. Some mediums used prayers focusing on words; others would feel the spirit guide approaching; and some were used to meeting their guide in a specific place they visualized and conversed with the spirit, or they just immersed themselves in silence. Through practice, the process gradually becomes faster so that an experienced *apará* may be able to enter a mediumistic state of consciousness in a matter of seconds. Describing the way he prepared himself to work in rituals, an elder master *doutrinador* in his sixties said:

> Since the moment you begin the preparation, you are in the state to engage in a ritual. You know that you are working with the assistance of spirits from the higher spiritual plane. To do this you need to mediumize yourself – that is ... become sensitive. What you feel then is a kind of euphoria, a different kind of vibration around and inside your body. You almost see ... you almost touch ... it is quite subtle but perceptible – a feeling that I could describe as a joy generated by the whole body.

The 'conscious mediumship' of the *doutrinador* is described as 'expanded consciousness' – which extends into his or her spirit mentors and those manifesting through the *apará* – involving increased attention, sharpened intuition and often sudden variations in thermoception, such as feeling heat in the hands or pervading the whole body. If the *doutrinador* experiences an enhanced sensory perception, the *apará* goes a step forward, as another elder master said:

> We [*aparás*] prepare ourselves through mediumization in the *Castelo do Silêncio*. When we leave the *Castelo* to go and sit in the *Tronos* for the ritual,

we are almost manifested with the spirit. The energies surround us – we are perfectly tuned with the incorporation. I don't hear much of the noises around me; I can see you but I feel as if I am far away from you. As I sit in the *Trono*, I close my eyes and the *doutrinador* invites the mentor, and then the manifestation is complete. When the spirit arrives, I feel my self moving onto the side to give access to my spirit mentor. When the manifestation is complete, I am just an observer and not many of the things that are said remain in my mind afterwards.

Thus, both *doutrinadores* and *aparás* experience increased perception; however, only the *apará* manifests the spirit. Mestre Diego described how the senses expand for both, though in different ways: 'The more the *apará* closes the eyes the more he sees, the more the *doutrinador* opens the eyes the more he sees. Each in his function, they both reach mediumistic trance; they both undergo an expansion of their vision, of their senses. They *feel* if there is really a *sofredor* or a *preto velho* manifesting'.

Whether 'conscious' or 'semi-conscious', what is addressed as 'mediumistic trance' in the Vale is a complex and changeable phenomenon that cannot be reduced to one comprehensive description, but it may be evoked through some of its various traits. In the case of the medium *apará*, not only does the level of consciousness vary between mediums but also within the same *apará* from one spirit incorporation to another, and even within the same incorporation. One *apará* described her mediumistic state of consciousness as a feeling that the mentor was 'dancing between consciousness and unconsciousness'. Another *apará* described it as a state of drowsiness, although remaining aware of what is happening and thus able to follow the reasoning of the spirit: 'when the entity leaves the body, the feeling is like waking up and trying to remember a dream'. The experiences of incorporation are also reported by *aparás* as being similar to dream sleep even though the body moves as if it is in a state of wakefulness. As psychologist Etzel Cardeña states, altered states of consciousness are not unchangeable and homogenous entities, as consciousness is an ever-changing process, so we should rather approach them as 'different modalities of experiencing' (Cardeña 2009). Although the levels of consciousness are constantly varying, through practice and intersubjective exchanges, mediums define and recognize what is part of the repertoire of mediumistic practice of the Vale.

### Towards an Extended Self and a Permeable Body

In my own experience of learning the modality addressed as 'semi-conscious mediumship' in the development, on certain occasions I felt as though I was sitting in a particular seat, but on opening my eyes, I realized that I had been sitting in a different place all along. In reporting this sensation to other mediums in development, as well as to the more experienced ones, they also reported having felt similar sensations of displacement during incorporation, such as 'seeing' themselves in another seat, or observing the ritual from a side perspective. It gradually emerged that these experiences of partial displacement appeared to be more recurrent than experiences of leaving the body to visit other dimensions. I highlight 'partial' because the feeling was described as being on one level somewhere else and on another still present in the body, suggesting a partial presence of proprioceptive sensations. The Adjunto Yumatá Mestre Caldeira, an elder master, then explained to me that the spirit of the medium is projected about one and a half metres out of the body while spirits project their aura into the medium's body. Thus, according to this conceptualization, this ability of the self to extend out of the body does not imply that the self would fully leave the body, as body and self are interwoven in the solar plexus of the incarnated being. Jorge, an *ajaná* in his thirties, used the metaphor of a car to describe his incorporation of the *preto velho*: 'Have you ever had a conversation in a car with a friend? The voices sound different as you are so close in that space that you can feel the breath and the smell of the other person, but when you get out of the car you hear the voice in a different way – that is when you leave the *preto velho* working with the patient'. In some cases, the self was described to me as also moving into a distinct space within the body. Beth, for instance, was a European yoga teacher in her thirties who was in the initial stages of mediumistic development as an *apará* in the Templo Mãe. One day, while discussing mediumistic experiences in the development, I asked her where she felt her spirit guides during the incorporation, and she said,

> It is in that space where I am in that moment; it is like a space which is created inside of me and from there I can safely incorporate. In my previous [yogic] meditation, I had a lot of *samadhi* experiences, when the mind is transcended and you are in a universal awareness, and in this I have a space where I have to enter to incorporate safely. There are some guards that close the door; it is like a temple really ... The work in the Vale is actually grounding for me because before I set my path always meditating, being in the clouds ... also a shaman told me I had to accept having a body, as it was always easy for me to go in *Samadhi* ... Here I feel that my all force and energy that are transmitted from the higher planes needs this kind of body. Here I have begun to feel that the physical manipulation is very necessary because we are on a physical plane ...

It is remarkable that Beth described her spiritual experiences in the Vale as 'grounding'. Since spiritual trance has been mostly associated with transcendence, amnesia or out-of-body experience, one would seldom expect mediumistic experience to be 'grounding'. Mediumistic development in the Vale brought about a new feeling and perception of her bodiliness, as she continued to explain her experience to me:

> everyone here feels these subtle worlds in the physical reality, even *doutrina-dores* feel the energies. I have always distinguished the physical reality from the beautiful soul, but here I appreciate that the dimensions are interacting with each other ... Here the spirits come through your body; you can experience them in your body, you can work with them in your body, but they are actually from a different dimension so everything gets interwoven. That was the feeling I was missing; I felt as not having any borders, but now I understand that if you have other dimensions inside of you as experience rather than knowledge ... then ... you see with many New Age people ... some people who took ayahuasca said that they visited other dimensions and then they came back and did not know how these different dimensions could come together.

This new feeling has produced a new conceptualization of her body and self. Beth described her self as being in a space created inside of her, where different dimensions are interwoven in the body in precise ritualistic moments, and where spirit guides may come to communicate with her and perform their work with patients. The development of the skills of spirit discernment was also informing the perception of having semi-permeable bodily boundaries and the definition of a sense of self as she became aware of her multidimensionality:

> Here you can probably see it [the body] more as a semi-permeable membrane where it is very clearly defined in which space the spirit comes through. If you work with a shaman in the jungle, for example, how do you know what comes through? I sometimes felt as though they didn't know what they were calling. So it is like a semi-permeable membrane where in certain spaces it is allowed for this energy to come through the physical space and in certain places not. So it is very clearly defined and that is actually very healthy. Because otherwise there is this thing always travelling around dimensions not knowing how and where, and that is the difference here, it is clearly a protection. With the *doutrinador* ... there is a channel that is opened, and now it is allowed to come through, and then it is closed again, then it is opened again, and closed. You know, it is really a matter of safety. I feel that this is the best thing for me, to feel the protection, not to just flow around, but there are times when you are physical, times when you are a medium, and whatever comes through your body is very precise. I feel that this gives me a sort of stability, and this is also what I mean by being more embodied.

Spiritual practice in the Vale is indeed precise and highly ritualistic: following formalized ritual scripts and specific symbols and colours of vestments, intended to channel specific kinds of energies through each detail, with the *doutrinador* performing the role of delimiting the boundaries where and when the spirit can manifest.

> Besides, this ability that I have to be in contact with spirits – the communication with other dimensions ... it is not something random, making me suffer to be in this earthly plane, but it is actually something useful that can help others. That's the most grounding part of it if you have this sensitivity and you don't know where to bring this energy and you think 'What shall I do with it?'

At the time of this conversation, Beth was in the initial classes of mediumistic development. Only later in her advanced stage of development did she learn that, according to Tia Neiva, the three dimensions – body, soul and spirit – are located within the body in the solar plexus and enveloped by an energetic membrane, whilst the self is extended through several planes – physical, etheric, astral, and so on (N.C. Zelaya 1984: 105; Sassi 2003: 50). Therefore, as Beth also stressed, this kind of 'knowing' was grounded primarily in experience. She recognized the ability of her self to extend out from the physical dimension in meditation but also be immersed in the space within during mediumistic trance. She perceived her body as a 'semi-permeable membrane' able to be crossed by spirit energy in specific ritual times and spaces.

Similarly, an Italian *doutrinador*, recalling his past experiences of altered states of consciousness before encountering the Vale along his spiritual route, told me that when he tried *ayahuasca*, on several occasions, there was a somewhat episodic and provisional opening of consciousness in which he could experience other dimensions only for that moment after ingesting the tea. As a *doutrinador* in the Vale, he felt as if through practice his consciousness was continuously and gradually amplifying to accommodate other dimensions in his everyday life. These emerging conceptualizations of the body and the self are further articulated through the relationship with spirits, which is gradually established by means of a multisensory experience.

### Extended Senses and Multisensory Images

During the first sessions of the development, *aparás* often experience certain difficulties in letting the spirit communicate through their voice. These difficulties are an outcome of the expectation, pretty much common among developing mediums, that the spirit will completely take over the medium's body and intentionality. One medium in the development classes I attended was formerly a *doutrinador* who suddenly began to incorporate, so he had to restart the development as an *apará*. He told me that his recent experiences of incorporation contradicted his initial thoughts – cultivated from years of practice as a *doutrinador* – that the *apará* would leave his body to the spirit, who would also take over control upon communication. Explaining the phenomenology of spirit communication, however, Mestre Caldeira told me that the spirit projects communication energetically in the form of thoughts in the *apará*'s mind, then the articulation through language relies on the *apará*'s brain processes, although the tone of voice and accents are attributed to the spirit. Other instructors also explained that this telepathic-like communication might sometimes take the form of visual or auditory images that are then articulated in words and sentences by the *apará*. Thus, *aparás* must find their own key to unlock this communication, and instructors encourage them to release it by saying the first words that come to their mind, which may be in the form of greeting spirits (*saudações*). Once the *apará* releases the first words, the process speeds up and the message flows rapidly, sometimes leaving no time for the *apará* to follow it, in that the time it takes to articulate a complex thought in language in an ordinary conscious state is reduced to a few seconds during a spirit incorporation. As Jorge described it, 'you begin a sentence, which is then followed by a text; then you say the last word, but you are not able to tell the semantic relation'. Something similar has been highlighted in Catholic ecstatic states, characterized by 'an increase both of mental activity and sensory input (increase in the volume of information for time unit that reaches consciousness), and of data processing (mental and psychic activity)' (Gentili 2006: 199).[1]

What precedes verbalization may imply the activation of what can be understood as 'extended senses', referring to those senses that are not directly dependent upon the organs to which they are ordinarily attributed. They are commonly addressed collectively as the 'extra-sensorial', but since the categorization of senses is cultural and these are part of mediums' everyday life experience, they may be conceived as 'extended': they are conceived as inner, but they are also depicted as extending beyond a physical organ, the physical body or a physical source. Thus, *aparás* may, in some cases, see an image as a snapshot or a succession of interconnected images with their eyes closed. A wide range of feelings accompany these images. They may hear, feel, touch, smell or perceive the temperature of what they claim to be an immaterial source, or a material one that is not physically present. They use expressions such as 'my spirit mentor showed me … (or told me …)' not only in the ritual practice but also in everyday activities.

The ethnographic literature illuminates several similar phenomena in different cultures, and long-term fieldwork tends to lead anthropologists to distinguish these images from pathological hallucinations. In a study on Evangelical Christianity, Tanya Luhrmann makes such a distinction, preferring the term 'sensory override' to refer to moments in which 'people experience a sensation in the absence of a source to be sensed', emphasizing a lack of distress accompanying these experiences (Luhrmann 2011: 73–74). This definition complements what I am describing. Additionally, she relates these experiences to absorption – which she understands 'as the mental capacity common to trance, hypnosis, dissociation, and much other spiritual experience'– which may be learned and produces greater 'internal sensory experiences with sharper mental-imagery and more sensory overrides' (Luhrmann, Nusbaum and Thisted 2010: 74).

In the case of Shamanism, Richard Noll approached mental imagery among shamans as an ability achieved through altered states of consciousness and which can be cultivated as a skill in shamanic training (1985: 444–447). He specifically refers to metaphors of inner vision – such as 'the development of an inner or a spiritual eye' in different 'shamanic cultures' (1985: 446) – and argues that visual imagery enhancement is a cultural phenomenon. Visual imagery, Noll noted, was the most reported modality in the ethnographic literature on different societies. Likewise, Luhrmann has pointed out that the predominance of one sense in unusual sensory experiences is cultural, such as vision for Catholics and Hindus, and hearing for Protestants (2011: 77). Indeed, besides these ethnographic instances, we should consider that the use of absorption, and its relation to the development of extended senses, is not restricted to Shamanic practices but has also been advocated in sacred texts of world religions as the pre-condition to opening oneself up to the sacred, in practices of meditation, prayer and devotion, such as the Ignatian Exercises in Christianity.

In the case of the Vale do Amanhecer, visual mental imagery may be encouraged during the process of mediumization that leads to spirit incorporation. However, these sensory images, which emerge during mediumistic trance states and are a common feature of mediums' narratives about their experiences, are not particularly addressed by the instructors in mediumistic development. They rather understand them as a bodily means through which the spirit mentor communicates, emphasizing the spontaneity of their emergence to mediums' awareness. Visual and auditory images may be predominant in some mediums but not in others. Other sensory modalities may interact or stand out. In this sense, I draw upon Csordas, who, in order to avoid the focus on visual imagery as a dominant sensory modality in his study of glossolalia, proposes the term 'multisensory imagery' (1990: 13), describing the imagery process as resulting from the 'integration' of different senses (ibid.: 42). However, Csordas assumes that the phenomena attributed to a sacred otherness ultimately result from the pre-objective experience of the 'socially informed body' (ibid.: 33–34). It should be considered that, in pre-objective experience, mental imagery is largely culturally patterned and the body is socially informed, inasmuch as the interpretation of the body response to a stimulus. This paradigm could perhaps account for the fact that some mediums in development in Italy initially identified their *preto velho* with the name of an Italian Catholic Saint preceded by the Brazilian suffix defining the spirit's category (e.g. Vovó Caterina da Siena, where *vovó* defines the spirit of a *preta velha* followed by the name of Saint Catherine of Siena) or their *médico de cura* as the spirit of a Catholic priest (e.g. Padre Andrea – that is, 'Father Andrew'). But this wasn't the case entirely, and not only because these were just a few cases among many in which spirits were identified within the Vale's Brazilian repertoire. Cognitive explanations of unusual body images and somatic sensations do not necessarily undermine the local explanation of an external spiritual source just because particular brain processes are involved in the phenomenon (Krippner 1987; Cardeña 1989; Hageman et al. 2010). Indeed, if we treat intangible sacred otherness as agents understanding their affects upon human tangible worlds, instead of reducing them to symbols and projections dismissing practitioners' claims (Blanes and Espírito Santo 2013), it emerges that also spirits are considered by mediums as having a 'socially informed body'. In fact, the Brazilian instructors were claiming that local spirits belonging to the Italian land were incorporating and needed to be instructed to come under the cultural manifestation of a *preto velho*, a *caboclo* or a *médico de cura*. Thus, both bodies – the spiritual body of the spirit mentor and the physical one of the medium – are cultivated in the learning process, in an ongoing intersubjective production of a mediumistic body.

Furthermore, most multisensory images arising while the *aparás* incorporate a spirit with their eyes closed consist of vivid images and details that are closely associated with the patient's particular biographical situation, which the cultural pattern paradigm may only in part account for. As in the case of Gloria, the psychologist medium, many *aparás* claim that while incorporated they may have access to knowledge of details of the patient's life events, and patients confirm the accuracy of this information as being specific to their situation rather than generally applicable to different people. Mostly, these images even precede the beginning of the conversation between patient and spirit, thus they are not triggered by the patients' narration of their stories or needs. When mediums explained to me their ideas about the phenomenology of these images, their interpretations referred to a shared somatosensory experience between them and their spirits. Some mediums said it is the spirit sensing these details and others thought that the spirit shows them through the mediums' somatosensory apparatus. The more mediums advance in the development, the more their perception expands, and multisensory images involving precognition may also occur beyond the spirits' incorporation. As Mestre Guto said, 'it gets to a point in which even without wearing the uniform in rituals it's not easy to say whether you are incorporated or not because you begin to tell people things and you know that it is not you talking'.

The way mediums visualize their individual spirit mentors may also be considered as multisensory images, since they are constructed by a mixture of physical feelings about their attributes: such as facial expression, whether contracted or relaxed; touch, through feeling the hands increasing in dimension and becoming rough when incorporating a *preto velho*; and bodily sensations that reveal the robustness or fragility of the body, suggesting a younger or older appearance. These details combine to form an image of the incorporated spirit. They may appear as embodied images, as one may form an image of oneself from an awareness of one's body. They may also appear as external to the body, as an image of the spirit approaching or standing beside the body. Marilza, for instance, felt water spraying in her face while incorporated, then said that she saw her *preta velha* telling her she was not from the People of the Waterfalls (*Povo das Cachoeiras*) but from the People of the Waters (*Povo das Águas*) and identified herself as Vovó Amélia das Águas.

While spirit categories are necessary to discern between different types of spirit specializations and for the medium to connect to their specific energy, individual experiences of incorporation sometimes stand out as being different from the referential image of those categories. There is a general consensus among mediums that not all *pretos velhos* (old blacks) are old with African traits. Julio felt his *preto velho* to be in his thirties, whilst Camila said that she was able to see face traits of her *preta velha* that suggested she was a white woman in her late eighties. Joana initially saw her *preta velha* as an old African robust woman, but after six months in development she said that she looked thinner and younger. Indeed, the way the spirit moulds its appearance is changeable and often depends on its evolution through the practice of charity in rituals with its medium, as Lucas told me. Lucas, as a *doutrinador*, said that if one were to look for the images of spirits one should seek an inner vision:

> Images are simultaneously within and without my self... it is not the physical eye that sees something spiritual, but the spirit guides give me the frequency to tune in so that the spirit world can show up to me. I used to think that the images that I was seeing were created by my imagination, then I understood that things are within my self – the universe is both within and without my self. Then, when you understand that the great occult mystery is within every being, another dimension opens up, another kind of knowledge.

An *apará* called Ana affirmed that the image she formed of her *preta velha* while incorporated was half way between her own appearance of a white woman in her forties and that of an African woman. Although she recognized the implications of her physical sensations in this image, she felt as though a part of her self was connected to her mentor beyond the incorporation event. This sense of continuity between spirit and medium is remarkably illustrated by Diana Espírito Santo in addressing mediumistic development in Cuban Espiritismo Cruzado (2011, 2015). Espírito Santo has highlighted how in mediumistic development both spirit and medium are produced in this interaction, and a developed medium produces 'the smoothest possible overlap or entanglement between her senses and cognition and those of her spirits' (Espírito Santo 2011: 104).

The *apará* embodies the pain and anger of the obsessor as much as the more positive emotions attributed to a spirit of light, such as the calm of the People of the Waterfalls. He or she also embodies the principles of the doctrine of tolerance, humility and love, feeling them through the attitudes of the spirit mentors. During their practice, mediums experience a wide range of emotions and feelings that are shared with the spiritual agent at a bodily level. The understanding of the body as a platform of shared emotions and feelings is key to establishing the conceptualization of the self as extending into non-material beings, allowing oneself to be transformed by them.

Goldman addresses possession in Brazilian Candomblé as a 'dynamic system that not only classifies but also aims to produce specific types of persons not, certainly, in the sense of generating "personalities" or "psycho-logical types", but generating a certain conception of the human person-hood' (1984: 168).[2] In Candomblé initiation, a particular type of person is thus made that is 'multiple and "layered", composed of a series of material and immaterial elements. These include the main *orisha* to which the person belongs ... the secondary *orishas*, as well as ancestral spirits, a guardian angel, a soul and so forth' (Goldman 2007: 111). It is in a Candomblé trance that the different layers converge, 'raising humans to almost a divine status' (ibid.: 112).

In Chapter Four, I explored the discourses on the articulation of notions of the body and the self as multidimensional. I looked at their extensi-bility through their composition, fluids, substances and field of relations in flux across different dimensions. In this chapter, the mediums' nar-ratives of their experiences emphasize a conceptualization of the self as constituted by multiple layers, some of which are described by mediums as partially displaced by extending out of the body during mediumistic states of consciousness although still maintaining a connection with it. The self also extends into spiritual beings, through multisensory images. The body is permeable; it may be penetrated by other extended selves of spirits. Therefore, I argue that in a reciprocal movement bodily experience in rituals shapes the sense of self, providing the notion of the self with attributes of extensibility and multidimensionality. This notion in turn informs the mediums' conceptualizations concerning the phenomenology of 'mediumistic trance' – that is, the extension of the medium's spirit out of the body and the extension of the spirit's aura inside the body, which leads to the experience of the body as a platform of shared emotions and feelings (Pierini 2016a). As the articulation of the notion of self occurs at different levels, I shall now examine the process of learning mediumship, by unpacking its various dimensions.

## The Process of Learning: Knowing and Enskillment

The primacy of bodily experience over conceptual transmission in the Vale do Amanhecer's mediumistic development is effectively captured in the expression often used by initiated mediums: 'our doctrine is more practical than theoretical'. When referring to 'doctrine' or 'doctrinal knowledge', mediums addressed principles and notions with a revelatory character – either contained in the Gospels or transmitted by Tia Neiva through her clairvoyance – and particularly those grounded in practical experience. The temple itself is understood as a place where mediums may actively practise 'doctrinal knowledge' by serving patients through their mediumship. Rather than a place for meditation and contemplation, mediums describe their temple as 'spiritual first aid', a place where they rapidly pass from one ritual to another in order to assist patients and indoctrinate disincarnate spirits.

Mediumistic development frames the experiences of mediumistic phenomena of those who arrive in the Vale as either already spontaneously manifesting or needing development. However, this does not imply a pregiven corpus of propositional knowledge that is passed down to mediums. I address the process of mediumistic development in the Vale as learning a way of knowing through lived experience, through a process of 'enskillment' (Ingold 2000), as an ongoing education of perception initially guided by instructors, situating the practice locally – that is, in engagement with the environment. In fact, another widely used expression is *'tem que sentir'* ('you have to feel it'), where *'sentir'* means both 'sensing' and 'feeling'. Drawing on neuroscientist Antonio Damasio's definitions, I refer to 'emotion' as a bodily response to a stimulus, and 'feeling' as the subjective perception of emotion (Damasio 2000). Different dimensions of learning spring from these ideas, which I have identified as being predominantly: embodied learning (somatosensory), intuitive learning (in which mediums attribute the source of intuition to spiritual beings), performative learning (ritualistic), conceptual learning and intersubjective learning.

Cognitive approaches alone have addressed the mind almost independently from the bodily dimension of religious experiences (Boyer 2001; Cohen 2007, 2008). Recent ethnographic approaches to religious learning consider the body precisely as the source of knowledge and experience – as being at the core of religious transmission (Berliner and Sarró 2009; Halloy 2015). As Vasconcelos has proposed in his research among mediums of a Brazilian Spiritualist Doctrine in Cape Verde, namely Christian Rationalism, 'that sense of revelation, of intimate certainty, which is usually called belief only springs when getting ideas about spiritual entities and being moved by them come together' (2009: 130). Likewise, Luhrmann distinguished between learning categories and learning practices in Pagan Magic, whereby Pagan cognitive categories were not straightforwardly accepted by the new practitioners but 'They confirmed those ideas in their everyday experience of their world, and when their practice led them to experience magical power in their bodies, the discourse seemed much more real' (Luhrmann 2010: 220).

Among the elder masters I met in the Vale – mostly those who were among the first to be consecrated Adjuntos de Povo Raiz by Tia Neiva in 1978 – many recalled their first day of development in the 1970s as an immediate immersion in spiritual work, with Tia Neiva handing them a *fita* (the yellow and purple string worn around the medium's chest) and telling them to go and indoctrinate spirits. The current instructors in the development bring forth Tia Neiva's ideal that the medium should 'learn by doing'. As Mestre Diego told me, 'you have to feel spiritual knowledge: it is not a study (*estudo*), it is a state (*estado*)'. Hence, cosmology and spiritual knowledge become significant for mediums because of the way they are perceived and experienced and by the way they are embodied and act upon mediums, producing a transformation in their cognition. In other words, the practice and experience of teachings precede cognitive transformation in beliefs.

'Performative learning' relies on the repetitive practical execution of rituals. Ritual performances in the Vale are highly repetitive and formalized, following prescribed written scripts that refer to both the verbal and the choreographic elements of the performance, indicating the different sequences of opening, invocations and spirit incorporations, among other things. Mediums in development receive a short summarized explanation of the ritual sequence, which they may refer to before participating to the ritual, but to a greater extent the experiential aspects of the repetitive practice are at the core of learning how to perform a ritual.

'Conceptual learning' is addressed in the advanced development classes – in preparation for the initiations – and more substantially in the last course that leads to the third initiation called *Centúria*, when mediums already possess a certain amount of practical experience (that is – between six months and a year of practice) in assisting patients in rituals. During this course, the instructors explain the meaning of ritual actions in greater detail and their effects upon life beyond matter. The rigidity of ritual scripts and more or less controlled bodily postures may be a common aspect with Afro-Brazilian religions, particularly in Candomblé Ketu and in the Xangô in Recife, whereby the mediumistic public learning process of the latter entails what is called 'indoctrinating the body' (Halloy 2015). However, the explanation of the meaning of ritual actions is almost absent from the initiatory process in Afro-Brazilian religions. Learning in Candomblé, as Goldman has pointed out, does not entail a coherent set of teachings received from a master but requires putting together details gathered over years of learning the practice (2009: 109). Conversely, the Vale's advanced stage of mediumistic training features a 'doctrinal mode of transmission' (Whitehouse 2000; Whitehouse and Laidlaw 2004) with master instructors explaining aspects of what is referred to as 'doctrinal knowledge', such as: the dynamics of forces in rituals, the phenomenology of incarnation and disincarnation, descriptions of the afterlife, the spirit worlds and the categories of spirits, the aetiology of illness and different kinds of spiritual healing. They also explain the joint reincarnations of the Jaguars in different ancient civilizations and the purpose of redeeming their karmic debts from past lives through the spiritual healing of others. In this sense, conceptual learning in the Vale contributes along with other dimensions of learning to the articulation of notions of the self, adding a layer of discourse to somatic knowledge.

My use of the term 'intuitive learning' draws upon claims made by mediums that they received teachings from spiritual mentors by means of intuition: in some cases by the spirits they incorporated; in other cases by those incorporated by other *aparás* or during states of mediumization. Some *aparás* affirmed that they retained certain memories of the *pretos velhos*' teachings passed on through them to patients, especially when these teachings were relevant to a situation that they themselves were experiencing. They held that the spirit mentors select patients who are going through similar situations to those of the mediums assisting them, so that all participants can learn something from the spirit. Another case is that of Marco, a *doutrinador* in his thirties born and raised in the Vale, who held that, during the beginning of his development, for each ritual the same spirit of Pai João de Enoque (Father John of Enoch) used to incorporate and instruct him on how to use his mediumship inside and outside the temple. He said he was advised by the spirit guide on techniques to protect himself when perceiving negative vibrations or places, such as using thought and images to create 'magnetic fields' around him, and how to transform negative energies into positive ones in order to cleanse social and physical environments. For instance, he said that once he perceived that an argument among a small group of people was being caused by a spirit, and he was able to transfer the spirit into the ritual of *Mesa Evangélica* through a visualization of the sacred space with the ritual being performed, which suddenly transformed the situation. One *apará* told me that she had a series of encounters with her spirit guide during a state of mediumization in which he taught her techniques to avoid losing connection with the spirit whilst in a mediumistic state of consciousness, and these techniques involved the visualization of a specific symbol that would immediately intensify that state of consciousness. Another medium held he had dreams where he attended group lectures delivered by a spirit mentor, during which he received some spiritual teachings.

From the beginning of the mediumistic development, spirit mentors, according to instructors, are responsible for teaching their mediums and 'shaping them as a crystal'. The above cases are not isolated, but they form the basis of most relationships between mediums and their individual spirit mentors, creating a bond that fosters the production of knowledge during mediumistic trance states. Mediums claim that the doctrine of the Amanhecer itself has a revelatory origin, as Tia Neiva claimed she was learning with spirit mentors such as Pai Seta Branca (Father White Arrow), Pai João de Enoque, Tiaozinho and Amanto. Similarly, in Shamanism, the initial role of spirits is that of teachers (Noll 1985: 449).

This spiritual knowledge, which mediums held they received intuitively in their relationship with their spirits, becomes relevant beyond an individual level once it is shared between mediums along with other spiritual experiences. The expression used in the Vale *'mestre ensinando mestre'* (master teaching master) refers to both the relationship between the instructor and the developing medium and to the form of intersubjective sharing of a lived-through knowledge that happens between mediums in informal situations. Knowledge transmission is not merely oral, but it is primarily experiential, with embodiment at the core of this process; notions before being accepted are sensed and then eventually shared.

In this sense, I propose to understand the process of learning spirit mediumship in the Vale as learning a way of knowing. Especially when considering that what matters to mediums is talking about their *experiences* of spirits rather than describing their *belief* in spirits. In fact, I have introduced this chapter by affirming that newcomers are not being transmitted a belief in the existence of spirits, but they learn how to feel and discern spirits. And this is a specific mode of knowing that urges us to shift our analytical stance from 'belief' to 'experience'. I thus moved beyond mind-centred approaches to explore the intertwining of cognitive, sensory and emotional processes in the articulation of notions of the body and the self during the process of learning to become a medium. But how does the articulation of the sense of self become crucial in the mediumistic development of the Vale do Amanhecer? If 'learning' as 'enskillment' implies situating the practice – that is, a practice that requires the medium to both extend into the spirits and discern between his or her self and the spirits that need to be controlled – through the education of perception (Ingold 2000) then mediums need to develop their sense of self.

In the next chapters, I broaden the perspective in order to understand the role of mediumistic practices in the Vale do Amanhecer in relation to the wider Brazilian context of spiritual healing. I argue that the development of an embodied relation with the sacred and of a specific notion of the body re-establishes spiritual commitment within a context of intense religious mobility. Then, I will show how bodily enskillment and embodied knowledge are crucial in cases in which the mediumistic development is used as a complementary therapy for addictions and mental disorders. Finally, I will illuminate another kind of discernment between pathological and spiritual experiences and show how therapeutic trajectories may lead patients to an initiatory spiritual path.

## Notes

Earlier versions of different parts of this chapter were originally published as: Pierini, E. 2016. 'Becoming a Spirit Medium: Initiatory Learning and the Self in the Vale do Amanhecer', *Ethnos* 81(2): 290–314; and Pierini, E. 2016. 'Embodied Encounters: Ethnographic Knowledge, Emotion and Senses in the Vale do Amanhecer's Spirit Mediumship', *Journal for the Study of Religious Experience* 2: 25–49.
  1. Translated from the original in Italian.
  2. Translated from the original in Portuguese.

*Chapter 8*

# SPIRITUAL ROUTES

The Brazilian religious meshwork presents diversified spaces for experiencing the sacred, proposing different ways of being-in-the-world according to the different experiences, cosmologies and values that constitute both established and emergent religions and spiritual groups. On the one hand, Brazilian religiosity features an intense mobility, marked in part by a continuous passage of some religiously inclined Brazilians from one spiritual practice to another, and in part by their often simultaneous participation in different religions. On the other hand, this mobility is accompanied by an ongoing transit of symbols, ideas and practices between religions (Pierini 2009). The way Brazilians move within and between religions has been addressed by Brazilian scholars as religious 'transit', 'wandering', or 'itinerancy' (Amaral 1993; Pierucci 1997; Camurça 2003; Siqueira 2009), primarily through the perspective of social inclusion. According to Brandão, the diversified 'religious offer' experienced in everyday life reflects different modalities of the self 'coated with an aura of sacredness', as well as different social identities, such as one being 'a convert, a believer, a worshipper, an affiliate, a fanatic, a militant, a sectarian, a suppliant … an environmental-esoteric-vegetarian-announcer of the New Age, a sorcerer, a seeker, a saint, and even an unbeliever' (2004: 279).[1] In this 'Brazilian religious field', Camurça envisions 'hybrid religious spaces' as working 'in opposition to an unequal and exclusive society, offering plenty of healing, refuge and identity', referring to the Vale do Amanhecer in this context as one of the 'most genuine' Brazilian religion that has succeeded in this purpose (2003: 51).[2]

Besides scholars approaching the phenomenon of religious mobility through the lens of the need for social inclusion, there are studies that focus on the dynamics of 'religious consumption' through the perspective of a 'religious marketplace', discussed in Chapter One. According to Greenfield,

> Brazilians trek from one religion group to the next until they obtain what they request, but once they convert, there is no guarantee they will remain loyal. Should their next crisis not be resolved by the spirits of the group whose rituals they practice, they will turn to another group and still other until satisfaction is eventually obtained. Consequently, the average Brazilian may become a member of several religions over the course of a lifetime, giving us at the socio-logical level a pattern of individuals moving, or circulating, from religion to religion over the time. (Greenfield 2008: 151)

This perspective can be read in line with sociological approaches proposing that individuals are trained as consumers looking for instantaneous satis-faction in many spheres of their lives, including religion (Bauman 2004). Prandi refers to a sort of 'religious consumer' rather than a 'convert', whose commitment to religion is significantly reduced (2000: 38). Hence, he sug-gests that the increased mobility of people from one religion to the next undermines the idea of 'conversion': changing religion is no longer per-ceived as a drastic change in one's personal life (ibid.).

It is possible to envisage a third perspective, which approaches religious mobility as closely related to an ongoing construction of a sense of self. Whilst the 'social inclusion' model tends to consider religion as compen-satory, the 'religious marketplace' one focuses upon a sort of transaction. Both these models highlight the pragmatic aspect of religious behaviour, which certainly is a conspicuous trait informing religious choices. However, these perspectives downplay the role of spiritual experience. In this chapter, I will address the movement across religions as 'spiritual routes' and 'tra-jectories' so as to avoid the use of terms that evoke a sense of planning, which is seldom part of spiritual experience in Brazil. Conversely, 'routes' and 'trajectories' can be redesigned and reoriented and convey the sense of transition, of 'moving through', and the repositioning of choices according to life events at any given time. I will explore the spiritual routes that spon-taneously emerged from mediums' narratives as they revealed an ongoing construction of their sense of self. I will also examine how these mediums position their experiences within the Vale do Amanhecer, through their mediumistic practice. In doing so, I will illuminate how the Vale attracts and accommodates people with such different backgrounds and religious experiences through the global character of its discourse.

## Spiritual Routes

In the temples of the Amanhecer I visited, both in Brazil and Europe, when a medium talked about their spiritual experiences, they frequently began by recounting a story of their route through different religions and spiritual practices, eventually marked by a transformative encounter with the Vale do Amanhecer and the spirit world. What triggered them to undertake their own spiritual routes away from mainstream religions? How did they experience and make sense of such different practices? What these narratives shared in common was an emphasis on the empirical, participative, ritualistic and bodily aspects of their experiences. More specifically, those who embarked on spiritual routes to encounter the divine and who eventually came to experience mediumistic practice sought immediate and embodied forms to experience such an encounter and tended to experience those religions that supported an idea of the multiplicity of the self. Particularly, some mediums told me that before developing mediumship in the Vale do Amanhecer, they were looking for a religion that could provide them with an active participation in rituals, identifying Catholic and some Evangelical rituals as marked by 'passive' participation, focused mainly on 'listening'. João, a young medium *doutrinador* in his twenties, told me that in his view,

> In the Catholic Church there is God. In the Vale do Amanhecer we have the same God. The main difference is that in the Church you pray to the saints, but they seem to be unreachable. In the Vale do Amanhecer, through the incorporation of these spiritual entities, the contact between the person and the entity is restored. A contact that is more direct, sensed and emotionally felt.

The immediacy of the relationship with the divine – that is, non-mediated by a religious authority – was a crucial point also in Aldemir's experience. Aldemir was a *doutrinador* in his thirties who moved to Brasília to live in the Vale, before opening a Temple of the Amanhecer in Cambridgeshire, UK. In telling me about his previous experiences in Catholicism and several Protestant churches, he said he used to perceive a sort of authority in the priest or minister that seemed to be too 'earthly' compared to the spiritual experience he was longing for. In his opinion, 'the need for a closer contact with the sacred arises from the spiritual anxiety of those whom are in search of a sense of self, their origins and their mission in this life'. The contact with spirits of light, he said, could encourage self-awareness and inner knowledge; and by establishing a causal relationship between different past incarnations, it is possible to trace the reasons of present sorrows and to encounter one's life-path to follow for one's moral and spiritual evolution. These words resonated with what another medium once told me: 'since I arrived in the Vale do Amanhecer, it seems as though I have opened a book and this book is narrating my story'.

Carol initially travelled with her husband from the US to Brazil to visit Abadiânia, the centre of the medium João de Deus (John of God), where they had their 'first experience of the invisible forces of spirits' and began working on themselves and decided to quit their jobs in the US and start a new life in Brazil. After two years living in Abadiânia, they decided to travel across Brazil. Having heard about the Vale from a friend in Abadiânia, they visited the temple and subsequently decided to develop their mediumship. They both initiated as *doutrinadores*. Carol describes the two years she spent in the Vale as a transformative experience, a shift in the sense of self:

I think that what I wanted from the Vale was the training. I felt that it was time to let go of an intermediary, of someone who had the ear for the entities, which is sort of the old model, whether it is the priest, the doctor, the Pope … it is always like 'oh, I am not good enough, they are special, I am not'. I developed my intuition. I felt, as a psychotherapist, that I would be more of a *doutrinadora*: speaking, helping, making sense of things to people … but I wanted to directly experience it. At the time, I thought that the medium 'downloading' things is the true medium, like being possessed by the spirit. But the *doutrinador* 'uploads' the energy, so I thought that is not a real medium; it is a second-class medium. It was kind of difficult, but then what really happened – it was that intuition … I felt that there was more than just a voice with me, that looking back it has always led me. We did the development in a year and a half, so I think that the evolution happens alongside that. Something created itself within me, no matter where I am, there is something with me always, not just when I wear the clothes and go to the temple. I felt a shift in health, well-being, sense of self, empowerment, rebirth.

I understand more that I am here to fulfil a destiny. I was a rebellious person just searching … very heavy … it is pretty much the opposite now. I feel that it is such a miracle that this could happen in a life. I see many people now able to shift their sense of self, going from a reactive human being in a situation they didn't like so much, to understanding themselves as a spiritual being in a situation that they welcome. Everything is sort of shifting and I think that is because I am remembering things. I don't really have 'oh, yes, in 1630 I was this and that …', it is about bringing from all of the past lives so that now I can use them in this life time, and it is so transformative. The Gregas' [Greeks, her phalanx] energy to me always felt so powerful; what is now showing up is the sacred feminine powerful person, so are the dresses also. Also because the phalanx has very powerful women, they are so chummy, but a lot of these ladies are also like 'out of my way!' and I like that!

The question of the ongoing construction of a sense of self is at the core of contemporary spiritual experiences. When this process takes the form of a spiritual quest, this quest usually features a frantic passage through different religious groups and spiritual practices that propose what scholars have addressed as a 'sacralization of the self' (Csordas 1994; Heelas 1996)[3]– especially, I suggest, by experimenting with those religions that support a conceptualization of the multiplicity of the self. Maria's experience may well illustrate this. Maria, an *apará* in her thirties, presented one of the most complex religious biographies I came across. In her childhood, she firstly attended with her family a Catholic Church and then a Baptist one, passing to the Mormons in her teenage years and then spending two years in the Christian Church of Brazil. She said that when she got married she was asked to leave that church, since her husband was a 'non-believer'. She experienced Tibetan Buddhism and the Buddhism of the Soka Gakkai, but since her belief in spiritual beings was not part of these religions, she moved on to Kardecism, where she developed her mediumship. She then began to accompany her husband to the Anglican Church he attended. While studying Philosophy and Theology at University, she went on to learn about many other religious groups, including Gnosticism, Rosicrucians and Afro-Brazilian religions, although without fully participating in their practices. Through an encounter with the Franciscan Fathers, she had what she defined as 'a mystic involvement' with St. Francis of Assisi and participated in charitable social works with street children. After graduating, she travelled abroad teaching English, experiencing other cultures and religions. Years later she was diagnosed with Leukaemia and sought treatment with three different doctors when a friend invited her to visit the Vale do Amanhecer. She maintained that in passing through rituals her illness disappeared. She continued to attend rituals as a patient and three months later a *preto velho* told her she was going to have a daughter, which she thought was impossible after many failed attempts and treatments. Soon after, she fell pregnant with a daughter and later, again, with a son. Once she developed her mediumship in the Vale as an *apará*, she felt she could continue her route of 'learning through religion' within the Vale do Amanhecer.

Sitting on the floor of the porch of her house in the Vale while playing with her children, Maria summed up her spiritual route, telling me how she learned from Eastern religions to see things as a whole through the law of karma. Through Taoism, she embraced a view of the collective dimension rather than an individual one. She learned spiritual transcendence through Amerindian beliefs, and the importance of humility and charity with the Franciscans. In Kardecism and Umbanda, she received teachings from the spirits and became conscious of her self-development. However, she noted how in the passage from one religion to another, the new belief could clash against her previous experiences, creating an inner conflict. She stressed that in the Vale do Amanhecer she did not need to renounce her religious past. She did not need to renounce Buddhism as she worked on redeeming her karma with the Oriental line of spirits and forces from the Himalayas; nor Kardecism, because the Vale is grounded in a Spiritualist philosophy; nor Umbanda and Candomblé, as she incorporated *pretos velhos* and *caboclos*, and she works the forces of Yemanjá and other *orixás*. In the rituals, she called upon the forces of Ancient Egypt with Amon-Ra and the forces of Ancient Greece invoking Apollo and the Pythia through the work with her phalanx, while she praised Jesus Christ to release the spirits and heal the patients.

Mestre Antônio, a *doutrinador* in his thirties, along his spiritual route had experienced Catholicism, Spiritism, several esoteric groups and Afro-Brazilian religions. He said that the Vale do Amanhecer represented for him the space where he could manifest his religious identities simultaneously: 'As you arrive in the Vale do Amanhecer', he said, 'you find the religious knowledge that you already own, but with new answers'. Similarly, José affirmed that when he arrived in the Vale about twenty years earlier he felt as if he was in 'a spiritual and thematic complex' that he had already known. Visually, the familiarity of symbols contributed to this perception. What really caught his attention, though, was that both mediums and spirits respected his free will, and so he felt as if he was the 'master of himself' because the Vale provided him with 'the conditions to acquire a map to find the answers to the big questions around the self and the spirit world'.

Tereza, a social scientist retired from a university, was advised by a colleague to bring her sick father to the Vale about thirty years earlier. She said she was a catechist in a Catholic Church at that time, but she felt she had to follow an 'external model of knowledge'. In contrast, she said that since she developed as a medium *doutrinadora* in the Vale she felt free to create and follow her own 'inner knowledge, which emerged from the inside out', as well as her own pattern of participation. Because of the doctrinal principle of respecting free will, she explained, mediums experience a great freedom of participation, and once trained in how to conduct themselves in and outside rituals they are considered to be ultimately responsible for themselves, so they may choose when to go to the temple and which ritual to participate in by following their intuition.

I used to visit another scholar and friend, Carlos, a *doutrinador* in his late thirties who lectures in history of religion at a university, engaging in long conversations ranging from doctrinal discourses to scholarly debates on Brazilian religions. Although he came from a family with a Catholic background, he never held a strong relationship with the Church. He rather explained his spiritual quest through these words:

I felt the lack of mysticism and explanation of the spirit world. Since I was a teenager, I have read a lot, and I became interested in other religions. During my spiritual quest, I passed through Spiritism, some initiatory groups and Afro-Brazilian religions. So I have always had religious references other than Catholicism, and I was looking for a space where I could express them altogether, and this is what the Vale do Amanhecer represented for me. The encounters with spiritual beings, the confirmations they give us, represent our evidence and ground us in this mystical universe of the Amanhecer. This relation with the extra-human world grounds our truths and our being in the doctrine.

The sense of affinity with a particular kind of spiritual practice and the possibility to understand it through the lens of past lives marked Victor's first approach to the Vale. Victor, in his fifties, was a doctor working in a local hospital who had developed his mediumship as an *apará* twenty-five years earlier. Recalling his arrival in the Vale, he told me he was initially Catholic and how along his spiritual route he began incorporating spirits while attending Umbanda ceremonies. Then, he passed through Kardecism, after which he went on to learn about various Evangelical churches, such as the Congregação Brasileira and the Baptist Church. Eventually, he visited the Vale's temple, seeking healing for his daughter in rituals. He said he was look-ing for a form of faith that could bring him closer to God. 'Kardecism', he said, 'is an excellently codified doctrine, with a lot of study and lectures and less ritualism'. In the Kardecist centre, though, the manifestation of his *preto velho* from Umbanda was not accepted. Thus, as he moved on to the Vale, not only was he able to incorporate his *preto velho* but he also felt a greater affinity with a highly ritualistic practice. He then thought it was his *preto velho* who brought him to the Vale. Moreover, the idea that his social and professional status would not determine his hierarchical position emphasized the feeling that he was just one medium and missionary working among other mediums. He stressed that at first glance the Vale appeared to him as a mixture of the religions of the present; he then understood that it is rather about fragments of past epochs in which the Jaguars lived. Since then, he said he felt 'localized within the doctrine, as a way to transform one's karma from past lives and to understand one's self and what is happening in present life'.

Different levels of spirituality, affinity and participation emerge from these mediums' narratives with a great emphasis on the empirical and ritu-alistic aspects. When religious teachings were transmitted, they were not merely passively accepted, but they were actively reinterpreted through the framework of past experiences and subjectively rearticulated. That is, along the routes that led them to the Vale, they seemed to have selected some discourses, practices and teachings of each experienced religion that were more compatible with their experiences, which have then been eclectically reinterpreted within the construction of a sense of self. Indeed, along these passages in and between religions, they experienced a state of 'liminality', engaging themselves in a self-reflexive process; and liminal states produce the highest pitch of self-consciousness (Turner 1974: 255).

Their initial interest in the Vale do Amanhecer was certainly facilitated by the sense of familiarity that they experienced upon arrival. Those elements already encountered in their religious past, in terms of ideas, symbols and practices, soon became points of access to their route undertaken within the Vale. Such a process of familiarization involved an 'interpretive drift' – that is, a progressive 'shift in the interpretation of events' (Luhrmann 1989: 312). At a discursive level, not only did new mediums progressively rearticulate their sense of self transcending the present life but also their own biographical narratives through the broader narrative of the Jaguars with their joint incarnations in different civilizations. The doctrine's narrative is, thus, interwoven in mediums' personal narratives through a process of 'emplotment' (Ricoeur 1984: 54), in which discordant elements, such as the clashing beliefs previously experienced in their routes, are rearticulated in a meaningful narrative, the time of which also reconfigures mediums' temporal experience. The re-incarnational narrative of the Jaguars bridges past lives in different cultures and religions to the present one. Thus, the sense of self becomes transhistorical, extending beyond the single lifespan when calling upon forces from one's past incarnation, wearing ritual vestments representing those incarnations, or discussing with spirits events from past lives for the purpose of karmic release. Indeed, as Jaguars, mediums are redeeming their individual and collective karma by rescuing spirits.

## Beyond Ritual: Extensibility and Emotions in Mediumistic Experience

In the previous chapter, I proposed that the idea of a multidimensional and extended self is not merely transmitted but is experienced beforehand at a perceptual level in mediumistic practice. Here, I intend to expand the perspective upon rituals to include the levels of lived experience and discourse in order to highlight the pervasiveness of the idea of extensibility in mediumistic experience.

Anthropologists have given relevance to the complex processes occurring before and after the performance of rituals, understanding rituals as points where these trajectories interweave (Rosaldo 1984, 1993; Favret-Saada 1990). Assuming that the processual trajectories meeting in confluence with ritual are, in this case, the spiritual and therapeutic routes of participants, ritual then becomes the space-temporal dimension in which these trajectories intersect. Then, through the concurrent expression of different aspects of the self, the sense of self is reconfigured, producing an inner transformation. This transformation is, thus, possible as ritual helps integrate different aspects of one's self and previous experiences. Particularly those elements perceived as conflicting, causing a sense of unease, frustration and incompleteness, seem to acquire coherence in the Vale do Amanhecer, as I have illustrated with the experience of Maria during her own spiritual route. Primarily, these aspects have the possibility to be expressed and manifested simultaneously and poly-phonically without being denied, releasing emotions in rituals.

Mediums' discourses about rituals are consistently permeated by the idea of the extensibility of rituals beyond their physical and performative boundaries. The healing work is not confined to the ritual alone, nor is it concerned with the physical level, but it is directed to the evolution of incar-nated and disincarnate spirits. Indeed, even though rituals in the Vale have a precise structure with fixed opening and closing formulas to concentrate the forces, the specific work with incarnate and disincarnate participants is held to begin before and to continue after its physical enactment by mediums. Instructors explained that the spiritual mentors begin work with mediums and patients long before they arrive at the temple: patients' energies are worked on by spirit guides in the long queues of people waiting to enter the ritual. *Obsessores* and *sofredores* are also said to be pre-treated before entering the ritual space. Then the ritual continues in dimensions beyond physical matter, where, according to Tia Neiva, the spirits released by mediums continue to receive treatment by spirits of light with the assistance of mediums who visit the Red Channel through astral projection at night while asleep. For this reason, mediums say that 'the Jaguars work twenty-four hours a day', and some reported vivid memories of their experiences in the etheric plane during sleep states (Lacerda 2010).[4] Ritual is thus under-stood as being a physical manifestation, a kind of apex of broader processes occurring beyond matter and involving all its participants. Ritual spaces are also considered to extend into the etheric plane and into specific sectors of the Red Channel and also beyond the higher astral plane, where healing forces are said to originate. This idea of temporal and spatial extensibility triggered by a ritual informs mediums' experiences and being-in-the-world.

In a practice that features rigid ritual scripts, I found myself asking what, then, makes the performance of a ritual different from another? Ritual creativity was experienced by the mediums I spoke to as the possibility to perceive the forces in the form of emotions and feelings and to express them, along with their multidimensional self, through their emission and chant. As a nymph said: 'Through the emission and chant, we invoke the forces of our transcendence that we left in past lives, in the spirit world, so I am projected towards other dimensions and the feeling of these emotions and vibrations remain with us even for days after the ritual'. I could not quite grasp the intensity of rituals when they comprised of more than ten consecutive emissions until I was trained to become aware of the perceptual dimension through mediumistic development. Before then, I found it quite hard and tiring to sit for three hours or more to follow the rituals of *Turigano* or *Leito Magnetico*, which comprised over thirty emissions and chants, including those of each phalanx summoning the forces from the past lives of the Jaguars. Affect and emotions in the ritual shape the different ways it is experienced at each performance. In the case of spirit incorporation, the uniqueness of each ritual is enhanced by the emotional and verbal content conveyed by the spirit's manifestation. Mediums experience each incorporation with a varying intensity – that is, according to the state of each medium, the people participating and the spiritual beings intervening in ritual, both manifested and not. Each position occupied by a medium is also significant for the diversified experiences it may offer. For a *doutrinador*, representing and projecting the forces of a *Cavaleiro da Lança Vermelha* (Knight of the Red Lance, representing disobsessive healing) 'feels different' from representing the *Cavaleiro da Lança Lilas* (Knight of the Lilac Lance, representing spiritual healing) even though both spirits belong to the same hierarchy. Feeling and sensation underpin ritual experience as much as learning mediumship and constructing a relationship with spirit guides involve bodily experience.

## Rehabilitating Commitment in Contemporary Religious Experience

In Chapter Three, I anticipated a distinction between mediumistic experience in the Vale and New Age spirituality. I should now develop this distinction in the light of the discussion of my interlocutors' spiritual routes. The question is to understand why mediums reject the association some visitors and researchers made with the 'New Age Movement' and why adopting this analytical category could be inappropriate and problematic. Even though the Vale frequently attracts spiritual seekers involved in the New Age Movement, who may visit the temples and participate in rituals as patients, many of these when considering to be initiated have expressed their discomfort with the issues of hierarchical structure, highly ritualized practice with defined scripts and exclusive commitment at the level of ritualistic practice. Explaining this distinction is crucial to understanding the peculiarity of the Vale do Amanhecer in the context of Brazilian religiosity.

Even though commitment in the Vale is not related to the frequency of attendance at the temple – as both attendance and the decision to enter or leave the Order are down to the free will of the medium – it is rather understood as responsibility towards a practice directed to patients, and the body becomes relevant to this discourse. The instructors in the development explained that each religious ritual practice works with a different energetic frequency, and through the initiatory path the body of the medium is developed to accommodate and work with a specific frequency. Mediums may visit and interact with other religious groups; however, they are advised that they should avoid participating actively in other kinds of ritual practices. This means that, if invited, mediums may attend a mass, a wedding, and so on, but they should avoid participating in the performance of the ritual, as they would feel in their bodies the change of energies and forces acting in other rituals. The impact of different forces would then be felt as a form of unbalance or bodily discomfort, which has consequences for mediumistic practice in rituals and hence for patients. To explain this, instructors often used the metaphor of an electric device plugged in to a socket with a different voltage. Thus, mixing energies by participating in different spiritual practices is not conceived as integrating new forces; it is rather perceived as damaging the device (*aparelho*) – that is, the medium's body in its various dimensions (physical, etheric, spiritual and so on). This precaution indirectly interrupts the dynamic of moving from one religion to another, resulting in a spiritual experience exclusively immersed in the Vale. Such an interruption is similar to a process described by Luiz Eduardo Soares when assessing Santo Daime in the context of what he called a 'New Religious Consciousness' (2014). Whilst initially appearing as a manifestation of that phenomenon, through closer involvement, Soares came to reject the view of Daimistas as 'new agers'. He had to reconsider Santo Daime as 'establishing a point of inflation of the dynamics of the field' from which it emerged and as urging 'a proto-institutionalizing or routinizing pause, a suspension of the mystical circulation' typical of spiritual wandering, proposing a place for permanent and intense spiritual commitment (Soares 2014: 67).

As we have tackled in depth notions of the body as articulated by mediumistic development, it should be noted how central the body was to my interlocutors' narratives of their spiritual experiences. Those who presented a past spiritual route – intense religious mobility in seeking an embodied relation with the divine – before choosing to be initiated affirmed that the Vale helped them draw together the elements and experiences of their past spiritual routes, engendering new meanings. They experienced the highly ritualized practice as a way to engage their bodies and live through their mediumship in a safe and protected setting. Since at each initiatic stage the body is prepared to support different kinds and increasing amounts of energy, they also understood hierarchy and rituals with prescribed scripts as protection from unsolicited energies and interferences, which may be better controlled by more experienced mediums holding higher ranks. For this reason, the long lines of mediums in rituals follow a hierarchical classification, so that the bodies of those in front with higher classifications are more prepared to face the impact of strong energies that are gradually distributed down the rest of the line. In this sense, the questions of hierarchy, prescribed ritual scripts and exclusive commitment, which differentiate the Vale from the New Age Movement, become meaningful through the bodily grounding of this spiritual practice.

One should consider that rather than viewing new members' past spiritual routes as contributing to a supposed growing hybridity of the Vale's rituals, differently to many new religious movements, individual contribution such as the creation of new rituals or the inclusion of new elements drawn from past experiences is strongly discouraged, for it is considered to undermine Tia Neiva's teachings and her discourse about the spiritual origins of the doctrine. Since Tia Neiva's death, a centralized hierarchy favours strict control over the maintenance of the formal ritualistic system left by its founder. Members of the Vale consider individual intervention to be undermining not only to Tia Neiva's revelations and her legitimizing role but also to ritual efficacy. For this reason, the execution of rituals follows a precise script (both verbal and choreographic) contained in the 'Livro de Leis e Chaves Ritualisticas' (Book of Laws and Ritualistic Keys), which elder masters present as being compiled in 1977 by Tia Neiva channelling the instructions of the spiritual mentors of the doctrine, such as Pai João de Enoque. After Tia Neiva's death, a tendency towards separation and the creation of new small-scale groups derived from the Vale prevailed over the accommodation of new elements.[5] Attempts to change even the wording of rituals have contributed to the emergence of internal conflicts – such as the schisms presented in Chapter Two – which interested those in higher ranks in the hierarchy – occupied by *Adjuntos Arcanos* and *Trinos* and including Tia Neiva's sons – rather than new members. Some flexibility is observed in external temples, but it is limited to changes in the number of mediums composing a ritual, adaptation of sacred spaces and execution of special spiritual works in response to the specific physical arrangement and availability of people to ensure ritual performances and does not extend to new elements from participants' past spiritual experiences in other religious groups. Those who join the Vale are in some sense invited to participate in a ritualistic system presented as having 'originated in the spirit world' and that although rigorous in its formal aspects undergoes an ongoing revitalization through highly emotional encounters and interactions with the spirits. Those who challenge the appropriate behaviour either by participating in other spiritual or religious rituals or making use of alcohol or drugs are rarely formally sanctioned because of the principle of free will. Sometimes, especially in smaller temples, they may not be permitted to work directly with patients. Mostly, they lose the trust of the community, as other mediums may consider their mediumistic practice as less effective or even harmful in some cases and avoid working with them. In most cases, they are advised by instructors to continue to pass as patients and speak to the *pretos velhos* about their situation to see if the Vale is the right place to practise their mediumship.

To visitors and newcomers, the Vale do Amanhecer stands out distinctively for what is perceived as its prominent hybridity – expressed through its strong visual impact and being grounded in a discourse developed from the mediumistic experiences, visions and revelations of the founder. Due to its global character, this discourse attracts people from different backgrounds, articulating and localizing through rituals a great variety of contemporary religious experiences (Pierini 2016a, 2016c).

Most interestingly, if the mobility of people through religions undermines 'commitment' (Prandi 2000), in the entanglement of human-spirit trajectories of the Brazilian religious meshwork, the Vale do Amanhecer re-habilitates 'commitment' as meaningful for its spiritual practice. It does so through a multilayered learning process that cultivates a particular sensory experience informing specific notions and understandings of the body and the self. Indeed, spiritual routes and therapeutic trajectories converge in the mediumistic development, and the process of learning approaches both through the production of embodied notions. If along their journeys my interlocutors experienced liminal states that produced the highest pitch of self-consciousness, my point is that it is precisely through the process of learning that the new notions of the self were articulated through bodily experience.

## Notes

1. Translated from the original in Portuguese.
2. Translated from the original in Portuguese.
3. Heelas (1996) refers to the affirmation of the spiritual potential of every human being as part of a divine essence.
4. Mestre Lacerda has gathered together written memories of his experiences that he defines as 'beyond matter' in his book *A Vida Fora da Matéria* (Lacerda 2010).
5. A first instance occurred after Tia Neiva's death, when Mário Sassi with a restricted group of mediums began to develop a ritual manifestation of a new category of spirits known as the Great Initiates, supposedly predicted by Tia Neiva but interrupted by her death. This practice encountered the strong opposition of the other *Trinos*, which resulted in Mário Sassi's departure from the Vale in order to found the Universal Order of the Great Initiates in 1990. He ultimately returned to the Vale towards the end of his life.

*Chapter 9*

# THERAPEUTIC TRAJECTORIES

## Therapeutic Trajectories Intertwining with Spiritual Routes

For many of those attending the temples of the Amanhecer, the Vale goes beyond being a new spiritual practice to experience. Their first approach was that of patients arriving in a 'spiritual first aid' (*pronto soccorro spiritual*). As a medium told me, what was meaningful to him in his first experience in the Vale as a patient was the fact of receiving free spiritual treatment and, especially, understanding that he himself was able to help others through mediumship. Realizing that one is able to help and heal others is often described by my interlocutors as being a 'revelation', a turning point in their lives, as it reverses the role of someone who is in need of help to one of being healer. Some experiences of spiritual routes, then, interweave with therapeutic trajectories and vice versa – trajectories that variably unfolded between biomedicine and other spiritual approaches to well-being.

As anticipated in the previous chapter, Victor, besides his spiritual quest through religions, had also experienced a therapeutic trajectory with his daughter. Upon his return from travelling in the Middle East, his one-year-old daughter spent eight months with severe dysentery. Being himself a doctor, he said he had tried every possible medical resource and consulted several specialists without finding any scientific explanation for the persistence of the disease. Since he already had a Spiritualist background and had heard of the Vale, he decided to visit the temple with his daughter to pass through the rituals. They passed together through the rituals of *Tronos* and *Cura*, and as soon as the ritual of *Junção* began, his daughter suddenly began to scream in acute pain and fainted. They rushed her to the hospital, and the doctor said she was asleep in a stable condition. The morning after, the symptoms had disappeared. He said that as a doctor he had no medical explanation for her sudden recovery, but as a medium he understood that through the disobsessive mechanism of the ritual an *obsessor* spirit that caused the physical disease had been removed, even though the process of disconnection had been quite painful. In this case, illness was considered to be caused by a spirit for karmic purposes, rather than as a result of a mediumistic disorder, such as in the next case.

Denise, a retired school teacher who has spent over thirty years in the Vale as an *apará*, was raised in a Catholic family and studied in a convent school. As a teenager, she said she began to experience mediumistic phenomena and attended an Umbanda centre, where she sought an explanation but felt unsure about developing her mediumship there so she opted for Kardecism when she moved to Brasília. However, she felt that the process of development in Kardecism was too slow for her needs, as she began to experience increasing symptoms, such as body tremors, tachycardia and drowsiness during the day followed by anxiety at night, which she had initially interpreted as physical illness. She consulted several cardiologists and psychologists without receiving any diagnosis. Thus, as she began losing control over those symptoms, which were also affecting her job, a colleague suggested that she attend the rituals of the Vale. Since she began developing her mediumship in the Vale in the 1980s, she has felt an increase in self-confidence and self-awareness through learning how to handle many different forces and has developed physical and emotional control and a kind dedication to others, which has changed the way she socially relates to people. In her words: 'When I feel heaviness, I participate in rituals where I can release suffering spirits. When I feel a pressure on my chest, I know that I need to incorporate my *caboclo*. I feel the need to work in rituals for a complete physical, emotional and spiritual realization, knowing that the greatest benefit is for patients'.

In several cases, mediums told me how they came to the Vale accompanying a relative or a friend and eventually experienced a sense of revelation through the highly emotional encounter with spiritual beings, or with Tia Neiva when she was alive. Conceição, an *apará* in her sixties, used to live in the nearby town of Planaltina since the 1950s. When she was twelve years old, she fell ill with what according to her doctor was a congestion, but she then entered into what she described as a 'coma-like' state for two days. Her parents' friends, who had recently opened a Spiritist centre in Planaltina, thought it was a spiritual illness and gave her a *passe magnético* (that is, the application of magnetic force to her body). As soon as they applied the *passe*, she suddenly woke up screaming and started smashing things around her. She considered this episode to be her first spiritual phenomenon. When she got married, her six-month-old daughter fell ill so she took her to a local hospital where she was mistakenly treated for asthma. As her conditions worsen, she was hospitalized for eighteen months in Brasília for heart disease and pneumonia. One day, Conceição was visited by her neighbour, who told her, 'I am a Spiritist and I have to give you a message: your daughter's illness is a spiritual problem, and she needs a spiritual intervention. I know that a woman, Dona Neiva, just moved to live in a farm out of town, and I think she can help her. João is going to take you there by carriage'. As Conceição told me,

> Eventually, he accompanied me to meet this woman. As I arrived in the Vale, there was absolutely nothing around there; no roads, only a straw hut where she received people. It was 1969, and Tia Neiva had just moved there about two months earlier. Suddenly, she saw me from the distance; she came to me dressed in white and asked if my daughter was ill and if I wanted to talk to her. She invited me to sit. She looked at me for a while and said, 'It is not your daughter's problem, it has to do with your spiritual mission. You have a great spiritual mission and this is a call for you'. I told her I was afraid of spirits. She said, 'from now onwards, you are not going to be afraid anymore'. I went back on the Saturday and a ritual of *Cura* was performed for my daughter by the spirit of Dr Ralph incorporated in a medium. A week later, a doctor looked at my daughter's ECG and said that there was a mistake; they couldn't be her results. He asked if he could repeat the test once again, and twice there was nothing at all. He said it could only be a miracle because she was cured. Today she is 42 years old and she had no heart problems since. Soon after her recovery, I began my mediumistic development as a *doutrinadora*, as Tia Neiva suggested, anticipating that I would change to an *apará* afterwards. This happened after eight years, and I am still an *apará* today.

Healing is a consistent feature of the practices of many different religious groups. Besides those people who find no solution for their infirmities in biomedicine, the lack of trust in the public health system and the limited access to the private one is such that some people seek complementary or alternative assistance through spiritual approaches to healing. Sônia Maluf noted how the Brazilian context features a 'therapeutic pluralism' involving a variety of informal practices as well as ritual practices with a therapeutic dimension that may lead to religious conversion (2005: 150). Moving on from a similar standpoint, Sidney Greenfield suggests that Brazilians move across religions seeking healing and 'only if the consumer is satisfied he or she is committed to make payment. This payment involves affiliating with the community' (2008: 100). In Greenfield's view – which is based on economic models of market analysis – Brazilian religious groups 'choose to offer healing or other forms of help by their supernatural(s) as the primary tools in their competition for converts' (ibid.). This kind of reciprocity may be true for some religious groups whose cosmologies are based on relationships of exchange and compensation between human and supernatural beings, or it may also be derived from Catholic tradition – as Greenfield suggests (ibid.). Whilst I do not exclude the fact that in some cases a sense of gratitude for recovery informed a person's decision to be initiated in the Vale, seldom has initiation in the Vale appeared as a 'payment in exchange for a service'. The Vale's cosmology departs from this dynamic. As instructors explain, when patients are invited to develop their mediumship, they do not owe anything to the Order, the mediums or spiritual beings, but by helping others by means of their mediumship for free, they may pay their own karmic debts, whether they would choose to do this in the Vale or in other religious groups. Through a deeper analysis of individual experiences, this decision is more relevantly related to the question of healing being perceived as an 'evidence' or 'confirmation' of the spirit world's intervention in a person's life and, thus, of having been given the opportunity to become the means, oneself, through which this intervention is made possible for others. Moreover, this practice becomes related to a particular form of construction and expression of selfhood. Therefore, I argue that the intertwinement of therapeutic trajectories with spiritual routes informs an initiatory path.

Spiritual healing is a broad field of scholarly interest, with a primary focus being that of the social aspects of patients' participation in healing practices and rituals and its results on a clinical level. Yet, little attention has been paid to those patients who have chosen to undertake an initiatory path for therapeutic purposes. Among the mediums participating in my research, a small minority had experienced mental disorders or alcohol and drug addiction before their mediumistic development. In this chapter, I will address this particular group so as to illustrate the complementary use of techniques of mediumistic development in the treatment of these particular cases. In doing so, I will explore those presented as the therapeutic aspects of the process of initiatory learning. More specifically, I will examine the ways in which this process acts upon cognitive, bodily and biographical levels, engendering a particular kind of embodied knowledge that was relevant in the therapeutic process.

# Mediumistic Approaches to Mental Disorders and Alcohol and Drug Addiction

*The Temple in the Mountains: From a Therapeutic Trajectory to a Spiritual Mission*

Between 2010 and 2013, I conducted fieldwork in temples of the Amanhecer in Northeast Brazil for approximately two months once or twice year. During my stays, I had the opportunity to be hosted on various occasions by a family running a small temple in the mountains. When I first visited their temple, it was at its first stage (called the evangelic stage), which means it was working as spiritual first aid, with the forces and ritual spaces suitable for a small number of rituals.[1] The temple was a small house with another two small buildings either side, one used as a dressing room and for other services, and the other one as the private house of the president of the temple. It was located on the outskirts of a village lying on the slopes of smooth green mountains covered by dense tropical vegetation, interspersed by banana plantations and crossed by several streams forming scattered waterfalls. Being used to the town of the Vale do Amanhecer with its ongoing flow of people, I was fascinated by the cosy atmosphere and simplicity of that temple. Mediums and patients attending rituals were locals – mainly peasants and housekeepers. What struck my attention was that in order to work in the temple most of them would walk for miles and miles down the mountains to catch an old truck that would drive them there, and they would only leave late in the evening to walk up the mountain again in the dark. Seldom were they interested in discussing doctrinal knowledge, but their experience was certainly an embodiment of faith.

Francisco, a middle-class man in his early sixties, came from the city. He encountered the Vale twelve years earlier through a health issue due to alcohol addiction. One day, while walking in a shopping centre with his wife, he came across an old friend married to a medium of the Vale. A few days later, his wife, led by the curiosity of that unexpected meeting with the medium, asked him to join her on a visit to the local temple of the Amanhecer in the city. Upon entering the temple, as a first reaction he wanted to leave as soon as possible, so he told his wife that she was free to attend as many times as she liked, but he would not return again. At the time, he was a non-practising Catholic and associated spirit rituals to some kind of evil practice.

Some years went by, and he had a career advancement that improved his financial situation to such an extent that he earned enough to build his own house. Yet, his wage increase also resulted in him spending more money on alcohol at weekends. One weekend, he realized he had lost control over his drinking and he was having severe pain in his stomach. He went to see a doctor, who referred him for a series of tests. It soon became clear that his health condition had significantly deteriorated, and his pain was caused by five ulcers in his stomach. The doctor told him and his wife that he was not aware of any available treatment for his condition, which was already at an advanced stage; he could only prescribe him an expensive medicine that would not cure him but could allow him to live for around ninety additional days. Francisco described his reaction as being more rational than emotional, since he went back home and began to sort out his job, investments and insurance so that he could ensure a comfortable living situation for his wife and sons even in his absence.

His wife then persuaded him to visit another temple of the Amanhecer, consisting of a small and simple house on the outskirts of the city. He passed into the ritual of *Tronos* with the spirit of a *preta velha*. Differently from the first time, he felt protected and 'touched', so continued to visit the temple on Wednesdays and Saturdays. He would sit without talking to the spirits; he just listened to their messages and regularly drank the temple's water and took the painkillers prescribed by the doctor. Ninety days later, the *preta velha* said he could repeat the tests so he went back to the doctor, who performed another endoscopy.

> When the doctor performed the endoscopy, he called the nurse and said she had given him the wrong medical records, but she insisted that they were the right ones. I had nothing. Interestingly, he said he had never seen anything like it: healing without leaving any scars. This is what intrigued him more, and he said that my health condition was better than his. He told me that it could not have been the medicine, because in that case it would have left a scar. He had never given me hope that the remedy would cure me. He said immediately, 'I don't know any remedy able to cure you'. I was healed and that's it. So I took the test results to another doctor. He asked what remedy I had taken so that he could prescribe it to his patients. I didn't say that I was drinking the water of Seta Branca; he would not believe it, but he said that it was a miracle. I went back to the Vale do Amanhecer, for I knew I was cured. That day, for the first time, I talked to the *preta velha*. I had to thank her, I told her my story, I told her about my illness and that I repeated the tests and there was nothing left. For the first time since the medical diagnosis, I cried. Then I told my wife I wanted to find a new job; I wanted to go back to work.

He then went back to the Vale and explained to a *preto velho* that he had lost his job because of his illness, and the *preto velho* said that before the end of that week he would send someone to get him to take him back to work. On the Friday, the president of his company sent a car to pick him up, and he went back to work for the same company for the next twelve years.

Not long after, he went back to drinking; this time, rather than beer, he was into whiskey. Meanwhile, his wife was also attending the Vale as a patient and decided to begin her mediumistic development as *doutrinadora*. She asked him to drive her to the temple regularly so that she could undertake her development sessions. He would accompany her, pass through as a patient, but then go for a drink afterwards. Two years and four months later, after receiving many invitations from the spirits to develop his mediumship, a *preta velha* told him that it was time to give up drinking. He eventually decided to take the test of mediumship and entered into the process of development as a *doutrinador*. He has not had any alcohol since.

After the third initiation of *Centúria*, he received a 'mission' by the spirits to establish an external temple and to coordinate it as president. He received all the hierarchical classifications he needed that same same night, instead of having to wait four to five years to begin his mission. Then, Francisco and his wife, accompanied by a group of other mediums, went looking in a small town a couple of hours away from the city for land to build a temple. They visited several places until a spirit called Vovó Irene do Oriente (Grandma Irene of the Orient) incorporated in an *apará* and told them they had to build the temple on that particular land. With their own life savings, they built a simple structure in bricks, with no electricity, water or proper street access, and they began to receive over a hundred patients every Saturday.

Francisco recalled the beginning of the work at the temple as featuring a consistent number of patients arriving with a variety of problems including severe obsession, self-harming, suicide attempts and uncontrolled spirit incorporations. He attributed those intense phenomena to the spiritual legacy of the area, which in colonial times was a place of slavery and several riots. He said that some spirits remained trapped and, having formed phalanges in the darkness over the centuries, were obsessing the living. Some patients claimed that they were healed after their full mediumistic development, and some of them were still practising mediums in that temple. Nine years later, the temple had grown in size. During my visits, there were over three hundred initiates, and the small house could not accommodate them all. The spirit mentors had then demanded that the temple should pass to an initiatic stage, so Francisco began the construction of a larger building following the plan for an initiatic temple, which includes all the sacred spaces (*castelos*)[2] for the rituals that a temple in that phase should have in order to move the 'initiatic force' of the *corrente mestra* (master force). I accompanied this transition and the efforts involved in the physical construction of the building. Given the social condition of the members, it was hard to collect the financial resources to buy materials. Several social events such as a gipsy festival were organized for the members, along with a regular market of second-hand clothes. Francisco's son was making handicrafts, such as small statues of the spirit guides, to be sold to other temples in the region to buy some bricks. Physical and financial efforts went hand in hand with an increase in cases of obsession phenomena arriving at the temple and attended to through special works (*trabalhos especiais*). There was a time when forces were understood to be acting beyond the temple's boundaries, affecting Francisco's family home, with *aparás* suddenly feeling sick and drowsy. The house was regularly cleansed with incense through a *defumação*, and several rituals were performed at the temple to cleanse the energies for all the community. Francisco then inaugurated the initiatic temple, which became a referential point in the region and often attends to cases of alcohol and drug addiction. A few of these patients developed their mediumship under his guidance and work regularly at the temple. He described his journey as being 'tough but rewarding and filled with confirmations' of the highest spirit worlds' action upon his life as much as others' lives, through the healing he had both experienced and witnessed.

### The Mansão Ypuena

When I first visited the Adjunto Ypuena Mestre Lacerda, I walked into his office with some specific topics in mind that I wanted to explore through an interview with him, but as I began to perceive that his answers were not related to my questions, I suddenly asked myself whether he was really listening to me. But then I realized that it was me who was not really listening to what he was telling me. In fact, he had something else to tell. So I began to visit him regularly to listen to his explanations about disobsession, karma and life beyond matter. No matter who he had in front of him, whether a researcher, a journalist, a medium, a patient or an alcohol addict, he had his mission as an *'evangelizador'* (evangelizer), which he intended as that of clarifying life beyond physical matter; specifically the influences of spirits that a person might have hurt in past lives on present obsessions and the ways to help them through Christic principles – thus, through everyday actions of love, tolerance and humility. The role of the evangelizer was indeed intended in this context to mean someone who unveils the dynamics beyond physical matter, rather than someone who advocates a cause to make converts. Each of the Adjuntos de Povo Raiz consecrated by Tia Neiva[3] seemed to hold a specific sphere of action. For instance, among others, the Adjunto Yumatã Mestre Caldeira would be more inclined to explain in detail the technical aspects of mediumship and the action of forces in rituals. The Adjunto Amayã Mestre Guilherme Stuckert would discuss healing, as he represented the Knight of the Lilac Lance (*Cavaleiro da Lança Lilas*), the force of spiritual and physical healing.

When I first met Lacerda, he was in his seventies. He had long grey hair tied in a ponytail, deep eyes and pronounced facial features, which altogether suggested the nickname '*o indio*', as some people would call him, as they said he reminded them of a native North American. He told me that although religion was very much present in his life – he had been brought up as a Catholic and then attended the Messianic Church – from his teenage years up to his thirties, his life was 'dominated by addictions and violence'. He sought medical treatment, but the effects of *cachaça* liquor on his organs were already so severe that the doctors did not believe a recovery was possible. In 1970, he was living in Brasília when his partner at the time took him to the Vale do Amanhecer to meet Tia Neiva. Tia Neiva told him that it was almost too late for his case, but through her support, he decided to be spiritually treated. Through his mediumistic development as a *doutrinador*, he said he became self-conscious and aware of his body and of what he could change and improve. Particularly, he said he immediately began to 'dominate the intuitions'. On a spiritual level, he learned how to indoctrinate the obsessing spirits considered to be causing addictions:

The *obsessores* that attack through drugs and alcohol are difficult to control – they come from our past lives and live in the double of the physical plane and the etheric, feeding themselves on the vital force we generate. Through this feeding we begin to obey them; we become slaves, and the only way out is one's sense of will. It all depends on intuitive perception. We need to be capable of discernment.

In 1978, he was consecrated by Tia Neiva as one of the first *Adjuntos de Povo* (*Adjuntos Koatay 108 – Arjuna-Rama*), the roots of which thousands of mediums affiliate with, and from which other peoples originated, such as the Ypuena People, one of the largest groups in the Vale. He became a firm and respected Adjunto de Povo, acting as a caring father for many. Occasionally, to the people closest to him, he would show the legacy of his past as a rocker in the form of rock songs that he was still writing. Mostly, he considered it his spiritual mission to devote his life to assisting people recovering from alcohol and drug addictions, and for this purpose he founded the charitable institution called *Casa Transitória Povo Ypuena* (CTPY, Transitory House of the Ypuena People), also known as *Mansão Ypuena* (Ypuena Mansion), named after his spiritual minister, Ministro Ypuena. Since its foundation, the Vale has been engaged in social assistance, initially by opening an orphanage, then offering assistance to the homeless. Founded by Lacerda and a group of mediums, the CTPY developed in parallel to the Order (OSOEC), although as an independent entity. Being a philanthropic institution, it is funded by the voluntary donations of some of the residents of the Vale's town or components of the Ypuena People. It provides social and community assistance to the town of the Vale do Amanhecer (such as professional courses aimed at the social reintegration of patients and a soup kitchen for those in need), and it hosts people with mental disorders and alcohol and drug addictions for short periods free of charge. These cases are addressed by integrating treatment from a professional physician and psychologist with spiritual treatment provided by the rituals of disobsessive healing in the temple. Treatment through the weekly visits of medical professionals includes psychological counselling, prescriptions, and, where appropriate, a mediation with local medical institutions is arranged. At a social level, the CTPY also offers opportunities for community work. It is an open system, based on the respect of patients' free will. Discipline in cohabitation in the house and being willing to receive spiritual treatment as patients in the temple's rituals – intended as a complementary part of the therapy – are the conditions for the patient's stay. Indeed, the staff of volunteers constantly works towards increasing the patient's personal responsibility and spiritual awareness, especially because, being an open system, patients may find chances to relapse in being able to exit the CTPY onto the streets nearby. Whilst passing through rituals of disobsessive healing, patients are not expected to embrace this spiritual practice, but if they choose to do so, they may begin the mediumistic development.

Since I was regularly visiting Lacerda and occasionally helping him with some tasks, I was spending time at the CTPY, and he and the other staff members who were coordinating patients' activities agreed that I could talk to some of the current and former patients to grasp an understanding of the mediumistic approaches to these therapeutic trajectories. Among the residents in the house, the average period of stay varied between seven and nine months. Seven out of ten people hosted presented problems with addiction, while the remaining three had mental disorders. Lacerda used to explain that the CTPY was connected to a *casa transitória* (transitory house) for spirits in the spirit world and both houses were working together for incarnated and disincarnate spirits. For my morning visits, he would often invite me to stay for lunch at the *Mansão*; indeed, the kitchen played a central role in the house, as he said that his Ministro Ypuena would project his forces onto the food, which is served free of charge to those in need; and the charitable work in the kitchen preparing and serving food to the homeless was also part of the therapy of resident patients, who benefited from the ongoing projection of spiritual healing forces. Daniel was one of them. He worked in the kitchen during the months of his stay. He arrived at the *Mansão* after thirty days of hospitalization for alcohol and drugs. Besides his work in the kitchen, Daniel chose to develop his mediumship and was then initiated as a *doutrinador*. After one year in development, he received all the initiations and regularly practised as a medium in the temple. Meanwhile, he said that he had gained control over his life, leaving the *Mansão* with a job and moving into a new house with his new partner.

One day, a patient arrived. He said that as soon as he passed over the threshold of the Vale, he began to feel sick, experiencing headaches and tiredness, and sometimes feeling a sense of rage rising within, which could explode aggressively at any moment. What brought Miguel to the *Mansão* was his five-year-long drug addiction. He soon began his mediumistic development as an *apará*, but after twenty-two classes he was only incorporating *sofredores* and *obessessores*, rather than his spirit guides. Once I was walking along the temple's aisle and all of a sudden I saw him incorporating an *obsessor* while he was sat in the patients' waiting seats; three *doutrinadores* arrived and began indoctrinating the spirit while trying to elude his punches. When he eventually disincorporated, he said he felt a negative force approaching him and an impulse to attack whoever was in his way. After consulting with the *pretos velhos* about his lack of control over the incorporations, he was exceptionally authorized to change his development from *apará* to that of *doutrinador*. Gradually, during the first seven classes of the development, he calmed down, stopped incorporating and gained more control, progressing towards the various stages of initiation. Throughout the development, he was also helping the *Mansão Ypuena*, doing voluntary work in the kitchen. One year later, when I returned to the Vale, I met him wearing his uniform of Jaguar while he was coming out of a ritual in a stage of centurion. We sat outside the temple, and he began to tell me how things had changed since he developed his mediumship as a *doutrinador*. He told me that the aggressive episodes and involuntary incorporation disappeared; he had had no relapses with drugs, and his social relations had benefited from his greater self-control and confidence. He said that learning about his past incarnations in different rituals allowed him to understand himself and the meaning of some events in his present life and to contextualize them within a new broader frame. He gained new strategies to deal with problems and perspectives that he was hopeful he could use for planning his future. He then told me about his past experience of moving across several religious groups, particularly emphasizing the episode of a visit to a centre of Umbanda. He said that the members of that centre told him that they would not let him participate in the rituals because he was accompanied by the spirit of an Amerindian who was telling them that Umbanda was not the right place for him, and that he would not permit the unfolding of rituals if his son would remain there. Thus, Miguel told me that because the spirit guides had recently revealed to him that the spirit was Pai Seta Branca, he felt that the episode was a confirmation of his 'spiritual mission'. Healing is thereby perceived as 'evidence' or 'confirmation' of the spirit world's intervention in a person's life and, thus, of having been given the opportunity to become the means, oneself, through which this intervention is made possible for others.

The perception of having a 'spiritual mission' was a trigger point also for Thiago's therapeutic trajectory. Thiago told me he was formerly in the army and had an accident that left him with some disability. He consequently lost his job, and he and his wife got divorced. He became an alcoholic, drinking around a bottle of *cachaça* a day, and got involved in crime. He spent four years travelling across Brazil as a homeless outlaw, as he was accused of the illegal possession of weapons, drug dealing and armed robbery. The first time he passed into the Vale's rituals, he said he felt uncomfortable being surrounded by 'crazy people wearing funny costumes'. Then he sat in the ritual of *Tronos*, where the *preta velha* Vovó Catarina das Cachoeiras (Grandma Catherine of the Waterfalls) suddenly began to recount to him the story of his life, to which he reacted with a highly emotional cry. He arrived at the *Mansão*, where he began doing some voluntary work and saw a psychiatrist, who prescribed him medical treatment that he refused to take. Fifteen days after his arrival, he began to develop his mediumship as a *doutrinador*. He spent six months in treatment in the *Mansão* without relapses. Meanwhile, his court case was filed, and he met someone who helped him to find another job. Another six months later, he met a woman and they got married. He said that those who could see his transformation from outlaw and alcoholic to 'missionary' in the Vale would think it was a miracle. He attributes his process of redemption to the work of spiritual beings and to being aware of both his pursuit of moral conduct based upon the practice of doctrinal principles and his firm psycho-physical control.

One of the staff members who was helping Lacerda in the coordination of patients explained to me that the most severe cases of schizophrenia or mental disorders are considered to be forms of obsession by a *cobrador* spirit and are linked to karma. She explained that, because of this reason, for those who in addition to passing as patients decide to develop their mediumship, it is preferable to develop as a *doutrinador* straight away, otherwise the *cobrador* may take advantage of the vulnerability of an *apará* in the initial phase of the special development intended for these cases. In some cases, once they are able to control different forces, after receiving all the initiations and having achieved increased balance, the medium may restart the development as an *apará*. The patients with schizophrenia that have been hosted in the house, she said, needed to have the 24-hour assistance of their carers (or a family member), who accompany them in the temple rituals and make sure they continue their medical treatment with a psychiatrist. Those who were able to develop their mediumship followed a special group of development for *doutrinadores*, dedicated to those who have special needs and may require more than ten classes of preparation to reach the stage of initiation. After the initiations, she said, they begin showing evident improvements in communication skills, in personal care and control, but even if they reach a certain degree of autonomy they may not work directly with patients as they are still what she defined as 'mediums in treatment'.

Forty-year-old Luísa was already at an advanced stage of mediumistic practice in the Vale when she told me about her experience from ten years earlier, when in a fortunate period of her life all of a sudden she began to suffer nervous disorders. At that time, she went from being unemployed to winning a large sum of money at the bingo that she used to build a new house. Soon afterwards, she found a new job and settled down with a good standard of life when she suddenly began to experience her body twisting. It began rapidly and developed as an ongoing involuntary con-traction of her limb and face muscles, resulting in a constant jaw grinding, while feeling her heart in her throat. After visiting several specialists, such as an orthopaedic, a cardiologist and a psychiatrist, she was diagnosed with a severe panic disorder. She had a constant fear of dying as she was suffering five to ten attacks per day. She said that her neurological system was affected up to a point where she had to use a wheelchair. She was treated with benzodiazepine drugs without showing any improvement. Then she also sought assistance in religious groups, attending the meetings of the Japanese Seicho-no-ie and several Evangelical churches. Her disorder seriously affected her marriage and so she moved to Brasília where her sisters could look after her. Once in Brasília, she re-established contact with her other sister, who was living in the Vale do Amanhecer. She went to visit her and never left. The first time she was taken to the temple, she entered the patients' queue and fainted. She described it as a feeling of her spirit moving away from her body and floating. She was passed into three *Tronos* with three different *pretos velhos* as part of a *trabalho especial* (special work) when she herself incorporated a *preta velha*, Vovó Catarina das Cachoeiras (Grandma Catherine of the Waterfalls). After the ritual, she understood that she had to begin her mediumistic development immediately in order to gain control and balance. She then understood her bodily symptoms as the action of a *cobrador* spirit that was affecting her nervous system, and through the development of her mediumship and her spiritual work to help others she said she was able to release her *cobrador*. Luísa claimed that she has had no panic attacks since her third initiation of *Centúria* eight years ago and that she has learned to see things with a wider perspective, feeling as if she is 'a spirit living a human experience'.

## The Therapeutic Uses of Mediumistic Development

Most mediums I encountered in my research arrived in the Vale as spiritual seekers or looking for spiritual assistance for a wide range of emotional, material or health issues. Among the health issues, some mediums reported a past history of schizophrenia, anxiety, panic disorders or alcohol and drug addictions. When they arrived as patients presenting symptoms of mental disorders or addictions, they were advised by spirit guides to develop their mediumship in the Vale or in other spiritual groups. It is worth reminding the Vale's understanding of mediumship as having a bodily dimension: an energy common to all human bodies, originating in the blood flow; if this energy is produced in excess it accumulates, affecting the person physically, whilst when this excessive energy is distributed to others it may help healing. Through mediumistic development in the Vale do Amanhecer, one may learn to become aware of one's mediumship, to control it and to direct the energy in excess for the healing of others. Then, through ongoing spiritual practice, mediums become aware of their bodily and emotional responses and, thus, of how to maintain their mediumship in balance.

When a patient decides to undertake the development for therapeutic purposes in the Vale, this practice is understood as being complementary to the biomedical therapies of each particular case – namely, patients undertaking treatments in biomedicine are advised to continue to follow the medical advice. Mediums in the Vale discern between phenomena provoked by undeveloped mediumship and mental disorders. They explained that the disturbances caused by undeveloped mediumship may disappear during the development and through the practice of mediumship, thus their nature is transitional. Regarding mental disorders, these may be part of a process of karmic redemption determined in a past life, and thus they are understood as having a spiritual origin, such as an obsession by a *cobrador*, but the effects on the psycho-physical level are such that they require clinical treatment. In these cases, the mediumistic development may provide the person with some control over the symptoms, but it may not be treated completely without clinical intervention. Whilst some cases will follow the regular development sessions, other cases may require special development, consisting in a greater number of sessions, and their mediumistic practice may not involve patients.

The staff of the CTPY observed how, in cases of addictions, the chance of a relapse was lower when progressing along the development and the initiatory steps. They noted that among those who received assistance in the CTPY passing as patients through rituals 10 percent of them recovered, whilst 90 percent presented at least one relapse. Recovery rates, however, increased when patients decided to begin the process of mediumistic development and learn to perform for themselves disobsessive healing: 70 percent would recover without relapses and 30 percent presented at least one relapse. The percentage of relapses was higher between the *emplacamento* and the first initiation, but it drastically fell after the last initiation of *Centúria* as a consequence of the enhanced control, self-awareness and personal responsibility that the medium seemingly acquires at that stage. As far as I was able to discuss with mediums who developed for therapeutic purposes, I would agree with these figures.

Unlike many other systems that deal with addiction, the treatment did not include discussion groups. Those who had previous experiences in other groups (they cited the Alcoholics and Narcotics Anonymous, Catholic and Evangelical institutions, among others) stressed that what made the difference in their recovery was the combination of mediumistic development and disobsessive healing. Spiritual approaches to addictions are indeed quite widespread in Brazil, and drug addicts seeking spiritual treatment present better recovery rates than those treated exclusively by conventional medicine, according to a study conducted in São Paulo (Sanchez and Nappo 2008).[4] Frederico Camelo Leão and Francisco Lotufo Neto, while observing clinical improvements in people with mental disorders participating as patients in Spiritist mediumistic sessions, made the subtle distinction between 'cure', intended as complete recovery, and 'healing', which concerns the process of 'getting better', proposing the latter as a paradigm within which they could frame their results (Leão and Lotufo Neto 2007: 27). From the perspective of healing, one may approach the cases of schizophrenia that were seeking complementary treatment in the Vale. Whereas those who undertook the process of development for nervous disorders claimed their complete recovery. Both healing and cure in these cases, however, are not just dependent on the release of a spirit or the medical treatment of a symptom but actively involve the patient's development at several experiential levels.

My interlocutors' accounts of their experiences illuminated the therapeutic use of mediumistic development, with its process of initiatory learning, particularly the way it acted upon the cognitive, the bodily and the biographical levels. Their spiritual experiences of encountering and communicating with spirits triggered a highly emotional response through what they described as 'revelations' – that is, for example, becoming aware that they were mediums: that not only their bodies produced their mediumship but that their mediumship may also help others. The spirits' messages helped reframe their illness in a broader perspective of karmic redemption, emphasizing personal responsibility and moral principles in one's thoughts, actions and relationships with others.

In order to become aware of and control their phenomena, these patients decided to begin their mediumistic development. When new mediums are introduced to the development, instructors stress that alcohol and drugs pollute the blood and, consequently, the medium's ectoplasm used by spirits to heal patients. Thus, the conceptualization of the medium's body gradually changes through notions of cleansing and pollution. Yet, it is the development of techniques of bodily control – their bodily enskillment during the development – that reshapes their ways of knowing, transforms their perception of the body as permeable and transforms their sense of self as multidimensional and extensible towards their spirit guides and beyond the single lifespan. As one medium *doutrinador* in development for therapeutic reasons told me, 'When I say that spirituality is important for my recovery, I don't mean just praying but in the sense of practising, because it is the practice that gives me a direct psychophysical help'.

The emphasis on control and discernment promoted in the development sessions was indeed crucial for cases of mental and nervous disorders. This embodied knowledge seemed to have contributed to a healing process, which was then reinforced by the shift of their social role from patients to mediators of healing able to help others, enhancing their sense of responsibility. Scholars have explored ritual healing in terms of the patients' rhetorical transition from a condition of illness to a new phenomenological reality differing from both pre-illness and illness realities (Csordas 1983; Greenfield 1991, 1992, 2003, 2008). In the case of the Vale do Amanhecer, the patient is moved into a new reality not only rhetorically but experientially: those who choose to undertake the mediumistic development experience a new role as 'mediator of healing' or 'missionary', devoted to helping others through the lived Gospel. This transition from patient to mediator of healing, however, becomes effective for therapeutic purposes if supported by a particular kind of embodied knowledge and emotional experience.

This analysis is not intended as an exhaustive explanatory paradigm of what is a complex process of spiritual healing. I rather intended to focus upon embodied knowledge to illuminate specific dynamics that emerged from my interlocutors' narratives upon the therapeutic uses of mediumistic development; and I did so in the light of my approach to the processes of initiatory learning as a multilayered experience – which is embodied, intuitive, performative, conceptual and intersubjective, articulating particular notions of the body and the self. The discussion of these cases remarked the centrality in peoples' therapeutic trajectories of the process of learning a particular practice that informs both notions of body and selfhood. Further investigation is certainly needed in this direction, involving a larger number of case studies[5] over a longer period of time and, possibly, combined with a comparative analysis involving mediumistic development in other contexts.

Two subsequent considerations emerge at this point. In the first instance, the need for different fields of scholarly and medical intervention to reposition the early approaches to spirit mediumship and possession as 'pathology', exploring more closely and cross-culturally the implications of the processes of learning in mediumistic development. Secondly, further attention should be paid to a phenomenon in which therapeutic trajectories are intertwined with spiritual routes determining new patterns of religious affiliation and initiatory paths.

## Notes

Some sections of an earlier version of this chapter were published in the article: Pierini, E. 2018. 'Healing and Therapeutic Trajectories among the Spirit Mediums of the Brazilian Vale do Amanhecer', *International Journal of Latin American Religions* 2(2): 272–89.

1. *Mesa Evangélica, Tronos, Cura Evangélica, Junção Evangélica, Linha de Passe, Defumação.*
2. That is, initiatic temples, including: *Area Evangélica* with *Pira* and *Mesa Evangélica, Radar, Tronos, Castelo do Silencio, Cura Iniciática, Junção, Castelo do Doutrinador, Indução, Oráculo de Simiromba, Sudálio/Linha de Passe, Cruz do Caminho* and *Randy.*
3. The *Adjuntos de Povo Raiz* (*Adjuntos Koatay 108 – Arjuna-Rama*) represent the spiritual roots of all 'peoples'. They were consecrated by Tia Neiva in 1978.
4. Their study is based on in-depth interviews with eighty-five former alcohol and drug addicts in São Paulo, Brazil, who sought non-medical treatment. Evangelical Christians and Catholics sought treatment exclusively in religion, whilst Spiritists sought complementary treatment both in medical and spiritual therapies. Besides the role of faith, they highlighted the importance of community support during their process of recovery.
5. The case studies presented in this chapter were selected from among those participants who arrived in the Vale with a history of addiction or pathology. Moreover, at the time of my fieldwork in the Vale do Amanhecer, the *Mansão* offered limited spaces for patients, since it lacked voluntary caregivers to assist additional patients; therefore, I could only follow a limited number of cases.

# CONCLUSION

## The Extended Self: Transhistorical and Multidimensional

Developing and practising mediumship in the Vale do Amanhecer is a highly transformative process for mediums in many ways. It is not something that happens straightforwardly in people's lives; it is rather negotiated along life trajectories, often unfolding across the fluid Brazilian religious meshwork, whether seeking spirituality or healing. For many, approaching mediumship means delving into new sensations and feelings and learning to discern and control them. It opens up a new horizon of relationships with human and non-human beings and dimensions as much as with other histories that become one's own history. Through these relationships, histories and mediumistic trance, the self undergoes an extension through its substances and its narratives beyond the body, beyond the single lifespan. In the Vale do Amanhecer, these experiences are not prompted by meditative practices or the study of sacred texts; they are rather cultivated through a ritual practice aimed at assisting humans and spirits in need, with the temple as a place to actively engage the body from one ritual to another in the practice of mediumistic work rather than worship spiritual beings or deities. In this sense, the self is constantly articulated intersubjectively in relation to human and non-human others and to its threads extending into the past lives.

In my discussion, I have addressed the interrelational character of learning and the articulation of the self on an intersubjective level through the experience of the relationship between mediums and spirits, as also noted by Goldman (2009) and Espírito Santo (2011) in Afro-Brazilian and Afro-Cuban religions, respectively. I have illustrated how in the Vale do

Amanhecer this relationship between mediums and spirits is established in trance states through 'multisensory imagery' (Csordas 1990). Exploring the intertwining of cognitive, sensory and emotional processes, I have shown how the different layers at work in the process of learning mediumship inform a multilayered articulation of the self.

At the level of discourse, in Chapter Three I have discussed Tia Neiva's revelations on the lives of the Jaguars in different historical times. I have proposed that the principle of reincarnation articulates elements known in other religions as well as the sense of self. That is, when mediums call upon the forces of Apollo, Ramses, Amon-Ra, the Spartans, the Mayans, the Franciscans and so on, they are also calling upon the forces of their lives in those times, making threads of their selves from the past along with different histories converge in rituals to be co-performed for their karmic redemption and healing. When these threads are enunciated by *emissão* (emission of ectoplasm, the individual invocation of one's own transcendental forces) they form a meshwork to catch forces and spirits that need to be released. The mediums' histories from past lives may also be accessed through communications with both spirit guides and disincarnate spirits in special rituals, in which episodes from past lives and their consequences in the present one are discussed and transformed, so that the medium becomes aware of different aspects of the self in the past, as part of the 'spiritual tribe of the Jaguars'. When a nymph, a female medium, works in a ritual as a member of the phalanx of the Mayans, she is not just representing the Mayans; she is that part of her self that lived as a Mayan. Tia Neiva instructed that the Jaguars have had an average of nineteen different incarnations, making the medium's self transhistorical.

When I propose to consider the self in transhistorical terms, I also imply that we need to expand our ways of thinking about history and how we forge relationships to the past (Palmié and Stewart 2016), as well as expand our ways of thinking about the self. Palmié and Stewart stress the plurality of repertoires of historicity in societies around the world that cannot be reduced to the Western one. The alternate forms of making history to which they refer depart from the intellectual ways in which the relationship to the past may be conceived, in order to explore culturally specific modalities in which societies shape histories. They use Bakhtin's concept of 'chronotopes' (1981), implying that 'a plurality of senses of space and time become not only thinkable, but also potentially psychologically and socially inhabitable ... They are modal switches that activate – often unintentionally and spontaneously – particular pasts in joint or individual attention ... In chronotopic switching, affectivity takes precedence over reference'; past and present may become fused in rituals through trance-inducing dances, images, olfaction and so on (Palmié and Stewart 2016: 218–19). Looking at the temporal orientation of the self, Hallowell maintains that self-related experience may be broadened to include dreams, such as among the Ojibwa Indians, and to move beyond the limits of the behavioural environment through space and time along with non-human selves: 'This implies the notion of self-continuity as one of the ubiquitous aspects of self-awareness' (1955: 98). This was well illustrated by Luíza, in Chapter Nine, who having arrived in the Vale with a panic disorder and then developed her mediumship said she was feeling as 'a spirit living a human experience'. According to mediums who undertook a therapeutic trajectory in the Vale, this understanding of past lives helped them see things in a wider perspective. During their therapeutic process, they also began to rewrite their stories as Jaguars. Andrew Strathern argued that 'when trance with possession is found much of the therapeutic performance consists of the presentation of a historical consciousness[1] on the part of those possessed' (1996: 153). He looks at ethnographic cases such as the Songhay people of Niger as presented by Stoller (1989, 1994), whereby spirit families represent different historical periods of sociocultural crises, and he notes the consistency of an idea of 'appropriation of power from the past' (Strathern 1996: 167). Stoller understands the body as a reservoir of cultural memory and the spirits in Songhay possession as an embodiment of the past (1994, 1997). In the Vale, the spirit mentors incorporating in mediums are said to belong to the different historical periods in which the Jaguars were incarnated together. Therefore, the encounter with other-than-human selves (spirits), ritual performance and the uniforms of the phalanges trigger access to different chronotopes in order to: reframe the relationships of the past; bring forces and substances from the past into the present for healing; and learn about different past lives to transform the self in the present. Grounding the sense of identity of the Jaguars as a spirit group results in the expansion of selfhood both diachronically through time and synchronically through space. The process of learning mediumship in the Vale do Amanhecer is, indeed, a process of becoming: becoming aware of the multidimensionality of self and becoming a Jaguar.

The self is also multidimensional. In Chapter Four, I have presented Tia Neiva's conceptualization of the human being and Sassi's analysis of the multiplicity of its composition. The self extends from matter to the etheric, to astral and spirit, becoming more subtle and co-existing in different planes and thus not reducible to the experience in the physical world. It may be conceived as an organism, in that its body, soul and spirt are connected by fluids, membranes and substances as a field of relations in flux. It is multi-faceted – comprising different 'minor selves' from past lives – and mutable, changing its spiritual clothing every eighty days, when one clothe from a past life predominates over the others bringing along in the present the spiritual relationships from that past. The Vale illustrates in detail how spirits move along the geographies of the spirit worlds from one life to another, which is also the case with Kardecism. It also focuses on how the spirit simultaneously extends towards other planes through its substances, such as ectoplasm or magnetic animal fluid, which is also a concept found in nineteenth- and twentieth-century Spiritualism. Taking up the example of the *emissão*, the medium's own invocation is described as an extension of the self into the spirit world through ectoplasm, emitted by words. It is simultaneously an extension of the spirit world through the forces it projects on the medium – an interpenetration of human and spirit worlds. These substances when uncontrolled or overproduced, as explained in Chapter Five, may result in illness or psychological disorders, but they are also considered to be constitutive of mediumship and its varying typologies as illustrated in Chapter Six.

At a somatosensory level, in Chapter Seven I have discussed how the self extends partially out of the body – through the expanded consciousness of the *doutrinador* or in the mediumistic trance of the *apará*, letting the spirits' selves project onto their bodies–while still being grounded in the body. Rather than transcendence, Beth, for instance, has experienced a feeling of being more embodied as a being during her mediumistic development. The body is thus described as a 'semi-permeable membrane', a platform for shared emotions and feelings, interweaving different dimensions together to overcome dualist views of the self.

In discussing the process of learning in the Vale, I have shown how mediumship is not a belief that happens in peoples' minds but develops through the body. Likewise, what precedes the transmission of propositional knowledge about notions of the self is learning a way of knowing that is affective and sensorial. In mediumistic development, the transformation of the self is felt along with the transformation of the body through pain as well as other emotions, feelings and affect in the embodied encounters with spirits. Hence, I have argued that notions of the body and self are co-produced and in turn they inform the mediums' conceptualizations of the phenomenology of 'mediumistic trance'. Ingold has proposed an approach to 'the human being not as a composite entity made up of separable but complementary parts, such as body, mind and culture, but rather as a singular locus of creative growth within a continually unfolding field of relationships' (2000: 4). 'Enskillment', in Ingold's view, implies a 'practised ability to notice and to respond fluently to salient aspects of the environment', rather than 'the acquisition of conceptual schemata for organizing sensory data into higher-order representations' (2000: 166). Learning to attend to spirits in the Vale do Amanhecer requires that the medium learns to both extend into spirits and discern between his or her self and those of different spirits. Thus, the articulation of the self becomes crucial for the skill of discernment, which relies on emotions, feelings, intuitions, words and gestures cultivated among the mediums in the development as a shared feeling that constitutes collectively and relationally the mediumistic body (*corpo mediúnico*) of the Jaguars. The multilayered articulation of the self in the Vale results from a multilayered process of learning mediumship, which is embodied, intuitive, performative, conceptual and intersubjective.

Finally, in Chapter Eight and Nine, I have shown how the bodily enskill-ment and notions of mediumship, body and self forged during the medi-umistic development and practice were relevant in the mediums' narratives of their spiritual and therapeutic trajectories in the broadest sense for re-establishing commitment and belonging in the fluidity of Brazilian religios-ity and in informing the processes of healing.

## Beyond Belief, Unsettling the Pathological: Mediumistic Development and Healing

Addressing the cases of mediums in development for therapeutic purposes, in the last chapter, I have argued that the articulation of the body and self through mediumistic development has implications for healing in the Vale. A focus on experience and the articulation of the body and the self unsettles early views that reduced too straightforwardly phenomena of spirit medium-ship and possession to pathologies through the lens of Western psychiatric categories. These views were informed by a focus primarily upon altered states of consciousness and the association of the alterations of behaviour with hypnotic states, hallucinations, hysteria, schizophrenia, epilepsy, neuro-sis and psychopathology (Oesterreich 1930; Nina Rodrigues 1935; Kroeber 1940; Devereux 1961; Ward 1989). Some of these pathological explanations were permeated by evolutionist ideas about race. Traugott Oesterreich (1930) considered spirit possession as a form of autosuggestion characteristic of the instability of a 'primitive' personality. His theories based on racial psychol-ogy have now been dismissed given the speculative assumption of an existing correlation between mental illness and an alleged 'primitive' race. Likewise, 'spirit possession' in Afro-Brazilian religions was presented by Brazilian psychiatrist Raimundo Nina Rodrigues (1935) as resulting from '"hysteri-cal phenomena" allowed by the "extreme neuropathic and hysterical" and "profoundly superstitious" personality of the Negro' (in Krippner 2008: 4). Several studies have suggested that schizophrenia is generated by similar cog-nitive processes as shamanic behaviour, although it is interpreted differently in Western societies (Silverman 1967; Bourguignon 1989). Yet, the 'negative association' related to possession is currently considered to be a legacy of either a colonial perspective or of the early scholarly focus on aspects of pain and suffering, which led to interpretations of possession as 'evil' through a Judeo-Christian perspective (Huskinson and Schmidt 2010: 8).

Hence, developed mediumship should not be reduced to being a case of 'controlled pathology' or mediums themselves reduced to the category of 'wounded healers', in the same way as Lewis has advocated that 'We cannot treat all shamans as simply self-healed neurotics. As in psychiatry, this may be the case for some practitioners, but it is not true for all' (1971: 187). Indeed, several cross-cultural studies stressed the absence of mental disorders among initiated shamans or participants in possession practices (Eliade 1964; Lewis 1971). Shamanic states and schizophrenia cannot be considered 'as transcultural versions of the same psychological state' because the former does not meet the criteria for the diagnosis of the latter; thus, the schizophrenic metaphor is untenable (Noll 1983: 447). The shaman voluntarily enters altered states of consciousness, which requires a strong sense of self, and his or her activity is balanced with social activities. The shaman is also able to make a distinction between the two worlds he or she inhabits, a distinction that the schizophrenic cannot make (Noll 1983: 454). Ethnographic approaches have urged that these phenomena cannot be reduced to any psychiatric category:

> To emphasize 'pathology', 'mental illness', 'psychosis', and 'neurosis' in case of spirit possession ... is to raise essentially misleading, though culturally expectable, responses to an 'uncanny' encounter ... Such diagnoses may well blind us to the dynamic of spirit possession. The question that must be asked is this: what, besides a protective shield, do we gain from calling a shaman schizophrenic ..., an individual possessed by a spirit a paranoid ..., a neurotic..., or a hysteric? (Crapanzano 1977: 13–14)

Crapanzano argued that the spirit idiom should not be reduced to the Western psychological one, because self-articulation is oriented within the individual in the Western perspective and outside the individual in societies that use the spirit idiom. Hence, because spirits are located outside the individual in non-Western societies, he maintains that we should not consider them as if they are merely projections of inner feelings and desires that are not recognized by the individual; we should rather analyse the ways in which the idiom is constructed and used in different societies (Crapanzano 1977).

Exploring mediumship and possession through notions of the body and the self allows us to broaden our perspective to include their multiple dynamics and their place in people's lives and therapeutic trajectories. Researching 'possession' in Afro-Brazilian Candomblé, Márcio Goldman proposed investigating it from the standpoint of notions of personhood, rather than reducing it to a 'pathology' such as dissociation of personality, which, he noted, is a term reliant upon the Western notion of an indivisible self (1985: 30). Rather, pathologies may lead a person to a religion; and 'If we assume that a disease may be lived through as an experience of division of the person, we may understand possession as a technique of its symbolic construction' (Goldman 1985: 50).[2]

Besides the anthropological approaches, recent developments in psychiatric research have advocated the need to discern between spiritual and pathological experiences. Among the causes of the explanatory reductions of mediumship and possession to pathology, Hageman et al. identified 'methodological pitfalls' in psychiatry, such as: 'assuming that experiences based on superficial similarities are identical' (e.g. mediumship and dissociative identity disorder) and identifying a particular brain region as the cause of a spiritual phenomenon merely because it is involved in the experience and without considering that bodily experiences may have different aetiologies (2010: 87). Brazilian psychiatrists Alexander Moreira-Almeida and Francisco Lotufo Neto proposed methodological guidelines specifically for the study of ASC that include: avoiding pathologizing the unusual; multiplying the concepts of 'pathology' and 'normality'; extending research into non-clinical populations; considering the cultural contexts as well as the cultural meanings of terms; considering the limitations of psychiatric classifications; and wherever possible using phenomenological description (2003: 24).

Neurological experiments based on EEGs of mediums in Brazil have excluded abnormal electrical activity in the temporal lobes or epileptic disorders (Hageman et al. 2010: 105). Clinical studies exclude psychopathological perspectives, revealing that people with mystical experiences score higher than control groups on the psychological well-being scale (Lukoff, Lu and Turner 1992; Moreira-Almeida 2009). One study in particular, involving 115 mediums selected from different Kardecist centres in São Paulo, demonstrated that mediums had a low prevalence of anxiety, mental disorders, borderline personality symptoms and use of mental health services; and that they had a high socio-educational level, employment and good social adjustment (Moreira-Almeida, Lotufo Neto and Greyson 2007; Moreira-Almeida, Lotufo Neto and Cardeña 2008).[3] Among these mediums, twelve participants were presenting symptoms of schizophrenia and so they were interviewed, along with a control group of twelve, using a Dissociative Disorders Interview Schedule (DDIS) and Schedules for Clinical Assessment in Neuropsychiatry. The results ruled out schizophrenia and dissociative identity disorders, since the cases failed to meet the criteria for the assessment (ibid.). Criteria were thus proposed for a differential diagnosis between spiritual experiences and mental disorders of religious content, such as: lack of suffering, lack of social and occupational impairments, short duration of the experience, critical attitude about the objective reality of the experience, compatibility with the patient's cultural or religious group, absence of co-morbidities, control over the experience, personal growth, and an attitude aimed at helping others (Menezes and Moreira-Almeida 2009; Moreira-Almeida 2009).[4]

In light of this discussion, my point is that an ethnographic approach that takes into account lived experience along with intersubjective, embodied knowledge may assist in facilitating this kind of discernment. In fact, both clinical studies and ethnographic data from different cultures around the world stress a distinction between spiritual and psychopathological experiences. The non-pathological character of mediumistic experience becomes even clearer through the use of ethnographic methods that examine lived experience and notions of the body and the self. Within this focus, we should also consider these notions as being the product of an initiatory learning process in a specific historical and cultural context and of a particular embodied experience, which in turn inform the interpretation of mediumistic experience itself. Furthermore, I suggested that these notions along with bodily enskillment, articulated by initiatory learning, also informed the healing process in some particular cases in which mediumistic development was used as a complementary treatment in patients with mental disorders, alcohol and drug addiction.

Mediumistic development addresses, through its mechanisms, a variety of experiences, ranging from the spiritual to the therapeutic. Amongst those who arrived in the Vale via a spiritual or therapeutic trajectory, a sense of self is developed through learning how to enter into a relationship with various spiritual entities and with past lives. The mediums I met understood this learning process as a possibility to develop, practise and experience one's mediumship in a safe way while alleviating karma and helping others and discerning the different spiritual agents interacting in their lives and relationships. In learning mediumship, they came to perceive their body as permeable and their sense of self as multidimensional and extensible. These embodied notions triggered these mediums' process of healing, intended both as 'recovery' and as a process of 'getting better', which was reinforced by the shift in their social role from former patients to medium-healers.

Studies on mediumship and possession have explored the therapeutic effects of these phenomena, and there has been a noticeable expansion of interest in the question of selfhood. Further attention, however, should be paid to the process of learning mediumistic practices, for it may provide us with deeper understandings of both experiences of therapy and the articulation of the self. The discussions in this field should also carefully consider the use of 'belief' as the main analytical category, as this category may create hierarchies of claims concerned with questions of healing, drawing boundaries between 'spiritual' and 'pathological' experiences. If we look at 'experience' instead, we may understand that in people's lives boundaries are more blurred than they seem; therefore, we may illuminate the fluid, relational, embodied and lived-through character of the notions involved in the therapeutic process.

In referring to 'belief' as a territory of contested categories, I am also calling into question the idea of cultural translation. Rita Laura Segato notes that what is not directly intelligible in the process of making the strange familiar, or what does not fall under a supposed correspondence or 'coherence' between belief and society, tends to be ignored if it is not consistent with Western rationality (1992: 126). In doing so, anthropology flattens the world, attenuating the accents of human experience that are meaningful to and eventually foreground a particular religious group. She proposes that rather than resolve difference, anthropologists should be exhibiting it in the ethnography (Segato 1992: 133). The idea of translation is problematic if intended as a direct transposition of one set of categories into another, which may result in explaining away our interlocutors' assumptions as 'imaginative interpretations' or metaphors of a pre-given reality (Henare, Holbraad and Wastell 2007: 1). Holbraad suggested that when native categories clash with our own assumptions, we should recognize that 'our conceptual framework' and categories are often inadequate to describe native concepts because they are not 'rich enough to comprehend all the others' (Holbraad 2009: 86). He rather proposes as part of the analytical task of the anthropologist that we rethink our own assumptions and produce new concepts that reflect native ones, namely 'inventive definitions' or 'infinitions':[5] 'a speech-act that inaugurates a new meaning by combining two or more previously unrelated meanings' (Holbraad 2012: 220).

Approaching the process of mediumistic development as learning a mode of knowing, as illustrated in Chapter Seven, allowed me to explore how categories were articulated and shift the analysis from belief to experience, which was a necessary step, since mediums' narratives of bodily experience of spirits outshone descriptions of a belief in spirits. Moreover, undermining the notion of 'belief' in favour of that of 'experience', according to Goldman (2003), allows to move beyond the differences, in terms of the belief, between the categories of the researcher and those people he or she studies. Both Jeanne Favret-Saada and Márcio Goldman stressed the primacy of 'being affected' over belief, for 'being affected' provides another kind of access to different spheres of experience, knowledge and dynamics of participants (Favret-Saada 1980, 1990; Goldman 2003, 2005, 2006). Goldman, in particular, suggested that the anthropologist's main task is that of producing 'ethnographic theories', namely theories produced from a local context that may render intelligible other contexts.

In this work, I proposed to explore the entanglements between experience and discourse, reframing cognition within the body, with its senses and emotions, so as to understand rituals and cosmologies as they are lived through as a part of human experience. Rather than being taught new concepts, I have argued that new mediums, through an education of perception, learn a mode of knowing, experiencing notions through their bodies. Spirits, for mediums, are not something to believe in, or metaphors or representations of something else. Mediums learn spirits through their experience of their relations with them, occurring through the mediumistic body. They are guided by their instructors to experience what it *feels* like having a mediumistic body, before being passed the knowledge of how different dimensions are interwoven in their solar plexus. This specific mode of knowing shapes their lived experience and articulates bodies and selves. In order investigate this process in depth, it was necessary to re-educate my own body, becoming skilled in this mode of knowing. The ethnographic method provides the researcher with a particular kind of access to other ways of knowing. In this sense, in the ethnographic task, the process of knowing gains centrality over cross-cultural translation. Namely, we are not just translating or contextualizing native propositions. What distinguishes ethnographic knowledge is the ability to illuminate the processes through which theories, notions and categories are articulated and lived through in different contexts; firstly by participants and then by the researcher. The way the ethnographer may illuminate these processes is through a discerning analysis, making explicit the ways in which local categories and theories may differ from those in use in the scholarly debate; and then considering how local categories are articulated and lived through, informing lived experience and thus moving from belief to experience. The ethnographer's experience of enskillment should then enter the analysis when deemed methodologically relevant to understanding the variety of embodied experiences of the encounter with otherness, whether it be our interlocutors in the field or that which occurs between our interlocutors and those experienced as non-human selves.

## Notes

Some sections of an earlier version of this chapter were published in the articles: Pierini, E. 2018. 'Healing and Therapeutic Trajectories among the Spirit Mediums of the Brazilian Vale do Amanhecer', *International Journal of Latin American Religions* 2(2): 272–89; and Pierini, E. 2016. 'Embodied Encounters: Ethnographic Knowledge, Emotion and Senses in the Vale do Amanhecer's Spirit Mediumship', *Journal for the Study of Religious Experience* 2: 25–49.

   1.  Strathern intends 'consciousness' to mean 'communication to the others of identity and intention on the part of an actor' (1996: 153).

2. Translated from the original in Portuguese.
3. Mediums were interviewed using the Self-report Psychiatric Screening Questionnaire (SRQ) and the Social Adjustment Scale (SAS). The SAS score was within the range of the general population and better than psychiatric patients. The SQR score showed a low prevalence of mental disorders – lower than in other Brazilian studies using SRQ in non-clinical population (Moreira-Almeida, Lotufo Neto and Greyson 2007: 57).
4. Adair Menezes Junior and Alexander Moreira-Almeida (2009) identified these criteria through a survey of 135 medical articles.
5. Holbraad coined the term 'infinition' (inventive definitions) to designate concepts 'under permanent ontological reconstruction' (2008: 101).

# APPENDIX

## The Missionary Phalanges

From 1975 until 1985, Tia Neiva established the twenty-one missionary phalanges of the Vale do Amanhecer. These are groups of mediums with specific ritual functions and 'spiritual affinity'. They may be compared to the orders of the Catholic Church, such as Franciscan, Benedictine, Carmelite, Dominican and so on. Each phalanx has a foundation narrative, called 'transcendental origin', transmitted through Tia Neiva's clairvoyance. She recounted that each phalanx is representative of a spiritual phalanx working in the spirit world, and its members among mediums are connected through joint past incarnations, during which they formed groups with a specific aim or affinity that continued in the spirit world and through the next incarnations. The mediums' vestments, chants and symbols are means to facilitate access to the forces left in the past incarnations they shared as Jaguars, in order to draw them into rituals for healing. Two phalanges are intended for men; the rest are for women. Mediums choose their phalanx in most cases after the third initiation of *Centúria*, and from then onwards they may work in rituals either individually or with other members of their group, wearing vestments representing specific forces of the phalanx. Each phalanx has specific ritual functions that are in many cases exclusive of its members and so their presence is necessary for the performance of that ritual. Members, however, may participate in many different rituals, wearing the vestments of their phalanges. The *cortes* are processions formed by members of the different phalanges lined up in a specific order (*chamada oficial*, meaning 'official call'), and they are aimed at cleansing energies in the temple through the *mantras* (hymns) and opening the way to the *mestres* participating in rituals.

## *Nityamas*

The first phalanx, established by Tia Neiva in 1975, is comprised of two groups: the *Nityamas*, unmarried nymphs, and the *Madruxas*, married ones. Tia Neiva recounted that the *Nityamas* had a joint past life in the Peloponnese:

> A group of young women gathered around a pythoness called Magdala, Godmother of the Devas, who brought from India a powerful priestess-hood with esoteric knowledge, herbal treatments and spiritual healing ... They used to make bonfires, invoking the spirits, asking protection for men engaged in battles, and, after a long absence they safely returned home from war ... Within a gypsy tradition, they danced around the fire, from which they received energies, they read hands, making prophecies and staging theatre performances, always covering their face with veils, which would be lifted only at the time of their wedding. They were feared in that region because, as Daughters of the Devas, they had the power to control the meteorological conditions, invoking the gods, causing storms. The men who remained at the village, disabled or too young to fight, began to help the *Nityamas* and were consecrated *Magos* (Magis), *Filhos de Devas* (Sons of the Devas), having developed their mediumship and acquiring spiritual powers. ... Once married, the Nityama becomes a Madruxa. Madruxa is the god-mother of the Nityamas. (Silva 2010: N)[1]

In rituals, they lead the *Cortes* (procession of mediums singing the mantras); light the 'Flame of Life' (*Chama da Vida*) in the *Turigano* with the *Magos*; and work in the ritual of *Estrela Sublimação* (Sublimation Star) for the entrance of the *Ismênias*. The *Nityama* wears a dress comprised of a skirt made out of coloured strips (red, yellow and blue), a black corsage with the symbols of the fire and a golden sun for the *doutrinadora*, or the silver moon and stars for the *apará*, and a belt with three chains. She also wears a cloak of organza, made by two layers (blue and red) and tied with bracelets to the wrist, black gloves and a white veil fixed with a tiara to cover the face during rituals. The dress of the *Nityama Madruxa* differs from that of the *Nityama* in the skirt, which is made up of ten strips in different colours (yellow, black, red, white, pink, light blue and blue); the shape of the corsage is larger, the cloak has black and blue layers of organza and the *pente* has coloured veils.

## *Samaritanas* (Samaritans)

According to Tia Neiva, their spiritual origin is related to the Gospel's episode of the Samaritan who gave Jesus water to drink (John 4, 4–18). The phalanx evokes the spirit of charity and dedication and is led by Tia Neiva's daughter, Vera Lúcia Zelaya. They work in rituals, consecrating and serving salt, perfume, water and non-alcoholic wine. They wear purple and orange cloaks and a dress with the symbol of the amphora, from which Jesus drunk the water, sewn at the level of the chest. They also wear a sun or moon and stars symbols according to the type of mediumship, purple gloves and a *pente* with purple, orange and black veils.

## *Gregas* (Greeks)

Tia Neiva narrated that in Delphi the Pythia would send a group of young girls to the battlefields to gather the weapons of the dead soldiers and carry them to be consecrated at the Temple of Apollo, so that the spirit of the soldier could follow his journey to the spirit world. The *Gregas* were guards of honour in rituals and with their lances they defended Helen of Troy. They form the *Cortes* (processions) in rituals and invoke the forces of Apollo, Kali and Policena in the *Turigano*. The *apará* wears a one-shoulder teal dress with a silver moon and stars, a teal and white cloak and *pente* and white gloves. The *doutrinadora* also wears a one-shoulder dress, white with a golden sun, a white and yellow cloak and *pente* and yellow gloves. They always carry a lance in rituals.

## *Mayas* (Mayans)

According to Tia Neiva, their origins belong to the Mayan civilization and the sacrifices of the virgins. They form the *Cortes* (processions) in rituals and invoke the forces in the *Chama da Vida* (Flame of Life) in the *Turigano*. The *Mayas* wear a coloured skirt (purple, red, white, blue and yellow) with a weaved belt of purple and yellow laces, a black corsage with the symbol of the chalice, a purple and yellow cloak, black gloves and a *pente* with coloured veils.

## *Magos* (Magi)

Tia Neiva established this phalanx for men and recounted that the *Magos* shared a life with the *Nityamas* invoking the forces of nature in Greece. Then they incarnated as the Magi, wise priests travelling across lands and sea disseminating their astrological and astronomical knowledge, gaining religious and political relevance as they influenced the kings of the Persians, Assyrians, Chaldean and Medes. The biblical Magi also belonged to this phalanx. In rituals, they work in *Cortes* (processions) and light the *Chama da Vida* (Flame of Life) with the *Nityama* in the *Turigano*. They wear a blue shirt with the symbol of the jaguar and a golden sun for the *doutrinador* or a silver moon for the *ajaná*, brown trousers and a blue cloak with the cross of the *doutrinador* or the red triangle of the *ajaná*.

## *Príncipes Mayas* (Mayan Princes)

The second phalanx for male mediums, according to Tia Neiva, had its origins in the Mayan civilization in Yucatan, where they held scientific knowledge and communicated with other spiritual planes. In another incarnation, they were Spartan warriors. The aim of the phalanx is to bring into rituals the forces left in that past. In rituals, they work in the *Cortes* (processions) and as guards of honour to the incorporations of Pai Seta Branca. They wear a yellow shirt with large sleeves and brown trousers with a red belt (which is said to recall another incarnation as gypsies). The *doutrinadores* wear a brown cloak with the symbol of the cross, and the *ajanás* wear a green cloak with the symbol of the red triangle.

## *Yuricys*

Tia Neiva had initially established this phalanx for *doutrinadoras*, as in their life in Delphi they were selected by Pythia (one of Tia Neiva's incarnations) to help her in the Temple of Apollo, but they did not incorporate. They rather rescued soldiers in the battlefields and prepared the phalanges of *Muruaicys* and *Jaçanãs* to incorporate as Pythias. The name *Yuricys* in the spirit world means 'field flowers'. The *Yuricy Lua* (Moon, *apará*) was then established to gather the *aparás Yuricys* in order to represent Koatay 108 Tia Neiva in rituals. The *Yuricy Sol* (Sun, *doutrinadora*) invoke forces in specific rituals, whereas selected *Yuricys*, called *Jandas*, are specially trained to invoke the forces in the opening of major consecrations and in the second initiation, manipulating through their chant the first and stronger forces arriving in the rituals. They invoke the forces of the *Cavaleiros da Luz* (Knights of the Light) in the ritual of *Cruz do Camino*. Along with the *Príncipes Mayas*, they are guards of honour to the incorporation of Pai Seta Branca. The *Yuricy Sol* wears a black dress with a golden sun, black gloves and cloak and a *pente* with coloured veils. The *Yuricy Lua* wears a black dress with a silver moon and stars, a belt, an Egyptian-like collar, black gloves and cloak and a *pente* with coloured veils.

### Dharman-Oxintos

According to Tia Neiva, in the spirit world the name *Dharman-Oxinto* means 'On the Path to God', which is also the name of the first initiation of mediums. The phalanx is said to have originated from the Egyptian priestesses of Horus and Amon-Ra. They had incarnations in Delphi, in the Roman Empire, in Palestine, as aristocratic women in Hungary, in a medieval nunnery in Aquitaine, France, as Andalusian gypsies and in colonial Brazil. In the temple, they are responsible for the *Castelo de Autorização* (Castle of Authorization), where patients invited by *pretos velhos* to develop their mediumship are directed to get the authorization to undertake the Test of Mediumship. The *Dharman-Oxintos* are therefore responsible for providing patients with the information they need before deciding to develop their mediumship. Their work is also related to the initiation; indeed, the first initiation is called *Dharman-Oxinto*. They are guards of honour of Yemanjá in the ritual of *Cruz do Caminho*, and they serve the wine (grape juice) in the Oracle of Pai Seta Branca. The nymph *Dharman-Oxinto* wears a black dress with a triangular ornament similar to a shield on the chest (golden for *doutrinadoras* and silver for *aparás*), black gloves and cloak and a *pente* with coloured veils.

### Muruaicys

According to Tia Neiva, the phalanx was created by the Pythia in Delphi, where they were prepared by the *Yuricys* to incorporate in the Oracle of Apollo. They also had incarnations in Ancient Egypt, Rome and the Andes. In the spirit world, the phalanx uses its disobsessive force to open the doors of caves, working with the phalanges of the *Madalenas* and *Cayçaras* to rescue spirits without light entrapped in hatred, which are then taken by the knights Ypuena into the ritual of *Estrela Candente*. The phalanx is led by Tia Neiva's daughter Carmem Lúcia Zelaya, and it is responsible for opening the gates of the ritual spaces. In the ritual of *Turigano*, they are guards of honour and incorporate Mãe Yara. They wear a white dress with the symbol of the *Chama da Vida* (Flame of Life), a red and purple cloak with the ankh, which is a symbol of the key to eternal life, purple gloves and a *pente* with red, yellow and white veils. The symbol of the *Chama da Vida*, also called *Cabala* (Kabbalah), comprises of two moons and a chalice representing the body of the medium. The wine represents the blood, which is understood to produce 'magnetic animal fluid' or 'ectoplasm', while the flame on top of the chalice represents the *prana*, the 'vital force'.

## Jaçanãs

The phalanx was created by the Pythia in Delphi along with the *Muruaicys* to represent Pythia incorporating in the Oracle of Delphi. In the temple, they incorporate Yemanjá in the *Turigano*; in the ritual of *Cruz do Caminho*, they are responsible for putting the *morsas* (white scarfs) around the neck of the *doutrinadores*. They wear a black dress with a long shield-like ornament on the front decorated with the golden sun for the *doutrinadora* and the stars for the *apará*. They also wear black gloves and cloak and a *pente* with coloured veils and velvet stripes.

## Arianas da Estrela Testemunha (Aryans of the Witness Star)

Tia Neiva traced their origins back to Persia, the land of the Aryans. They also had incarnations in Ancient Greece and Egypt, and as healers and missionaries preaching the Gospel. In rituals, they invoke the forces of the Oracles of Ramses, Amon-Ra and Akhenaten, and of the force of the Witness Star, witness of the mission of the Jaguar. They are also guards of honour in the Wedding ritual. They wear a black dress with a 'coat of arms shield' in the shape of the *Mesa Evangélica* with seven coloured rays representing the forces of the Jaguar, and the symbol of the sun (*doutrinadora*) or the moon and stars (*apará*). They also wear a belt with three chains, black gloves and cloak, and a *pente* with coloured veils.

## Madalenas de Cassia (Magdalenes of Cascia)

In their previous incarnations, they were nuns in a convent in the Middle Ages in Europe, where they used to help noblewomen running away from their families and arranged marriages. They work under the protection of the missionary guide Madalena de Cassia, who according to Tia Neiva was the Mary Magdalene of the Gospels. In the temple, they work as guards of honour in the wedding ritual and in the *Turigano*. The nymphs *Madalenas* wear a black dress with a shield-like symbol of the *Cabala* (or *Chama da Vida*, 'Flame of Life') on the front. The symbol is golden with the sun for the *doutrinadora* and silver with the stars for the *aparás*. They also wear black gloves and cloak and a *pente* with coloured veils.

## *Franciscanas* (Franciscans)

This phalanx represents the forces of the incarnation of Pai Seta Branca as Francis of Assisi. They shared several incarnation as valiant warriors rescuing and healing other warriors buried alive and injured in battles; they were also war nurses; landowners in the colonial era in Angical; queens, princesses, prostitutes and gypsies; and wives of Roman centurions and gladiators, poor or rich. In 1181, they were Clarisse, Poor Clare nuns, in Assisi, Italy, and in 1981 they returned as *Franciscanas* to the Vale do Amanhecer. In rituals, they accompany the patients in the Oracle of Pai Seta Branca, and they work in the Sacred Way of the ritual of *Turigano*. They wear a brown dress representing the Franciscan legacy, a white vest over the top of it with the symbol of the golden cross with a purple shroud and a golden sun for the *doutrinadoras* or a silver moon and stars for the *aparás*. They also wear a Franciscan cord tied around the waist, a brown and green cloak evoking the forces of earth, brown gloves, and a *pente* with brown, yellow, white and green veils.

## *Narayamas*

The phalanx works specifically with the forces of three Oracles of Simiromba, Obatalá and Olorum in disobsessive rituals. These three forces are represented in the pink 'coat of arms' shaped as a triangle on their black dress with the inscription '*Koatay 108*', representing also the forces of Tia Neiva, along with the sun for the *doutrinadoras* and the moon and stars for the *aparás*. They wear a black collar-like ornament around the neck with the symbols -0-0-, a three-chain belt, black gloves, a black and pink cloak and a *pente* with black, pink and white veils.

## *Rochanas*

The phalanx has its origins in Ancient Greece, in a rocky island in the Aegean Sea, where a group of women whose husbands left for the battle-fields lived hidden in caves, as they were being persecuted by a local queen who was jealous because the king fell in love with one of them. In the ritu-als of the Vale, the *Rochanas* represent the forces of the rocks and stones, and they work specifically in the *Estrela Sublimação*. They wear a red and purple dress, the colours of disobsession and healing, respectively, with golden and purple rays and a sun for the *doutrinadoras* and silver and purple rays and a moon for the *aparás*. They also wear red gloves and a red and purple cloak and veils.

## *Cayçaras*

Tia Neiva narrated stories about the *cabocla* Cayçara, an Amerindian leader who sacrificed herself in order to save her people from persecution by their neighbours. In the spirit world, the *Cayçaras*, along with the *Muruaicys*, the *Madalenas* and the knights Ypuena hunt the spirits of the lower planes with their magnetic nets to bring them into the ritual of *Estrela Candente* and help with their release. For this reason, they work primarily in the ritual of *Estrela Candente*, and they wear a purple dress, representing healing, with the symbol of the *Estrela Candente* and the ellipse on the solar plexus, and the sun for the *doutrinadoras* or the moon and stars for the *aparás*. They also wear a collar-like ornament, purple gloves and a purple and green cloak and veils.

## *Tupinambás*

According to Tia Neiva they represent the Amerindian people amongst whom Pai Seta Branca had his last incarnation on earth. Their specific function in the temple is to dedicate themselves to the social assistance of patients and those in need arriving at the temple. The image of Pai Seta Branca appears on their blue dress along with the golden sun for the *doutri-nadoras* and the silver stars and moon for the *aparás*. They also wear blue gloves, and blue and yellow cloak and veils.

## *Ciganas Aganaras* (Aganara Gypsies)

The roots of this phalanx, according to Tia Neiva, are to be traced among a nomadic people originally from Leningrad, Russia, who travelled across Europe. They were known as the Katshimoshys, and they included healers using herbs and potions, fortune tellers, horse and jewellery traders, musicians and dancers. Because of the disobsessive force attributed to gypsies in the Vale, the *Ciganas* work specifically in rituals of *Aramê* and *Julgamento* (Judgment) of prisoners, where they represent on earth the phalanx in the spirit world responsible for the release of mediums' *cobradores* spirits of their past lives. Their dress is made of a black top and a coloured skirt (yellow, purple, red, green and pink) representing the gypsy past, with the symbol of the sun for the *doutrinadoras* or the moon and stars for the *aparás*. They wear a round ornament around the neck, black gloves and a red and black cloak and veils.

## *Ciganas Taganas* (Tagana Gypsies)

According to Tia Neiva, the *Taganas* had incarnations in Delphi, then at the time of Jesus and as gypsies. Because of their transcendental force as gypsies, as with the *Ciganas Aganaras* they also work in the ritual of *Aramê* and *Julgamento* (Judgment) of prisoners for the release of their *cobradores* from past lives. They wear a black and green dress with the symbols of the chalice, the sun (*doutrinadoras*) or the moon (*aparás*), a collar ornament with chains on the chest, green gloves and a green and black cloak and veils.

## *Agulhas Ismênias*

This phalanx originated in Ancient Egypt and incarnated amongst the Incas. Recalling the sacrifices of the Incas, the phalanx represents the symbolic sacrifice of the *Ismênias* in the ritual of *Estrela Sublimação* – that is, they carry the negative charges of past lives into the sacred space to be released in the ritual while they activate the forces projected by the Oracles of Oxalá, Obatalá and Olorum through Agamor. They wear a white dress with symbols representing ancient hieroglyphs, the sun (*doutrinadoras*) or the moon and stars (*apará*), a belt, white gloves, and a red and white cloak and veils with a coloured braid around the head.

## *Nyatras*

Tia Neiva recounted that as a phalanx they used to help the families of the women sacrificed to the deities in ancient civilizations and rescued the bodies of the Virgins of the Sun trying to heal those who survived. In the ritual of *Estrela Sublimação*, they accompany the *Ismênias* in the sacred space. They wear a black dress with either the sun (*doutrinadoras*) or the moon and stars (*aparás*), a belt, a black veil with sacred symbols around the shoulders and head then extending down the left side of the dress, black gloves, a black and green cloak and a *pente* with coloured veils.

## *Aponaras*

'Aponara' was the denomination through which Tia Neiva called the nymphs of the *mestres* with the hierarchical classification of *Adjuntos Arcanos*. The 22nd phalanx was created only in 1998, years after Tia Neiva's passing, by the Trinos Triadas Presidentes to group the nymphs of the presidents of external temples, with the function of coordinating their temples (the local members of the phalanges in particular), and it is led by Nair Zelaya, wife of the Trino Ajará Gilberto Zelaya. Since 2009, the work of the phalanx is limited to the external temples of the CGTA. They wear a red dress with the symbol of the sun (*doutrinadoras*) or the moon and stars (*aparás*), a belt, a purple mantle around the shoulders and extending down the left side of the dress, red gloves, a red and purple cloak and a *pente* with coloured veils.

## Note

1. Translated from the original in Portuguese.

# GLOSSARY

*Adjuntos Koatay 108:* 'Adjunct Koatay 108'. A title received by male mediums after the third initiation of *Centúria*, when they become representatives of their spiritual Minister (*Ministro*) on earth.

*Adjuntos Koatay 108 Arcanos de Povo:* 'Adjunct Koatay 108 Arcana of People' or simply *Adjunto de Povo* (Adjunct of People). A high hierarchical position representing the roots of a people.

*Ajanã:* after the second initiation, an *apará* medium is referred to as an *ajanã*, although the term is often used to designate male *aparás* in particular.

*Alabá:* a ritual of communication between patients and *pretos velhos* taking place in the *Aruanda de Pai João* in front of the temple every month during the week of the full moon.

*Apará:* a medium that incorporates spirits in a mediumistic state defined as a 'semi-conscious trance'.

*Aparelho:* 'device'. A term often used to designate the medium of incorporation, the *apará*. The metaphor of the radio device is used to describe how the medium may tune in with different spirits.

*Armas:* 'weapons'. The symbols on the uniforms that are considered to protect the medium from different energies.

*Aruanda de Pai João:* sacred space in front of the temple used for the ritual of *Alabá*.

*Aruanda:* a specific sacred space or a city (or colony) in the spirit world inhabited by the *pretos velhos*.

*Aspirantes:* 'aspirant mediums'. Mediums in development before their initiation.

*Caboclo:* a term used in Brazil to designate a person with mixed indigenous Amerindian and European origins. In several Brazilian mediumistic religions, including the Vale, it is also used to designate spirits of Amerindians incorporated by mediums that work with the forces of nature.

*Canal Vermelho:* 'Red Channel'. A dimension in the spirit world for the adaptation of the spirits between lives.

*Canto:* 'chant'. Whilst the *emissão* (emission) is an assertion of identity of the medium presenting himself or herself to the spirit worlds to receive the forces vertically, the *canto* is the horizontal emission of transcendental forces from the past, either of a phalanx or of the individual medium. Each phalanx has its own chant.

*Capelinos:* highly evolved spirits from the Planet Capela with the mission of helping humans.

*Casa Grande:* 'big house'. The former house of Tia Neiva is currently a museum of the history of the Vale do Amanhecer.

*Cassandras:* a row of yellow seats closed off by a chain along the aisle of the Templo Mãe. Members of different peoples (groups of mediums) that are represented by a spirit called *Ministro* (Minister) sit here and act as projectors of that *Ministro*'s forces around the temple. The ritual itself is called *ritual de Cassandra*. '*Cassandra*' also refers to ships transporting spirits between the planes.

*Castelo:* 'castle'. Ritual rooms inside the temple.

*Cavaleiros:* 'knights'. Spirits of high hierarchy acting as personal guides that protect male mediums and rescue suffering spirits.

*Cavaleiros da Luz:* 'knights of the light'. Spirits of high hierarchy depicted as Roman centurions that represent specific healing powers intersecting in rituals, namely: *Cavaleiro da Lança Vermelha* (Knight of the Red Lance) for disobsessive healing; *Cavaleiro da Lança Lilás* (Lilac Lance) for physical healing; *Cavaleiro da Lança Verde* (Green Lance) for mental healing; *Cavaleiro da Lança Rósea* (Pink Lance) for unconditional love; *Cavaleiro da Lança Azul* (Blue Lance) for inner peace and balance; *Cavaleiro da Lança Aurea* (Golden Lance) for universal peace; *Caveleiro da Lança Reino Central* (Central Kingdom Lance); *Cavaleiro da Lança Negra* (Black Lance) for final justice.

*Cavaleiros de Oxossi:* 'knights of Oxossi'. *Caboclos* consecrated in the spirit world in order to hunt spirits wandering in the etheric plane and bring them into the rituals so that they can be released to follow their path of evolution.

*Centúria:* the third initiation by which the medium becomes a *Centurião* (Centurion).

*Charme:* the divine energy that links the spirit to the foetus and remains on earth after the bodily death, and thus it is also understood as karmic energy from past lives.

*Chaves Iniciáticas:* 'initiatic keys'. Pre-fixed ritual formulas composed of a precise number of words that are considered to produce spiritual processes.

*Ciganos:* gypsy spirits.

*Cobradores:* 'debt collectors'; 'creditors'. Disincarnate spirits from a past incarnation that died with a desire for revenge. They may obsess directly upon the person or interfere in their material, social or emotional life, causing difficulties that reflect the karmic debt until they consider the debt to be paid. Human beings may also be incarnated *cobradores* from one's past life.

*Corrente Indiana do Espaço* and *Correntes Brancas do Oriente Maior:* 'Indian Current (or Chain) of the Space' and 'White Currents (or Chains) of the Greater East'. The first is described as a Christic force projected by the Great Indian Initiates, whereas the latter represents the joint action of the earthly forces from the Himalayas and the rays projected from the Oracle of Obatalá. The spirits working in the Vale do Amanhecer are said to be positioned in hierarchies along these two currents.

*Cruz do Caminho:* 'Cross of the Path'. Healing ritual involving the incorporation of Yemanjá, deity of the sea, the forces of the *Cavaleiros da Luz* and the *médicos de cura*. As a sacred space, the *Cruz do Caminho* hosts also the rituals of baptism and wedding.

*Cura:* 'healing'. It might also refer to the ritual of *Cura*, the second healing ritual along the temple's ritual itinerary, or to the sacred space in which the ritual is performed.

*Cura desobsessiva:* 'disobsessive healing'. Mediumistic practice involving the release of disincarnate spirits affecting the patients.

*Desenvolvimento mediúnico:* 'mediumistic development'. A learning process organized into different stages and initiations through which one develops spirit mediumship and learns to discern and control spirits.

*Doutrinador/a:* a 'conscious medium' that indoctrinates disincarnate spirits and releases them into the spirit world.

*Ectolítero:* described by Tia Neiva as a membrane enveloping the three spheres of body, soul and spirit, located in the solar plexus.

*Ectolítrio:* the energy emitted by the *ectolítero*, which acts continuously through the body, determining the vibratory pattern of the person. It also triggers the throat chakra, allowing the medium to issue his or her ectoplasm.

*Ectopía:* the process of emission of ectoplasm.

*Ectoplasma:* 'ectoplasm' or 'magnetic animal fluid'. Ectoplasm is considered to be produced by the human body and to carry the energies emitted by the person. Its balance and distribution ground, define and regulate the practice of mediumship. Unlike physical mediumship in Anglo-Saxon Spiritualism, ectoplasm is not visible in the mediumistic practice of the Vale do Amanhecer.

*Elevação de Espadas:* 'Elevation of Swords'. The second initiation of mediums.

*Elipse:* 'ellipse'. The elliptical shape of the main symbol of the Vale illustrates the flow of the energy emitted by the spirit worlds, which is manipulated for healing purposes by the Jaguar (appearing at the bottom of the symbol) and ultimately returned to the spiritual planes. The ellipse is also considered a portal of the disintegration and reintegration of forces between two worlds.

*Elítrio:* a spirit deformed by rage incarnating together with the person in debt from a past life. It is attached to an organ or to the nervous centre, causing major illnesses associated to karmic debts.

*Emissão:* 'emission'. Working as an invocation of forces, the emission is an identification of the medium before the spirit world, in which the medium affirms his or her position in the Order, stating their individual features such as: type of mediumship, phalanx of masters, people, missionary phalanx, adjunct, classification, knight or missionary guide, star and working shift. It is said to enable the opening of a channel that reaches the higher dimensions of the spiritual planes permitting the passage of forces.

*Emplacamento:* a ritual in which mediums in the first stage of development receive the badge (*plaquinha*) with the name of their main spirit mentor, which enables them to work with patients in rituals.

*Equitumans:* according to Tia Neiva, it was the first civilization of spirits from the 'Planet Capela' incarnating on earth with the mission of preparing it for future civilizations.

*Espíritos de Luz:* 'spirits of light', spirits from the high spiritual planes. They may be spirit mentors and guides, manifesting as *pretos velhos, caboclos, médicos de cura,* knights, missionary guides, ministers and so on.

*Espíritos sem Luz:* 'spirits without light', spirits from the lower spirit worlds. They are deemed to affect human beings or to be causal agents of obsession and illness. They are distinguished in the categories of *sofredores* (sufferers), *cobradores* (debt collectors) and *obsessores* (obsessors).

*Estrela Candente:* 'Candescent Star'. A ritual performed three times a day in the homonymous open-air sacred space, aimed at removing from the earth those spirits that may cause major problems to humanity.

*Estrela Sublimação:* 'Sublimation Star'. A sacred space setting of the homonymous ritual of healing that draws upon forces of ancient civilizations, and of Apollo, Ramses and Amon-Rá.

*Filho dos Devas:* 'Sons of the Devas'. Mediums responsible for the rituals of initiation, the hierarchical classifications and the administration of members of the Order.

*Fita:* the yellow and purple 'string' diagonally encircling the medium's body to represent an ellipse. As a mandatory part of each uniform, the *fita* is said to act on the medium's body as a portal of disintegration of forces, protecting the body from different kinds of energies. By wearing it, the medium carries on the body the meaning of mediumistic practice – wisdom and healing (or science and faith) – which are respectively codified in the yellow and purple colours of the *fita*.

*Guias Missionárias:* 'missionary guides'. Spirits guides belonging to the high spiritual hierarchy protecting female mediums.

*Incorporação:* 'incorporation' of a spirit.

*Indução:* 'Induction'. A ritual that disintegrates negative energetic charges acting upon material life, and the sacred space in the temple where this ritual is held.

*Iniciação Dharman-Oxinto:* 'Initiation on the Path to God'. The medium's first initiation.

*Jaguares:* 'Jaguars'. The third civilization of spirits described by Tia Neiva as having incarnated on earth as a group with the mission of shaping the social forces. They incarnated among ancient civilizations and different cultures and geographical regions across the centuries until they incarnated in the present life to redeem their karma as mediums in the spiritual mission led by Pai Seta Branca.

*Junção:* 'Junction'. A healing ritual aimed at releasing the *elítrios*, who cause karmic illnesses, and the sacred space in the temple understood as being an extension of the ritual of *Cura*.

*Mãe Yara:* 'Mother Yara'. Among the main spirit mentors of the Vale along with Pai Seta Branca, with whom she incarnated as Saint Clare of Assisi. She is considered the godmother of the *doutrinadores*.

*Mantras:* hymns sung by mediums in rituals.

*Médicos de Cura:* 'doctors of healing'. Spirits of doctors of the late nineteenth and early twentieth century who incorporate in mediums to perform healing rituals.

*Mediunidade:* 'mediumship'. Considered in the Vale as an energy produced by bodies that determines the universal ability to connect to the spiritual planes, to receive and transmit different forces.

*Mediunismo:* 'mediumism'. The way the mediums of the Vale refer to any technical and doctrinal system aimed at the development and practice of mediumship.

*Mediunização:* 'mediumization'. A practice of 'concentration' through which mediums become more perceptive to spiritual phenomena and enter specific mediumistic states of consciousness.

*Mesa Evangélica:* 'Evangelical Table'. A ritual in which the *apará* mediums sit around a white triangular table for the incorporation of the *sofredores* (suffering spirits), who are indoctrinated and released into the spirit world by the *doutrinador* mediums.

*Mestre:* 'master'. A title given to mediums (both male and female – although female mediums are usually called 'nymphs') after the second initiation of *Elevação de Espadas* (Elevation of Swords).

*Ministros:* 'ministers' (of God). Spirits of the highest spiritual hierarchies responsible for individual or groups of mediums forming a people (*povo*) and represented on earth by male mediums, who receive the title of *Adjunto* (Adjunct) of their Minister.

*Neutrom:* an energetic barrier described by Tia Neiva as a cloud delimiting the borders that divide the visible from invisible worlds, functioning also as a protection for humans against seeing disincarnate spirits. The *doutrinadores* develop the ability to open the *neutrom* through initiatic keys to pass disincarnate spirits to the spirit worlds.

*Ninfa:* 'nymph'. A female medium.

*Obsessão:* 'obsession'. Refers to the action of a disincarnate being in a low stage of evolution upon a person, which produces psycho-physical imbalances.

*Obsessores:* 'obsessors'. Disincarnate spirits that feed themselves with human ectoplasm and act with a more or less constant vibration upon the person, establishing a spiritual relationship based on an energy exchange. They are considered to be causal agents of most alcohol and drug addictions and emotional and mental disorders.

*Oráculo:* 'oracle'. A point of emission of forces in the highest spirit worlds projecting its rays upon the earth. Oracles act in rituals and upon the medium's body at various stages of mediumistic development.

*Oráculo de Pai Seta Branca:* 'Oracle of Pai Seta Branca'. The sacred space in which Pai Seta Branca is said to project his forces in *ajanã* mediums who have been specially prepared to receive and distribute them in the temple.

*Orixá:* African deity in Nago-Yorubá tradition. In Brazil, *orixás* work predominantly in Afro-Brazilian religions. In the Vale, only some *orixás* are included in the group of spirits working in the rituals, Yemanjá being the only one incorporating in mediums. Moreover, the medium commanders that open and close the temple ritual sessions each day are called *orixás do dia* (*orixás* of the day) and represent the means through which the highest spiritual forces may flow and spread through the rituals.

*Pai Seta Branca:* 'Father White Arrow'. The main spirit mentor of the Vale do Amanhecer. Represented as an Amerindian chief, he is said to have had also incarnated as Saint Francis of Assisi.

*Pajé:* 'shaman' among Brazilian Amerindians.

*Passes:* 'pass'. Intended as a transfusion of the magnetic force of the *doutrinador* from his or her plexus into the patient's body to re-establish an energetic balance. The *passe* is applied by the *doutrinador* with a movement of his or her hands in front of the patients' plexus, a touch to the forefront and a light pressure on the back of the shoulders.

*Pente:* is the veil worn by the *ninfas* (female mediums). It represents the energy projected from the spiritual planes flowing from the medium's coronary chakra. The base of the veil, which is fixed to the hair, is shaped as an elliptical cone aimed at concentrating energies around the crown chakra.

*Pequeno Pajé:* 'little shaman'. Children in the Vale do Amanhecer, who participate in Sunday meetings where the Christian principles are passed on in a ludic way. They may also sing in the temple, but they cannot practise spirit incorporations.

*Pira:* 'Pyre'. A panel at the centre of the temple comprised of various symbols, including those of the *apará* and *doutrinador*, and representing the Divine

Presence in the temple. In front of the *Pira*, mediums open and close their sessions of *trabalhos espirituais* (spiritual works).

*Piramide:* the 'pyramid' standing on the shore of the Lake of Yemanjá is considered to work as the power plant of all the temples of the Amanhecer.

*Pousada:* guesthouse or bed and breakfast.

*Povo das águas:* 'people of the waters'. Spirits of light, including mermaids and other water spirits, incorporating in rituals aimed at a collective cleansing.

*Pretos velhos:* 'old blacks'. Spirits of African slaves. They are spirit mentors of the *aparás*, incorporating in their mediums to provide patients with words of hope for overcoming difficulties in their lives.

*Princesas:* 'princesses'. Spirit mentors of the mediums *doutrinadores*, namely: Janaína, Jurema, Iracema, Juremá, Iramar, Jandaia and Janara.

*Quadrante:* 'Quadrant'. A ritual performed daily along the north shore of the Lake of Yemanjá. It is aimed at channelling the forces of the universe. There are seven *Quadrantes*, one for each day of the week, represented by the seven *princesas*.

*Radar:* 'radar'. The position in the temple from which the mediums *comandantes* (commanders) *orixás do dia* (orixás of the day) direct the rituals of the day.

*Recepção:* 'reception'. A group of mediums specially trained to deal with the logistics of the temple, such as welcoming and orienting patients and visitors and accompanying disabled patients around rituals. Some *recepcionistas* (receptionists) are also in charge of assisting journalists and researchers, providing them with the basic information about the Vale's doctrine, symbols and rituals.

*Salve Deus!:* 'Hail God!' An expression used both in ritual enunciations by spirit guides and as a form used by mediums to greet each other in the Vale. These words are said to have the power to disintegrate negative energies.

*Setores de trabalho:* 'working sectors'. Another way of referring to sacred ritual spaces.

*Sofredores:* suffering disincarnate spirits wandering on earth who are often not aware of their death and feed themselves with the energies of the living ones.

*Solar dos Médiuns:* 'Solar of the Mediums'. Open-air sacred complex situated around the artificial *Lago de Yemanjá* (Lake of Yemanjá) and comprised of three ritual spaces: *Estrela Candente* (Candescent Star) *Quadrantes* (Quandrants) and *Piramide* (Pyramid).

*Sudálio,* or *Linha de Passe:* sacred space and ritual for the incorporation of *caboclos,* aimed at disobsessive healing.

*Templo Mãe:* 'Mother Temple'. The main temple near Brasília where the doctrine and sacred spaces were developed.

*Terreiro:* Afro-Brazilian religious centre.

*Trabalho Especial:* 'special work'. A special disobsessive ritual performed for emergency cases during the night when the temple is closed.

*Trabalhos espirituais:* 'spiritual works'. Another way of referring to rituals.

*Trinos:* 'Trines'. The highest hierarchical title, meaning that the medium is receiving three rays of the Oracle of Simiromba.

*Trinos Triadas Presidentes:* presidents of the Order.

*Trono Milenar:* 'Millennial Throne'. A ritual of communication with ancient spirits belonging to the lower spirit worlds that are indoctrinated and helped to be released by the *doutrinadores.*

*Tronos:* 'Thrones'. A sacred space located at the centre of the temple, with small red or yellow tables and seats that host mediums and patients in the ritual of communication with *pretos velhos* (*Ritual de Tronos*).

*Tumuchys:* the second civilization of spirits, described by Tia Neiva as having incarnated on earth as a group with the mission of building megalithic monuments at different geographical points in order to attract extra-planetary energies.

*Turigano:* sacred space adjoining the temple and setting of the ritual of *Turigano,* which draws upon the ancient forces of Delphi. The space is also used for other rituals, including the *Entrega das Energias* (Delivery of Energies) of the mediums who participate in the *Estrela Candente.*

*Vovó* and *Vovô:* 'grandmother' and 'grandfather'. Refers to the suffix used in the individual names of spirit guides to indicate that they are *pretos velhos* (e.g. Vovó Catarina das Cachoeiras/Grandma Catherine of the Waterfalls).

# REFERENCES

Álvares, B. (ed.). 1991. *Mensagens de Pai Seta Branca*. Vale do Amanhecer, Planaltina: OSOEC.
———. 1992. *Tia Neiva: Autobiografia Missionária*. Brasília: Vale do Amanhecer.
Amaral, L. 1993. 'Os Errantes da Nova Era e sua Religiosidade Caleidoscópica', *Cadernos de Ciências Sociais* 3(4): 19–32.
Armond, E. 1986 [1949]. *Os Exilados da Capela: Esboço Sintético da Evolução Espiritual do Mundo*. São Paulo: Ed. Aliança.
Aureliano, W. 2013. 'Terapias Espirituais e Complementares no Tratamento do Câncer: A Experiência de Pacientes Oncológicos em Florianópolis (SC)', *Caderno Saúde Coletiva* 21(1): 18–24.
Bakhtin, M. 1981. *The Dialogic Imagination*. Austin: University of Texas Press.
Bastide, R. 1978. *The African Religions of Brazil: Toward a Sociology of the Interpenetration of Civilisations*. Baltimore: Johns Hopkins University Press.
———. 2004. 'Problems of Religious Syncretism', in M. Leopold and J.S. Jensen (eds), *Syncretism in Religion: A Reader*. London: Equinox, pp. 113–39.
Bateson, G. 1972. *Steps to an Ecology of Mind*. New York: Ballantine.
Bauman, Z. 2004. *Identity: Conversations with Benedetto Vecchi*. Oxford: Polity.
Berger, P. 1967. *The Sacred Canopy: Elements for a Sociological Theory of Religion*. New York: Doubleday.
Berliner, D., and T. Sarró (eds). 2009. *Learning Religion: Anthropological Approaches*. New York; Oxford: Berghahn Books.
Blanes, R., and D. Espírito Santo (eds). 2013. *The Social Life of Spirits*. Chicago: University of Chicago Press.
Blavatsky, H.P. 1999 [1877]. *Isis Unveiled: A Master-Key to the Mysteries of Ancient and Modern Science and Theology*. Pasadena, CA: Theosophical University Press.
———. 2011 [1888]. *The Secret Doctrine: The Synthesis of Science, Religion, and Philosophy*. New York; Cambridge: Cambridge University Press.
Boddy, J. 1988. 'Spirits and Selves in Northern Sudan: The Cultural Therapeutics of Possession and Trance', *American Ethnologist* 15(1): 4–27.
———. 1994. 'Spirit Possession Revisited: Beyond Instrumentality', *Annual Review of Anthropology* 23: 407–34.
Bourguignon, E. 1967. 'World Distribution and Patterns of Possession States', in R. Prince (ed.), *Trance and Possession States*. Montreal: R.M. Bucke Memorial Society, pp. 3–34.
———. 1979. *Psychological Anthropology: An Introduction to Human Nature and Cultural Difference*. New York: Holt, Rinehart and Winston.
———. 1989. 'Multiple Personality, Possession Trance, and the Psychic Unity of Mankind', *Ethos* 17(3): 371–84.

Bowie, F. 1997. 'Equilibrium and the End of Time: The Roots of Millenarianism', in F. Bowie (ed.), *The Coming Deliverer: Millennial Themes in World Religions*. Cardiff: University of Wales Press, pp. 1–26.

———. 2011. 'Miracles in Traditional Religion', in G.H. Twelftree (ed.), *The Cambridge Companion to Miracles*. Cambridge: Cambridge University Press, pp. 167–83.

———. 2013. 'Building Bridges, Crossing Boundaries: Towards a Methodology for the Study of the Afterlife, Mediumship, and Spiritual Beings', *Journal of the American Academy of Religion* 81(3): 698–733.

Boyer, P. 2001. *Religion Explained: The Human Instincts That Fashion Gods, Spirits and Ancestors*. London: Heinemann.

Brandão, C.R. 2004. 'Fronteiras da Fé: Alguns Sistemas de Sentido, Crenças e Religiões no Brasil de Hoje', *Estudos Avançados* 18(52): 261–88.

Brumana, F.G., and E. Martínez. 1989. *Spirits from the Margin: Umbanda in São Paulo: A Study in Popular Religion and Social Experience*. Uppsala: Acta Universitatis Uppsaliensis.

Camargo, C.P. 1961. *Kardecismo e Umbanda*. São Paulo: Pioneira.

———. 1973. *Católicos, Protestantes e Espíritas*. Petrópolis: Vozes.

Camurça, M.A. 2003. 'Espaços de Hibridação, Desubstancialização da Identidade Religiosa e Idéias Fora do Lugar', *Ciências Sociais e Religião* 5: 37–65.

———. 2014. 'A Religião e o Censo: Enfoques Metodológicos: Uma Reflexão a partir das Consultorias do ISER ao IBGE Sobre o Dado Religioso no Censo', in R. de Castro Menezes and C.V. da Cunha (eds), *Religiões em Conexão: Números, Direitos, Pessoas*. Rio de Janeiro: ISER, pp. 8–17.

———. 2017. 'A Teoria do "Continuum Mediúnico" de Candido Procópio Camargo nos anos de 1960–1970: Atualizações e Transformações Contemporâneas', *Religare* 14(1): 5–27.

Cardeña, E. 1989. 'Varieties of Possession Experience', *AASC Quarterly* 5(2–3): 1–2; 12–17.

———. 2009. 'Beyond Plato? Toward a Science of Alterations of Consciousness', in C.A. Roe, W. Kramer and L. Coly (eds), *Utrecht II: Charting the Future of Parapsychology*. New York: Parapsychology Foundation, pp. 305–22.

Carvalho, V.L.M. 2002 [1993]. *Violetas na Janela (pelo Espírito de Patricia)*. São Paulo: Petit Editora.

Cavalcante, C.L.C. 2000. *Xamanismo no Vale do Amanhecer: O Caso da Tia Neiva*. São Paulo: Annablume.

Chiesa, G.R. 2016. *Além do que se vê: Magnetismos, Ectoplasmas e Paracirurgias*. Porto Alegre: Multifoco.

Clastres, H. 1978. *Terra sem Mal: O Profetismo Tupi-Guarani*. São Paulo: Brasiliense.

Clastres, P. 2003. *A Sociedade contra o Estado*. São Paulo: Cosac & Naify.

Claus, P.J. 1979. 'Spirit Possession and Spirit Mediumship from the Perspective of Tulu Oral Traditions', *Culture, Medicine and Psychiatry* 3: 29–52.

Cohen, E. 2007. *The Mind Possessed: The Cognition of Spirit Possession in an Afro-Brazilian Religious Tradition*. Oxford: Oxford University Press.

———. 2008. 'What is Spirit Possession? Defining, Comparing, and Explaining Two Possession Forms', *Ethnos* 73(1): 101–26.

Comaroff, J. 1985. *Body of Power, Spirit of Resistance: The Culture and History of a South African People*. Chicago: University of Chicago Press.

Crapanzano, V. 1977. 'Introduction', in V. Crapanzano and V. Garrison (eds), *Case Studies in Spirit Possession*. New York: Wiley, pp. 1–40.

Csordas, T.J. 1983. 'The Rhetoric of Transformation in Ritual Healing', *Culture, Medicine and Psychiatry* 7: 333–75.

———. 1990. 'Embodiment as a Paradigm for Anthropology', *Ethos* 18(1): 5–47.

————. 1993. 'Somatic Modes of Attention', *Cultural Anthropology* 8(2): 135–56.

————. 1994. *The Sacred Self: A Cultural Phenomenology of Charismatic Healing*. Berkeley: University of California Press.

Damasio, A. 2000. *The Feeling of What Happens: Body and Emotion in the Making of Consciousness*. London: Vintage.

Da Matta, R. 1979. *Carnavais, Malandros e Heróis: Para uma Sociología do Dilema Brasileiro*. Rio de Janeiro: Zahar.

————. 1985. *A Casa e a Rua: Espaço, Cidadanía, Mulher e Morte no Brasil*. São Paulo: Editôra Brasiliense.

Da Silva, V.G., and F.G. Brumana. 2016. 'Candomblé: Religion, World Vision and Experience', in B. Schmidt and S. Engler (eds), *Handbook of Contemporary Religions in Brazil*. Leiden; Boston: Brill, pp. 170–85.

Dawson, A. 2007. *New Era New Religions: Religious Transformation in Contemporary Brazil*. Aldershot: Ashgate.

————. 2010. 'Taking Possession in Santo Daime: The Growth of Umbanda within a Brazilian New Religion', in B. Schmidt and L. Huskinson (eds), *Spirit Possession and Trance: New Interdisciplinary Perspectives*. London; New York: Continuum, pp. 134–50.

De Andrade, O. 1928. 'Manifesto Antropófago', *Revista de Antropofagia* 1(1): 6–7.

Deleuze, G., and F. Guattari. 2004. *A Thousand Plateaus: Capitalism and Schizophrenia*. London: Continuum.

Desjarlais, R. 1992. *Body and Emotion: The Aesthetic of Illness and Healing in Nepal Himalayas*. Philadelphia: University of Pennsylvania Press.

Desjarlais, R., and C.J. Throop. 2011. 'Phenomenological Approaches in Anthropology', *Annual Review of Anthropology* 40: 87–102.

Devereux, G. 1961. 'Shamans as Neurotics', *American Anthropologist* 63(5): 1088–90.

Donovan, J.M. 2000. 'A Brazilian Challenge to Lewis's Explanation of Cult Mediumship', *Journal of Contemporary Religion* 15(3): 361–77.

Dowling, L. 1908. *The Aquarian Gospel of Jesus the Christ*. Los Angeles: Leo W. Dowling.

Eliade, M. 1964. *Shamanism: The Archaic Techniques of Ecstasy*. London: Routledge & Kegan Paul.

Engler, S., and Ê. Brito. 2016. 'Afro-Brazilian and Indigenous-Influenced Religions', in B. Schmidt and S. Engler (eds), *Handbook of Contemporary Religions in Brazil*. Leiden; Boston: Brill, pp. 142–69.

Engler, S., and A.C. Isaia. 2016. 'Kardecism', in B. Schmidt and S. Engler (eds), *Handbook of Contemporary Religions in Brazil*. Leiden; Boston: Brill, pp. 186–203.

Engler, S., and B. Schmidt. 2016. 'Introduction', in B. Schmidt and S. Engler (eds), *Handbook of Contemporary Religions in Brazil*. Leiden; Boston: Brill, pp. 1–29.

Espírito Santo, D. 2011. 'Process, Personhood and Possession in Cuban Spiritism', in A. Dawson (ed.), *Summoning the Spirits: Possession and Invocation in Contemporary Religion*. London; New York: Tauris, pp. 93–108.

————. 2015. *Developing the Dead: Mediumship and Selfhood in Cuban Espiritismo*. Gainesville, FL: University Press of Florida.

————. 2016. 'Clothes for the Spirits: Opening and Closing the Cosmos in Brazilian Umbanda', *HAU: Journal of Ethnographic Theory* 6(3): 85–106.

————. 2017. 'Possession Consciousness, Religious Individualism, and Subjectivity in Brazilian Umbanda', *Religion* 47(2): 179–202.

Espírito Santo, D. et al. 2010. 'Around the Mind Possessed: The Cognition of Spirit Possession in an Afro-Brazilian Religious Tradition by Emma Cohen', *Religion and Society: Advances in Research* 1: 164–76.

Evans-Pritchard, E. 1976 [1937]. *Witchcraft, Oracles and Magic among the Azande.* Oxford: Clarendon Press.

Fabian, J. 2001. *Anthropology with an Attitude: Critical Essays.* Stanford, CA: Stanford University Press.

Fausto, C. 2007. 'If God Were a Jaguar: Cannibalism and Christianity among the Guarani (16th–20th Centuries)', in C. Fausto and M. Heckenberger (eds), *Time and Memory in Indigenous Amazonia: Anthropological Perspectives.* Gainesville:

Favret-Saada, J. 1980. *Deadly Words: Witchcraft in the Bocage.* Cambridge: Cambridge University Press.

———. 1990. 'About Participation', *Culture, Medicine and Psychiatry* 14: 189–99.

Ferretti, M. 2001. 'The Presence of Non-African Spirits in an Afro-Brazilian Religion', in S.M. Greenfield and A. Droogers (eds), *Reinventing Religions: Syncretism and Transformation in Africa and the Americas.* Lanham: Rowman and Littlefield, pp. 99–111.

Ferretti, S. 2001. 'Religious Syncretism in an Afro-Brazilian Cult House', in S.M. Greenfield and A. Droogers (eds), *Reinventing Religions: Syncretism and Transformation in Africa and the Americas.* Lanham: Rowman and Littlefield, pp. 87–97.

Firth, R. 1967. *Tikopia Ritual and Belief.* Boston: Beacon.

Freyre, G. 1945. *Brazil: An Interpretation.* New York: Alfred Knopf.

———. 1968. *Brasis, Brasil e Brasília.* Rio de Janeiro: Grafica Recor Editôra.

———. 1986 [1933]. *The Masters and the Slaves: A Study in the Development of Brazilian Civilization.* Berkeley, Los Angeles; London: University of California Press.

Frigerio, A. 1989. 'Levels of Possession Awareness in Afro-Brazilian Religions', *AASC Quarterly* 5(2–3): 5–12.

Galinkin, A.L. 2008. *A Cura no Vale do Amanhecer.* Brasília: Technopolitik.

Gentili, A. 2006. *Le Ragioni del Corpo.* Milano: Ancora.

Gerber, J. 1932. *Communication with the Spirit World: Its Laws and Purpose: Personal Experiences of a Catholic Priest.* New York, NY: John Felsberg.

Giumbelli, E. 2003. 'O "Baixo Espiritismo" e a História dos Cultos Mediúnicos', *Horizontes Antropológicos* 9(19): 247–81.

Goldman, M. 1984. 'Possessão e a Construção Ritual da Pessoa no Candomblé'. Dissertação de Mestrado. PPGAS-MN: Universidade Federal Rio de Janeiro, Brazil.

———. 1985. 'A Construção Ritual da Pessoa: A Possessão no Candomblé', *Religião e Sociedade* 12(1): 22–54.

———. 2003. 'Os Tambores dos Vivos e os Tambores dos Mortos: Etnografia, Antropologia e Política em Ilhéus, Bahia', *Revista de Antropologia* 46(2): 446–76.

———. 2005. 'Jeanne Favret-Saada, os Afetos, a Etnografia', *Cadernos de Campo* 13: 149–53.

———. 2006. 'Alteridade e Experiência: Antropologia e Teoria Etnográfica', *Etnográfica* 10(1): 161–73.

———. 2009. 'How to Learn in Afro-Brazilian Spirit Possession Religion: Ontology and Multiplicity in Candomblé', in D. Berliner and R. Sarró, *Learning Religion: Anthropological Approaches.* New York; Oxford: Berghahn Books, pp. 103–19.

Goulet J.G.A., and B. Granville Miller. 2007. 'Embodied Knowledge: Towards a Radical Anthropology of Cross-cultural Encounters', in J.G.A. Goulet and B. Granville Miller (eds), *Extraordinary Anthropology: Transformations in the Field.* Lincoln: Nebraska University Press, pp.1–14.

Gow, P. 2001. *An Amazonian Myth and its History.* Oxford: Oxford University Press.

Greenfield, S.M. 1991. 'Hypnosis and Trance Induction in the Surgeries of Brazilian Spirit Healer-Mediums', *Anthropology of Consciousness* 2(3–4): 20–25.

————. 1992. 'Spirits and Spiritist Therapy in Southern Brazil: A Case Study of an Innovative Syncretic Healing Group', *Culture, Medicine and Psychiatry* 16: 23–51.

————. 2001. 'Population Growth Industrialization and the Proliferation of Syncretized Religions in Brazil', in S.M. Greenfield and A. Droogers (eds), *Reinventing Religions: Syncretism and Transformation in Africa and the Americas*. Lanham: Rowman and Littlefield, pp. 55–70.

————. 2003. 'Can Supernaturals Really Heal?', *Anthropological Forum* 13: 151–58.

————. 2008. *Spirits with Scalpels: The Cultural Biology of Religious Healing in Brazil*. Walnut Creek, CA: Left Coast Press.

Groisman, A. 2016. 'Daime Religions, Mediumship and Religious Agency: Health and the Fluency of Social Relations', *Journal for the Study of Religious Experience* 2: 50–70.

Hageman, J. et al. 2010. 'The Neurobiology of Trance and Mediumship in Brazil', in S. Krippner and H. Friedman (eds), *Mysterious Minds: The Neurobiology of Psychic, Mediums, and other Extraordinary People*. Santa Barbara, CA: Greenwood, pp. 85–112.

Hallowell, A.I. 1955. *Culture and Experience*. Philadelphia: University of Pennsylvania Press.

Halloy, A. 2015. *Divinités Incarnées: La Fabrique des Possédés dans un Culte Afro-brésilien*. Paris: PETRA Editions, Collection Anthropologiques.

————. 2016. 'Full Participation and Ethnographic Reflexivity: An Afro-Brazilian Case Study', *Journal for the Study of Religious Experience* 2: 7–24.

Halloy, A., and V. Naumescu. 2012. 'Learning Possession: An Introduction', *Ethnos* 77(2): 155–76.

Halperin, D. 1995. 'Memory and "Consciousness" in an Evolving Brazilian Possession Religion', *Anthropology of Consciousness* 6(4): 1–17.

Heelas, P. 1996. *The New Age Movement: The Celebration of the Self and the Sacralization of Modernity*. Oxford; Cambridge, MA: Blackwell.

Henare, A., M. Holbraad and S. Wastell. 2007. 'Introduction: Thinking through Things', in A. Henare, M. Holbraad and S. Wastell (eds), *Thinking through Things: Theorising Artefacts Ethnographically*. New York: Routledge, pp. 1–31.

Hess, D.J. 1987. 'The Many Rooms of Spiritism in Brazil', *Luso-Brazilian Review* 24(2): 15–34.

Holbraad, M. 2008. 'Definitive Evidence from Cuban Gods', *Journal of the Royal Anthropological Institute (N.S.)*: 93–109.

————. 2009. 'Ontography and Alterity: Defining Anthropological Truth', *Social Analysis* 53(2): 80–93.

————. 2012. *Truth in Motion: The Recursive Anthropology of Cuban Divination*. Chicago; London: University of Chicago Press.

Hollan, D. 1992. 'Cross-cultural Differences in the Self', *Journal of Anthropological Research* 48(4): 283–300.

Holston, J. 1989. *The Modernist City: An Anthropological Critique of Brasília*. Chicago: University of Chicago Press.

————. 1999. 'Alternative Modernities: Statecraft and Religious Imagination in the Valley of the Dawn', *American Ethnologist* 26(3): 605–31.

Huskinson, L., and B.E. Schmidt (eds). 2010. *Spirit Possession and Trance: New Interdisciplinary Perspectives*. London; New York: Continuum.

Hutton, R. 2001. *Shamans: Siberian Spirituality and the Western Imagination*. London; New York: Hambledon Continuum.

IBGE. 2010a. *Censo 2010: População Residente no Vale do Amanhecer – Planaltina – Brasília – Distrito Federal*. Brasília: Instituto Brasileiro de Geografia e Estatística-IBGE.

———. 2010b. *Censo Demográfico: Características Gerais da População, Religião e Pessoas com Deficiência*. Rio de Janeiro: Instituto Brasileiro de Geografia e Estatística-IBGE.

Ingold, T. 2000. *The Perception of the Environment: Essays on Livelihood, Dwelling and Skill*. London: Routledge.

———. 2010. 'Bringing Things to Life: Creative Entanglements in a World of Materials', NCRM Working Paper Series. ESRC National Centre for Research Methods. Retrieved 10 March 2016 from http://eprints.ncrm.ac.uk/1306/1/0510_creative_entanglements.pdf.

———. 2011. *Being Alive: Essays on Movement, Knowledge and Description*. Abingdon, Oxon; New York: Routledge.

———. 2013. *Making: Anthropology, Archaeology, Art and Architecture*. Abingdon, Oxford; New York: Routledge.

Kardec, A. 2010 [1857]. *The Spirits' Book*. Brasília: International Spiritist Council.

Kern, Y. 1995. *De Akenaton a JK: Das Pirâmides a Brasília*. Brasília: Coronário Editora Gráfica.

Kern, Y., and E.F. Pimentel. 2001. *The Secret Brasília: Enigma of Ancient Egypt*. Brasília: Pórfiro Editora.

Knibbe, K.E., and E. van Houtert. 2018. 'Religious Experience and Phenomenology', in H. Callan (ed.), *The International Encyclopedia of Anthropology*. New York: Wiley, pp. 1–10.

Krippner, S. 1987. 'Cross-cultural Approaches to Multiple Personality Disorder: Practices in Brazilian Spiritism', *Ethos* 15(3): 273–95.

———. 2008. 'Learning from the Spirits: Candomblé, Umbanda, and Kardecismo in Recife, Brazil', *Anthropology of Consciousness* 19(1): 1–32.

Kroeber, A. 1940. 'Psychotic Factors in Shamanism', *Journal of Personality* 8: 204–15.

Lacerda, M.F. 2010. *A Vida Fora da Matéria*. Goiânia: Corel Editora.

Lambek, M. 1981. *Human Spirits: A Cultural Account of Trance in Mayotte*. Cambridge; New York: Cambridge University Press.

Leacock, S. 1964. 'Fun-Loving Deities in an Afro-Brazilian Cult', *Anthropological Quarterly* 37(3): 94–109.

Leacock, S., and R. Leacock. 1972. *Spirits of the Deep: Drums, Mediums and Trance in a Brazilian City*. Garden City, NY: Doubleday.

Leão, F.C., and F. Lotufo Neto. 2007. 'Spiritual Practices in an Institution for Mentally Disabled', *Revista Psiquiatria Clínica* 1: 23–28.

Lemoyne, G.B. 1907. *Memorie Biografiche di Don Giovanni Bosco*, Volume 16. Torino: Libreria Salesiana.

Leopold, A.M., and J.S. Jensen (eds). 2004. *Syncretism in Religion: A Reader*. London: Equinox.

Lewgoy, B. 2004. *O Grande Mediador: Chico Xavier e a Cultura Brasileira*. Bauru, SP: EDUSC.

Lewis, I.M. 1971. *Ecstatic Religion: A Study of Shamanism and Spirit Possession*. Harmondsworth, Middlesex: Penguin Books.

Lienhardt, G. 1961. *Divinity and Experience: The Religion of the Dinka*. Oxford: Oxford University Press.

Luhrmann, T.M. 1989. *Persuasions of the Witch's Craft: Ritual Magic in Contemporary England*. Cambridge, MA: Harvard University Press.

———. 2009. 'How do You Learn to Know that Is God Who Speaks?', in D. Berliner and R. Sarró (eds), *Learning Religion: Anthropological Approaches*. New York; Oxford: Berghahn Books, pp. 83–102.

———. 2010. 'What Counts as Data', in J. Davies and D. Spencer (eds), *Emotions in the Field: The Psychology and Anthropology of Fieldwork Experience*. Stanford, CA: Stanford University Press, pp. 212–38.

———. 2011. 'Hallucinations and Sensory Overrides', *Annual Review of Anthropology* 40: 71–85.

Luhrmann, T.M., H. Nusbaum and R. Thisted. 2010. 'The Absorption Hypothesis: Learning to Hear God in Evangelical Christianity', *American Anthropologist* 112(1): 66–78.

Lukoff, D., F. Lu and R. Turner. 1992. 'Toward a More Culturally Sensitive DSM-IV: Psychoreligious and Psychospiritual Problems', *Journal of Nervous and Mental Disease* 180: 673–82.

Maluf, S. 2005. 'Da Mente ao Corpo? A Centralidade do Corpo nas Culturas da Nova Era', *Ilha: Revista de Antropologia* 7: 147–61.

Marques, E.G. 2008. 'Ritual e Gênero no Vale do Amanhecer'. Paper presented at the Conference Fazendo Gênero: Corpo, Violência e Poder. Universidade Federal de Santa Catarina, Florianópolis, Brazil.

———. 2009. 'Os Poderes do Estado no Vale do Amanhecer: Percursos Religiosos, Práticas Espirituais e Cura', MA dissertation. Universidade de Brasília: Departamento de Antropologia.

Menezes J.A., and A. Moreira-Almeida. 2009. 'Differential Diagnosis between Spiritual Experiences and Mental Disorders of Religious Content', *Revista de Psiquiatria Clínica* 36(2): 75–82.

Merleau-Ponty, M. 1962. *Phenomenology of Perception*. London: Routledge & Kegan Paul.

Métraux, A. 1927. *Migrations Historiques des Tupi-Guarani*. Paris: Librarie Orientale et Américaine.

Miller, B. 2007. 'The Politics of Ecstatic Research', in J.G. Goulet and B. Granville Miller (eds), *Extraordinary Anthropology: Transformations in the Field*. Lincoln: University of Nebraska Press, pp. 186–207.

Moen, B. 1998. *Voyage beyond Doubt*. Charlottesville, VA: Hampton Roads Publishing.

———. 2005. *Afterlife Knowledge Guidebook: A Manual for Art of Retrieval and Afterlife Exploration*. Charlottesville, VA: Hampton Roads Publishing.

Montero, P., and E. Dullo. 2014. 'Ateísmo no Brasil: da invisibilidade à crença fundamentalista', *Novos Estudos CEBRAP* 100: 57–79.

Moreira-Almeida, A. 2009. 'Differentiating Spiritual from Psychotic Experiences', *British Journal of Psychiatry* 195: 370–71.

Moreira-Almeida, A., and F. Lotufo Neto. 2003. 'Diretrizes Metodológicas para Investigar Estados Alterados de Conciência e Experiências Anômalas', *Revista Psiquiatria Clínica* 30(1): 21–28.

Moreira-Almeida, A., F. Lotufo Neto and E. Cardeña. 2008. 'Comparison of Brazilian Spiritist Mediumship and Dissociative Identity Disorder', *Journal of Nervous and Mental Disorder* 196: 420–24.

Moreira-Almeida, A., F. Lotufo Neto and B. Greyson. 2007. 'Dissociative and Psychotic Experiences in Brazilian Spirit Mediums', *Psychotherapy and Psychosomatics* 76: 57–58.

Motta, R. 2001. 'Ethnicity, Purity, the Market and Syncretism in Afro-Brazilian Cults', in S.M. Greenfield and A. Droogers (eds), *Reinventing Religions: Syncretism and Transformation in Africa and the Americas*. Lanham: Rowman and Littlefield, pp. 71–85.

Natale, S. 2011. 'A Cosmology of Invisible Fluids: Wireless, X-Rays and Psychical Research around 1900', *Canadian Journal of Communication* 36: 263–75.

Nimuendajú, K. 1987. *As Lendas da Criação e Destruição do Mundo como Fundamentos da Religião dos Apapocúva-Guarani*. São Paulo: HUCITEC & EDUSP.

Nina Rodrigues, R. 1935. *O Animismo Fetichista dos Negros Bahianos*. Rio de Janeiro: Civilização Brasileira.

Noll, R. 1983. 'Shamanism and Schizophrenia: A State-Specific Approach to the "Schizophrenia Metaphor" of Shamanic States', *American Ethnologist* 10(3): 443–59.

———. 1985. 'Mental Imagery Cultivation as a Cultural Phenomenon: The Role of Visions in Shamanism', *Current Anthropology* 46(4): 443–61.

*Nosso Lar*. 2010. Motion Picture. Directed by Wagner de Assis. Brazil.

Notovitch, N. 1916 [1890]. *The Unknown Life of Jesus Christ*, 4th edn., trans. A. Loranger. Chicago: Indo-American Book Company.

Ochs, E., and L. Capps. 1996. 'Narrating the Self', *Annual Review of Anthropology* 25: 19–43.

Oesterreich, T.K. 1930. *Possession, Demoniacal and Other, among Primitive Races, in Antiquity, the Middle Ages, and Modern Times*. New York: R.R. Smith.

Okely, J. 2007. 'Fieldwork Embodied', in C. Shilling (ed.), *Embodying Sociology: Retrospects, Progress and Prospects*. Oxford: Blackwell, pp. 65–79.

———. 2012. *Anthropological Practice: Fieldwork and the Ethnographic Method*. London; New York: Berg.

Oliveira, A. 2007. 'Nova Era à brasileira: New Age Popular do Vale do Amanhecer', *Interações-Cultura e Comunidade* 4(5): 31–50.

Palmié, S., and C. Stewart. 2016. 'Introduction: For an Anthropology of History', *HAU: Journal of Ethnographic Theory* 6(1): 207–36.

Pessar, P.R. 2004. *From Fanatics to Folk: Brazilian Millenarianism and Popular Culture*. Durham, NC: Duke University Press.

Pierini, E. 2009, 'Identità Ibride: L'Esperienza Religiosa nella Vale do Amanhecer', *Quaderni di Thule IX. Rivista Italiana di Studi Americanistici* 9: 215–20.

———. 2010. 'Aspectos Sócio-culturais dos Cultos de Matrizes Afros e Afro-brasileiras no Distrito Federal', in E. Pierini and M. Reis, *Identificação dos Lugares de Matrizes Africanas e Afro-Brasileira no Distrito Federal e Entorno, Inventário Nacional de Referências Culturais Lugares de Culto de Matrizes Africanas e Afro-Brasileiras no Distrito Federal e Entorno Fase II*. Brasília: Instituto do Patrimônio Histórico e Artístico Nacional, pp. 56–94.

———. 2013. 'The Journey of the Jaguares: Spirit Mediumship in the Vale do Amanhecer', Ph.D. dissertation. Department of Archaeology and Anthropology: University of Bristol.

———. 2016a. 'Becoming a Spirit Medium: Initiatory Learning and the Self in the Vale do Amanhecer', *Ethnos* 81(2): 290–314.

———. 2016b. 'Fieldwork and Embodied Knowledge: Researching upon the Experiences of Spirit Mediums in Brazil', in B. Schmidt (ed.), *The Study of Religious Experience: Approaches and Methodologies*. London: Equinox, pp. 55–70.

———. 2016c. 'Becoming a Jaguar: Spiritual Routes in the Vale do Amanhecer', in B. Schmidt and S. Engler (eds), *Handbook of Contemporary Religions in Brazil*. Leiden: Brill, pp. 225–32.

———. 2016d. 'Embodied Encounters: Ethnographic Knowledge, Emotion and Senses in the Vale do Amanhecer's Spirit Mediumship', *Journal for the Study of Religious Experience* 2: 25–49.

———. 2018. 'Healing and Therapeutic Trajectories among the Spirit Mediums of the Brazilian Vale do Amanhecer', *International Journal of Latin American Religions* 2(2): 272–89.

Pierini, E., and A. Groisman. 2016. 'Introduction: Fieldwork in Religion: Bodily Experience and Ethnographic Knowledge', *Journal for the Study of Religious Experience* 2: 1–6.

Pierucci, A.F. 1997. 'Interesses Religiosos dos Sociólogos da Religião', in A.P. Oro and C.A. Steil (eds), *Globalização e Religião*. Petrópolis: Vozes, pp. 249–62.

Pink, S. 2009. *Doing Sensory Ethnography*. London: Sage.

Pompa, C. 2004. 'O Profetismo Tupi-Guarani: Um Objeto Antropológico', *Revista de Indias* 230: 141–74.

Prandi, R. 2000. 'Religião, Biografia e Conversão: Escolhas e Mudanças', *Tempo e Presença* 310: 34–42.

Pressel, E. 1974. 'Umbanda, Trance and Possession in São Paulo, Brazil', in F. Goodman, J.H. Henny and E. Pressel (eds), *Trance, Healing and Hallucination: Three Fields of Studies in Religious Experience*. New York: John Wiley and Sons, pp. 113–26.

Rabelo, M.C.M. 2007. 'Religião e a Transformação da Experiência: Notas sobre o Estudo das Práticas Terapêuticas nos Espaços Religiosos', *Ilha: Revista de Antropologia* 7: 125–45.

Reichel-Dolmatoff, G. 1975. *The Shaman and the Jaguar: A Study of Narcotic Drugs among the Indians of Colombia*. Philadelphia: Temple University Press.

Reis, M.R. 2008. 'Tia Neiva: a Trajetória de uma Líder Religiosa e a sua Obra: O Vale do Amanhecer (1925–2008)', Ph.D. dissertation. Instituto de Ciências Humanas, Departamento de História: Universidade de Brasília.

Ribeiro, D. 1995. *O Povo Brasileiro: A Formação e o Sentido do Brasil*. São Paulo: Companhia das Letras.

Ricoeur, P. 1984. *Time and Narrative Vol. 1*. Chicago: University of Chicago Press.

Rocha, C. 2017. *John of God: The Globalisation of Brazilian Faith Healing*. New York: Oxford University Press.

Rocha, C., and M. Vásquez (eds). 2013. *The Diaspora of Brazilian Religions*. Leiden; Boston: Brill.

Rosaldo, R. 1984. 'Grief and Headhunter's Rage: On the Cultural Force of Emotions', in E. Bruner (ed.), *Text, Play and Story: The Construction and Reconstruction of Self and Society*. Washington, DC: American Ethnological Society, pp. 178–95.

———. 1993. *Culture and Truth: The Remaking of Social Analysis*. London: Routledge.

Sanchez, Z. van der Meer, and S. Nappo. 2008. 'Intervenção Religiosa na Recuperação dos Dependentes de Drogas', *Revista de Saúde Pública* 42(2): 265–72.

Santos, M.G. 2014. 'Os Limites do Censo no Campo Religioso Brasileiro', in R. Menezes and C. V. da Cunha (eds), *Religiões em Conexão: Números, Direitos, Pessoas*. Rio de Janeiro: ISER, pp.18–33.

Sarró, R. 2018. 'Between Writing and Art: The Invention of Mandombe', *Terrain* 70, DOI: 10.4000/terrain.17289.

Sassi, M. 1974a. *No Limiar do Terceiro Milênio*. Brasília: Editora Vale do Amanhecer.

———. 1974b. *Sob os Olhos da Carividente, 2ª Edição*. Brasília: Editora Vale do Amanhecer.

———. 1999. *Vale do Amanhecer: Sob os Olhos da Clarividente*. Brasília: Editora Vale do Amanhecer.

———. 2003. *2000 a Conjunção de Dois Palnos*. Brasília: Editora Vale do Amanhecer.

Sassi, M. (ed.) 1985. *Minha Vida Meus Amores*. Brasília: Vale do Amanhecer.

Saunders, N. 1998. *Icons of Power: Feline Symbolism in the Americas*. London: Routledge.

Schaden, E. 1974. *Aspectos Fundamentais da Cultura Guarani*. São Paulo: E.P.U. & EDUSP.

Schmidt, B.E. 2006. 'The Creation of Afro-Caribbean Religions and their Incorporation of Christian Elements: A Critique against Syncretism', *Transformation: An International Journal of Holistic Mission Studies* 23: 236–43.

———. 2010. 'Possessed Women in the African Diaspora: Gender Difference in Spirit Possession Rituals', in L. Huskinson and B.E. Schmidt (eds), *Spirit Possession and Trance: New Interdisciplinary Perspectives*. London; New York: Continuum, pp. 97–116.

———. 2016. 'Spirit Possession', in B. Schmidt and S. Engler (eds), *Handbook of Contemporary Religions in Brazil*. Leiden; Boston: Brill, pp. 431–47.

Segato, R.L. 1992. 'Um Paradoxo do Relativismo: O Discurso Racional da Antropologia frente ao Sagrado', *Religião e Sociedade* 16(1): 114–33.

Silva, J.C.N. 2010. 'Observações Tumará', Unpublished archive of the Trino Tumará Mestre José Carlos do Nascimento Silva. Brasília: Vale do Amanhecer.

Silva da Silveira, M. 1994. 'Cultos de Possessão no Distrito Federal'. Dissertação de Mestrado. Programa de Pós-graduação em Antropologia do Instituto das Ciências Sociais: Universidade de Brasília.

Silverman, J. 1967. 'Shamanism and Acute Schizophrenia', *American Anthropologist* 69: 21–31.

Siqueira, D.E. 2002. 'Novas Religiosidades na Capital do Brasil', *Tempo Social* 14(1): 177–97.

———. 2009. 'O Labirinto Religioso Ocidental: Da Religião à Espiritualidade. Do Institucional ao não Convencional', *Sociedade e Estado* 23: 425–62.

Siqueira, D.E., M. Reis, J. Zelaya Leite, R.M. Ramassote. 2010. *Vale do Amanhecer: Inventário Nacional de Referências Culturais*. Brasília DF: Superintendência do IPHAN no Distrito Federal.

Soares, L.E. 2014. 'Santo Daime in the Context of the New Religious Consciousness', in B. Labate and E. MacRae (eds), *Ayahuasca Ritual and Religion in Brazil*. Oxon; New York: Routledge, pp. 65–72.

Souza, V.F., and I. Damião. n.d. *Manual Prático do Recepcionista*. Brasília: OSOEC.

Stewart, C., and R. Shaw. 1994. *Syncretism/Anti-syncretism: The Politics of Religious Synthesis*. London; New York: Routledge.

Stoller, P. 1989. *Fusion of the Worlds: An Ethnography of Possession among the Songhay of Niger*. Chicago: University of Chicago Press.

———. 1994. 'Embodying Colonial Memories', *American Anthropologist* 96(3): 634–48.

———. 1997. *Sensuous Scholarship*. Philadelphia: University of Pennsylvania Press.

Strathern, A. 1996. *Body Thoughts*. Ann Arbor: University of Michigan Press.

Taves, A. 1999. *Fits, Trances, & Visions: Experiencing Religion and Explaining Experience from Wesley to James*. Princeton: Princeton University Press.

———. 2016. *Revelatory Events: Three Case Studies of the Emergence of New Spiritual Paths*. Princeton: Princeton University Press.

Tedlock, B. 1991. 'From Participant Observation to the Observation of Participation: The Emergence of Narrative Ethnography', *Journal of Anthropological Research* 47(1): 69–94.

Throop, J. 2003. 'Articulating Experience', *Anthropological Theory* 3(2): 219–41.

Turner, V. 1974. *Dramas, Fields and Metaphors: Symbolic Action in Human Society*. New York: Cornell University Press.

———. 1987. *The Anthropology of Performance*. New York: PAJ Publications.

*Vacancy*. 1998. Directed by Matthias Müller. Germany [16mm/DVD].

Vasconcelos, J. 2009. 'Learning to be a Proper Medium: Middle-Class Womanhood and Spirit Mediumship at Christian Rationalist Séances in Cape Verde', in D. Berliner and R. Sarró (eds), *Learning Religion: Anthropological Approaches*. New York; Oxford: Berghahn Books, pp. 121–40.

Vásquez, M.A., and J.C.S. Alves. 2013. 'The Valley of Dawn in Atlanta, Georgia: Negotiating Incorporation and Gender Identity in the Diaspora', in C. Rocha and M.A. Vásquez (eds), *The Diaspora of Brazilian Religions*. Leiden: Brill, pp. 313–37.

Vicente, C. 1977, 'O Vale do Amanhecer', in *Atualização Revista de Divulgação Teologica para o Cristão de Hoje*. Belo Horizonte: Instituto dos Missionários Sacramentinos de Nossa Senhora, pp. 95–96.

Ward, C. 1989. 'The Cross-Cultural Study of Altered States of Consciousness and Mental Health', in C. Ward (ed.), *Altered States of Consciousness and Mental Health*. Newbury Park, CA: Sage, pp.15–35.

Whitehouse, H. 2000. *Arguments and Icons: Divergent Modes of Religiosity*. Oxford: Oxford University Press.

————. 2004. *Modes of Religiosity: A Cognitive Theory of Religious Transmission*. Walnut Creek, CA: Alta Mira Press.

Whitehouse, H., and J. Laidlaw (eds). 2004. *Ritual and Memory: Toward a Comparative Anthropology of Religion*. Walnut Creek, CA; Oxford: Alta Mira Press.

Xavier, F.C. 2000 [1939]. *A Caminho da Luz (pelo Espírito Emmanuel)*. Brasília: FEB editora.

————. 2000 [1944]. *Nosso Lar, The Astral City: The Story of a Doctor's Odissey in the Spirit World (through the Spirit André Luiz)*. New York: GEAE Grupo de Estudos Avançados Espiritas. Retrieved 10 October 2011 from http://www.spiritist.com/arquivo/books/eng/AstralCity.pdf.

Zelaya, C.L. 2009. *Os Símbolos da Doutrina do Vale do Amanhecer: Sob os Olhos da Clarividente*. Brasília: Tia Neiva Publicações.

————. 2014. *Neiva. Sua Vida pelos meus Olhos*. Brasília: Tia Neiva Publicações.

Zelaya, N.C. 1960. 'Carta 1º Janeiro 1960'. Letter.

————. 1977. 'Carta Reino Central 7 Agosto de 1977'. Letter.

————. 1979. 'Lei do Adjunto', *Acervo Doutrinario da Clarividente Vol.1*. Unpublished archive of the Adjunto Yumatã Mestre Caldeira. Brasília: Vale do Amanhecer, p. 170.

————. 1979b. 'Brasil Celeiro do Mundo. Carta 11 Dezembro de 1979'. Letter.

————. 1980. 'Ectolítero, Ectolítrio e o Ectoplasma', *Acervo Doutrinario da Clarividente Vol.1*. Unpublished archive of the Adjunto Yumatã Mestre Caldeira. Brasília: Vale do Amanhecer, pp. 26–29.

————. 1980b. 'Carta do 1º Maio 1980'. Letter.

————. 1981. 'A Energia dos Rituais. Carta 14 Agosto 1981'. Letter.

————. 1984. 'Carta do 3 Junho1984'. *Acervo Doutrinario da Clarividente Vol.1*. Unpublished archive of the Adjunto Yumatã Mestre Caldeira. Brasília: Vale do Amanhecer, pp. 103–6.

————. 1985. *Minha Vida Meus Amores*. Brasília: Vale do Amanhecer.

Zelaya, R. (ed.). 2009. *Cultura dos Ajanãs e Ninfas Sol na Partida Evangélica*. Brasília: Vale do Amanhecer.

# INDEX